LONG AGOS AND WORLDS APART

Popular Music History

Series Editor: Alyn Shipton, Royal Academy of Music, London.

This series publishes books that extend the field of popular music studies, examine the lives and careers of key musicians, interrogate histories of genres, focus on previously neglected forms, or engage in the formative history of popular music styles.

Published

An Unholy Row: Jazz in Britain and its Audience, 1945–1960
Dave Gelly

Being Prez: The Life and Music of Lester Young
Dave Gelly

Bill Russell and the New Orleans Jazz Revival
Ray Smith and Mike Pointon

Chasin' the Bird: The Life and Legacy of Charlie Parker
Brian Priestley

Desperado: An Autobiography
Tomasz Stanko with Rafał Księżyk, translated by Halina Maria Boniszewska

Eberhard Weber: A German Jazz Story
Eberhard Weber, translated by Heidi Kirk

Formation: Building a Personal Canon, Part 1
Brad Mehldau

Handful of Keys: Conversations with Thirty Jazz Pianists
Alyn Shipton

Hear My Train A Comin': The Songs of Jimi Hendrix
Kevin Le Gendre

Hidden Man: My Many Musical Lives
John Altman

Ivor Cutler: A Life Outside the Sitting Room
Bruce Lindsay

Jazz Me Blues: The Autobiography of Chris Barber
Chris Barber with Alyn Shipton

Jazz Visions: Lennie Tristano and His Legacy
Peter Ind

Kansas City Jazz: A Little Evil Will Do You Good
Con Chapman

Keith Jarrett: A Biography
Wolfgang Sandner, translated by Chris Jarrett

Komeda: A Private Life in Jazz
Magdalena Grzebalkowska, translated by Halina Boniszwska

Lee Morgan: His Life, Music and Culture
Tom Perchard

Lionel Richie: Hello
Sharon Davis

Mosaics: The Life and Works of Graham Collier
Duncan Heining

Mr P.C.: The Life and Music of Paul Chambers
Rob Palmer

Out of the Long Dark: The Life of Ian Carr
Alyn Shipton

Rufus Wainwright
Katherine Williams

Scouse Pop
Paul Skillen

Soul Unsung: Reflections on the Band in Black Popular Music
Kevin Le Gendre

The Godfather of British Jazz: The Life and Music of Stan Tracey
Clark Tracey

The History of European Jazz: The Music, Musicians and Audience in Context
Edited by Francesco Martinelli

The Last Miles: The Music of Miles Davis, 1980–1991
George Cole

The Long Shadow of the Little Giant (second edition): The Life, Work and Legacy of Tubby Hayes
Simon Spillett

The Ultimate Guide to Great Reggae: The Complete Story of Reggae Told through its Greatest Songs, Famous and Forgotten
Michael Garnice

This is Bop: Jon Hendricks and the Art of Vocal Jazz
Peter Jones

This is Hip: The Life of Mark Murphy
Peter Jones

Trad Dads, Dirty Boppers and Free Fusioneers: A History of British Jazz, 1960–1975
Duncan Heining

Two Bold Singermen and the English Folk Revival: The Lives, Song Traditions and Legacies of Sam Larner and Harry Cox
Bruce Lindsay

Vinyl Ventures: My Fifty Years at Rounder Records
Bill Nowlin

Long Agos and Worlds Apart

The Definitive Small Faces Biography

Sean Egan

SHEFFIELD UK   BRISTOL CT

Published by Equinox Publishing Ltd.

UK   Office 415, The Workstation, 15 Paternoster Row, Sheffield,
      South Yorkshire S1 2BX
USA   ISD, 70 Enterprise Drive, Bristol, CT 06010

www.equinoxpub.com

First published 2024

British Library Cataloguing-in-Publication Data

A catalogue record for this book is available from the British Library.

ISBN-13   978 1 80050 537 7   (hardback)
          978 1 80050 538 4   (ePDF)
          978 1 80050 604 6   (ePub)

Library of Congress Cataloging-in-Publication Data

Names: Egan, Sean, author.
Title: Long agos and worlds apart : the definitive Small Faces biography /
   by Sean Egan.
Description: Sheffield, South Yorkshire ; Bristol, CT : Equinox Publishing
   Ltd, 2024. | Series: Popular music history | Includes bibliographical
   references and index. | Summary: "A revealing, impartial, exhaustive and
   definitive account, Longs Agos and Worlds Apart lays to rest several
   myths about the Small Faces while at the same time seeking to redress
   the lack of credit accorded a truly great band"-- Provided by publisher.

Identifiers: LCCN 2024017352 (print) | LCCN 2024017353 (ebook) | ISBN
   9781800505377 (hardback) | ISBN 9781800505384 (pdf) | ISBN 9781800506046
   (epub)
Subjects: LCSH: Small Faces (Musical group) | Rock
   musicians--England--Biography. | LCGFT: Biographies.
Classification: LCC ML421.S6134 E43 2024 (print) | LCC ML421.S6134
   (ebook) | DDC 782.42166092/2--dc23/eng/20240416
LC record available at https://lccn.loc.gov/2024017352
LC ebook record available at https://lccn.loc.gov/2024017353

Typeset by Sparks – www.sparkspublishing.com

Contents

Introduction

The Small Faces epitomised the maxim, "Never mind the width, feel the quality."

In their brief original lifespan, they released just three official albums and a dozen-and-a-half authorised non-album singles and B-sides. Five decades after the London quartet's split, however, the phenomenal quality of that compact body of work has ensured a continuing and unassailable musical esteem bordering on legend.

Gut-bucket vocalist Steve Marriott brought a bluesy grit both to compositions of gravitas and effervescent pop numbers. Bassist Ronnie Lane collaborated with him to form one of the most formidable songwriting partnerships of the era. Ian McLagan was an exhilaratingly blurred-fingered keyboardist. Kenney Jones brought up the rear with blistering drum patterns, with his rolls often used to provide an explosive fanfare to Small Faces singles. Such a talent-oozing line-up was virtually predestined to conjure excellence. 'Tin Soldier', their exquisitely sophisticated psychedelic-soul release of 1967, regularly appears in polls to decide history's greatest singles. However, the band are just as much loved for rip-roaring power-pop like 'Sha-La-La-La-Lee' and 'Hey Girl' and storming instrumental B-sides such as 'Grow Your Own' and 'Almost Grown'. Their acknowledged masterpiece is *Ogdens' Nut Gone Flake* (1968), an album that was not only artistically superb but groundbreaking. Its second-side narrative suite paved the way for rock operas such as the Pretty Things' *SF Sorrow* and the Who's *Tommy*. Regardless of style, quality and innovativeness, the Small Faces' music was characterised by a life-affirming joyousness.

The breadth of their talents helps explain why their catalogue is endlessly recycled via deluxe and anniversary editions and why their corpus has been disproportionately inspirational: the Small Faces were clear or acknowledged influences on David Bowie, Paul Weller, Quiet Riot, Blur, Oasis, Ocean Colour Scene and even Led Zeppelin. Even so, the band are often overlooked.

1

Documentaries and dedicated biographies are comparatively thin on the ground, while their failure to tour the United States has resulted in that country being largely oblivious of them.

Long Agos and Worlds Apart covers the Small Faces' full, tumultuous story. It explores the group's 1965 formation, their Sixties glory years, the redistribution of the band's members at the turn of the Seventies into Humble Pie and the Faces, the ill-fated but grimly fascinating Small Faces reunion of the late Seventies, and the little-known but worthy 1981 Small-Faces-in-all-but-name project the Majik Mijits. A closing section brings the story up to date and summarises the group's extraordinary legacy.

The book draws on lengthy new interviews, including ones with Kenney Jones, Lane's close friend Pete Townshend and original Small Faces member Jimmy Winston. It features contributions from many associates and intimates, including managers, agents, publicists, songwriters, auxiliary musicians, fan-club personnel, recording engineers, journalists, friends and wives. It also draws on numerous interviews the author conducted down the years with both Jones and McLagan, much of which material is previously unpublished.

Longs Agos and Worlds Apart attempts to be a revealing, impartial and definitive account. While it strives to lay to rest several self-aggrandising myths about the Small Faces, it also seeks to redress the lack of credit accorded a truly great band.

1   All Our Yesterdays

"The Faces looked like they were straight out of the cradle," says Kenny Lynch, onetime songwriter for and producer of the band. Precocity was certainly a hallmark of the Small Faces. Drummer Kenney Jones was only 15 when they first started playing together in January 1965, and the definitive line-up had an average age of just 21 when it split in early 1969. The band's frontman had gotten used to fame even younger than that.

Stephen Peter Marriott was born on 30 January 1947 in East Ham, East London and was raised in nearby Manor Park. He was the son of a newspaper-compositor father and factory-worker mother. "A very good job," notes Marriott's future colleague Jerry Shirley of his father's profession. Home life was perhaps not quite as fortunate. David Arden, son of the Small Faces' original manager Don, was close to Marriott. Although he says of the adult Marriott, "Everybody loved him, he was a very popular chap," he also says that he always found him a troubled character. "He could get up people's noses a lot because of his weird attitude," he notes. "From what I can gather, he did not have a good home life." In his leisure time, Marriott's father was a talented pianist and may have been the source of his musicality, but nobody testifies that father and son were close. Arden, though, thinks Marriott's mother was the real source of his problems. "I remember [my] old man distinctly thinking that she was quite a vile creature. Stevie would apparently on occasions be thrown out the house as a kid ... He was always disturbed about Steve's mother. There was a lady who wrote a musical on the Small Faces and she portrayed Stevie's mother in that as being a right bag. I said to the lady, 'Was that how she was?' She went, 'Well, yeah. And everybody that I know that knew her [thought] she was horrible.'"

Jenny Rylance, Marriott's onetime wife, notes that Marriott got on well with Kay, his younger sister by five years, and "he really loved his gran," but saw a relationship with his parents that she felt "slightly stilted." While keen to emphasise that Marriott's mother "probably had a hard life" and his parents "were thrilled when he became successful," she also says, "Things were not great with his mum. He left home quite young." Marriott's son Toby, who lived with his father's parents for the majority of his childhood, has said that he never saw any cruelty from his grandparents and pointed out that Marriott buying them a house in the early Seventies hardly suggests antagonism. Rylance's ambiguous riposte to that is, "He wanted to do the right thing for them."

Whatever their source, original Small Faces keyboardist and guitarist Jimmy Winston is someone who agrees that Marriott was burdened with demons. (Like several interviewed for this book, Winston has since passed away. For reasons of stylistic consistency and clear attribution, the present tense has been maintained when deploying interviewees' quotes whether still with us or otherwise.) "He could go very moody, get upset very easily, if what you were doing was outweighing what he was doing," recalls Winston. "Throughout his life, this thing got in the way."

People would later marvel at the way Marriott commanded the stage in the Small Faces and Humble Pie, but that ability to hold an entire venue, no matter how big, in the palm of his hand becomes more understandable when one realises that he was – unlike so many rock and pop musicians – a trained performer. That he was a child star is a relatively little remarked-upon aspect of Marriott's life, something that seems primarily down to Marriott's own disinclination to discuss the matter. However, his father Bill was happy to expound on the subject to *Mojo*'s Cliff Jones in 1994, three years after his son's premature death. When his boy was twelve, Bill saw an advertisement seeking auditionees for the original London production of Lionel Bart's Dickens musical *Oliver!* Few who bore witness to Marriott's 'gor-blimey' schtick – whether it be in real life or on recordings like 'Lazy Sunday' – will be surprised by the fact that the role for which Marriott applied was the Artful Dodger. Nor by Bill's revelation to Jones, "He got the part without even finishing the audition." "You always hear people refer to comedians being 'on', well Steve seemed 'on' 24 hours a day, playing the cockney," noted Marriott's adult friend and colleague Mick Grabham. For a character like Marriott, Oliver Twist's streetwise ragamuffin mate was the archetypal part he was born to play. However, David Arden, who went to stage school with Marriott, cautions, "Although he took the role many, many times, he was understudy for it." Arden may actually mean that Marriott was part of a pool, for the law at the time restricted the number of consecutive days under-sixteens could work. (In the first six months of *Oliver!*'s run, the other Artful Dodgers included David Jones, who went on to become one of the Monkees, and Tony Robinson, now a knight and chiefly famous for being Baldrick in *Blackadder*). Nevertheless, the role saw him handsomely rewarded for his age, the £8 per week wage being the equivalent of approaching £200 in today's money. Marriott didn't appear on the original cast recording of the show released in 1960. However, on a 1962 cast recording released by mail-order budget-price label World Record Club,

'Stephen Marriott' was given the spotlight. His scattering of tracks find him sounding as pugnacious, confident and dexterous as Small Faces fans would one day come to know and love, with the only thing missing from that pre-adolescent voice the gravelly quality that would make him one of the finest of all adult pop/rock singers.

Marriott attended the famous Italia Conti School of Acting, where his tuition was free but recoupable against any earnings from jobs the school secured for him. Arden was a few years older than Marriott and they were at the school together for only a couple of terms. Moreover, "We didn't see too much of him anyway in that last term because they were being tutored in the theatre." However, he got to know Marriott quite well, partly because he had another friend in *Oliver!* whom he would visit at the Lyric Theatre where it was staged. When towards the end of Arden's first Italia Conti term the two began to talk a little bit, Marriott was mightily impressed to discover that Arden's father, in his capacity as a music promoter, was the man who had brought Little Richard over for a UK tour. "He was showing signs then," says Arden of Marriott's interest in making music. "He brought his guitar to school a couple of times, strummed out a couple of things. Of course, he could always sing ... Stevie was such a huge talent."

Arden in fact says of Marriott in general "He was one of the stars of the school," noting, "He'd been in a movie with Peter Sellers, *Heavens Above!*" He also notes, "And he was popular. It was a mixed school, lots of beautiful girls." Arden recalls Marriott leaving Conti's when he was sixteen and his last term being the end of 1963.

Because of the fact of him sharing the screen with a legend like Sellers, *Heavens Above!* (1963) was the gig of which Marriott's parents were particularly proud. However, he racked up numerous others, including appearances in radio soap *Mrs Dale's Diary/The Dales*, television shows *Dixon of Dock Green* and *Mr Pastry*, and motion pictures *Live It Up* and *Be My Guest.* "It was acting which gave me the confidence in myself in front of cameras which is so useful to me now," Marriott told journalist Keith Altham in 1966. Yet despite both this and the fact that he allowed that his time playing Shakespeare with the Old Vic repertory company was "educational," he otherwise dismissed his acting days. He told Altham three years later that he had never thought of returning to acting "... because I was never very good at it ... In all my early films I just played myself." Altham now theorises of Marriott's dismissal of his thespian hinterland, "I think he just thought it was childish, which in some respects it was because he had a young face and he was small and he played characters quite often that were much younger than he actually was. I think he thought it was a kids' thing." Jerry Shirley was a friend of Marriott in the Small Faces days and later his colleague in Humble Pie. Of Marriott's attitude to his thespian years he says, "He dissed it: 'Nah, nah, I hated it.' But he was just born to be on the stage." While tap dancing and other skills the young thesp Marriott acquired may not have been much use in the rock world, Shirley insists that as a consequence of acting Marriott worked a stage more schematically and adroitly than a standard music-group frontman. "He was just a master at it."

Marriott's lack of interest in the acting life was laid bare when he obtained an audition at the Old Vic with no less a figure than Laurence Olivier. Marriott told his parents that he'd fluffed the audition, but the next morning an irate call came through demanding to know why he hadn't turned up for it. "I had a real go at Steve," Bill Marriott told Jones. "'You don't mess Olivier about, my boy. This is the biggest break you'll ever get.' All he said was, 'Dad, I want to be a musician.'"

Marriott's musical pursuits dated from at least the age of eight, when his father bought him a plastic ukulele. He taught himself to play it, as well as harmonica and piano. He won several talent contests and – according to early Marriott publicity – developed sufficiently swiftly to receive a guitar as a Christmas present aged twelve.

Musical artists Marriott loved included blues and R&B masters like Ray Charles, Booker T and the MG's, Muddy Waters and Jimmy Reed. Numbered amongst his white heroes were rock 'n' roll artist Buddy Holly and British rhythm and blues pioneer Long John Baldry. He also had tastes that were less obvious and well-known. "This guy's knowledge of music – his internal jukebox – was immense for a young man," says Shirley, who met Marriott when the latter was nineteen. "Particularly – here's the bit a lot of people don't realise – country music. His knowledge of Hank Williams and George Jones and Patsy Cline was huge. He could sing 'em beautifully too."

By the age of sixteen, Marriott was a recording artist. Having started writing songs, he tried to interest music publishers in his composition 'Imaginary Love', a musical tribute to a female object of desire. His aunt Sheila was secretary to Jack Hylton, then a well-known showbusiness producer and impresario. Hylton introduced Marriott to a music publisher. The latter liked his song but was even more impressed by his voice. In July 1963, 'Imaginary Love' appeared on the B-side of Decca single 'Give Her My Regards'. That 'Imaginary Love' is mannered and polite in a way no future Marriott would be is demonstrated by its opening line, "As fragrant as a wild rose in Spring." The A-side was a hiccupping number in the style of Marriott's hero Buddy Holly. It was written by Kenny Lynch, a black British songwriter-cum-family entertainer who would be a significant figure in the early stages of Marriott's musical career. For his part, Marriott later told Jim Green of *Trouser Press* that 'Give Her My Regards' was "fuckin' awful, really the producer's dream." The record flopped, but Marriott reasoned to Altham, "I reckoned it was good experience and that I was still young enough to hope for another chance on disc."

Meanwhile, Marriott honed his gifts and persuaded people who admired them to provide him a helping hand. Paul Banes was assistant DJ to Tony Calder at London's Ilford Palais, and the two would later be colleagues at the Small Faces' second record label, Immediate. "I started to work with Tony back in '63 and Tony already was in contact with Steve," Banes recalls. Calder gave Marriott a job as part-time assistant. He also became Marriott's agent. Banes: "Steve had different groups that most people ignore but we came up with an idea in the Wimpy Bar in Ilford one night for Steve Marriott's Moments and not that long after he came and played live at the Ilford Pally. Steve at the time was more into R&B, like the majority of the English bands. They were all doing 'Hoochie Coochie Man' and 'Smokestack Lightning'. He used to play harmonica a lot." Marriott was never considered a virtuoso on any instrument – especially by himself – but for Jerry Shirley musical ability was in his DNA. "You hand him an instrument that he's never played before, he'll within five minutes have a tune out of it," he asserts. "He was very, very gifted," concurs Jenny Rylance. "I remember he wanted to get a sitar and we went to this lovely Indian family and he would sit at [our] cottage teaching him to play the sitar. He obviously wasn't Ravi Shankar, but it was wonderful. He could do anything. That's an extraordinary gift."

Marriott found a miniature fame with the Moments: their seven-month UK tour of 1964 inspired the fanzine *Beat '64* and caused one Anne Marshall of Essex to set up a fan club for them. That was about as far, though, as their success went, even though Steve Marriott and the Moments' 'You Really Got Me' was possibly the first-ever Kinks cover. Although it was prepared for US single release in late 1964, it doesn't seem to have progressed beyond promo-copy stage, thus failing in its attempt to hit the States before the original by composer Ray Davies' band could. Intended B-side 'Money Money', written by Alan Caddy, is better, although notable for featuring the first use of Marriott's slightly preposterous early-Small Faces vocal trademark "Come on children," which he had cribbed from James Brown who most famously used it on 'Night Train'. It sounded less incongruous coming from the mouth of a man-of-the-world soul star than someone who from certain angles still looked around twelve...

Marriott's miscellaneous pre-Small Faces recordings also include 'Tell Me', a cover of a song written by Rolling Stones Mick Jagger and Keith Richards. It was advertised in early 1965 as a Decca release but no copy has ever surfaced, although rumours persist of a 7" promo. Marriott later mentioned the record in an interview, stating that it was produced by Andrew Loog Oldham. Oldham confirms, "Yes, he did 'Tell Me', over the same track that's on *The Rolling Stones Songbook*." He adds, "It's unreleased and in my vaults. As is another '64 solo Stevie outing entitled 'Maybe', written by myself and Lionel Bart." Marriott also claimed to have released a version of Cliff Richard's hit 'Move It' with the Frantiks. There is no concrete evidence of it, although again some believe a promo copy was pressed and Marriott insisted it was released "in Malaysia or somewhere." He also claimed to have recorded under the aegis of Decca a version of Timi Yuro's 'Maybe' and, through the grace of Troggs' manager Larry Page, an unnamed Sonny Boy Williamson number.

Marriott reflected of the Moments to Jim Green, "Aside from demos, nothing was really happening so they got despondent and kicked me out to get a better singer — another boy they knew who was five years older than me. I don't really blame them." By early 1965, Marriott – a semi-famous ex-actor and to some extent a *bona fide* recording artist – was reduced to working as a sales assistant at a musical instrument shop, the J60 Music Bar in Manor Park, East London.

While a return to civvy street might be considered a humiliating comedown, it was here on Saturday 23 January 1965 that he had a fateful meeting with future Small Faces colleagues Kenney Jones and Ronnie Lane. This was not – contrary to some reports – the first time he'd encountered Lane. More than one account has him making Lane's acquaintance when the latter's band the Outcasts shared a bill with the Moments in Summer 1964. However, one part of the myth holds true: it was after this meeting that the Small Faces as a band coalesced, ensuring life would never be the same again for any of them. Jones recalled to Cliff Jones of the visit, "This helpful little geezer comes bounding up … and starts chattering away about music. Almost immediately we knew something was up. It was electric, like we all knew in our heads that this was it."

Kenneth Thomas Jones would be the baby of a precocious bunch. The son of a father who was a lorry driver and warehouseman, he was born on 16 September 1948 in Whitechapel and raised in Stepney. Magazine articles contemporaneous with the Small Faces' original Sixties lifespan render the pet version of Jones' Christian name as 'Kenny'. The unusual but now more familiar two-'e' spelling derives from the fact that, once the Small Faces' career got underway, he needed to ensure safe delivery of monies due him. "In the Sixties, there was about five Kenny Joneses, a few band leaders and God knows what, and we were all getting each other's royalties or PRS," he recalls. "[I said], 'Well, stick an "e" in mine, because that way you'll know the difference' … It was there right from day dot." He was always aware that the extra 'e' was missing on early record sleeves but "didn't really care at that time." Others have been more vexed on his behalf. "If anyone spells it over the years without the 'e', all the fans just go up in the air."

Although Jones says of his original fellow Small Faces, "We were all born East London," he also observes, "I'm the only one that's a cockney. I was born within the sound of Bow Bells." He was thirteen when he started playing drums and is entirely self-taught on the instrument. "Most drummers in those days never had any lessons," he points out. "When you got no money, it's the only way to learn." He was dedicated in his practice, getting behind his kit before school, at lunchtime and for two hours in the evening. What education he did have came from listening to the drum patterns to be heard on records. "Not so much copying them, just playing along with them … Turned out all right." He notes, "Sometimes I have to give a lesson for charity. I say, 'Look, it's very important that you find your own style. If you want to have lessons after that, great, but find your own style first, and stick with it.'" The particular style he developed was a blazing one. "I'm known for being one of the loudest drummers in the business, so they tell me," he says. "I'm very fit and quite strong. I don't hit the drums hard, funnily enough. It's actually very martial-arty, if I have to analyse it."

He met Ronnie Lane two months after he began playing (they'd briefly encountered each other as children but had forgotten the fact) and they formed the Outcasts. This ensemble was succeeded by the Pioneers. Jones was fifteen and had just left school when he and Lane encountered Marriott.

Ronald Frederick Lane was born in Plaistow on 1 April 1946. As well as Ronnie, he would be known as 'Plonk'. The explanation for the latter nickname is shrouded in the myth and misunderstanding engendered by a bygone censorious culture. Or is it? "We call him Plonk because he plonks instead of plinks on his bass," Jones stated to *Rave* in late 1965. "It's a name that just happened in the days when he first started 'plonking' the guitar!" stated a Small Faces fan club newsletter from early 1966. Pop paper journalists proffered another explanation relating to a penchant for wine. However, when the coy era of the band's original lifespan had long been subsumed into the modern permissive age, Ian McLagan felt able in his 1998 autobiography *All the Rage* to baldly explain of the nickname, "...he had a big knob, that's all!" Pete Townshend, who would become Lane's best friend, is still under the impression that "Ronnie Lane was called 'Plonk', because he didn't have a particularly distinctive bass style or sound." Told of McLagan's assertion, he says, "It's one I haven't heard about. Also, I don't know that you can trust anything that Mac said. He was a latecomer, too." He adds, "I don't know that I ever saw Ronnie's knob." However, Lane's future wife Sue Hunt, while not confirming McLagan's story, doesn't seem surprised to be asked about it, simply saying, "I'm not going to comment on that." "It's both," says Jones. "Plonked on the bass and plonked on his knob."

With that momentous issue out of the way, we can turn to Lane's musical development. His father Stanley was an amateur singer and drummer, and gifted him a ukulele when his son was six, on which Lane gained sufficient proficiency to make money busking for amused passers-by. It was Lane, Sr. who told Ronnie, "Learn to play the guitar, son, and you'll always have a friend." Lane said that his father was so "tickled" by his learning some chords that he bought him an acoustic guitar. By the time he crossed paths with Marriott at the J60, Lane was actually seeking to switch instrument. "Ronnie said, 'I don't want to play lead guitar anymore, I want to play bass,'" recalls Jones. "So I said, 'Let's go to the shop where we both bought our instruments and see what they've got.'"

Odd, even mystical, coincidences are said to have attended the Small Faces story. "There's something a little bit magical about the Small Faces," Marriott asserted to John Pidgeon. Lane told the same author, "There were some funny little things about it that sound almost fictional. I think the four of us definitely had it in our destiny." This day is a case in point. Jones – who was familiar with Marriott's face from his acting career – had previously had a dream about appearing with Marriott on TV pop show *Thank Your Lucky Stars*. Ultimately, that dream would come true. Then there is the fact that Jones, Lane and Marriott were all of unusually diminutive stature, five-and-a-half feet or less.

Another common element among the trio is that all were mods. To some extent, mod is a notion that defies definition. This is not least due to the fact that it has been subject to revival and is sometimes adhered to by the middle-aged, both of which facts undermine an original concept of a youth cult oriented around modernism. However, Pete Townshend proffers one characterisation by way of the Who's first manager, Pete Meaden, who turned that group into mods for purposes of wider exposure. Says the guitarist, "He described it as a kind of a lifestyle philosophy: 'clean living in difficult circumstances.'"

Jones provides another definition, if one less pithy. "Basically, I grew up in black and white," he says. "In the East End, there was no colour after the Second World War. It was either grey or black. No one wore any reds or blues or anything striking. There were no shops or anything to sell things like that. Also, you got foggy London Town. That was really fucking true, that was. I couldn't see a hand in front of my face once crossing Commercial Road. They had iron foundries and stuff like that. That's how it got foggy, because it was very industrial. The old ladies – my nan, various other old ladies – all wore black. First time I go to the pie and mash shop, I thought, 'Fuckin 'ell – they all look like nuns.' Then they take their teeth out to eat the jellied eels." On a bus trip to Aldgate, Jones happened to see a red caravel in a shop window. "It stood out like a sore thumb. I thought, 'I've gotta have that.' So I went in the shop and said, 'How much is that?' They said, 'Thirty bob.' So I went back home and I saved up for a couple of weeks and started to wear colour for the first time in my life. I got some red socks. I dyed my Levis white. So there I was with Hush Puppies, red socks, and my jeans were shrunk so you could see my socks. That's how my look started. Everyone more or less did the same thing. People of my age just broke free. We needed to wear colour, we needed to cheer ourselves up, we needed to get away from this drab look … The mod fashion happened so quickly. It spread to the upper classes. Anyone who was a teenager got into it."

Jones and Townshend agree that mod was a Continental import. Jones cites the influence of the stylish children of post-war Italian immigrants. Townshend additionally detects a French connection. "I remember talking to a guy who I suppose I would have regarded as a 'face'. He said that he'd gone to Paris with a group of young men and [they] were really struck by the fact that the young kids in Paris, the young boys, were wearing their hair in this feminine style with a back-comb so that their hair leapt up at the back, but they were also wearing really nicely cut clothes. They were wearing American jeans and really beautifully cut shoes. They were all really affected by it and felt scruffy by comparison. He said there was a kind of decision that they made collectively, which was that they couldn't really continue to look at boys like this and just kind of go, 'They're queer.' There was something about them that made it clear that they weren't homosexual. If they were, it wasn't what was important about what these kids were saying. In Milan, they saw pretty much the same thing happening … These guys just thought, 'We want some of that.' The gang came back to London and they were responsible for starting it. The look of it and the style of it."

With their short, neat hair and jackets and ties, Mods might on the surface resemble the average office dogsbody, especially compared to the flamboyance of the teddy boy's drape jackets or the anti-conventionality of the rocker's leather and jeans get-up. However, their top-of-the-range suits and careful coiffures gave them a peacock gleam alien to the average Joe's black-and-whites and short-back-and-sides. Mod also had another aspect, not so much resplendent as exclamatory: candy-stripes, check patterns and loud colours. Some claim that this latter version of mod was a bastardisation of the original vision, but be that as it may it was the one to which the Small Faces gravitated.

"We were mods from day one," says Jones. "Before the band got together. We loved clothes, we loved the style. No one told us what to wear. We were completely natural." Although the latter couldn't really be said of their peers the Who, who adopted the mod look as a career move, Jones doesn't subscribe to the view that the Who were phonies: "I looked upon them as a mod band same as us." Perhaps surprisingly someone who differs on this is Townshend. "No, I concur with that," he fesses up. However, he adds of the plastic-mods charge, "I do also think that you are what you want to be. There was no register for who was mod and who wasn't. The problem that Pete Meaden had with the Who was that I was the only one who really got it and who really wanted to be a part of it. I had mod friends at art college. We were victims of cool."

For Townshend, mod was a movement that began dying almost as soon as it was birthed, primarily because of the mods-versus-rockers clashes that famously took place at British seaside resorts on Bank Holidays in the mid-1960s. "When there were fights on the South Coast, a lot of mods became very disenchanted with the whole mod idea," he states. "It felt uncool to be getting involved in battles with motorcyclists who were wielding bicycle chains and it sort of just came apart and drifted." However, the media gave the ailing movement the equivalent of a defibrillator application, specifically because of a mod-friendly music TV programme. "What actually happened was that the Small Faces were riding on the crest of that wave, which was drifting up through the UK as a result of it being supported by Vicky Wickham on *Ready Steady Go!*" says Townshend. "It gave the mod movement an extra breath."

The J60 boasted that it was "run by musicians for musicians." The legend is that Marriott took that fraternal principle a little too far when, after the

Jones–Lane–Marriott trio had jammed for several hours on the shop floor, he sold Lane his first bass with such a deep discount that it shortly got him the sack. From what Jones says, this idea may have stemmed from band members gilding the lily in interviews. "I'm not quite sure he [didn't have] to do a deal with the manager of the shop," says the drummer. "I think Steve's wangled something." Moreover, there were legal niceties necessary in an era where the age of majority was 21. Jones: "Ronnie's dad went there – he had to – a bit later. Sign the HP agreement."

The developing bond between Lane and Marriott was deepened that afternoon when the former went to the latter's parents' home to hear some of his extensive record collection. Lane and Jones were currently members of an outfit named the Muleskinners. Lane invited Marriott to bring his harmonica to this band's next gig, taking place that night at the British Prince in Bermondsey. There, Marriott ended up switching from harmonica to piano, which he proceeded to pound with more enthusiasm than skill. Pound being the literal description. His Jerry Lee Lewis act was so destructive that the band were thrown out of the pub, leading the other members to refuse to talk to Lane. Jones told Andy Neill, "We were sitting on my drum kit outside on the curb, the three of us just looked at each other and burst out laughing and that's when we decided to form a band together." Marriott told Paolo Hewitt, "When we formed the Small Faces, it was out of error. It wasn't a planned thing at all. It was a case of me getting Ronnie and Kenney slung out of their group."

According to the Outcasts' Ron Chimes, the Jones–Lane–Marriott axis asked that band's guitarist Terry Newman to join them in their new musical venture but the latter declined. The fourth member became instead Jimmy Winston, who as it happens was domiciled in the same street as the J60. "His dad had a pub called the Ruskin Arms with a bit of a ballroom at the back," explains Jones. "It was a place to rehearse." The pub was a three-minute walk from the J60. Adding to the cosiness/incestuousness, Marriott's father had once run a fish stall opposite the Ruskin.

"I was born in a pub," says Winston. "I grew up in a pub in Stratford called the Pigeons Hotel." That birth took place on 20 April 1943. (Sixties sources stating 1945 were disingenuous.) Residency in hostelries like the Pigeons and the Ruskin Arms went with his father's publican profession, which Winston says was both advantageous and disadvantageous: "The work involved, for what you got paid, was a joke, because it's seven days and nights a week." However, he does concede, "You could say, in desperate times, that there's a few bonuses that come from running a pub. Everyone wants to know you and wants to come in and a have a drink. So my dad was never short of meat from the butcher's, if you know what I mean."

Winton was actually born James Edward Winston Langwith but would adopt one of his middle names as a surname for professional purposes. "You can spend so long spelling it out to people that in the end I just thought, 'For the sake of music, I'm going to change my name,'" he reasons. Winston's musicality was forged in the late-Fifties skiffle boom. "I started like a lot of us really about the age of 14, the Lonnie Donegan period and all that type of thing. Playing guitar and playing at school. After 16, 17 I got the first band together, called the East Enders. We did alright for a bit. We played one date at the Cromwellian and Rod Stewart was there when he used to sing with Long John Baldry. It was all Chuck Berry stuff and things like that." However, he explains of music, "It was an on-and-off thing for me. I became a lighterman in the London docks, went in a different route. Then I went to Jersey to live, like a lot of young guys did then. Sort of 17, 18. You lived out there on your wits really ... I was out in Jersey for about one-and-a-half years." Winston then decided he had acting ambitions, a career choice assisted by someone he met in the Channel Isles. "He said, 'Come back, we've got contacts with Central Casting and all that, we'll get you some work.' I started doing extra work and stuff. I went to drama school. Theatre Workshop, E15. So that was all fairly well ingrained in me then. A few weeks after leaving there, getting ready to form a career, is when Stevie and Ronnie came in the Ruskin Arms. I worked in the pub sometimes ... I was up just singing some songs with the current little band that was there. Stevie came up after a bit, said, 'Can I play some harmonica?' He played for a bit, and we did a few songs, then we sat down together." The intended course of his life promptly changed: "One minute you're going to be an actor ..."

Just as Marriott and Lane's supposed initial meeting was almost certainly not the first time they made a connection, so this probably wasn't the first time Marriott and Winston had actually coalesced: Moments member Allen Ellett has recalled that ensemble rehearsing at the Ruskin Arms, while both Marriott and Marriott friend/bandmate Denis Thompson actually said that Winston was once a member of the Moments. A friendship was logical, with Winston and Marriott having not just musical and clothing tastes but their acting background in common. Whatever the case, after a visit by Lane and Marriott to the Ruskin, the trio repaired to a house Winston was renting in nearby Stratford. During what Winston recalls as a "thoroughly good night," they played guitar, listened to records and engaged in other activities "which I won't get into too much." He says, "It was a long night and in the morning the band was on. Probably within a few days, we'd started rehearsing ... We had a week round my house, we were playing guitar all night and just improvising. And then we started rehearsing at the pub, upstairs in the hall." Musically – as with most mods – the new friends shared a penchant for black American rhythm & blues and soul, with a tinge of twelve-bar blues and jazz. Mutually fondly regarded labels were Stax, Tamla and Atlantic and well-regarded artists included Ray Charles, Bobby Bland, Booker T and the MG's, Ray Charles, John Lee Hooker, Howlin' Wolf, James Brown, Otis Redding and Jimmy McGriff.

Winston remembers a communality about those early days. "Stevie was still living with his parents in Manor Park and Ronnie and Kenney were living in the East End … They stayed over at the pub a few times because we rehearsed and did things late. My mum would look after them all, cook for everyone and so on. It was a bit of a community, the pub at the time. We'd go up in the hall and rehearse and one thing and another, then maybe go out in the evening."

That Winston towered over his three new colleagues by several inches wasn't the only palpable difference between he and the rest of the group. Although Winston was the tender age of 21, approaching 22, he had three years on Lane, the second eldest in the band, and five years on Jones. Such age gaps seem significantly greater at that age and Winston does indeed say that he felt he had a "slightly different outlook" to the rest of the group. "I was more streetwise in a sense."

It has to be said that Winston's perception of himself and his status in the band was not necessarily shared by his new colleagues. "I have good, fond memories of him, but he never really fitted in the band," says Jones. "He couldn't play anything. It was Steve that actually had to teach him how to play something. He was also taller. And older." Jones has claimed that the band saw Winston as a friend who was helping them out with a rehearsal space and that it came as a bit of a surprise when he purchased a Vox organ and began joining in the rehearsals. Jones also notes, "Jimmy's brother had a van, this old ex-police one, so we had transport to get around. It was all a bit like that: kind of Jimmy helping out."

Those rehearsals, incidentally, were slotted in between the outstanding commitments of the Moments, whose name Marriott had retained after his ousting and for which he had hired a new line-up. Another indication of an overlap in activity that suggests that the Small Faces were then far from Marriott's be-all-and-end-all is that he was auditioning for other groups and his solo 'Tell Me' single was scheduled, even if it wasn't ultimately released.

"We were all learning," says Winston. "This thing had come together, but everyone was in the early space. They hadn't reached their point of efficiency, let's say." However, while virtuosity lay over a fairly distant horizon, and the Small Faces could never really be said to be a band that paid their dues, it can also be stated that competence and collective tightness seems to have been a hallmark of the group almost from day one. Notes Jones, "We were all so keen. We all learned to play instruments virtually at the same time and we were always trying to improve ourselves. We just played naturally. We had a great telepathy between us all and constantly wanted to please each other." He adds, "We used to love playing instrumentals and that probably helped us in our natural way of playing and finding arrangements. We could actually play everything from jazz to blues to rock to whatever and we just combined a little bit of everything." The sheer energy of the band's music, meanwhile, can possibly be attributed to Jones' unusual methods: "I was never really playing with bass, although Ronnie was a great simple bass player. The way I used to play was to and with the lead guitarist and vocalist. That's my style of drumming. My foot naturally went with Ronnie, but I was more influenced and more honed by what was going on lead-wise."

The pursuit of the band as a truly serious proposition was something that occurred as a consequence of Lane getting sacked from his job at Selmer's amplifier factory in High Holborn. This was down to the fact that it was discovered that Marriott had been provided a free amp by way of reciprocation for the discount he'd arranged at the J60. Some reports have it that Jones got his cards from Selmer's on the same day. The drummer has recalled that following this bombshell they drifted to the Giaconda café in Denmark Street, London's Tin Pan Alley: "[We] called up Steve and said, 'Right, let's go professional.'"

Following some unpaid performances at the Ruskin Arms, Winston's recollection is that, "The first gig was Kensington [Road] Youth Club, which was a rehearsal really, but all the kids in there enjoyed it." Authors Keith Badman and Terry Rawlings have dated this historic East Ham show to 6 May 1965. From there, Winston says, Marriott's already considerable experience and range of contacts in showbusiness meant that "it escalated fairly quickly." Their first manager was a character named Maurice King, to whom they were recommended by up-and-coming white blues singer Elkie Brooks. Winston: "Stevie had spoken to a few agents, trying to just see what work was around. We'd go off to Birmingham and play for a night for nothing virtually and sleep in the van." Despite being active on the live circuit, the band was still nameless.

The not-yet-Small-Faces musical line-up on these early gigs consisted of two guitars, bass and drums. Jones' comment about Marriott having to teach Winston parts seems to be related solely to keyboards. Marriott later said of Winston, "He was proficient on guitar, more so than me." Winston says of he and Marriott, "We were both in a sense equal on guitar. Never decided. It's like, 'You do this and you do that.' It's probably a part of the problem. The thing came together rapidly... Some of these bands have been together for years, from when they were young, and they all know one another and have discussed things a lot more." He dates his move to keyboards to a point just prior to the band's debut single that August, and even then suggests only a partial switchover ("I played it on certain tracks"). Winston avers, "I wasn't a keyboard player and I never professed to be." He offers no argument when it's suggested that it was Marriott who was pushing for keyboards to be an element of the group's sound. As Marriott was more proficient on keys than him, it would have been logical for him to play them when needed but Winston says a Spencer Davis Group set-up wasn't feasible. That contemporaneous ensemble also featured a great white blues singer – Stevie Winwood – but one who did his gritty routine from behind a Hammond B-3. "He was great, but he didn't jump about," says Winston. "[Marriott] was a jump-abouter. That was a part of his thing. I never, ever saw him stand still and sing a song … He loved to perform and the way he performed and moved and did what he did really was made for guitar."

The band's early set essentially consisted of variations on around just half a dozen songs. It's possible that their first number at their first gig was an instrumental iteration of the song which would appear on the first Small Faces album as 'E Too D', essentially a string of well-worn blues and R&B musical motifs and vocal phrases. Other staples of the early Small Faces repertoire were 'You Need Loving', 'Baby Don't You Do It' and 'Jump Back', often stretched to transparency and never played the same way twice, a function of the fact that the early Small Faces were a jam band. "Some of them, we'd stretch it for ten, fifteen minutes," says Winston. "You stumble on something and you discover a new little bit you can put in the song. It's how blues developed, in a way."

The band's swiftly intensifying gigging schedule was made possible by Frankie Langwith. Jimmy Winston's brother invested considerable time and money in the Small Faces even though, Winston says, "My brother used to work in the pub – he had no fortunes." Winston explains "We were running round trying to do gigs, not a lot of money, trying to get to places. I had a little Jeep at one point. We used to go about with our equipment on the back – open, there was no cover on it, which wasn't a great idea. So my brother volunteered to buy a van, drive us, do all the transport and everything and we'd pay him a commission from what we earned. And obviously for him that was based on if it was successful, otherwise to drive to Birmingham and back for two quid in a van you've bought is not really a lot of fun. In the end, they all agreed … He spent all the money he had on a van. We couldn't have got around without it … Back in those days, you gotta realise that a van for five, six hundred pound was a lot of money. A lot of money." Winston claims that his brother's renumeration rate of ten per cent of the band's gig earnings was a formalised arrangement. "My brother did a contract, because he's certainly not daft." Jones told Pidgeon, "Jimmy's brother bought us a van for five or ten per cent of our earnings for life – we actually signed a bit of paper."

A group name had still not been settled on, with the guise under which they played sets sometimes devised by Marriott on the spot. They alighted on a permanent appellation one evening when visiting the flat of an acquaintance. Nobody has ever managed to definitively identify this fabled individual, but she occupies a significant footnote in musical history for bequeathing the group a handle (and by extension its successor band, the Faces). "It's strange, innit?" says Jones. "I would have thought she would have come forward." She has been remembered only by her first name, variously Annabella, Annie or – most commonly – Annabelle. Some sources claim she worked at pirate station Radio London. It has been asserted that she also signed the hire-purchase agreement to enable the underage Marriott to obtain a Marshall amplifier. Marriott recalled that she lived in the upmarket south-west London district of Chelsea. Jones vaguely recalls that "she was trying to be an actress" and suspects that she was an alumnus of Italia Conti "because that's where Steve met all the posh people." Winston's equally vague recollection is that she was one of three girls cohabiting in a flat off Old Brompton Road, which is located if not in Chelsea then the adjacent and equally upmarket South Kensington, although he says she was "middle class, not posh-posh." He recalls, "You were either rehearsing, making your music, or chasing women ... A lot of people used to go to see other people because they had a bit of dope to smoke." The latter intoxicant may have had something to do with Annabelle's momentous suggestion, which Jones recalls as, "'Oh, you've got little faces. Why don't you call yourself the Small Faces?'" Jones says, "We just fell about laughing. We took the piss out of it," but he adds, "Ended up sticking with it."

"To begin with, the name was an embarrassment!" Marriott told Keith Altham. "I mean, Small Faces – it's a joke, isn't it?" Yet joke or not, the handle was highly apposite. Not only was 75 per cent of the group's membership diminutive, but 100 per cent were modernists. The mysterious Annabelle may not have been cognisant of the fact, and the band themselves may not have instantaneously alighted on the significance, but in the mod lexicon a 'face' was a notable figure on the scene, a style icon. "[Pete Meaden] was the one who came up with the definition 'faces' and 'numbers'," says Pete Townshend. "Faces were the fashion leaders and the style leaders and the numbers, the tickets, were the people that followed." (Meaden composition 'I'm the Face' had been the B-side of 'Zoot Suit', released by Who-precursor band the High Numbers in July 1964.) Moreover, the juxtaposition involved in the title Small Faces – the boastfulness of the second word qualified by the first word – was again, intended or not, the quintessence of the band's impish, irreverent sense of humour.

Winston says he never saw Annabelle/Annabella/Annie again after that juncture. However, he feels fairly sure that she was aware of her walk-on role in music history. He reasons, "If you'd have suggested that and then, within a month, the band's had a record out with that name..."

The name was something that seemed to become less an embarrassment and more a virtue with each passing day. "It's like 'The Beatles,'" says Winston. "When you first hear the name, you think, 'What's happening?' Also, what's easy to remember is a bonus for the band." He adds an afterthought which – although he doesn't say it – may have played into the reason for the group settling on the name. "In the East End, the Jack the Lads were the 'faces' – certain people who could either really have a fight or [were] a little bit known for something."

The emphasis in the pronunciation of the name was always supposed to be on the first word. Ian McLagan was amused to be told by this author that some pronounce it Small *Faces*: "That's funny. That's very Irish. 'The Post *Office*' instead of 'The *Post* Office.'" On a related note of pedantry, Winston says, "It was just Small Faces." However, the fact that there was no definite article in the group's handle won't be reflected in this text because – as with the Buzzcocks, the Eagles, the Skids, et al – band members didn't practice in speech/interviews what their album billings preached. It should also be noted that the "small" part often wasn't even enunciated: long before there was a group of the name fronted by Rod Stewart, colloquially and informally the Small Faces were frequently referred to as simply "the Faces."[1]

The group were first advertised as the Small Faces on 5 June 1965 when they started a five-week Saturday residency at the Cavern in the Town club in the Notre Dame building off Leicester Square. "We played there once and then got booked for four weeks," recalls Winston. "It was like the big moment." Ostensibly, it was a moment for which the group were not quite ready. Not only did their repertoire still consist of a handful of songs, but – Jones later recalled – "By this time we'd already given up trying to make it … We were terribly impatient." Marriott said the same thing to Pidgeon, stating, "We'd've been happy to just to play weddings and pubs and relax. We weren't out to prove anything."

One of the people who came to see the group at the venue was in fact Pete Townshend, a comparatively grizzled veteran even discounting the High Numbers record: the Who were by now two singles – both hits – into their recording career. He had gone on the recommendation of Elkie Brooks. "The musicianship seemed pretty good to me," he says. "Jimmy Winston was on guitar and he was really, really copying me. He was swinging his arm, he had a Union Jack on his Marshall amp. But despite that, they were pretty fucking remarkable … Ronnie Lane was very competent … There's not much to it, playing bass well, but part of it is humility … Kenney Jones was a drummer I liked from straight off. He was really straight-down-the-middle, very, very solid drummer … But I think it was really about Steve Marriott." Of the latter, he marvels, "Stevie's voice was just spectacular. It was a proper blues voice. The other big blues voices in London at that time were Chris Farlowe, Rod Stewart, Long John Baldry. Everybody was on the lookout for these great blues voices and Stevie just had that. It was really all the band needed."

Of their repertoire, Townshend notes, "They were playing some of the songs we used to play. We were playing some James Brown songs. In fact, we recorded one on our first album, 'Please, Please, Please'. They played it brilliantly." He adds, "What I do remember about the Cavern was that it wasn't full up by any means but the crowd that were there seemed to be quite elitist mods."

It wasn't only Townshend who was impressed. The newly christened Small Faces were spotted by someone working at Contemporary Records, owned by one Don Arden. "It could have been either Ian Samwell or Pat Meehan,"

---

[1] The subtitle of this book ('The Definitive Small Faces Biography') is deliberately designed to circumnavigate the issue of the definite article, lest fans of the band, as Jones puts it, "go up in the air."

says David Arden. Marriott claimed in fact that it was Arden's secretary, with whom he was familiar, that championed the band to Contemporary. He is backed up by Moments guitarist Graham Dee, who was a flatmate of the young lady in question. In any case, as with so many people with whom Marriott would work, ranging from Ronnie Lane to Tony Calder, Arden is a man on whose radar the singer may have already registered, in his case because the Moments had supported Arden's clients the Nashville Teens. Whoever first alerted the company, Winston says, "Pat Meehan came down to see the band. He was like Don Arden's report man." Winston says that Meehan announced his presence and its purpose "but very briefly – he was a man of few words." He adds, "Shortly afterwards we got the call to go up and see Don."

That the owner of that business was the father of Marriott's ex-stage schoolmate David Arden was a coincidence, but the latter notes that Marriott made a point of informing Arden, Sr. of his past acquaintance with his son.

Don Arden was born Harry Levy in Manchester in 1926. "He was brought up to be a very religious Jew," says David. "He was going to be a cantor, the man who leads the prayers in synagogue, because he had a fantastic voice. He had such a fantastic voice that he went on the stage." "I was in the office one day and he played me [something] he'd recorded, 'My Yiddishe Momme'," says Jimmy Winston. "He had quite an operatic voice." Arden's Judaism began to peel away as he got older. Despite this, and the fact that many have attested to his dishonest or violent behaviour, Arden – according to David – considered himself to have a moral core. "He said, 'Son listen, there's only ten things you gotta know – ten commandments.' That's how I was brought up."

Arden plied a trade as both singer and stand-up comedian until his late twenties, when he switched to promotion and management on the grounds that there was more money to be made from other people's talents. In a still primitive industry where the power of the fist or threat thereof had greater currency than negotiation or law, he was well equipped for his new role. "You either loved him or hated him," notes David. "If he walked in a room, heads would turn. He had a presence." Yet David insists that his father obtained what he wanted by insinuation and bluster rather than brute force. "His face would look grotesque and scary and he could tell you what he was going to do. Not that he ever did it. If anybody ever says they received physical punishment from him, they're liars. I've only ever seen him in two fights." Did the man he called 'Pops' believe in corporal punishment for his kids? "No. Absolutely not. Family man." David insists that Arden's powerful presence was essential to protect his and his clients' rights. It should be noted, though, that Don Arden would sometimes seem to view his rights and his clients' rights as in opposition, something that would be a bone of contention for more than one of his artists, the Small Faces among them.

"The first big rock artist he managed officially was Gene Vincent," says David. Musical luminaries whose UK tours Don Arden promoted included Chuck Berry, Ray Charles, Sam Cooke, Fats Domino, Jerry Lee Lewis, Carl

Perkins and Little Richard. All these artists hailed from the United States, a country suffused with the sort of glamour and excitement that at the time it seemed inconceivable could originate in drizzly, low-key Great Britain. However, in the early 1960s, Arden's fortunes experienced a downturn when Britons inexplicably began turning up their noses at American artistes in favour of something that had not too long before been considered oxymoronic: British rock 'n' roll.

Ironically, he could have got on this gravy train at an early stage when he was tipped off about a pre-recording contract Beatles. David Arden: "It was Little Richard kept saying to the old man, 'Oh man, you should look at them.' [To] the old man in those days, Americans were the top artists. He always thought the English were second best. The old man wasn't interested." Arden even warned off others. Arden's future colleague Ron King ran booking agency Galaxy Entertainments. "Brian Epstein was standing in that office of mine in Oxford Street," King recalls. "At that time, Don Arden and me were starting to get work together. I phoned him up and said, 'I've got a man called Brian Epstein here and he wants me to be the agent for a group called the Beatles.' 'Daah, they're a bag of shit,' he said. 'With a name like that... He's been all over London trying to get somebody to take them. Don't even think about it.' I repeated that to Brian Epstein. He said, 'Thank you' and walked out."

Asked when it was that his father realised his mistake in spurning the British scene, David Arden says, "Soon as he was losing every penny he'd ever earned with all the Yanks. He brought over the Everly Brothers and Bo Diddley and the tour was dying. It was the Rolling Stones' first tour. He had to call up Little Richard and say, 'Richard, please come on over and join this show' just to get bums on seats ... He was slow to take it up, but it didn't take him long. The next thing was the Animals and the Nashville Teens."

Although Mike Jeffery had already nabbed the Animals' management role, he needed an established promoter to help turn popularity in their native Newcastle into national success and to that purpose turned to Arden. It was the latter who put the band in touch with record producer Mickie Most. The recording career the latter supervised had, by their second single, facilitated international success: 'The House of the Rising Sun' (1964) was a transatlantic number one. Although a lucrative gig, Arden's ownership of the Animals' concert rights came to an end after a disagreement with Jeffery, a slightly murky figure who might be posited as one of the few people in the business who could not be intimidated by Arden. For a brief moment, Arden's management of the Nashville Teens touched Animals-level success: 'Tobacco Road' was also a UK and US hit.

Part of Arden's strategy for capitalising on the newly hot British music scene involved locating himself in Carnaby Street. "Carnaby Street in those days was the place to be seen in," notes King of the short, narrow thoroughfare in Soho, central London that was then stuffed with 'boutiques' frequented by those enamoured of the era's brightly coloured, flamboyantly tailored mod fashions. It was therefore fitting that his next attempt at jumping on the British beat-boom bandwagon should involve the Small Faces.

Arden's interest in the band wasn't shaken by the fact that when they made their way to Carnaby Street to present themselves to him they didn't look quite as elfinly attractive as they probably had when Meehan attended one of their gigs. Due to an altercation when out the previous night, they arrived covered in bruises and stitches. Undeterred, Arden put the band on a summer season bill at Margate Winter Gardens with the Nashville Teens and the Pretty Things. "As soon as they walked on stage you could tell they were something different, something special," he recalled. "Four Oliver Twists." If that sounds like the naïve verdict of an older man not interested in their kind of music, he is backed up by someone younger and hipper. Says Jerry Shirley, "They were the only band that you could say in the early days rivalled the Who for sheer power and excitement on stage." For his part, David Arden says that while his dad was partly motivated by "success at all costs," he was also no philistine: "If you had talent, he adored it. He adored Stevie. If you were an arsehole and you were talented, he'd do anything for you. You'd get away with anything ... Not only did he love talent, he could help nurture it. He recognised it in its raw state and got a buzz out of bringing it along. He wasn't too good on soundboards, but [he was on] lighting plots, presentation, running order for a set."

The Small Faces had, it so happened, also attracted the interest of Kit Lambert, who as co-manager of the Who was on the surface a more enticing prospect than Arden. Not only that, but there was a rather disturbing portent on the day the Small Faces went to Arden's offices to discuss his overture. There they were surprised to meet the Animals, who had just managed to extricate themselves from their professional relationship with Arden. "As we knocked at the door, they started to walk out," recalls Winston. Eric Burdon, Animals lead singer, addressed the newcomer. Winston: "[He] said, 'What you going to do?' 'We're going up to sign with Don.' And the look on his face. He went, 'Oh, fuck. You must be crazy. We just managed to get out from that so and so.' And they all walked off laughing." Although Winston says this encounter was "a shock," he candidly admits it was scant deterrence to he and his colleagues. "Because you were so – let's be honest – enthusiastic to get on."

It has been suggested that the reason the Small Faces did plump for Arden over Lambert or anyone else is precisely because of Marriott having known his son at stage school. If true, it might be argued that a fatuous rationale ended up costing the band dearly. Winston, though, offers alternative reasons. One was Arden's own performing hinterland, the other, "Don Arden's company had an agency attached to it, Galaxy." David Arden himself has a different theory. For Marriott, Don Arden's reputation as a heavy would be far from a demerit. "Stevie loved to be around tough guys," David says. "The old man was not a gangster, but he was a tough guy in terms of if you fucked with him you'd pay the price." He reflects of Marriott, "I guess it must be his East-End upbringing. The last person involved with him that I knew of was Laurie O'Leary and Laurie used to run the Charlie Kray agency." Charlie Kray was a brother of notoriously vicious Sixties villains Reg and Ronnie Kray. Winston says of Arden, "He looked like the Mafia," and doesn't necessarily mean it as an insult. He notes, "You walk into an office... Big desk, he's sitting there, smoked a cigar – you just start considering it as success."

The Small Faces signed to Arden's Contemporary Records on 10 June 1965. Despite its name, it was not a music label but a production company. It would finance recordings which would then be leased to a music label. The beauty of this unconventional arrangement was that the rights of those recordings could be sold to record companies in different territories. Moreover, those rights would eventually revert. "That's something that he learnt from Mickie Most, with the Animals and the Nashville Teens," says David. "The old man was extremely bright."

Arden arranged for publicity photos, engaging the services of Gered Mankowitz, who had previously shot the Nashville Teens for him and whose work was soon to grace the front of the Rolling Stones' latest LP *Out of Our Heads*. "When he called me to do a session, I always had to remind him that he hadn't paid me for the previous [one]," Mankowitz notes. As for this particular session, he says, "The shoot was my usual sort of mixture of a couple of backgrounds. I've only got black and white. Don't know whether I shot colour. They had a funny little puppy. It had its leg in a cast. Very typical of the Small Faces even then, they managed to persuade me to put the dog in some of the pictures. In the shots where I did Jimmy forward, he makes the others look small, but where he's just a little bit behind the line and leaning back, which is possibly something I asked him to do, the height difference isn't really that pronounced. I don't think I saw it as being an issue. Maybe because I didn't really concern myself about the fact that they were called the Small Faces. They look awkward but very relaxed. Awkward just simply because the experience of having your photograph taken is a bit awkward. They were all dressed in a sort of mod-ish way. They all had jackets. Steve and Jimmy were wearing ties. Looking at the pictures, they seem to work really well together. They look very much a band. I was beginning to work with getting bands to work off each other, lean on each other, have quite physically close composition because, in photography, the gap between people is exaggerated. They responded very well to that."

As alluded to by Winston, there was a certain symbiosis between Contemporary Records and Galaxy Entertainments. Ron King's booking agency had recently moved from Oxford Street to offices across the corridor from Contemporary following an overture from Arden to take a share of the Carnaby Street building. King had graduated to agenting through running clubs. "I booked a couple of groups through his office, then it went on from there," King says. Although the Small Faces became one of his clients, "There was no contract, but I was the unofficial agent for them." King gainsays David Arden's assertion of his father's love of artistry: "He didn't appreciate anybody's talent. He was only interested in the money he could get out of it."

The Small Faces themselves were happy bunnies. Jones has recalled he had been earning £9 per week in his job at Selmer's. The £20 weekly wages on which Arden promptly put the group members, therefore, was not insignificant, especially to a group of kids only a couple of years removed from pocket money and paper-round wages and who had recently been surviving – Jones has averred – on brown-sauce rolls. It was also more than the average 1965 UK weekly wage and £350-plus in today's money. In addition to that, Arden provided the parents of Jones, Lane and Marriott an allowance of the same amount. The band members were also – notionally – to receive a 1.5 per cent royalty rate on their recorded product. The cherry on the cake for such clothes horses must have been Arden giving them the run of the top boutiques. "There was only three shops in Carnaby Street then," recalls Jones. "One was John Stephen, which Don's offices were above. A little bit further down the road was Toppers, the shoe shop. Then Lord John started up. We had accounts in those three shops, the only place to buy stuff." For mods-about-town to be able to breeze into such emporiums and depart with bulging carrier bags without spending a penny would have made for a heady feeling indeed. The fact that such expense was recoupable against future record royalties was a matter of hazy import, something that would become a motif in the band's story and their perception of themselves as having been ripped off.

Despite all this though, ex-Moments guitarist Denis Thompson was shocked to be told by Marriott of his remuneration level. Thompson was currently earning much more than that for his gig in Tony Jackson & the Vibrations. There again, neither Thompson nor Tony Jackson & the Vibrations could be said to have gone on to become major entries in the annals of pop. Not only did Arden facilitate that distinction for the Small Faces, but he did so inside an almost ridiculously short space of time. Within days of their signing to his company, Arden was able to tell the group that they were to be recording artists on the Decca label, home to among others no less than the Rolling Stones. "He had lots of friends in the business," explains David Arden. "When you've got a bit of a track record, which the old man had with the Teens and the Animals, people would go, 'Really believe in this?' and they'd do a deal with him ... Dick Rowe I believe did the deal." Rowe, of course, has been immortalised as the man at Decca who turned down the Beatles. Arden: "He did indeed. But you know what? He signed the Rolling Stones, Tom Jones, Englebert Humperdinck, and a whole list of others. And the Small Faces." Winston recalls that the Decca deal wasn't done 'sight unseen', saying that the group entered Pye Studio in Marble Arch for a couple of days. "We did what we did on stage, 'E Too D' and some of those tracks. They became in the end, with a bit of tidying up, tracks on those first two LPs."

With a healthy regular wage and a record release on the horizon – and all just around five months after forming – the Small Faces must have felt truly blessed. Life would never be so uncomplicated for them again.

2 Almost Grown

The Small Faces' debut release fashioned a silk purse from a pig's ear.

From what can be gleaned from conflicting and clouded recollection, 'Whatcha Gonna Do About It' started out as a Marriott/Lane creation that was simply an undisguised vamp on the staccato riff and first section of Solomon Burke's 'Everybody Needs Somebody to Love'. However, the group weren't so naïve that they thought it was a masterpiece in this state and were happy for Arden to bring in professional help to fashion it into something more chart-worthy. The men the manager chose were Brian Potter and Ian Samwell.

Potter was at the start of a songwriting and production career that would reach full bloom in the Seventies with his work for, among others, the post-Motown Four Tops. Samwell's name was familiar to any Briton with the habit of looking at the information in the parentheses beneath record-label song titles. A onetime guitarist for Cliff Richard, he had obtained immortality by writing the latter's 'Move It', the 1958 hit universally recognised as the first authentic (as opposed to pastiche or awful) British rock 'n' roll song. He'd turned to full-time composing after leaving Richard's band and would have material recorded by Joe Brown, the Drifters, the Isley Brothers, Kenny Lynch and Dusty Springfield. Cliff Richard, meanwhile, laid down a string of his creations. By the time he worked with the Small Faces, he had become London's first high-profile DJ, running regular sessions at, among other places, the Lyceum. According to Don Arden, both Potter and Samwell were then working for him on a weekly £25 retainer.

David Arden claims that it wasn't actually Samwell's impressive track record that secured him the Small Faces gig. "The old man was very fond of Ian Samwell," he says. "He felt very bad for him. Ian Samwell had been a very unlucky chap. He thought life had been a bit cruel to him." No less so, perhaps, than during an incident at the Scene Club in London in 1964 when Samwell tried to persuade an as-yet-unsigned Animals to make him their producer.

Arden and Mickie Most had just been in to see the band perform with a view to working with them and Most found Samwell's overture in progress when he nipped back to ask the group about a song they'd performed. Arden: "My old man went, 'Over my fucking dead body'. He runs down there: 'Oi! Fuck off, Ian!'"

Winston doesn't recall the Small Faces having any interaction with Potter. "We only ever dealt with Ian Samwell," he says. "He was living in a flat in Hampstead. When we met him, he looked fairly wasted, but he knew what he was doing. He'd taken this simple structure and turned it into a pop song." With or without Potter, Samwell reshaped the song and added a lyric. The band were perhaps too embarrassed about the song's second-hand nature to demand composing credit but Samwell/Potter cannily copped 100% of the publishing. 'Whatcha Gonna Do About It' – as Samwell/Potter refashioned it, the title itself stolen from a Doris Troy record – is unquestionably slight. Its melody is staccato, its chorus consists of one line enunciated four times and its lyric is quintessentially moon-in-June: it begins with "I want you to know that I love you baby" and its first verse culminates in the profound observation that the narrator is happy when the object of his affections is present and sad when she's not. The attributed writers deserve a modicum of credit for a competent piece of hackwork. That the Small Faces make 'Whatcha Gonna Do About It' sound anything but trite merits them the real hosannas, though – it is a true mark of their astonishing chemistry and precocity.

This is all evident from the opening second. Jones' extended clatter across his kit is an extraordinarily exciting and raw beginning for a single of the period, not to mention a wonderful and representative fanfare for the Small Faces' recording career – such percussive entrées would be a Small Faces signature. The second galvanising component is the strength of the vocal performance. Marriott had triumphantly transcended the hurdle that so many male child singers face when their voice breaks. That impish set of bellows to be heard on his *Oliver!* cast recording had, three years on, become an instrument no less powerful but utterly different. It is raspy and raunchy and – by a miracle of happenstance that also blessed the likes of the Animals' Eric Burdon and the Spencer Davis Group's Stevie Winwood – perfectly suited to the black music styles that happened to form his musical tastes. "He was an old man's voice in that young body," notes Ian McLagan. Marriott once let in Jerry Shirley on the secret of his singing prowess by inviting him to look into his mouth. Explains Shirley, "If you look down your throat in a mirror, the gap between the bottom of your tongue and that thing that hangs down from above it, it's quarter of an inch maybe, half an inch maximum. Steve's was, like, two inches. It was like a huge great big hole. And on top of that, of course, he'd been trained as an actor to sing properly. He sang from his stomach, he didn't sing from his throat. But he had that throat for the voice to come out of. It was so loud."

It so happened that another of Graham Dee's flatmates was Brian Potter. Dee has claimed that he was booked by Samwell to play on the track – Marriott telling him that their first choice Jimmy Page was unavailable – and that in two sessions at IBC and Pye Studios he performed the background guitar riff while Marriott handled the barre chords. (His memory also suggests that Tony McIntyre drummed on the first session, Jones the second.) Despite the alleged presence of someone more competent on the instrument that him, the most impressive guitar moment of the recording remains Marriott's solo. The first half of this instrumental break is a brutal, grinding run with a touch of feedback that presages both heavy metal and punk. Nothing is taken away from its power by the fact that it was rooted in Marriott's inadequacies on the instrument. "He wasn't the greatest guitar player, so the distortion thing was a way of putting an effect into it without having to do too much," notes Winston. He observes, "It was also inventive." Not just inventive but hardly designed for the sweet tooth. One has to remind oneself that this is a teeny-bopper's record, if not in the eyes of the artists then certainly their songwriters, manager and record company. In fact, one is somewhat surprised – even to the point of admiration – that Arden didn't put his foot down and insist on something blander. However, Winston says, "Don saw it as commercial." Pete Townshend, incidentally, doesn't think Marriott was particularly taking his cue from the Who's feedback-drenched recordings and stage act. "Dave Davies was doing it in the Kinks, Lennon had done a little bit of it on one of their songs," he says easily. "The actual musical thing about feedback and distortion was just something that was happening."

Just as much the product of limited ability was 'Whatcha Gonna Do About It''s staccato, two-note keyboard element. It was also an act of compromise. Says Winston of his ultra-basic motif, "Ian Samwell had written the idea but, as we didn't have brass, [we put] an organ on it." Although the keyboard part is rudimentary, according to Jones even this pattern required some coaching. "I'll never forget Steve telling Jimmy what to do," he says. "It's only like: der-der, der-*der* – two fingers." "It was enough to help 'Whatcha Gonna Do About It' be a hit," shrugs Winston. As was the record's overarching pugnacious, gritty quality. "It was just laid out right," says Winston. "It had just a constant sort of energy about it … 'Whatcha Gonna Do About It' is a good title as well."

Colloquial confrontationalism also attends the title of the B-side. 'What's A Matter Baby', written by Joy Byers and Clyde Otis, was first recorded by US female vocalist Timi Yuro (a name that will crop up again in the Small Faces' story), who scored a *Billboard* #12 with it in 1962. Carl Wayne and The Vikings had attempted to put it into the British hit parade in 1964 without success. Remarkably, the Small Faces' version of the song is superior to the one proffered by Yuro's skilled session men. It begins with another impressive exploration of Jones' kit, albeit one more measured than on the A-side, suiting the mid-tempo pace. Falsetto sha-la-la vocal frills are counterpointed by Marriott's abrasive guitar work. The lyric – exploring the schadenfreude felt by a cruelly spurned lover upon hearing that his ex has been dumped by her current partner – gives Marriott the opportunity to indulge in impressively lip-trembling passion.

Both sides of the disc boast polished production work, credited to Samwell. The formal credit is gainsaid by Winston, who says, "We did it ourselves." Unconversant with studio technology, though, the band would have had an engineer, and Winston recalls Glyn Johns fulfilling that role, as did (talking to Paolo Hewitt in the 1990s) Johns himself. Johns would work extensively with the Small Faces as engineer throughout their career, before graduating to the status of one of the world's most in-demand producers. "I think I made just about all their records," he later observed.

'Whatcha Gonna Do About It' inaugurated a peculiar Small Faces alternative-version tradition. Different iterations of Small Faces tracks consistently turned up on foreign EPs and albums. Some were not notably different to the familiar/official/domestic version, but some were aesthetically superior. An alternative version of 'Whatcha Gonna Do About It' makes such a virtue of Marriott's feedback that it actually begins with a blast of it rather than Jones' drums clatter. Winston points out, "[Small Faces fan] John Hellier sent me a couple of demo discs, 45s. He sent me a French one where there was a couple of songs I was singing, which usually Steve would sing. I couldn't remember where they got it from." Whatever the means, continental releases have become coveted items amongst fans, not least for their picture sleeves, which were then virtually unheard of in the band's home country.

The Small Faces' debut single was released in August 1965. It climbed to a respectable no.14, or at least it did in one chart. There was really no 'official' pop chart in Britain throughout the Small Faces' original lifespan. That eventuality only came about in 1969 when chart TV programme *Top of the Pops* began using the rundown featured in *Record Retailer* magazine (later renamed *Music Week*) when it began to be compiled by the British Market Research Bureau. The most authoritative of the several competing Sixties magazine charts was considered to be that of weekly music paper *New Musical Express* (the *NME*), but unless otherwise stated UK chart positions for the period used in this book are from *Record Retailer* simply because it is the chart that has long been employed by the compilers of the *Guinness Book of Hit Singles*, now viewed as the industry's chart bible. Admittedly, this latter fact is not without some controversy, most notoriously regarding the Beatles' 'Please Please Me', which disc is recorded as a no.2 whereas in other charts – as well as popular memory – it was a chart-topper. The Small Faces have also suffered from this anomaly. Today, it's widely held that 'All or Nothing' was the Small Faces sole no.1 in their home country. This came as news to McLagan, who says, "I thought we had a few. I know that we knocked the Beatles off number one with one." As for the *Guinness* book placing its faith in the chart to be found in the *Record Retailer*, he caustically notes, "Who read that? We used to read *NME* or *Melody Maker*." On a similar note, although the *Billboard* charts were considered at the time no more authoritative State-side than those of rival *Cash Box*, with whose stats it sometimes differed, the demise of the latter magazine in 1996 makes people feel it incumbent to defer to the historical placings of the surviving periodical.

Jones and Winston agree that the TV and radio exposure Arden obtained the group for their first release was top-notch. "He got hustling TV companies and all of a sudden we did TV [shows] with Cher and some of the big players," says Winston. "All of a sudden you've taken such a leap." The Small Faces made their BBC television debut on 6 September on BBC 2's mildly alternative pop show *Gadzooks*. Ten days later saw the occasion of their first *Top of the Pops* appearance. On an appearance on ITV's *Ready Steady Go!*, the Small Faces made the acquaintance once again of Eric Burdon. Winston: "They gave him the job of introducing us and he called us the 'New Faces'. Could you imagine: you're just going on to play. Everyone's hair went up." The latter incident and its like couldn't dampen the exhilaration of newfound fame and the sensation of going places. "I can remember when everyone was at the pub one day and it came on the radio the first time," says Winston. "All of a sudden you felt a part of that thing that's so much bigger." However, all this success and exposure was ultimately the result of manoeuvres murkier than Arden merely using his contacts.

"Don was a first-class hyper," says Winston. "That's what he was good at. Him and Galaxy, they were flyposting all round London. Everywhere you drove, there's posters up, stuck here, stuck there. You got these firms driving round in the night." Billposting is, of course, illegal. It's not, however, particularly frowned on because there is no corruption involved, nor the theoretical disadvantaging of others. However, other methods of bringing the record to the public's attention are not widely viewed with as much benevolence. Notes McLagan, "They used to list the stores in the very early Sixties, every store that they took the charts from, so all the [artists'] managers had to do is to go to those stores couple of days before and buy four or five records." Of course, there is a reasonable argument that if everyone was doing this, it wasn't so much cheating as levelling the playing field. Arden's own testimony, however, was that his own measures in this regard were somewhat more industrial. He later claimed that over the course of two years he paid £5,500 (£100k today) to two individuals to buy Contemporary artists' records from shops. Moreover, he claimed he went to greater measures than merely buying records. He said he paid staff members of music publications to amend chart positions, gave £2,750 (£50k) to chart fixers to hype Contemporary's records into the hit parade and £5,000 to £6,000 for Radio Caroline airplay (commonly known as payola). David Arden confirms part of the latter. "I used to run up to uncle Phil Solomon, who ran Radio Caroline, the business end of it, on a weekend with two hundred and fifty quid for the airplay," he recalls. "Phil lived in an apartment just off Park Lane and we were then living in Berkeley Square, not far from there. If we were short of money, he'd always say, 'Give

Phil a call, tell him you'll be up later.' The old man would hustle and bustle and get this money. It's a fair amount of money, especially where there was Radio London as well (which I had nothing to do with)." Interestingly, David sees this activity as something that underlines his father's integrity. "If he believed in an artist, he would beg, steal, borrow, spend all his own money. No ifs, ands or buts."

If the band had been aware at the time of the sums Arden later claimed to have invested in them, they might not have ultimately become so disgruntled with their own remuneration, but Don Arden himself said, "The Small Faces had no idea what went on." His son is not surprised by the idea that his father might not have communicated the fact of his investment to his charges even when he might be said to have a reason to do so. "Money was a horrible side issue," he reasons. "It wasn't something that he ever really wanted to deal with. It was like a necessary evil."

With the Small Faces' recording career having only just taken off, Steve Marriott received some devastating news. "Steve came up the office and admitted that he'd got a fan pregnant," says Val Williams, who was soon to start working for Contemporary Records.

Williams' source was Pauline Corcoran, who ran the Small Faces fan club for Arden and in whom Marriott had confided. "Pauline said he sobbed on her shoulder," Williams recalls. "He just didn't know what to do." The fan was Sally Foulger, aged sixteen. Sixties Britain has been posited as a swinging proposition, but its burgeoning libertarianism was really restricted to the young, or even just a sub-section of it. In this transitional period in history, the reins of power – including those of the Fourth Estate – were in the hands of largely censorious and judgmental elders. As such, the revelation that a pop star/role model had engaged in 'promiscuous' behaviour that had led to the impregnation of a young woman to whom he wasn't married was potentially career destroying. Williams says of Marriott, "He went in to see Don and Don said to him, 'Look, don't worry about it, we'll sort it out.'" Williams says the next thing Corcoran knew was, "Steve come up and he's got cigars and champagne and obviously the child had been born. She said, 'Nothing ever was mentioned [again] about this child at all.'"

The child was a girl, christened Lesley. In 2010, the now-adult Lesley told Mick Taylor of the Groping with a Stoker Small Faces Facebook group that she was given up for adoption at the age of fifteen months and spent around three months in a children's home before she was taken up by what she terms a "very caring" if "very strict" couple. She had a younger adoptee step-brother. When she was eighteen, Lesley tracked down her birth mother, who revealed to her who her father was. Lesley also claimed that her mother had filed a paternity suit naming Marriott as the father but that it was dropped. One wonders whether Arden was instrumental in the way this potentially serious problem somehow harmlessly evaporated, and whether this involved – like the bribes and payola – expenses that could never be declared on a balance sheet or income-tax return.

Just as Arden's damage limitation for and financial indulgence of his charges makes it difficult to unequivocally portray him as heartless and a thief, so other factors render it problematic to suggest that he cared not a jot for art. It's doubtful, for instance, that a philistine would have allowed the Small Faces to write both sides of their second single.

It's true that he stood to make additional money if the record was a hit: the band were signed as writers to his publishing company Contemporary Music Ltd. However, somebody determined to play it safe would have allowed the group only the B-side at most. Yet Jones recalls, "We said, 'Okay, we're song-writers and we make our own music' and Don Arden was all for it." "He just took a chance," says Winston. "We said, 'We've got this song.' He said, 'Well, just get in the studio and do it then.'"

Winston notes of the song in question, "He didn't hear it first ... He wasn't that sort of manager. I never believed he knew about song construction and stuff like that. ... His music was so different. When he played this version of 'My Yiddishe Momme', I thought he sang it well, but it was a different world." The song was 'I've Got Mine', a creation Winston recalls emerging from the Small Faces' habit of improvisation long into the evening and beyond. "The only one who used to go home early was Kenney," he says. The band borrowed a trick from the writers of their first record by seeking to deploy snappy and resonant colloquialisms. The title phrase of 'I've Got Mine' doesn't quite make sense in the context of third parties' lack of knowledge about the narrator's heartbroken state. Lane's response-call to the title phrase – "You've got yours" – is sung rather gormlessly (in contrast to his competent rendering of the title line of 'Whatcha Gonna Do About It'). However, while the lyric is sloppy and the subsidiary vocals suspect, the record's music is sophisticated and innovative.

A slow, ominous introduction takes us into a mid-tempo soundscape which features possibly the first recorded instance of a guitar riff played through a Leslie organ cabinet, a trick that would explode into a mini-craze during the course of the decade. Phill Brown, a recording assistant who would work with the Small Faces in later years, explains the process: "The Leslie originally was just the speaker system for the Hammond organ. It had varispeed so that the horns could go at different speeds to give you that kind of shimmer sound of a Hammond ... There's this little phono socket on the main metal slab of the frame of the Hammond and that gave you access into the circuitry. It's very dangerous because the whole thing's live, so people did get electric shocks and things, but if you put vocals through or guitar, you just got a whole different sound ... It was just a brilliant texture ... It was a way of getting another sound in the studio because we just didn't have effects that much."

It should be pointed out that this innovation came not through Marriott, as many might assume, but Jimmy Winston. Winston had bought the speaker from the J60, the very music store that had given birth to the Small Faces. The upshot of plugging his 12-string Rickenbacker guitar into an amplifier intended for a completely different instrument was what he terms a "nagging riff that rolls." Says Winston, "Even the chords were done through this Leslie, which did give it a nice mood. Just getting that chordey sound that floated." The only keyboards accompanying this ethereal, insistent motif are a hint of organ behind the vocal phrase in which Marriott explains that he's 'hurting'.

As might be expected, Marriott sings grittily and passionately. Even the fact that he sounds like he's got a cold doesn't detract from the performance because the tired, nasal effect ties in with the overarching vulnerable, chastened tenor. A third of the way in comes a delightful stop-start, with the restart galvanisingly prompted by a yell from Marriott. With the exception of Jones – who plays economical but intelligently portentous rolls and cymbal-heavy swells – the instrumentation is minimalist. The air of quasi-profundity is assisted by the fact that, at just under three minutes, the song is a full sixty seconds longer than the debut.

B-side 'It's Too Late' has a slightly different permutation of the Marriott/ Jones/Winston/Lane collective publishing credit to be found on the A-side, with Winston's (misspelled) name here coming first. Production of both sides of the disc is credited to the Contemporary house name. Whoever was really responsible deserves kudos. In a day and age of four-track recording, 'It's Too Late' seems to have no fewer than three separate guitar parts: both acoustic and electric rhythm work plus a picked electric component, the latter's chiming qualities a contrast with the growling timbre of the other plugged-in guitar. The spikey, stuttering guitar solo may even be a fourth. As with 'I've Got Mine', there is little evidence of keyboards. The song opens with yet another galvanising Jones drum roll, and his understated but propulsive work scuds like dark storm clouds throughout the proceedings. The song is just as mordant as 'I've Got Mine', with Marriott declaring to an unresponsive female that he was warned by his father about girls who don't reciprocate affection.

Says Jones of 'I've Got Mine', "We loved it. It showed us off in a different way and we wrote it, so we were very proud of it. I was proud of the drumming on it, I was proud of the performance and I liked the song. It was different. Also, you had that lovely guitar going through a Leslie." He adds, "And what happened? It was a flop."

Britain might have had a multiplicity of charts but, upon its release in November 1965, 'I've Got Mine' failed to register on any of them. Considering both the promising start the band had made with their debut single and the new record's excellence, it was a remarkably disappointing outcome. So what was the explanation? "It wasn't immediate," reasons Winston. "You had to think about it." Whether or not Arden agreed with the idea that the slow-burn nature of 'I've Got Mine' was the cause of its sluggish commercial start is not known but Winston says, "Don pulled it. He got cold feet about it. You could tell. We were all up for it, but a few times he just said, 'I don't know if this is going to happen.' He just didn't stick by it. It may be record sales, other people's feedback. I think the feeling at the time was that if he let it just go on the band might have just faded away ... I think with a bit more work, it could have been a hit on the level of 'Whatcha Gonna Do About It'." Jones doesn't concur with Winston on much, but says of 'I've Got Mine', "I think the reason it was a flop is because Don Arden didn't push it enough. He wanted it to be a flop." But why would he want that? "Because basically he wants a commercial song." In a comment that suggests Arden in fact made more from the publishing arrangement with Samwell/Potter, he adds, "He's getting an end of the 'Whatcha Gonna Do About It' songwriting." David Arden states that the record's failure is down to nothing more sinister than the fact that there were limits to his father's ability to hype a record. "You couldn't guarantee success every time," he shrugs. "He always said, 'You can only get it up so high for people to take note, and if it hasn't got its own legs by then – forget it.' You can nowadays but you couldn't in those days fool people."

However, there is a complication to the record's lack of success. It seems to have been the case that Arden was relying on the single receiving a promotional boost by its inclusion in *Dateline Diamonds*, a motion picture in which the band had non-speaking parts. Directed by Jeremy Summers, it was written by Tudor Gates based on an idea by music publisher Harold Shampan. The latter also served as executive producer. Almost inevitably his path had previously crossed with Marriott's: the latter had appeared in his 1965 production *Be My Guest*. Amusingly, considering what is now known about Arden, *Dateline Diamond*'s plot portrays fictitious Small Faces manager Lester Benson as a crook. Benson is blackmailed into assisting a diamond smuggling operation which involves an offshore pirate radio ship. Musical artistes Rey Anton & the Pro Form, the Chantelles, Kiki Dee and Mark Richardson are also featured in the film but the Small Faces get the most number of songs, with 'I've Got Mine', 'It's Too Late', 'Come on Children' and 'Don't Stop What You Are Doing' all being heard at various points, if as background. The only non-background Small Faces sounds come with a performance of 'I've Got Mine' which is posited as live but which is accompanied by the sound of the actual record.

Winston – seen miming to guitar on the latter song – says the band's filming work amounted to "only a couple of days" and that their interaction with other people in the film like actor Kenneth Cope and DJ Kenny Everett was nothing more intimate than exchanging hellos. He perceived that granting their new song exposure in such a venture was a good move at the same time as he could see that the film's approach was "so old it seemed like the Fifties." Also discernible to him once again was their manager's preternatural promotional power: there were plenty of much bigger bands around at the time who could have been granted the Small Faces' spot in the picture. "Don Arden had a strange sort of muscle," he reflects.

Unfortunately, this time something went awry with Arden's inordinate influence. That *Dateline Diamonds* was a black-and-white support to *Doctor in Clover* would not have been much of an issue: both monochrome and the B-movie were then still component parts of the experience of going to the pictures. What was a problem was the delay before the film made it to the screens. By the time it went on general release in April 1966, it was – at least as far as the Small Faces was concerned –utterly out of date. Not only had 'I've Got Mine' been and gone – the band had actually issued another single since its shooting – but so had the line-up of the Small Faces featured in the film. A few days before the release of 'I've Got Mine', Jimmy Winston was out of the group.

The perspective of Winston's three colleagues about his dismissal has been widely disseminated down the years and essentially boils down to the assertion that he was a deadly combination of mediocre, difficult and egotistical. An example of this viewpoint is Marriott's much-repeated anecdote regarding a promotional appearance on Thank Your Lucky Stars for the band's first single: "When we came to the guitar solo, which I was very proud of, Jimmy started acting crazy in his corner, waving his arms and stuff, so that the cameras turned to him." Says Jones, "Jimmy tried to be the frontman and pushing Steve to one side, which is a bit silly of him to do really."

Val Williams, who began visiting Don Arden's office in early 1966 and started working there a few months afterwards, got to know Winston better than the other band members. "Jimmy was trying to steal the limelight," she says. "He was a bit big-headed. Even I would say that. He did have a bit of an ego ... Because they got their fame quite quickly and, Jimmy being the older one, it did go to his head." Although she says another aspect of the clash was the fact that "they wanted to grow musically ... and Jimmy was holding them back," she got the impression that "the clash was mostly with Ronnie ... Pauline said that they came to fisticuffs one day in the office. There was a lot of tension there ... Rather than Steve, because Steve obviously was friends with Jimmy before the others got introduced to him ... So I've always thought it was a bit weird that it was Steve [who was] the one that didn't [want] Jimmy in the band."

Keith Altham offers a slightly different perspective. He never met Winston but does recall what Marriott told him later regarding the impetus for his dismissal. "Steve resented the fact that he was pulling rank, or pulling his age, and didn't quite fit in with the others," he says. He adds, though, "Steve, being the egotist that he was, wanted to take over and lead the band. He didn't like being told what to do and he didn't think Jimmy had the necessary credentials to tell him what was good and bad and what he could do and couldn't do onstage. It was almost a schoolboy thing."

"[I] never saw him as overly pushy," demurs David Arden of Winston. "I don't think he ever saw himself bigger than Stevie as a talent." He offers alternative reasons for Winston being deemed undesirable. "He was bigger, a lot bigger, than the rest of them, so visually he wasn't really fitting in. Secondly, musically his ability was not up to what Stevie wanted ... Stevie, as much as he was a nice guy, he was pretty ruthless when it came to his music ... and Jimmy wasn't the greatest on the keyboards." Hugh Janes has said Marriott's ruthlessness was something he'd noticed back in the Moments days. Nor would it be the last time it surfaced: some actually feel it ultimately consumed the Small Faces.

"If you think about it, it's bullshit," Winston says of the allegation that he was trying to steal the spotlight on the *Lucky Stars* appearance. "When you're playing, there's things you do." So why the scabrous allegations about him? "They came out of the bitterness after this breakup." He insists that the frictions that led to that breakup were rooted in something that was never widely aired. Arden, he avers, was unhappy with the fact that when he signed the Small Faces he was taking on what might be termed a sitting tenant in the shape of Winston's brother. Frankie Langwith's formal arrangement with the band regarding transportation may originally have amounted to remuneration in the vicinity of ten per cent of nothing, but now that the Small Faces were recording artists with a commensurately higher public profile it was liable to amount in the long term to considerable amounts of money. "Don didn't like the idea at all," says Winston. "We did some gigs up north, great big halls full of a few thousand people, and money is getting higher and higher. They might have gone to America and done big. [He] wants control back. The idea of my brother was that, if it got big and they needed bigger vans and all of that, he would go along with the process ... That conflict really started the agitation between us all." Winston claims that Arden undermined the arrangement by indirect means. "He was sort of priming everybody about 'This is not a good idea,'" he reflects. "Don had got into their heads, which made the rest of the band a bit bratty about the idea. So that's where we started to get edgy with one another and fall out. This was quite a big thing at the time. I stood up for my brother ... I'm a family person so I wasn't going to renege on my brother, because he stuck himself out to help us ... [I could have] said, 'Oh, Frank – forget it,' but I didn't. I thought he should have had some rights."

Some might find it unlikely that Arden would be able to turn Winston's colleagues against him simply by invoking an agreement they had willingly made. On the other hand, the misgivings that were retroactively expressed by the band about Winston's inadequacies as keyboardist were hardly logical if we accept that it was through Marriott's urging that Winston had adopted that role, one Winston himself had never particularly wanted. In any case, the latter issue could have been addressed in the traditional manner. "Hypothetically, I would have just learnt more keyboard," says Winston. He also points out that in a day and age of sessioners secretly contributing to many pop records, it need not be a big issue even in lieu of him succeeding in picking up said skills.

For Winston, there was also an underlying reason why Marriott at least would be amenable to whispers in his ear about him: that he resented Winston's abilities as a vocalist. Ronnie Lane once noted to Jonh Ingham of Marriott, "He used to moan at me every now and then to sing a song, because I never really wanted to sing." However, Marriott could afford to encourage Lane's vocal excursions because Plonk's pleasant but unremarkable voice wasn't a threat. Accordingly, Lane – says Winston – would sing "two or three" songs on stage. "['Shake'] was one of his main ones." Winston's singing was a different matter. It has been rather lost in the folds of history, but Winston played a more prominent role in the group than that of a musician situated silently adjacent to Marriott as he emoted into the mic. Winston says that his contribution on stage amounted to "a quarter to a third." There are only a few Small Faces recordings with a Jimmy Winston lead vocal, among them 'Baby Don't You Do It', which appeared on the 1967 compilation *From the Beginning*, 'Jump Back', which featured in 1999 on *The BBC Sessions*, and the alternative version of 'Don't Stop What You Are Doing' that was compiled on the 2015 *Decca Years* box set. They reveal him to have an effective and gritty voice. Winston feels that his vocal prowess did not go unobserved by audiences, and that said audiences' appreciation of his contributions did not go unnoticed by a resentful Marriott. Winston: "Certain places we played, some of the big concerts up north and that, you get your own little following and I know he wasn't happy … With *Ready Steady Go!*, you got two tracks. We did 'Whatcha Gonna Do About It', which was the going release, and I did 'Jump Back'. He wasn't happy with someone else also doing their thing, especially on TV … He wanted to be the only frontperson, really. I think that was a real part of the problem and the van thing was the kind of initiator. It set it all off, got him the grumps. I thought he felt threatened."

The resultant in-fighting began laying waste to the possibility of Winston remaining in the band long-term. It was here that Winston's apartness – the "slightly different outlook" he speaks of – worked against him. "The trouble is, if you don't know people that long and you have a fall-out, it's not so easy for recovery. When they got grumpy about it, they go off and chat about it in the corner … They were moaning to Don … Then Don, it was obviously on his mind to get that contract with my brother gone … I knew they were getting together on it and I got a call from Don. Went up to see him and we chatted about it. The first stage, he was just talking about what do you think's happening. I had another appointment with him to talk about it and then we started discussing if it's not workable what would come next … He said, 'Oh, this has all got messy, ain't it?' … To be honest, by then I was so fed up with the bickering … that I started to get happier about the idea … You get to a point where if you're not enjoying it, it's not a lot of good." What would come next was, Arden suggested, Winston's departure from the Small Faces.

This all might sound like a Machiavellian masterstroke on Arden's part, the end result of a scheme whereby his self-interested desire to remove from the picture an individual who was (indirectly) causing him to lose a portion of concert earnings had succeeded in sowing sufficient discontent in the ranks that that individual had become unhappy enough to leave of his own volition. For both David Arden and Winston, things are neither as clear-cut nor sinister as that. "He was terribly upset when they got rid of Jimmy Winston," David says of his father. "He liked Jimmy." "We seemed to get on quite well," confirms Winston. "I think I understood him a bit more, because growing up in the East End [I] used to go to the clubs the Kray Twins run and all of that." Additionally, "He had a good humour about him." Moreover, Arden wasn't suggesting that Winston's mooted departure from a successful group be uncompensated. Winston says the manager told him, "If you want to leave, form your own band, do your own thing, I'll give you a recording contract." He adds, "He also paid me a fair sum of money for this process to occur." He declines to say how much but does offer that it was both "more than adequate" and "a bit better" than the £20 per week wages that stopped after he left the Small Faces' ranks. Moreover, Arden's continued stewardship of Winston's career, both live and on record, was no mere grudging fulfilment of terms he'd felt obliged to offer in order to ease him out of the Small Faces. "We tried to do things with Jimmy off and on for a long time after that," says Arden's son. "Well into the Seventies."

While some may have no problem with the theory that Winston was eased out partly because of Marriott's jealousy – Marriott's sometimes almost hysterical insecurity is well-documented – such an explanation would hardly explain why Jones and Lane took against Winston too. "Kenney and Ronnie got a bit bitter afterwards," offers Winston, asserting that this bitterness was largely rooted in a civil action his brother brought against the band. Frankie Langwith had lost out on what was theoretically a good deal of money.

The case didn't reach court until 1969. His writ claimed that he had been promised a percentage of the Small Faces' earnings over five years in exchange for his transportation services. "It was so funny, going to the court in the Strand," says Jones. "I remember them questioning Ronnie. The judge said, 'Do you know what ten per cent is?' And Ronnie went, "Course I know what ten per cent is!'" The case was dismissed. Jones: "We were too young to actually even enter into that. Me especially." "If he'd been over a certain age, then my brother would have had a case," says Winston. "He stuck his neck out, and I've always loved and respected him for that, but he didn't get treated well."

Frankie wasn't the only member of Winston's family whom Arden eased out of a supporting role in the Small Faces operation. Before Pauline Corcoran was appointed to administer the band's fan club, it had initially been run by Winston's elder brother Derek. He was succeeded by family friend Fran Piller, whose husband ran a betting shop that neighboured the Ruskin Arms. Piller's son Eddie – who would go on to found Acid Jazz Records – has suggested that Arden terminated their involvement in a dispute over expenses. Val Williams says, "When Don Arden signed the band he wanted to bring the fan club in-house and employ someone who knew nothing about the band and was not a fan." Winston himself says, "Don wanted to have complete control of everything."

Despite entering into a series of discussions with Arden that culminated in him departing the group – and apparently leaving him convinced it was his decision to do so – Winston still got the shock of his life when news filtered through to him as October 1965 turned into November that he had been supplanted in the Small Faces' ranks.

The new arrival was Ian Patrick McLagan, known to all and sundry – at least outside his family – as 'Mac'. Born on 12 May 1945 in Hounslow, West London, McLagan's Scottish father was a car mechanic and his Irish mother a shop assistant. He had a younger brother, Michael. Although, unlike Winston, McLagan was an out-and-out keyboardist, his development on that instrument didn't start well. At his mother's insistence, he had weekly piano lessons at the age of twelve which he hated and soon started dodging. Music was in his destiny, though: like so many of his generation, he was caught up in the skiffle craze. "I had a guitar soon after that, but it went out of tune and it hurt my fingers," he told Ian Fortnam. "I had a saxophone for a while … I was really disappointed to find that it was only one note. It sounded horrible, it was loud and you couldn't practise at home. But the organ's the perfect thing …" His first keyboard was a Hohner Cembalet electric piano. His reverence for Booker T and the MG's motivated him, aged nineteen, to obtain a Hammond organ on hire-purchase terms, a richer-sounding electric organ than the cheaper but chintzy Vox Continental favoured and made famous by the Animals' Alan Price. Although a self-taught keyboardist, he was proficient enough after dropping out of art school to take up music professionally. "I was a rhythm guitarist in the first band I was in, but once I learned the basics that was it," he said in 2000. "Pretty much all I play now are guitar licks transposed onto piano keys." He served stints in the Muleskinners (no relation to Lane's band of that name), with whom he recorded a single, 'Back Door Man', and Boz and the Boz People. The latter tenure ended because, McLagan explained, "They were more into jazz and I wanted to play blues." It so happened he left the Boz People just at the point when the Small Faces keyboardist vacancy came up.

McLagan's entry into their world occasioned more of the mystical qualities that the Small Faces were so convinced attended their story arc. The first time McLagan had become cognisant of the Small Faces was a peculiar occasion. Upon the occasion of one of their television appearances, his father called him into the room and remarked on the bass player's visual similarity to him. McLagan agreed that he and Lane looked like brothers. Eerier things than that were afoot, though. Following the rupture with the Boz People,

McLagan was jocularly told by a friend that the Small Faces were in need of a keyboardist and that he should join them. By complete coincidence, the next morning he received a telephone call from Don Arden enquiring as to his availability. "I got the job because of a great review about Boz and the Boz People in *Beat Instrumental*," McLagan recalls. "The guys were looking for a Hammond player and here's a review of a guy who was in London, right there, he's just been reviewed, how great he is."

In another piece of serendipity verging on the miraculous, the Small Faces literally had no idea what McLagan looked like before he turned up at Arden's Carnaby Street offices. McLagan points out of the *Beat Instrumental* review, "The thing is, they put a picture of Boz in the review, head shot, but they put my name under the picture." As it happened, McLagan was reasonably good-looking (an issue for 1960s pop groups), but that was of little significance compared to his height, which – in another instance of uncanniness – was absolutely apposite. While Winston had an extra pair of inches on his bandmates, the man who took his place turned out to be of the same diminutive stature as the other three members. McLagan joining would confer on the band a permanent symmetry of image, something he recalls as occasioning some delight in the Small Faces' ranks. "I didn't get hired because I was short but the fact that I was short was just a mind blast," he says. "They [physically] picked me up!" "That was a fluke, really," says Jones. "That was strange. It is a bit like it was always meant to be." "I couldn't believe it," marvelled Marriott. "Here's a guy, standing right in front of us, who was already one of the boys." "It was about the first time that I've ever counted myself lucky to be small," McLagan told Keith Altham the following year.

The four found that as well as seeing the world from the same vantage point, they were on the same page music-wise. "One of my favourite records was *Muddy Waters Live at Newport*," recalls McLagan. "It was also Steve's. The first day we met, when we started talking music, we had the same influences. We all loved Otis Redding, Booker T and the MG's … We would listen to Ray Charles, Mingus, Muddy Waters, all the blues guys, Tamla Motown." Then there was the matter of personality. "He fitted in," notes Jones. "The chemistry between us was perfect," Marriott said. "His humour was perfect, his charisma was perfect. All I could do was hug him, because it was just like he was the missing part."

McLagan joining the Small Faces is analogous to Ringo being absorbed into the Beatles: like Starr, he wasn't an original member but he completed the definitive line-up, his presence unmistakably constituting a vital part of the band's musical, personal and visual chemistry.

That excitement regarding serendipity and symmetry aside, the height aspect perhaps shouldn't be overplayed, despite the band's name. Both Jones and McLagan denied to this writer that their universally diminutive statures engendered shared perspectives on life. Jones: "We never thought about being short – you know that, don't you? It's kind of weird that we ended up being the same size. We didn't say, 'We've got a gimmick, let's exploit it.' No, we never thought about it at all. We all felt like we were six foot tall." McLagan: "The thing is, we weren't short to each other. We were all the same height, pretty much. I forget that I'm short. The same with all four of us. You are who you are and it's not your main concern." It was left up to others to remind them of their unusual stature. Jones remembers an early gig: "Soon as we got out of the car I heard some of the fans go, ''ere, int they short!'"

While young women such as that might have been disappointed at the band's statures – especially in a more patriarchal culture when men were expected by both genders to be the dominant/towering partner – Jerry Shirley says that the Small Faces were all the epitome of the principle 'small but perfectly formed'. "They were all perfect clothes horses," he says. "Because that's what mods were all about: how it fitted, how it looked on you. The freak thing was, they were all exactly the same size. They all had these tiny bone structures and narrow waists, and everything that fitted them fitted them perfectly."

Asked if, despite this physical symmetry, any Small Faces members had visible small-man syndrome, Shirley says, "Steve suffered from it a bit, but he hid it well. Steve was always referring to himself and his friends as midgets." "I didn't think any of them were insecure," says Altham. "They were little guys with huge egos and big personalities. Kenney was a little bit laid-back, but even Kenney was quite a strong character." "I don't think he did," says Jenny Rylance of her future husband Marriott, although she does allow, "That may have been what drove him the whole time. It would make sense, because he was so big on the stage – the voice, etc. It didn't really occur to me. You sort of forget about it when you're with somebody for a long time." However, Lane admitted that the reason he disliked the collective name the four professionally adopted was "I was uptight about being little."

There were a couple of things McLagan did not have in common with his new colleagues. One was youth, relatively speaking. McLagan was just three weeks junior to Winston. However, this doesn't seem to have been an issue in the way that some aver it was with Winston, possibly because the fun-loving McLagan was not the type to come on like an elder statesman. Another difference was that the newcomer had no interest in mod. "For me, it was the music first," he says. "I don't know what the movement was about."

Nevertheless, McLagan was quickly apprised of the fact that clothes were central to the life of bona fide pop groups, particularly this one, especially fresh clothes. He was despatched to the boutiques so that he would be mod-correct when he joined the band in promoting 'I've Got Mine'. His new existence involved a considerable churn of outfits. "When you'd travel around England, you'd start seeing the shirt you're wearing on someone in the audience," he recalls. "You'd go, 'Oh no.' You used to retire a shirt after a TV show." A barber's appointment was made for McLagan so that he could be provided with a barnet in the Small Faces' singular style of a parting slightly off-centre and uncovered ears. As 'I've Got Mine' didn't have a significant keyboard part, he was also gifted a brand-new Fender Telecaster.

McLagan notes, "I joined them on November the 1st and on November the 2nd we played *Ready Steady Radio!*." Said Radio Luxembourg show was a bizarre proposition: a wireless programme on which bands lip-synched to their hits. "We mimed the record in front of a bunch of screaming girls," he says.

The show was staged at the Lyceum in London. There, the Small Faces were horrified to find Jimmy Winston banging on their dressing room door demanding to know why he had been ousted. Jones said he had to steer a tearful Winston into another room to discuss the matter. "They'd all gone a bit shy on me and I wanted to have a talk about it," says Winston. "I went to speak to them about it, but it wasn't going to be a lot to be said." As Winston had already made up his mind that he wanted out, the confirmation of his no longer being part of the Small Faces set-up wasn't the issue. "The thing that got me a bit uptight, it's just backhanded stuff," he explains. "The music industry can be a terrible old state of affairs. People are not always straight with one another … I've never liked stuff that's too undercover." However, he does concede that there was an element of hypocrisy in his outrage: "Me talking to Don about a new band was similar on the other side." Was he annoyed because they had sacked him before his secret plans to quit were put into operation? "Not really." He emphasises, "They like to use the word 'sack' from a slightly bitter angle … That's what was annoying, and never having the face or the front to discuss it." The incident passed without much further drama and both Winston and the Small Faces embarked on their respective, separate life journeys.

"The next day we went to Swindon, played our first gig," recalls McLagan. "We spent all afternoon playing and basically most of the set we did Booker T instrumentals. Jams." As the Small Faces hadn't even bothered to audition him, this extended practice session was the first time Marriott, Lane and Jones had heard McLagan play. If the group had been pleased about his image and personality, they were ecstatic at the mellifluous musical skills the day's proceedings revealed their new member to possess. "Someone who could play the bloody thing," enthuses Jones. "From my point of view as a drummer, soon as we heard that Hammond organ I was in seventh heaven. I just could not believe it. It just took the band into a different place. All of us were very much Jimmy McGriff fans, Booker T and the MG's, and we could really do it then. When you've got a Hammond there, you can play anything." Marriott later recalled, "I didn't like to expect too much but I was really knocked back; the Hammond really slew me, he was so good."

McLagan was just as enchanted with his new colleagues as they were with him. "I thought I was dead lucky to get in there," he says. "I was looking at three guys who were so talented and I always felt it I was trying to keep up, honestly. But I'm sure all four of us felt similar, because it was so constructive and so 24-hours-a-day. If we weren't playing music, we were listening to it or we were thinking about it. And then sometimes we slept." McLagan was also ecstatic at the whirlwind of accomplishment he was suddenly in the middle of. "When you get a little success, you'll work so hard, but you don't mind. It's what you want to do. That's what you been waiting for. Nobody gets up in the morning and goes, 'Oh fuck, another gig.' Nobody. People want to hear you play and want to see you. You walk into the room and people are excited. It's an amazing thing."

Pop and rock groups usually have to accept a trade-off between a musical alchemy and a lack of personal chemistry. By the law of averages, it's unlikely that everyone in a four- or five-piece outfit is going to get along. Moreover, many are the ensembles whose constituent parts can't stand each other but elect to bear each other's company because they realise they are each other's ideal professional partners. The finalised line-up of the Small Faces, however, was the great exception to this rule. They were that rarest of things in the industry, a happy camp. McLagan describes the four of them as, "great mates," adding, "That was the lovely thing. We were in each other's pockets for years. We actually lived together for a year – '66 – and later on when we had no money in '68 we lived together again – Ronnie, Stevie and me – and that was with our wives second time, and we still got on pretty good ... I don't remember us ever arguing about anything except at the very end, and that wasn't really an argument, just Steve told us what he wanted to do." When the Small Faces began working at Olympic Studios, Pete Townshend, who lived nearby, would often pop in to see them. "They just seemed to be laughing all the time," he says. This was a stark contrast to his own band: the Who's internal relations down the years were famously cordial at best, and frequently miserable. "Yes, it made me jealous," Townshend admits.

McLagan does at least concede that the good cheer could become strained as a consequence of Marriott's overwhelming personality. Although he says, "Steve was 'all about' – very funny man," he adds that this was sometimes too much of a good thing. "He wore us all down. You loved the guy, but it was sometimes a lot of work to be around him because he was never 'off'."

From Christmas 1965, the new line-up had a new base. Arden arranged for the Small Faces to inhabit, rent-free, a four-bedroomed property in Westmoreland Terrace in south-west London. Although a terraced house, it was four stories high and situated in upmarket Pimlico, adjacent to the very posh Chelsea. Also provided gratis was a cook, a cleaner and the use of a chauffeur-driven Mark 10 Jaguar. A piano was handily situated in the dining room. "That was always my dad's thing: if you were a star, you had to live like one," says David Arden. German maid Liesel Schiffer was only marginally older than the band members but seems to have acted as a surrogate mother for them.

Although contemporaneous press coverage made much of the band's communal living arrangements – possibly because it so resembled the fictional collective abode of the Beatles in the 1965 *Help!* movie – there was actually one member who declined participation in this set-up. Jones – who had just turned seventeen – decided to stick with his parents. He felt he was vindicated when he saw how Westmoreland Terrace became party central. "I didn't stay up all night and take that many drugs," he says. "I was just straighter than anyone. The most I would take is what me and Mooney [Keith Moon] used to take, which was blues. The little pills that kept you awake and made you speak a lot. I never tried anything else. My drug days were very short-lived." The fourth bedroom was instead taken by Mick O'Sullivan, a friend of Marriott's who proceeded to become a band gofer, although other people have different words for him. "He was a ponce," says David Arden. "The old man used to loathe him. Plonk and Stevie would always have hangers-on … Plonk and Stevie used to give him money. I think the old man was informed that he was the one that also supplied them all the drugs. I know this guy concerned the old man very much. He was very protective of artists. He hated these people that would come round kissing arse and giving out drugs." Regarding that issue, the drugs of which the band (or, rather, three quarters of it) partook were, according to McLagan, daily blasts of hash and, less regularly, speed. Later, LSD would be sampled, introduced to Marriott, Lane and McLagan by Brian Epstein and the Moody Blues via a laced orange.

The Small Faces being gathered together all in one place came with its own perils, whether it be the attention of teenyboppers or more unusual sexual interest. "Brian Epstein knocked on the door," says David Arden. "'Oh, hello. Just want to come round for a drink.' Sat down." The Merseybeat king wasn't looking for a new act for his roster. "If he was, the old man would have been more than annoyed at it. But he knew it wasn't … Anybody that was gay in the business wanted to be round the Small Faces."

It should be pointed out that while his new colleagues seem to have always taken for granted that he was a permanent member, McLagan had not assumed this himself, simply because this was not what he'd been told by Arden. McLagan: "When Arden asked me how much I was earning, I lied and told him £20." His gig with Boz and the Boz People had actually been garnering him £5 a week. "He wanted to impress me so offered me £30, and that after a month's probation I would get an even split with the rest of the lads," he says. "They didn't know I was getting more than them, and neither did I. It only came up a month or so later when I asked if I was in the band or not." Far from now being let into the "fortunes" he assumed his new workmates were enjoying, "my wages went down to £20. Big mouth!" McLagan kept this unexpected diminution in his wages to himself for the entirety of the Small Faces' original lifespan, only revealing it to his old colleagues in the Seventies.

Arden had more things to worry about than the odd tenner. The Small Faces' last record had been an unmitigated flop and, while the group might have been ecstatic about their new member, upheavals within pop groups were at the time considered risky as they raised questions about band legitimacy, hence jeopardising fan loyalty. Arden in fact may very well have considered the Small Faces' current situation to be a crisis. Says Jones of 'I've Got

Mine', "It wasn't a disaster to us but … Don Arden said, 'I'm not taking any more chances here, so I've called up Kenny Lynch and Mort Shuman and they've written a song and I've booked Decca Studios in West Hampstead.'"

Many people in the business were surprised that Lynch and Shuman were a composing team. Shuman hailed from glamorous, faraway America and was already a legend through being co-writer with Doc Pomus of neo-classics like 'A Teenager in Love', 'Save The Last Dance for Me', 'Sweets For My Sweet', 'Can't Get Used to Losing You', 'Suspicion' and '(Marie's the Name) His Latest Flame'. Briton Lynch was primarily a singer and if he was noteworthy for anything else it was being something then unusual: a black man with an indigenous accent. In his case it was London, him hailing from the self-same East End as three-quarters of the Small Faces. However, while he had made half a dozen appearances in the charts as a performer since 1960, Lynch had ambitions in other directions. He had stumbled into songwriting when an employee of music publisher Aberbach pointed out to him that placing a composition of his own devising on his B-sides could be very lucrative. Although he had never written before and had rudimentary musical skills, he rose to the challenge. No sooner had he embarked on this new avenue in 1962 than Lynch's songwriting career was catapulted into the stratosphere. "Paul Case, who was running the [publishing] office in the States, said 'Go down and meet Mort Shuman,'" he recalls. "I was only sitting there talking to him for an hour and he said, 'Do you fancy being my new partner?' I said, 'What's the matter with Doc?' He said, 'He's very ill, he's paraplegic.' I couldn't believe it. I thought that him and Leiber & Stoller and Bacharach & David were the best team in the world and all of a sudden I was a member of it. He didn't know who the hell I was." Lynch and Shuman's first effort was 'Follow Me', written for Lynch's idols, the Drifters.

Although Lynch does indeed remember being contacted by Don Arden, he recollects the phone call in question being about another act on his roster. "I actually wrote 'Sha-La-La-La-Lee' for Amen Corner," he says. He adds that Arden had a recent Greenwich & Barry-written hit in mind: "They asked me to write a song like 'Do Wah Diddy' … He said, 'I don't want no brain surgery, just a nice pop song.'" Shuman made his way to Lynch's Chelsea home. "I said, 'They want a silly song like that Manfred Mann thing', which we hated. So we sat down and he started banging the piano and I got this tune out of what he was doing. We must have written it in about five minutes. There was no lyrics at all. We had a tape recorder in my flat. We just put it straight on the tape, just piano and vocal and Mort was joining me in this piece of chorus that we'd got. He said, 'If you play that to that fella, I'm not coming with you. I don't want you to put my bloody name on it. It's absolute rubbish.' I said, 'It's got a sort of feel about it, it swings a bit.'" Don Arden sided with Lynch's point of view. "Then he phoned me up and he said, 'I love this song you've give me, but I'm gonna do it with the Small Faces.' I said, 'Okay, great. If you do it with *somebody*, I don't care.'"

"Bless him – old age gets to us all," says David Arden. "That's totally incorrect. He never had Amen Corner at the time ... I remember how it came about. The old man heard that song – I think it was actually Mort Shuman that played it to him – and he's gone, 'Oh, that's a fucking hit. We're having that.'" The two men's recollections don't necessarily contradict each other: at the time, the Amen Corner were managed by Ron King, separated from Arden during workdays by a corridor. Regardless of the route by which it ended up a projected Small Faces record, Arden's charges were somewhat less enthusiastic about the creation than their manager. David Arden: "They did not want to know. I don't think it was just the song, it was the fact that they were having to record somebody else's music. They were dead against it." "It was upsetting for them because they thought they would be writing their own stuff," McLagan says of Marriott and Lane.

While Lynch might not have cared who recorded 'Sha-La-La-La-Lee', he found that he very much did care about the quality of what was recorded. He recalls Arden had sent Ian Samwell into the studio with the band to lay down his song. "It was absolutely dreadful," he says of the results. His main objection was to the prominent drums. "Sounded like the Dave Clark Five." As the co-writer of an unreleased composition, Lynch invoked his mechanical-reproduction rights. "I said to Don Arden, 'I'm not letting you bring it out.' He said, 'I've got it scheduled for the week after next.' I'm talking to him on the phone, I'm in Rome. I said, 'I'll come back tomorrow and I'll do the thing. Book me a studio.'"

Marriott's career had of course already bisected with Lynch's with 'Give Her My Regards'. McLagan also knew Lynch. "I used to back him when I was with the Boz People," he points out. "We used to do the odd summer Sunday show." Although McLagan adjudged Lynch a "great character," like the rest of his colleagues his opinion of the song Lynch had proffered the Small Faces was less than favourable. "I joined an R&B band and suddenly the first record I cut with them is, 'What the fuck is this?'" he says. "It's a little pop for me ... We thought it was a bit of a throwaway really." No less for Jones, who says, "There we were doing the commercial shit and I thought, 'Oh Gawd. Doesn't feel right.' The reason we could bear it and we got through it was the fact that we had a great singer. It was a commercial song with a great voice on it. That's what saved the day."

Jerry Shirley could understand the band's disdain from the perspective of a fan. "You wouldn't imagine the Who doing something that was a bit on the twee side," he reasons. "They only made it good because of the way they played it and the way Steve sang it." When he graduated from fan to band friend, Shirley got a further insight into the group's reasoning about 'Sha-La-La-La-Lee'. "I'm pretty sure [Marriott] played me a demo of the song as it was before they got their hands on it," he says. " The original song was if you can imagine someone like Herman's Hermits or Dave Dee, Dozy, Beaky, Mick and Tich doing it." Promoting the record, Marriott revealed a hard-nosed attitude.

"We've sussed it all out," he told an unnamed *Melody Maker* scribe. "We've gotta make some bread. The whole point in recording a commercial record is to try and get our name really established. If we can score two or three big hits, then we'll start making the kind of records we want to ... I know 'Sha-La-La-La-Lee' is a long haul from it, but one day we hope to be doing right weird, far-out stuff."

Although like McLagan Jones expresses a personal fondness for Lynch, he had a miserable time during the evening spent obtaining a recording to the composer's satisfaction. He recalls, "I was really giving it some welly and ... Kenny Lynch pressed the buzzer from the control room and said, 'Kenney, don't play anything you can't mime to' ... I just thought, 'Fuck me, what have we got here?'" McLagan was also not a happy bunny that day. He detested the tip-toeing organ run he was instructed to play during the track's musical lull. He additionally disdained the falsetto harmonies provided by Lynch on the choruses. "His voice was so piercing," he winces. "In fact, you can hear his voice in the background louder than Marriott's – and that's saying something."

"Yeah, I did all the high notes," says Lynch. He offers by way of explanation, "I said to Stevie Marriott, 'Make sure it's in the right key. We've only got one evening on this and it's gotta be done, finished.' Then he came up to the box and he said, 'Kenny, I can't do the harmonies. It's too high. I didn't realise it was gonna be that high once I'd done the vocal track.' I said, 'I'll come down. I'll try to do it right.' I've got a deep voice. I did this falsetto thing and thought the only way we'd get away with it is if I track it. So I tracked it a couple of times. It just about worked." As for Jones' grievance, Lynch says, "The thing I hated about coming up in the dance bands, the jazz area, was I could never get miming together so I thought I would try to take that burden off of anybody that I worked with. I used to say that to everybody."

"I went in there at five o'clock in the evening," Lynch recalls of the session. "I came out at half past twelve with a tape." Despite what the Small Faces felt to be risible material and fatuous production methods, they had laid down a recording with which Lynch was happy and he accordingly presented it to their manager the next day. Lynch: "He couldn't care less. It was the same song, more or less. I went back to Rome the next morning. That was on about the Thursday or Friday of that week." 'Sha-La-La-La-Lee' was released in January 1966. Lynch: "The next Friday ... my manager rang up and she said, 'You know that song you did with the Small Faces? It's number one.' I said, 'That's really good – they only brought it out on Tuesday.'" Lynch's first instinct is modestly not to offer the quality of the record as an explanation for its rapid and remarkable success. Instead, he suggests, "They were playing football parks and stadiums before the game. That's how he got them famous. The kids were clamouring for these young mods." His attitude seems to be rooted in the fact that, despite his conviction that the song always had a certain "feel" and "swing," he thinks no more highly of it than do the Small Faces. "They hated that song. I hated it more." Despite this, he offers the standard popular songwriter's spiel when he reasons, "I don't think it's a great record but it's a very popular record and I think greatness is in the eye of the beholder. If people like it, it's a good song." He also notes, "[It's] the biggest song I've ever written. I think I've got 54 covers on it."

Not even the song's success could lessen the Small Faces' disdain for 'Sha-La-La-La-Lee'. When the record was descending the charts after its healthy tenure in the top ten, Lynch found himself with the band on *Ready Steady Go!*. "They came into my dressing room and said, 'Go and tell that producer we don't wanna sing that horrible song,'" he recalls. "They would never do it if they didn't have to." Part of the reason for Marriott's contempt seems to have stemmed from an incident at stars' London watering hole the Scotch of St James when the record was at its peak. He was hurt when his hero Long John Baldry sarcastically yelled out, "Look – here's Steve Marriott the soul singer – 'Sha-La-La-La-Lee'!" In fact, come the following May and the band's next single, 'Sha-La-La-La-Lee' was permanently dropped from the Small Faces' set. The band member most enthusiastic about the song was Lane, and the most he could muster was his 1991 comment to *Record Hunter*'s John Pidgeon that it was "quite a good little Saturday night dance record." Jones dismisses it as "another song we didn't write" and another "nail in the coffin" in terms of the band's attempts to avoid being blatantly commercial. "It pissed us all off, the fact that we were more and more getting away from what we wanted to play," he says.

All of this may seem an incredibly churlish response to a record that revitalised a career that had so recently seemed in danger of being over as soon as soon as it had begun. However, what makes said response even more perplexing is that, far from being the turkey everybody involved in its creation and recording regarded it as, 'Sha-La-La-La-Lee' is a cast-iron classic.

The song is certainly on the surface anodyne and juvenile. Its vocal refrain is gibberish, even if designedly so. The number is highly conventional in its depiction of romance – its wooing narrative climaxes in a wedding as though to anxiously remove any shadow of the buzzword pejorative 'promiscuity'. Lynch's falsetto backing vocals are oddly camp and corny. In all other respects, however, it is pop of a rip-roaring, life-affirming and truly elevated stripe.

The lyric captures superbly the bliss of being in love, from the fact that the narrator is giddily vague about the hostelry that he and his partner visited on their first date to his euphoric pride at being seen in her company. Melodically the song is deliciously stuffed with refrains, respites and switchbacks. Performance-wise, it contains multiple examples of the kind of delightful tiny moments that the music-lover sits and waits for with keen anticipation, in particular the title refrain (pure singalong), the instrumentation drop-outs when Marriott reveals that the answer to his query as to whether the woman will be his is "Oh yeah!"; the slammed strokes on guitar accompanying those "Oh yeahs"; and – yes – that polished organ crawl so detested by McLagan.

The recording reminds us that one of the reasons that Pete Townshend coined the term "power-pop" was to convey the idea of the Small Faces' sound. While the song almost schematically features the milder side of pop – a vista of chaste romance, a nursery-rhyme catchphrase and a melodic structure that fastidiously incorporates a middle-eight – it is also thumpingly visceral in a way not usually associated with pop convention. This begins in the record's very first second when raspy strokes on Marriott's guitar allied to a tattoo from Jones gives us the feeling of being swept up without ceremony into an aural whirlwind. From there the recording never lets up. It simply does not come across as – to use a pejorative of the era – soft. A large part of the power comes from the fact that Marriott gives his all vocal-wise. Nobody would know from hearing this recording that he didn't absolutely believe in the material he is roaring out.

"I don't think you can trust the artist in this context," says Pete Townshend of 'Sha-La-La-La-Lee'. "You have to trust the people that hear it and what they get from it. The other thing about the Small Faces' music is, unlike a lot of Who singles that were hits at the time in the UK, you could dance to them. That's because, unlike Keith Moon, Kenney played proper drums. It was rhythmic." Townshend echoes Lane's Saturday-night-dance-record comment when he continues, "In the clubs and the places that we hung out at in those days, that was important. It was part of the mating process. It was part of the time when you could walk over and pull a bird when you were trying to dance. So those kind of records are just as important as any other. I like it."

While there are many people who not just like but positively love 'Sha-La-La-La-Lee' – pretty much, in fact, everybody except the Small Faces and Lynch – many of those fans still prefer the other side of the disc, 'Grow Your Own'. (The sniggering title is the first of several Small Faces surreptitious drug references.) The writing of this track is credited to all four band members. This is a music-business tradition with instrumentals, one rooted in the fact that, with no vocal melody or lyric, all personnel on a recording *sans* singing could be posited as being equally responsible for its contents. 'Grow Your Own' inaugurated a Small Faces tradition of exquisitely percolating instrumental recordings in the style of their heroes Booker T and the MG's. In a way, it also properly inaugurated the McLagan iteration of the Small Faces. Although he can be heard (to his chagrin) here and there on the A-side, the flipside finds him absolutely front and centre, and moreover not with cute runs dictated by a third party but churning and swooping Hammond progressions of his own devising, ones of a type that would now become as much a signature of the band's sound as Marriott's gravelly vocals. His stylish, furious organ work is nicely counterpointed on 'Grow Your Own' by abrasive contributions from Marriott's fretboard.

Jones describes the Small Faces' instrumentals as, "make-it-up-as-you-go-along jam things but organised a bit." He says, "When Mac joined, we started doing more instrumentals because we had the Hammond organ." He is "very proud" of said instrumentals "because it sums up the band and the way we used to love jamming together." McLagan recalls them as one-take affairs: "I mean, there was some thought went into it, but Steve would have an intro and then, 'See you at the end.'" It is for this reason that fans know these tracks better than the band ever did. Getting to know a track inside-out through repeated plays makes listeners oblivious of the fact that material like 'Grow Your Own' were pieces of music forgotten about by the artists as soon as the process of intertwined composition and performance was over. Such songs were rarely played onstage by the Small Faces and it clearly amused/bemused McLagan that as a solo performer years later he would receive requests for them. "Someone said to me, 'Ah, do "Grow Your Own!"'" he scoffs. "Well, if I did, it would be completely different. It would just be tonight's twelve-bar."

As well as a Small Faces instrumental tradition, 'Grow Your Own' also inaugurated a custom of top-notch, standalone (i.e. not collected on an album) Small Faces B-sides, something which makes their catalogue far deeper than it at first appears. "All of their B-sides were great," notes Shirley. "They were famous for it."

Lynch had scored a hit immediately prior to 'Sha-La-La-La-Lee' with 'Love's Just a Broken Heart' by Cilla Black, a co-write with Shuman and Michel Vendome. "I was very pleased with myself, looking at the top of the charts," he says. Underlining the fact that these were the days of non-standardised charts, the *Disc* and *Melody Maker* tables stated the Small Faces record to have topped them, but *The Guinness Book of Hit Singles* registers it as peaking at no.3. What there is no disputing is that Lynch and Shuman had hauled the Small Faces back from the commercial brink. Following the deflation of fortunes caused by the failure of 'I've Got Mine', their appeal – to promoters, radio stations, record purchasers and teenage girls – now soared again.

The latter was always an ambiguous pleasure, though. While no 'red-blooded man' would not feel a frission of enjoyment at the fact of members of the opposite sex being excited at his presence, it was something that always worked to obscure a band's musicianship, something that would become an increasing irritant in the Small Faces' career. "We could really play," says Jones. "The tragedy is when we did gigs then, the most we could play for was about thirty-five minutes because the girls were just going nuts. It was real Beatles hysteria."

Beyond the lack of fulfilment, there is an unprepossessing aspect about being the objects of young female lust which has not been discussed much in pop history books but which McLagan addressed in his autobiography. He recalled, "Many of the young girls in the front rows, believing themselves to be in total darkness, had their hands inside their knickers, playing with

themselves while we played ... They had no idea we could see them mastur-
bating. As the curtains parted each night, the first thing we'd notice was the
smell of pussy wafting up at us ... Though we didn't much mind, it certainly
wasn't a turn on, it was bizarre to watch and it was a revelation to realise that
to some of our fans we were merely sex objects."

The success he had provided the Small Faces earned Lynch the role of their
guiding light. Although he never got a formal credit in this regard, he was
made their permanent producer as they set about completing their first album.
(Some sources claim that Mike Leander also produced for the Small Faces at
this juncture, but Jones disputes this.) "I did about eight tracks with them on
record," Lynch avers. It has to be said that that number is questionable, and
indeed that his memory in general wasn't highly reliable. For instance, he told
this author of 'Give Her My Regards', "I gave it to Jimmy Winston, not Steve. I
didn't even know Steve was in that band" ("Never heard of it," says Winston,
who said he didn't meet Lynch until after he left the Small Faces.) Lynch also
claimed that he "looked after" the band "for about a year and a half" following
'Sha-La-La-La-Lee', something not consistent with the known timeline. Not
in dispute, though, is that for a short while Lynch continued to provide the
band songs. He was now working with another tunesmith who was on the
pathway to the status of legend. Jerry Ragovoy, who often composed under
the pseudonym Norman Meade, had already written 'Time Is on My Side'
(recorded by, among others, the Rolling Stones) and co-written 'Girl Happy'
(Elvis Presley). He would go on to co-write 'Piece of My Heart', which would
be immortalised by Janis Joplin. Lynch feels an affection for his work with
this collaborator that he doesn't for 'Sha-La-La-La-Lee'. "I like the Jerry Ragovoy stuff," he says. "I thought I was going to take them into a new venture.
I was bringing songs back from the States that I was writing with Jerry like
'You Better Believe It'. I wrote that in New York in Jerry's house. I said, 'I'm
gonna do this with this group I'm doing in England.'" 'You Better Believe It',
a mid-tempo paean to romance, is like 'Sha-La-La-La-Lee' propelled beyond
its moon-in-June limitations by its infectiousness, joyousness, pleasing collo-
quialism and fervent band performance. Lynch: "I sent him [it]. He thought
the record was great. I thought it was the best thing we'd ever done because it
was getting into more 'song-ey' things." The other composition Lynch would
place with the Small Faces was his solo creation 'Sorry She's Mine'.

"Lynch was a right asshole," Marriott later told Jim Green of *Trouser Press*.
"When he'd come around with hundreds of song demos we'd all groan,
'Fuckin' 'ell, 'ere 'e comes again!' He'd play you 50 lumps of shit and you'd say,
'OK, sounds really good.' For a while we felt obliged to listen to him because
we'd had a hit with 'Sha-La-La-La-Lee' ... but I like to think Mort Shuman
had more to do with it than him." The disdain in which Marriott claimed the
band held Lynch's efforts may explain a strange scenario that Lynch recalls as
unfolding when he turned up at the Pimlico house one day. "I could see there

was something wrong," he says. "I said, 'What's the problem?' They said ... 'If we're gonna rehearse these songs, we want part of the writing.' I said, 'No, that's not fair. You don't write the songs, you don't get part of it ... You gotta rehearse 'em, otherwise how you gonna bloody play 'em?'... So they said, 'I think we should part company' ... We split in seconds ... I just left the house and after that I never worked with them again." McLagan has no recollection of the incident. "We would never have said any such thing," he retorts. "We would never have made any deals with anybody. We didn't know anything about publishing back then." One wonders whether the Small Faces members, rather than angling for payola, were simply indicating that they wanted to participate in the writing. One alternatively wonders whether the incident was a Small Faces ruse to provoke Lynch into storming out.

Lynch insists, "We were great friends still," and points out that he produced the 1985 recording of 'All or Nothing' credited to Spectrum on which Marriott appeared as a 'soloist', proceeds from which went partly to Lane's ARMS charity. He seems to harbour a pang of regret about their parting of the ways over and above the financial loss. "I was going to try and take the band in a different way," he reflects. "I wanted to take them more into sort of rock Beach Boys. Do more harmonies with them, which I think would have worked for them. I never even got the chance to talk to them and do it." Was he surprised that Marriott and Lane proceeded to become such a good songwriting team? "No, not really. I thought the stuff they done like 'Itchycoo Park' was great. It was basically going the way I wanted to go with them anyway, so maybe I'd spoken to them about it."

Lynch, whatever his abilities, was not renowned for being far-out. As such, his perception of his own influence on such an outlandish recording as 'Itchycoo Park' will seem to many a bit of a reach, if not outright laughable. However, it isn't too bizarre an idea that he left a noticeable legacy to the Small Faces' sound. Hallmarks of the work of the Marriott/Lane songwriting axis – henceforth the creative crux of the band – included gorgeous pop melodies and songs with a life-affirming timbre, which characteristics certainly apply to most of the cluster of tracks Lynch wrote and co-wrote for the group. It's true that examples of Small Faces songwriting beforehand are almost too scant to represent a control sample, but 'I've Got Mine' and 'It's Too Late' are cut from a notably different, more mordant cloth either to Lynch's 'Sha-La-La-La-Lee' and 'You Better Believe It' or to much of the Marriott/Lane compositions that followed them. Of their then-current self-written repertoire (stage or studio), only 'Don't Stop What You Are Doing' displays an out-and-out pop sensibility.

Once acquired, this sensibility never went away. The Small Faces were always much more poppy than peers like the Animals or the Rolling Stones, despite being no less enamoured of gritty musical genres. This fact would from here on give the Small Faces a unique sound. The band married the sweet melodies of white pop with the passion, structure and motifs of black stylings, if black stylings of a more modern stripe than the blues and R&B practised by the aforementioned staples of the British blues boom, namely Stax/Volt and Motown. The result was something that one might call pop–soul. "It wasn't conscious or anything," says McLagan. "Our influences came out. We'd be writing pop songs, but we would be playing with the same intensity." Jones: "We had a real soul singer, so it was a natural thing. It was a fusion that was meant to be."

In March 1966, seventeen-year-old Val Williams made the sort of transition that many British teenage girls literally fantasised about when she went from being a Small Faces devotee to working with the band on a daily basis.

"I'd always been a fan right from when their first single came out," she recalls. "I know there's all this thing about the girls screaming and they hated it and they thought that the girls were just there because they're four good-looking boys, but for me – and I'm sure a lot of other people – it was the music. That's all I was interested in. The drum introduction to 'Whatcha Gonna Do About It' just gets me every time. I just loved everything that they did. Even though some of it was poppy and put on them, I could look beyond that because I was into the R&B sound. And they were a bit rock-ey as well. They were just amazing when they played live."

Although Williams was born and bred in London, she and her family relocated to Chesterfield when she was twelve. When the Small Faces played a gig there in December '65, she naturally attended. She was highly impressed that evening by the caring attitude Marriott displayed to fans. "I hung about afterwards," she recalls. "Steve and the band came out with their driver. I said, 'Can I walk back to the car with you?' I was walking along and I said to Steve, 'Can I hold your hand?' He said, 'Yeah, 'course you can.' So he was holding my hand all the way along this alleyway and along this road up until they got to their car."

At the beginning of 1966, Williams's family moved back to London. "I didn't take any exams at school so my dad found me this really boring job in the City as a trainee typist," she says. She found refuge from the tedium by skiving off and heading to Arden's Carnaby Street offices. "They allowed the fans," she explains. "Don Arden was quite good in that respect. He didn't chase us away or anything. He had this double character, really. He was quite generous and he was quite good to the boys as well." She adds, "There wasn't hundreds of girls hanging around. There might have been one or two people. Quite often, I was on my own."

The Small Faces' fan club was situated within Arden's offices and run by Pauline Corcoran, who was around nineteen months Williams' senior. "I got to be friends with Pauline and [I'd] go in and help her sorting out all the letters and just doing anything that she wanted me to do," says Williams. "They were talking about getting her an assistant, because the mail was coming in by the sack load at this time." It goes without saying that Williams wanted more than anything else in the world to fill this potential position. Corcoran consulted Ricky Arden, Don Arden's stepson, who was the office manager. Williams: "He said, 'Don't know if dad'd like that.' The reason they employed Pauline was because she wasn't a fan of the Small Faces ... She was quite mature for her age ... They didn't want anybody who would be in awe of the band. Pauline kept on at them and she was quite forceful. Ricky eventually said to me, 'Look, I've had a word with my dad and yes, we will take you on, but you've got to promise you will not pester the boys, you won't talk to them when they come up to the office, you won't be a fan. You're here to work.'" Williams was engaged by Contemporary Records at the rate of six pounds a week as an office junior. "I was not only there to help Pauline but to be general dogsbody around the office as well." Don Arden gave the staff some additional, non-standard duties. "He would get us to go out to record shops to buy the record. You had to be careful. You'd only buy one, but you'd go round to different shops to get them."

Williams gained the impression that the fan club was run more as a means of promoting the group than as a money-making operation, noting that the five shillings annual subscription was possibly only sufficient to cover the manufacturing and postage costs of membership card, badge and bi-monthly newsletter. She adds, "Obviously they were selling photographs and badges, things like that. I don't think they had any t-shirts made, but they had all these odd little things that they were making money [from]." However, she also points out, "If you read the newsletters, Pauline is constantly [urging] the fans to write to magazines, to write to radio shows, to turn up at the airport so that there's a presence. To help the band along the way." The fan club's letterhead featured a distinctive florid 'SF' logo. "Kenney I think came up with the design," says Williams. "I vaguely remember seeing the original copy on one of his drum kits, but they – Don – probably got a professional to turn it into a useable logo." It has now become somewhat iconic ("Kenney had it trademarked").

At the end of 1966, the fan club was stated to comprise 10,000 members. Williams confirms that that was a genuine figure. "I had to write them all in a book by hand. As they came in, you'd get the membership form with the postal order and I'd have to separate them and then write down the person's name and address and that and give them a membership number." Her colleague had the more onerous workload, though. "I don't know how Pauline did it. She produced all those newsletters. She [opened] all these thousands of letters that used to come into the fan club every day."

Despite the hard work, there were privileges attached to the job. Williams: "They used to give me free tickets to concerts. I went to some of the industry parties as well." However, the relationship with the band continued to be an arm's-length one, with her never allowed backstage or to the Pimlico house. "I was very restricted in what I was allowed to do and be involved in. No pictures were ever taken of me in the office. Pauline would not mention me in the newsletters." Despite these restrictions, it was impossible for Williams not to get to know the band members on some level. Naturally, she formed impressions of each of them. "Steve was lovely," she says. "He was really friendly and just normal. Steve used to come up the office quite a lot. Out of all of them, he was up there the most. He would work with Pauline. He would go through some of the letters. I don't think any of them answered any of the fan mail – Pauline did that for them – but he did take an interest. He loved the fans. He was just really sweet. He wasn't outrageous at all. He has got this larger-than-life character when he was performing or when he had to assert himself with interviews and that, but behind the scene he was fairly quiet. Funny, as well. He did like to crack a joke. He was a bit of a leg-puller." She also asserts the existence of a quiet intelligence behind the Artful Dodger façade. "I wouldn't have put him down as not being smart. I think he was quite savvy with what he wanted." Jones was Williams's favourite. "He was quite shy, but he also had this really funny side. I still adore Kenney. He's such a great character. He's always friendly. He can be difficult, of course. He doesn't mince his words and he won't let anybody take advantage of him." Of Lane, she says, "I didn't take to Ronnie as much as I did to the others. He was quite cheeky. He was a bit of a flirt, as well." Not taking to Lane was one thing, but Williams so resented McLagan that she was actively aggressive towards him. "I didn't realise this, but I gave Mac a hard time," Williams ruefully reveals. "Pauline said to me, 'You used to treat him horrible. You used to push him out the way when he come in the office, actually physically push him out the way. I told you off and reminded you that I'd got you this job and to behave yourself.' Looking back, that is exactly the sort of thing that I would have done." Did she not like Mac? "Only because he'd taken Jimmy's place in the band. You have to remember, I was an original fan, so when Mac came along, I felt Jimmy's resentment and obviously put that on Mac. And Mac was a bit funny. He was, not offish, but he wasn't as friendly as Kenney and Steve were. [Even] Ronnie was okay sometimes. But eventually, I did get to accept him as one of the band members and loved him for the music that they were producing. There's no doubt he was more suited to be in that band, because he looked like the rest of them. Fated, it really was, that he was to become a member of the band … I think it worked better musically with Mac. There's no doubt that the stuff that they went on to do was so much better."

In McLagan's autobiography, he claimed that the joy of his recruitment was slightly marred by his frosty treatment at the hands of Arden's receptionist and that he later discovered that the root cause of it was the fact that said employee was the girlfriend of the man he was replacing. Although he didn't name the person, it became clear that he meant Williams when he publicly (though non-maliciously) named her during shows later on in his life. Williams says that the keyboardist's memory is faulty on this score. "I did take over reception probably a few weeks after I started working there," she says, but points out that her employment didn't commence until four months after

McLagan's retention. However, McLagan was sort-of right on the "girlfriend" score.

Although Jimmy Winston was no longer a member of the Small Faces when Williams began working for Arden he, as one of Arden's artists, was still visiting the office regularly. (Oddly this was never at the same time as his former band, leading Williams to suspect Arden made sure to warn them of his forthcoming presence.) These visits, Williams says, occasioned "cuddling" between Winston and herself. However, she adds, "It was probably only about six or eight months that we were together. I didn't see it as anything really serious. We weren't courting." Nonetheless, she was close enough to him to see the effect his departure from the band had had on him. "It did shake him a bit and he did lose his confidence," she says. However, this doesn't seem to have lasted long. "Jimmy was doing his own thing. He was doing quite well. It wasn't as popular as what the Small Faces were – they were huge – but he was still working and I think in some ways he was happier being the frontman."

Not only had Ricky Arden been dubious about allowing a bona-fide fan proximity to the Small Faces, but, says Williams, "Don was not happy about employing me." However, Arden, Sr. could see at least one benefit to the arrangement, as Williams found out when she was called into his office one day not long after she started working for him. Although she says Arden, Sr. was "quite a good boss," she also says, "He was a bit of a scary character. You wouldn't want to cross him at all. He did have a nasty side to him." As such, being summoned into Arden's sanctum "always gets you shaking because you think, 'Oh God, what have I done?'" On this particular occasion, though, Williams found Arden quite solicitous, as was the also-present Marriott. "Him and Don were talking about what the next single was going to be," she says. "They told me to sit down and said, 'Right, we're gonna play you two songs and we want you to tell us which one you like best.' This is probably one of those times they thought as I'm a fan she'll be able to say which one we should put out." One of the tracks she was played had a vocal, the other did not. "What I said first of all was, 'Oh, I like both of them. They're both really good.' They said, 'No, no, no – you gotta choose one.'" Williams dropped the diplomacy and nominated the track sans singing. "I loved the guitar playing and I thought they were so good with the instrumentals that they did." Even as she stated her preference, though, she admits she worried that "Steve might be offended, because he's not singing on it." The song with a vocal was a Marriott/Lane composition called 'Hey Girl'; the instrumental was a group-written effort that would ultimately be titled 'Almost Grown'. Reflects Williams, "A few weeks later, the single was announced and 'Almost Grown' was the B-side. I don't know to this day whether Steve won or Don won."

'Hey Girl' appeared on 6 May 1966, its production credited to Don Arden. McLagan saw the single as being in a direct, cold-blooded line from 'Sha-La-La-La-Lee'. He says of the latter, "We cut it and we weren't really happy with it. It came out and it was a hit. Because of that, they came up with 'Hey Girl' which is pretty similar. Don Arden liked that and [said], 'That'll work.' That did okay. That got Steve and Ronnie back in the songwriting deal."

One can see why McLagan alleges cynicism. The confection is meticulously constructed (first verse/second verse/bridge/instrumental break/third verse) and is sprinkled with a call-and-response pattern custom-designed to be infectious. Yet whereas in the hands of Freddie and the Dreamers or Gerry and the Pacemakers the creation would have sounded trite, here it sounds like nimble pop craftsmanship. Moreover, the fundamental heft and grit of Small Faces instrumentation lifts it beyond that, and that's without even taking into consideration Marriott's vocal, which as ever is gravelly and impassioned. The track begins and ends sublimely, one of Jones' blistering drum charges providing the intro and Marriott and Lane taking the record into the fade with some inspired and impressively sustained call-and-response singing which perfectly demonstrates the band's move into that aforementioned soul and pop nexus.

There is something else that takes the recording into another dimension impact-wise, something that had been present on 'Sha-La-La-La-Lee' and which would proceed to be forever a hallmark of the band's sound. The Small Faces' music was infused with a rare joyousness, a *joie de vivre* that made the listener feel glad to be alive for the duration of their records. In the pop universe, the Beatles were the only other artists whose output so consistently boasted this attribute. 'Hey Girl' is its quintessence. When Marriott's voice rises in the middle-eight to declare that when he thinks of what he's missed it makes him laugh inside ("All the girls that I ain't kissed just to keep my pride!"), it's impossible for the listener's heart not to swell.

'Almost Grown' is a Chuck Berry song, but if the Small Faces were alluding to it they were co-opting the title only because their own number is a sort of sequel to 'Grow Your Own'. It's much the same in construction as that predecessor, but more dynamic in its interplay, and just as wonderful. Naturally, its composition is credited to all four members, even if a few scattered lines of, possibly improvised, lyric prevent it technically being an instrumental.

However, the Marriott/Lane attribution of the A-side was the real indication of where the creative power of the band now lay. Many pop consumers of the day simply didn't know or care if their idols wrote their own songs (something unfortunately and embarrassingly communicated by the erroneous statement in the second edition of the Small Faces' own fan club newsletter that 'I've Got Mine' "was written for them for the film they are in …"). However, self-composition was very important to Sixties artists, and none more so than these ones. The impetus originally came from Marriott. "I hadn't even considered writing songs until Steve sat down and said: 'I've got an idea', and we started working on it," Lane told John Pidgeon. "I thought it was pretty amazing that this guy could actually think of his own material." McLagan would often bear witness to Marriott/Lane songwriting sessions when "the three of us would stay up all night on leapers." He notes that the juncture at which the pair would sit down together during the writing process "would be that stage of finishing the song." He elucidates, "'Itchycoo Park' was Ronnie's; 'Tin Soldier' was Steve's; 'Get Yourself Together' was Steve; 'Show Me the Way', Ronnie; 'Here Comes the Nice' was Steve. But it was both of them because Steve would come in with a song and Ronnie would have some other part that would go with it or offer some vocal ideas, and backwards and forwards like that." He added, "More and more as time went on, they wrote separately." The observant will notice that the main composer of 'Itchycoo Park' is not the person who sang it. Was there ever any dispute over who should take lead vocals? McLagan: "No. We knew we had a great singer." The observant will also notice that despite the nuances of the compositional *modus operandi* delineated by McLagan, it was not reflected in the publishing attribution. As with the most famous writing partnership in popular music – that of Lennon/McCartney – credits and proceeds were divvied up fifty–fifty regardless of the specifics of the relevant creative process. Lane admitted to Pidgeon, "A bigger percentage of the ideas came from him than me." "I asked Steve once why he credited Ronnie with the songs he wrote, when he could have had all the publishing money himself," Marriott's father told Cliff Jones. "Steve said, 'Dad, Ronnie keeps me going. If it wasn't for Ron I wouldn't stay up half the night trying to finish these bloody songs. He's my inspiration.'" Or as Lane put it, "We'd come up with something to knock each other out, I suppose..."

Keith Altham considered the two halves of the composing pair rather a contrast as people. "Ronnie was a dear character," he says. "He was a sweet boy." Of Marriott, whom he first met back in the early Sixties, he observes, "I think he was a slightly damaged kid. I don't know exactly why, but I always felt he was a little bit disturbed. Then of course he started to find drugs and then didn't help him much." However, the journalist says, "Each admired the other for what they did that the other didn't have. You usually find that in a band. Not exactly opposites attracting, but one providing the talents or the characteristics that the other doesn't possess."

Not long after Marriott and Lane wrote 'Hey Girl', Lane met for the first time one Susanna 'Sue' Hunt, a young woman with whom he would enter into both a romantic relationship and spiritual areas that would have a profound effect on him, an effect which some parties believe is the main reason for the ultimate rupture of Lane's relationship with Steve Marriott and by extension the split of the Small Faces.

Not that any blame can be attached for this to Hunt, a forgiving and widely liked figure. A Kent native, her background was completely different to Lane's. "I grew up on farms and Ronnie grew up in the East End of London," she notes. Like Lane, though, she had artistic leanings, something stemming from her performance aged around twelve in *The Mikado*. "They cast me in a big role and I completely fell in love with the whole idea of acting. It was definitely my thing. When I did go to London, that was what I was going for." Although acting was Hunt's preference, she also worked as a model. In addition, she secured a recording contract. "I had a manager who engineered the whole thing," she explains, although also says, "I was willing to do it because I thought that's a step in some directions." She chose as her recording guise Geneveve ("I liked the idea of only one name").

Hunt released a handful of singles, one of which – 'Once' – scraped the UK top 40. While her musical career may have been short, merely moderate in success and only half-heartedly entered into, if she hadn't embarked on it Hunt would never have met the man who for several years was the love of her life. "I was on tour in one of the East Coast seaside piers," she recalls. This would appear to be the Swinging '66 package tour which took in six consecutive Sunday dates at Blackpool's South Pier Theatre staring on 12 August 1966. "The seaside piers have theatres on them, or did. I was booked for a whole season opening the show. All these different big bands each week would be the headliner. One week it was the Small Faces. I was just standing backstage kind of hanging out waiting to go on and I suddenly saw this little figure standing there completely in his own world and thinking deeply and not too aware of what was going on around him. I don't know if we talked then or not."

Her impression of Ronnie Lane was of someone "very different" and "a special spiritual, deep person." Before long they were a couple, something partly facilitated by the fact that Hunt's bedsit home was in Chelsea's Sloane Square, a short walk from the Small Faces' Pimlico house. The question of whether she got the impression that Lane's lack of height bothered him amuses her. "No, not at all," she answers emphatically. As alluded to previously, she declines to discuss whether his lack of a complex might be down to the alleged fact that he wasn't short in all departments.

Before long, the pair were making the music press gossip columns (February saw the *NME* make the crack that Geneveve might cover the Beatles' latest single 'Penny Lane' as 'Plonk Lane'). In time, she naturally met Lane's family. "Elsie was frail," she recalls of his mother. "She had MS, but they didn't really know what it was in those days. She couldn't move well and couldn't do much. Ronnie's dad was just this lovely, gorgeous man. He'd worked like a slave all his life, hauling coal on his back and stuff. They lived in a little tiny house." She got the impression that the Lanes were the archetypes of poor-but-happy. "His dad was, in many ways, his inspiration. He was a very beautiful person. So loving. Very much like Ronnie, actually."

Being familiar with pop groups, she was able to observe that the Small Faces were a more harmonious crew than most. As to why two very different characters like Lane and Marriott were so close, she offers, "The muse. The creative force that they were able to participate in together. The purity of it was an extraordinary bonding of two souls who could create beautiful things together. It created a fantastic atmosphere. I'm not being overly romantic here. When you have a beautiful creative force what it really represents in its manifestation is love and love is, as we all know, a force that grows. It spreads out and has others feeling good too. It's contagious."

That 'Hey Girl' marked the first appearance of the 'Marriott, Lane' songwriting attribution was a milestone but only on a technicality: the single was originally intended to appear on the same day as the Small Faces' debut album, which contained other examples of that credit, but the latter was delayed by a week because of what were described as "technical difficulties".

When on 11 May 1966 the Small Faces' eponymous debut long-player did make its belated appearance, its tracklisting seemed to constitute a repudiatory statement on the part of Arden. 'It's Too Late' was included but – apparently pointedly – not its flop A-side, even though with a scant 33-minute playing time the LP could have accommodated at least two more tracks. Moreover, the album could have done with a track of the quality of 'I've Got Mine', for it was aesthetically rather patchy. Having said that, with 'Whatcha Gonna Do About It' closing the original first vinyl side, 'Sha-La-La-La-Lee' concluding its second, and 'It's Too Late' also present, fully a quarter of the disc's contents were already familiar; had 'I've Got Mine' also been included – especially at the expense of one of the new tracks – purchasers who had already bought the singles might have felt exploited.

"Our first album, we did it in an afternoon or a morning," says Jones. McLagan's recollection was slightly different: "We did it in two or three days." In actual fact, the album patently isn't the product of one block of recordings. Not only are 'Whatcha Gonna Do About It', 'It's Too Late' and 'Sha-La-La-La-Lee' of older vintage than the bulk of the tracks, but two further selections have a Winston co-writing credit that suggests they were cut prior to McLagan's arrival, possibly backing up Winston's claim earlier in this text that some of the material consists at least in part of the band's demo for Decca.

McLagan's recollection of the part of the album that he helped record was that it wasn't taken too seriously. "We were tripping on one of the days," he said. "Steve was standing on a chair screaming. We were just looning." No producer is credited, although Arden's Contemporary company receives a generalised billing on the back cover. Asked how seriously we can take Don Arden production credits – explicit or implicit – on Small Faces releases, his son David says, "In those days a record producer [was] like a movie producer. Compared to a record producer of today, I'd say no." For his part, Winston says, "Pat Meehan might pop in and pop out, but it was more of a case of just seeing how it was going." "He was very rarely in the studio," McLagan asserts of Arden. "Self-produced, I think," although adds, "We had good engineers." The main one of those engineers, the aforementioned Glyn Johns, was another in the Small Faces' circle whom McLagan had met before he joined their ranks, as he had engineered a demo recorded by the Muleskinners.

The album kicks off oddly with 'Shake'. Although the Small Faces version is reasonably lively, it's a surprising choice for Lane's sole vocal showcase herein, Sam Cooke's classic exhortation to dance being perfect material for Marriott's sandpapery larynx. As previously mentioned, the Lynch/Ragovoy 'You Better Believe It' is both corny and blissful. Lynch's staccato composition 'Sorry She's Mine' is of a different stripe, less good-natured and less melodic. Nonetheless, it's an enjoyable affair in which the narrator warns a rival in romance to back off.

Not only is Winston's name a component of the four-way writing credit of 'Don't Stop What You Are Doing', but he notes, "That's one of the ones I used to sing." In this instance sung by Marriott, It's also very good. Cooing harmonies, determined melodiousness and a romantic lyric so chocolate-box conventional that it sees a little bird flying in to tell the narrator of his girl's undying love for him don't preclude grittiness, primarily from Marriott's ever-abrasive vocal and raw guitar work.

The phrases "own up" and "own-up time" were vogueish in the Sixties. The sleeve of the Small Faces' debut LP lists the fifth track as 'Own Up' and states it to be a Marriott, Lane composition, while the label has it as 'Own Up Time' and written by "Marriott, Jones, Lane, McLagan." In the case of the writing credit, the label seems the more reliable source as the track is another variant on 'Grow Your Own'. Like all such organ-heavy Small Faces instrumentals, it's highly likeable, if in this instance – at less than two minutes – a little too fleeting.

In the context of the other material, 'One Night Stand' (Marriott, Lane) is arrestingly mature and solemn, from its sexually suggestive title downwards. It sees the narrator denounce a woman who only became truly interested in him once his name was in lights. The song comes to a clean close with the unapologetically blunt statement, "I'm leaving you behind." That the depths of the narrator's bitterness don't become immediately apparent is probably due to the song being built on another pretty pop–soul structure.

The feeling of overarching insubstantiality that afflicts this album is primarily engendered by a trio of tracks whose familiarity has a different quality to the excavation of the singles tracks.

That with 'Come on Children' (Marriott, Jones, Winston, Lane) Marriott turns the catchphrase he had appropriated from James Brown into a song title would not have been to the pleasure of Kenny Lynch. "I used to go mad with Stevie, because he always used to keep singing 'child'," he says. "I used to hate him doing that. All the time, he used to say, 'Come on children!' and 'Come on, child!' I used to say, 'Stop Stevie, you're only a fucking snotty-nosed kid yourself!'" "I think that was the cuteness of it, though," Jones demurs. "The fact that Steve was a young guy saying, 'Come on children'. It was a great line. A bit like the Beatles going 'Yeah, yeah, yeah.'" Lynch's particular beef, though, isn't the problem that most listeners might have with the track. 'Come on Children' is essentially 4¼ minutes of R&B vocal and instrumental motifs randomly strung together. Not only is it flimsy and second-hand but it's rather similar to side two's Marriott/Lane attributed tracks 'E Too D' and 'You Need Loving', which also arbitrarily appropriate vaguely generic riffs and phrases with the sole apparent aim of occupying a disproportionate amount of space – the three tracks cumulatively span over eleven minutes, roughly a third of the LP, where all the other tracks each come in under three minutes, some under two. These three tracks, though, do give a hint of the Small Faces' stage act, not least in being far looser and more fiery than their other recordings of the time.

'You Need Loving' also presents problems over and above listenability. Its Marriott/Lane composing attribution is debatable not just because of the aforementioned fact that jams – thinly disguised or otherwise – are usually given group composing credit. (It's certainly odd that this tradition is cleaved to for 'Come on Children' and not this one when it might be said that the two tracks are parts one and two of the same song.) More to the point, Willie Dixon might consider 'You Need Loving' to be his creation. Of course, Dixon's 1962 composition 'You Need Love' – recorded by Muddy Waters – was itself reminiscent of many antecedents: it being the case that the blues is black American folk music, components of the genre's songs were habitually passed down from generation to generation, or even appropriated – without much controversy or rancour – by musicians of the same generation. However, fairly or unfairly, a different psychology or morality is felt to apply when one party is white and the other black: in these cases, such borrowing can feel like exploitation. In any event, Marriott felt plagiarism immoral on a broader scale. He reflected to *Phonograph Record*'s Jon Tiven in 1971, "I really hate it when rock groups steal a song from an obscure artist and then not give him credit. When I was seventeen and with the Small Faces, we stole a Willie Dixon number called 'You Need Lovin'' [sic]. We didn't credit him, but I regret it now. I've grown up a lot since then." Having said all that, words-wise 'E Too D' does have some originality. Part of it is almost disturbing. In a lyric of extraordinary torment, the narrator confesses to a deep unhappiness. "Sometimes I look inside me and I don't like what I see" is not a sentiment one would expect to hear from a teenager, least of all an 'all-about' character like Marriott.

The album was housed in a sleeve featuring a smiling head-and-shoulders front-cover group photograph. Its aura of innocence dissipated a little upon inspection of the graffiti on the wall behind the band. Handiwork of the artists, it included a chalked face smoking a cigarette with a pinched end. The back cover featured the sort of gushing, banal sleevenotes standard for the era, these ones written by PR man Tony Brainsby. The album climbed to no.3 in the UK. It spent twelve weeks in the top ten and remained in the UK top 40 for just under half a year.

Of the fact of the record being bizarrely divided between pop tunes and jam-oriented, almost avant garde material, David Arden muses, "I think that was half of the Small Faces' problem. The girls loved them but Stevie didn't want that. He wanted to be cool. Which I always found a bit strange." Lane claimed that becoming a teenybop idol was a descent from the band's early days. "When we started out it used to be all boys that would come and see us," he told Jonh Ingham in 1972, "and then as we had hit records the boys petered off because all these girls were turning up and screaming and wetting their knickers." While acknowledging that on some level Marriott did like being the object of female fan worship, Arden says, "Stevie was a guy's guy, if that makes sense, but with musos. That's where he wanted to be. He would rather be out with the guys – fellow musicians – thinking about ideas."

This tension between teen idoldom and a deep-seated hankering for credibility may have meant that the Small Faces were doomed from the start.

3   I Can't Dance With You

The month after the release of 'Hey Girl' and *Small Faces* saw the start of Jimmy Winston's solo recording career. Val Williams confirms the sincerity of his comment, "Leaving and getting on with my own band [was something] I enjoyed a whole lot more."

Although McLagan had taken his place in the Small Faces in November 1966, the legal niceties surrounding his departure worked on a slightly different timeline. "I left somewhere like late December, beginning of January, where it got finalised," recalls Winston. "I tied up and did a new deal with Don for a new band." To this purpose, Arden introduced Winston and said new ensemble to Kenny Lynch, who says, "They came up to the office in Aberbach and talked to me. I gave them this song that I'd written." The song was clearly not Marriott's pre-fame record 'Give Her My Regards', as Lynch misremembered, but 'Sorry She's Mine'. This, though, didn't engender a long-term professional relationship. "I never really liked his songs," Winston says. One also wonders whether he was less than impressed when he found out come the release of his ex-colleagues' first album that Lynch had also given 'Sorry She's Mine' to the Small Faces. "I quite liked it," Winston nevertheless says of 'Sorry She's Mine'. "It had its energy to it." Had Lynch been present in the studio for Winston's solo interpretation, one suspects he might have raised an objection to Winston's tweaking of the lyric to replace the line "Hands off, fella" to "Hands off, sir." 'Sorry She's Mine' by Jimmy Winston and his Reflections appeared on Decca in June 1966 (i.e., a month after the *Small Faces* track) with a Winston-written B-side titled 'It's Not What You Do (But the Way That You Do It)'. It did not trouble the chart compilers. From what Winston says, Arden's usual muscle may not have been put behind it. "I was never sure how much good promotion I'd get. People like the record, but it's just one of those things."

Winston would have considerable success in his life, but in spheres outside that of recording artist. He would never again taste the thrill of presence in the hit parade or the holding of status of teen idol.

The Small Faces had issued singles about which they were dubious but with which they scored success or of which they were proud but which flopped. In August 1966, with 'All or Nothing' they were finally able to combine commercial achievement with artistic fulfilment.

"I wrote 'All or Nothing' the same day we recorded it," Marriott said to Jim Green. He also told the *Trouser Press* journalist that the track was one of only four Small Faces recordings that the band specifically intended at the outset to be a single. As to the subject of the song, Jerry Shirley says, "There are about four or five women on the planet that claim 'All or Nothing' was about them, because he was a rascal. The truth is he was courting a girl from Manchester and it wasn't going as well as he intended, so that's when he wrote 'All or Nothing'. A 'shit or get off the pot' type of thing." The girl in question was one Sue Oliver, whom Marriott is said to have met when she was working in the cloakroom of the Oasis Club when the Small Faces played there in late 1965. The pair at one point got engaged, although the relationship was apparently doomed by Oliver's mother's constant interference.

The narrator of 'All or Nothing' demands his partner give herself over to him completely ("If I could have the other half of you"). The recording has a dignified desperation, helped by a stately tempo, a thin, glittering guitar riff and a delicate variation on Jones' by-now traditional opening drum roll, one which involves a gradual build in volume. Yet the classiness is sometimes undermined. "Come on children" makes another regrettable appearance and if the variant of Otis Redding's "Gotta gotta gotta" signature that's also present isn't as gauche as that, it's equally derivative. Meanwhile, the instrumental break that sees Marriott chirruping in tandem with McLagan's organ may be cute but it also belongs to a recording that isn't making the tilt for sophistication that this one is.

Far better is the B-side, 'Understanding'. Like the A-side a Marriott/Lane composition with production credited to Arden, it's a recording whose sonics are as dark and cavernous as the A-side's are clean verging on sterile. A particularly brawny soul-stomper in which Marriott imparts his philosophy on love, it features thunderous drums, floorboard-vibrating piano, a towering melody and a lyric that tips over into grand statement. Meanwhile, as if to definitively nail down the life-affirming quality of Small Faces music, it actually features the phrase, "I love this life I live."

Despite 'All or Nothing' resembling a good album track rather than a top-quality single, it was considered by the band an artistic breakthrough. Marriott asserted at the time, "'Sha-La-La' and 'Hey Girl' were really nursery rhymes. We're now writing lyrics that mean something ..." It was also a chart-topper – an undisputed one this time – and knocked the Beatles'

'Yellow Submarine'/'Eleanor Rigby' off the summit.[2] Because it was the only Small Faces single to top the *Record Retailer* chart, 'All or Nothing' has now gone down in legend as the band's sole no.1, thus giving it an artificial pre-eminence in the band's canon. This underserved stature has also been helped by the fact that the title phrase has become a handy motif and easy headline for anybody writing an article, book or play about the group or Marriott, not least because the absolutist philosophy it articulates does rather seem to accurately sum up Marriott's attitude toward life.

Although David Arden was still only fifteen, courtesy of his history with Marriott and his work for his father, he had the privilege of hanging around the band.

Like his father, he was particularly fond of Marriott and Jones (the latter shared David's love of horses). David says of Lane, "I was friendly with him to a degree" and of McLagan, "I didn't know him very well." (His father's feelings on the latter he sums up as, "Plonk, he could take or leave" and "[He] wasn't very fond of Ian McLagan. I always put that down to the fact that he took over from Jimmy.") David would pay the band visits when they were recording, initially at Decca Studios, West Hampstead which he says "they had the run of; they were in there whenever they wanted." The Small Faces ceased using the record company's facilities because "they found out that IBC was a cool place to record." However, he says Don Arden's indulgence continued at their new recording venue. "Any artist that the old man had control of were given full rein," he asserts. "They were spoilt rotten, artistically."

One of the recording sessions at the independent IBC Studios in London's West End for what was intended as their second album involved a rendition of the 1961 Del Shannon hit 'Runaway'. David Arden chipped in on the track's handclaps. His father made a more significant contribution, providing a mock-operatic vocal introduction. Marriott later told Jim Green that "he ran out and started to do it. He was taking it seriously — singing used to be his gig — and we were all in hysterics ... We wanted to give a Bronx cheer..." David is sceptical of this recollection of piss-taking and says that Marriott was happy to take the singing advice his father would offer him: "I remember he always said, 'Put your finger in the middle of your forehead, get the note...'"

Following that night's recording, Arden, Jr. found himself invited by Marriott to the band's Pimlico home. "That's when he gave me my first joint," Arden says. "The old man [said], 'Alright, don't stay up too late.' Of course, I've gone out of me tree. I've never been able to smoke that stuff. Two o'clock

---

[2] On one week's edition of *Top of the Pops*, the aggregated chart the BBC used couldn't find sufficient difference in sales to separate the two aforesaid bands' records, resulting in an infamous draw wherein half-headshots of each band member (one side Ringo, one side Jones, etc.) were placed beside the legend "Number 1."

in the morning: BOM! BOM! BOM! The old man's knocking at the door. Or even three o'clock in the morning. I was fast asleep. He was like, 'Come on – you're coming 'ome!" Did he suspect the corruption of his child that had taken place? "Oh, he knew."

In October, the Small Faces were involved in controversy when on a UK package tour they two nights in a row refused to perform because of a dispute about the higher billing given to the Hollies. The *NME* proposed that they should have been less concerned with the fact that the Hollies had been made headliners than that fans had paid to see them, sardonically suggesting that 'Big Heads' might be a more appropriate name for the band. Marriott was asked by a reporter who he would choose to burn on forthcoming Bonfire Night and nominated the Hollies' Graham Nash, although it's unclear whether he was motivated by spite or Nash's current Guy Fawkes-like whiskers. Somehow, the conflagration wasn't career-destroying. By the end of the year, the *NME* felt obliged to eat their words when in their annual reader's poll the Small Faces came second only to the Beach Boys. "We salute them for the freshness and vigour which they have injected into the disc scene, and we hope they continue with the good work," the paper effused without apparent sarcasm. Another contretemps that was potentially far more damaging took place at the *Top of the Pops* studio that year. Marriott, under the erroneous impression that producer and co-creator Johnnie Stewart was moving on, had responded to his unctuous thanks for their latest appearance with the words, "I'm glad you're leaving – I always thought you were a major cunt." The Small Faces were promptly banned, thus beating to the punch by some margin every other act banished by the *Pops*, whether Serge Gainsbourg or the Sex Pistols.

The Small Faces had other things about which to worry in 1966. The Autumn of that year was supposed to mark the date of the band's first tour of the United States. It was a matter for some excitement. The USA in those days was for Britons shrouded in a certain mystique: more than a decade before cheap transatlantic flights, the fact that few working-class people knew anyone who'd been there lent it a faraway allure. For rock and pop musicians, it was even more appealing, being the birthplace of all the music they loved, even if that music had recently been refined with considerable artistic and commercial success by British players. The tour never transpired. "Cheap management," is McLagan's explanation. Jones concurs. The drummer believes that Arden was initially enthusiastic but lost interest when he realised the financial outlay involved, as well as the fact that local agents would have to be cut in. "I think Don Arden didn't want to let us out of his sights," says Jones. "He didn't want anybody else to grab his thunder." The band later publicly recalled that Arden started talking down his own idea, pointing out the drawbacks of a long trek on a cramped tour bus as a mere support band.

Before long, the Small Faces had even more about Arden's management with which to be unhappy. Securing the Christmas number one single in

Britain is an important accolade. As music journalist Siân Pattenden once perceptively observed, "It's like being crowned. It's like winning the year." Don Arden was possibly less interested in that symbolic achievement than in the attendant commercial benefits. Either way, come the winter of 1966, he was keen for a release from his charges that could vie for that position. In October, the music press had claimed that the group's next single was likely to be 'Mystery' (a song later renamed 'Something I Want to Tell You'). Regardless of specific track, the band didn't feel they had finished product yet. They told their manager that the point at which they would was not far off and offered up a token of reassurance-cum-proof of such. Marriott said, "We'd presented a bunch of demos, left them in Arden's office." Driving home from a gig one November night, they were horrified to find coming out of their vehicle's radio a rough mix of one of those songs, 'My Mind's Eye', along with the news that it was set for release imminently. "We hadn't finished with it and even if we had we wouldn't have wanted it as a single," Marriott averred. "I doubt very much that that would have happened without them knowing," disputes David Arden. "It might not have been the mix that they wanted, but to say it was a demo…" The band were naturally furious. Although they were helpless to prevent the release, they at least ensured that the initial pressings were supplanted by a newly-mixed version with more backing vocals. In truth, though, 'My Mind's Eye' was never destined to be a classic.

"That was Steve's song," says McLagan. "At least I'm sure the melody was. He was the one who knew that it was a nick … It came from a hymn." The hymn in which 'My Mind's Eye's chorus is melodically rooted is 'Angels from the Realms of Glory'. However, whereas said hymn contained flowery worshipful verse like "Angels from the realms of glory/Wing your flight o'er all the earth/Ye who sang creation's story/Now proclaim Messiah's birth," the Small Faces song's chorus is merely hummed. The patent derivativeness – most people would have known the source melody from school assembly, religious broadcasts or Sunday School – gives the recording a substandard, unoriginal air.

When it comes to the lyric, it's impossible not to assume that directly or indirectly Lane had a significant influence on it, for it bears a touch of something that was becoming an increasingly large part of his character: truth-seeking. The narrator talks of seeing things more clearly than before and of bewildered people around him feeling he has changed. He also boasts of an enlightenment with which others aren't blessed. This, though, is not the enlightenment associated with either conventional religiosity or the acquired knowledge of elders, both of which Lane's generation were busily rejecting, but instead of a more ancient and exotic wisdom. In other words the type of outlook that would shortly and briefly become fashionable via flirtations by the Beatles, the Beach Boys, Donovan, et al., with the likes of the Maharishi Mahesh Yogi. The mind's eye, of course, is a notion classically associated with such non-Western spiritual outlooks, a belief in disregarding the readily available senses for deep contemplation through which will come greater insight. It's essentially the same principle as "Turn off your mind relax and float downstream," a line from the Beatles' track 'Tomorrow Never Knows' released three months prior to 'My Mind's Eye'. John Lennon adapted that song's lyric from *The Psychedelic Experience*, pretty much a modernistic LSD user's manual but one harking back to the ancient Buddhist text *The Tibetan Book of the Dead*.

The previous September, Lane had amazed the *NME*'s Keith Altham by talking to him about telepathy, astral travelling and philosophy. "In the last six months I've completely changed my attitude to life," he said. "I suddenly realised that I had achieved my ambition of playing in a big group and life must hold something more ... There are other things that I'm finding out about – they're as old as time. It's just that I'm beginning to see them more clearly." "Ronnie became a Buddhist in '66, and that lasted for a while," said McLagan. "He was with this American girlfriend. She gave him this scroll of paper which she hung on his wall. She said, 'That's your soul.' We just laughed at him. Acid changed us all a little bit, but he was a seeker and he went on from there to Meher Baba, etc. etc. He said to me one day, 'You're going the opposite direction to me,' because I'd been a kind of spiritual guy and I'd given up on it. Ronnie became hard to deal with for a while there because he was confused and he was searching. I wasn't searching. I knew exactly what I wanted to do. I wanted to be in the Small Faces, cutting records and playing shows and smoking dope. It was all good for me. Ronnie was looking for something else." Lane's spirituality, it should be pointed out, didn't prohibit him stealing other men's girlfriends or getting involved in aggro (as with his colleagues, his stature didn't inhibit him squaring up to people). In fact, not only would his spirituality often be in conflict with this earthliness, it would sometimes comprehensively lose out to it.

Although it can't be denied that the song hints at development, 'My Mind's Eye is in truth a rather cack-handed version of pop's nascent mysticism, coming across for all the world like a toytown version of the likes of the aforementioned 'Tomorrow Never Knows'. The record's B-side is much worse. 'I Can't Dance with You' is either a literal lament by the narrator that his bopping partner has the proverbial two left feet or a (maybe earthy) metaphor about two lovers being out of sync with each other. It's difficult to care which because its mid-tempo instrumentation is staccato and functional. Only Marriott's vocal – as engagingly overly-committed as ever – grants any vitality to the proceedings.

Yet for all the single's faults, the A-side was unquestionably catchy. The hymn derivation and chanting interlude also lent it an apt Christmassy air. These facts ensured that it secured one of the healthiest of all Small Faces chart performances. Although it didn't secure them that cherished Yuletide top spot, it made it to no.4.

The Small Faces, though, were in no way inclined to celebrate. The fact of Arden releasing the record without their consent only underlined a dissatisfaction with the manager already rumbling through their ranks. The crucial component of that dissatisfaction was remuneration. Gone were the days when they were happy with a £20 wage, gratis accommodation and free threads. Expectations had gone up along with their profile. As Marriott noted to Jim Green, "We had a number one single and were still getting [£20] a week!" That their greater financial earnings were not feeding through to the band made them feel uneasy.

McLagan says that by '66, the Small Faces were earning £1,000 a night – around £18k today. "No way," retorts David Arden. "Is he mad?" Of his father, he says, "Yes, his accounting was the bloody worst, all that stuff, but at the end of the day they weren't playing Wembley. Two hundred, two-fifty. A thousand pound a night? There might have been one or two big gigs where they might have got close to that but, by and large, it was Dreamland Margate, Locarno, Twisted Wheel, Boston Gliderdrome – those kind of gigs. Any artist, not one of them would say they were getting a grand a night in those days, no matter how big they were … I started as an agent looking after big acts in '68, '69 and I'm booking the Move out [for] 250 to 300 pound a night. I was booking out the Ike and Tina Turner Revue, '68 I think that was. We brought them over for a tour round the clubs and they were doing two shows a night in different venues and they were getting 300 to 500 pound a show."

Yet Galaxy Entertainments' Ron King says of McLagan's assertion, "That is right, too. It was a lot of money, but they were worth it. They packed every time." He also says, "Galaxy took ten per cent if we did the bookings. … Don would take 25% of that. But he was only entitled in those days to ten per cent. I remember that as being a major dispute. But I never interfered with it because he was the manager. My office was clean and the boys were happy with that." He also admits of Arden, "Many times it was, 'Don't tell 'em what they got for that gig.' Not just the Faces; it could be anybody. He was as bent as a ladies' hairpin." King is also convinced that the Small Faces were being cheated on their record royalties. "I would say that they were lucky if they got ten per cent of what they were due … There was always arguments, always heavy discussions amongst the Small Faces, and sometimes they poured it onto me. What could I do? … There was a continuous dispute. They didn't like him, they couldn't get out of the contract, they could get out, they couldn't get out, they did get out, they had to go back – that went on forever and a day. Every time I ever saw [them], there was always a moan or a groan: 'We're not getting paid.' That's all I kept on hearing from day one to the time I left … They left him two or three times – or attempted to – but somehow or other he conned them back … They deserved to get rid of him. They never had any money while I was with them. I don't mean no money at all. I'm talking about they didn't present theirselves as having money as like the Beatles and the Stones, for instance. The Faces never had that sort of money that they could flash it around."

David Arden is having none of it, recalling that King was rumoured to have been guilty of various felonious activities, quite the least of which is appropriating equipment for Amen Corner from other bands. Arden does have something of a point. King says in apparent pride, "I was brought up with the Twins," a reference to Reg and Ronnie Kray. He also easily offers, "I nearly killed a guy in Dunstable. I got a conviction for grievous bodily harm on that one."

Arden, as may have been intended, picked up on the fact that the Small Faces were beginning to question their lack of riches. According to McLagan, his initial reaction was to try to scare them, introducing them to a very large gentleman he described as 'Mad Tom'. Recalls McLagan, "Steve said, ''allo, Tom' and Mad Tom grabbed Steve by the neck and lifted him off the floor up to his face and he said, 'Mad Tom to you.' We learnt there that, 'Ah, maybe we'd better watch ourselves.' It was not a very nice day for us." "He used to work for me in my clubs," explains King, who claims it was he who conferred the 'Mad' sobriquet. "He was one of my own bouncers and a friend of mine. He *was* mad. In a fight, he was a raving lunatic. But he was, with us, as good as gold." Again, Arden's son has a different perspective. David says Marriott "absolutely adored" Mad Tom and his roughhouse manner. "Being an East End boy, he liked having tough guys around him or being part of the whole tough-guy scene."

Mad Tom was one of the principals in a drama that occurred when Arden got wind of the fact that Robert Stigwood, manager of Cream and the Bee Gees, was sniffing around his disgruntled charges. Arden's response has gone down in showbusiness folklore, his 2007 *Guardian* obituary for example saying, "He and his heavies paid Stigwood a visit with Arden hanging Stigwood off his fourth-floor balcony as a warning." As with much folklore, though, facts have become distorted and confused via both the passage of time and deliberate mythmaking. This starts with how Arden found out about Stigwood's overture. Some have suggested his antennae twitched when he heard of a meeting between Lane and a colleague of Stigwood's. David Arden heard a different story at the family dinner table. "Robert Stigwood calls up the [Pimlico] house and I think Kenney spoke to him," he recalls. "He said, 'I was thinking, it's about time you got a new manager.' Kenney called up dad and told him … The old man always took it very personally. To him, it was somebody trying to take the food off his family's table … That's when the plot was hatched to go round to Stigwood's office and frighten the fucking daylights out of him … He had Mad Tom and a couple of film extras – Big Stan was one – and I'm pretty sure Pat Meehan, Sr. was there too. They all burst in … His office was in Cavendish Square on the first floor and he had [a] Romeo and Juliet balcony. He did take him to that and pushed his head over and went, 'Oi, you try and steal off me again and that's where you'll fucking wind up' …

When the old man took him to his window, they all shouted, 'Drop 'im, drop 'im, Don!'"

"The Stigwood affair – that was my job," says Ron King, who remembers things rather differently from his perspective as participant and eyewitness. "The same time that Don asked me to pay him a visit and take a couple of people with me, there was rumours that Stigwood was getting in to the Amen Corner," he recalls. "I never even asked the Amen Corner. Soon as I heard that rumour, that was like loading a gun to me. With Don telling me about Stigwood trying to get the Small Faces, that was like throwing petrol on a fire … There was Mad Tom, me and Don Arden. Went straight through his secretary at the front there, said, 'Don't worry, love. Don't interfere. We just want to see him.'" There was a fourth person present: "That man stayed outside," detaining the secretary on the grounds that such robust activity as they had in mind should never involve women. King continues, "Closed the door behind us. Stigwood's sitting near and he happened to be on the phone as we walked in. Fortunately, he just put the phone down and then Don started with his usual screaming and shouting. He had a big mouth with nothing to back it up with. He started denying it and I grabbed him and I smashed him against a wall and I said, 'I tell you what, you fucking arsehole, I'll throw you out the fucking window.' He didn't get hung out the window at all. I had him by an open window. Mad Tom was very calm. I said to him, 'Stand there, just in case something comes through that door.' He stood by the door, I got Stigwood by the window and I said, 'I'll throw you out there you fucking arsehole. You're [after] the Amen Corner.' Now, that was my only beef. The beef that Arden had was he definitely went into the Small Faces and he was trying to pinch them. Everybody knew." What did Stigwood say? "'I didn't, I didn't, I didn't.' He denied it completely, one hundred per cent, both cases – the Small Faces, Amen Corner. But he was well-known for that in the business. I know the man's dead, but nobody can ask me to say nice things about a guy that I know was crooked. He was bent."

King's version of events ties in with the fact that many, including some members of the Small Faces, think Arden was not as nasty or at least as directly involved in nastiness as some people – including Arden himself – depicted him as. "Don Arden wouldn't hang anyone out the window," doubts Jones. "He ain't got fucking enough strength." "I don't believe any of that happened actually," said McLagan of the notion of Arden breaking bones. "He would employ people to hurt you." "I've always found him not as bad as everyone made him out to be," says Jones. "He was the rogue he was, but he was a big teddy bear in a sense." Keith Altham notes, "I think he just played at being a crook a lot of the time. It was fairly characteristic that when you went to his office, the big picture on the wall, his hero, was Edward G. Robinson in the film *Little Caesar*. He venerated those old Hollywood gangsters, who weren't the real thing at all."

"Arden never had any balls," says King. "He survived with a big mouth, knowing he had my team. I had about forty men, all heavyweights. They worked my clubs. Arden never had any contacts with any heavyweights. They didn't want to know him. Keep in mind, in those days people were anti-Jewish. I was one of the very few non-Jewish people that made a success in the business. When it came to any problems, if anybody needed a visit, Don would phone me up or when we were in Carnaby Street, he'd come in and we'd talk about it and I'd arrange all that ... I helped him out of a big problem in Windmill Street. We used to eat salt beef sandwiches there. I was still in there. He'd walked out. He had about three guys round him was going to turn him over and he's called out, 'Ron! Ron!' Gutless prick. I had to solve the problem."

Even if Arden's version of the Stigwood events was true, he didn't consider the story dramatic enough when he later related it to a tabloid. "The old man did an article in the *News of the World* and it was called 'I'm the Al Capone of Rock,'" recalls his son. "That would have been back in '70." In this recounting even David admits that his father was embellishing the facts: "Stigwood wasn't named but he says, 'I hung him out the window by his ankles.'"

Whatever the exact truth about this encounter, Stigwood got the message that the Small Faces' contract was not up for grabs.

David Arden and Ron King are in concordance on one thing: the matter was not something that Arden could have readily solved by, as the saying goes, reaching for his lawyers. "This day and age, yes," says King. "In my time, it was, if you were a heavyweight you can handle it, if you weren't, you were out. Nobody talked about solicitors. If the Faces done a job for me in a club and the promoter didn't pay, after two or three phone calls asking for the money then I had to send two or three heavyweights go and collect it." "You couldn't rely on the police," says Arden. "For instance, illegal programme selling. (It was only the programmes back in the Sixties that they would sell. T-shirts weren't a big thing then.) He'd call up the police. They'd say, ''ee, lad, it's nothing to do with us. That's civil suit. You 'ave to sue 'em.' What you gonna do? He'd ask them nicely two or three times – then he'd hit him. Today, because it's big business, they've got their own police force that can literally walk into your house and put a freeze on everything without even a court order."

Wild-West methods are said to have been in operation again in mid-1966 when Jimmy Page – in those pre-Led Zeppelin days a humble session guitarist and producer – was trying to put together a group with Jeff Beck, John Entwistle and Keith Moon. The preferred singer for this putative talent-oozing line-up was Marriott. That Moon had approached Marriott about the idea filtered back to Arden. Page later recalled that the idea was dropped when Arden relayed the message, "How would you like to have a group with no fingers, boys?" Another stymied attempt to leave Arden's orbit involved the band members paying a collective unannounced visit to Yardbirds and Marc Bolan manager Simon Napier-Bell, who was aware enough of Arden's reputation to telephone him while the band were seated before him to suggest a deal in light of their clearly being determined to change managers: "I'll be their manager and you take half the income." He wrote that Arden was amenable to the suggestion and that Arden suggested that if the band weren't, "I'll break their bloody legs." The group "fled" before Arden could make his way over to discuss matters further.

Of the Small Faces' grumbles about remuneration David Arden observes, "I never heard it from any of them because by that time obviously they're getting busier and busier, but I would pick up things at home or being in the office, hearing the old man and Pat Meehan and sometimes my elder brother talking about it. Of course, it all came to a head with that meeting with the parents." It's a measure of how young the band members were (Jones: "The bands that were around in those days were definitely three to four years older") that it was the Small Faces' parents who directly challenged Arden about finances. They confronted him at his Carnaby Street offices and demanded to know why their famous and successful sons were not in clover. According to several Small Faces chronicles down the years, Arden's response was to come up with a quite despicable stalling tactic that involved him telling them that their boys had squandered their money on drugs. As hashish and marijuana weren't expensive and cocaine not common, the implication of his words was heroin. Naturally, the parents were both horrified and chastened and beat a retreat to confront their progeny.

Of the common theory that Arden's behaviour in this meeting was a distraction tactic to throw the parents off the scent, David Arden says, "That I know not to be correct." However, he does offer of his father's behaviour at the meeting that it was "the biggest mistake he ever made." It was a mistake with benign motives behind it. He claims that Arden's introduction of the subject of drugs was down to genuine concern for the band's welfare, if a concern shot through with naivety: drugs was something Arden, Sr. knew little about despite the fact that David says, "He was so anti-drugs, it wasn't true." Frankie Langwith had been replaced as the band's driver by Bill Corbett, who had previously worked in that capacity for the Beatles. Unlike Jimmy Winston's brother, he wasn't blood-related to any of the Small Faces so was also able to act as Arden's eyes. David Arden: "He was always coming and telling the old man, 'Oh, they're smoking all that funny stuff, Don. I can't drive sometimes, the smoke's going in me eyes.' So that was a big thing." For Arden, his father's raising of the drugs issue in the context of a financial meeting was simply a matter of him blurting out his anxieties. "They were asking why they weren't getting more than their [twenty] quid a week," he says. "'Don't you think it's about time you started being a bit more interested in your son's well-being? All these fucking drugs that he's taking.' The way the old man did it was a big mistake. That was the start of the Faces and dad falling out."

With supreme irony, Don Arden was unwittingly responsible for the Sixties pop aristocracy – including the Small Faces – having easy access to drugs, courtesy of his association with a doctor in Harley Street whom he had once asked to treat Gene Vincent. Says David, "He was always called Dr Bobby. Used to wear a bowler hat." The practice was augmented by a junior doctor when Dr Bobby's health started to fail, one who was happy to abuse his position to dispense recreational drugs to anyone who could afford it and who was surreptitiously immortalised in the Beatles' 1966 *Revolver* track 'Doctor Robert'. "My dad was responsible for [the junior] being the drug doctor to all the rock stars, because he took Gene Vincent to Dr Bobby, and then the Small Faces went there when the junior doctor came along, and then the Small Faces took the Who there, and then they took God knows who else."

Whether or not Arden's drugs comment was a distraction tactic, it cemented the idea in the minds of the Small Faces that Arden was a man of limited honesty and integrity. As soon as they had reassured their mums and dads that they weren't on smack, the band members were at the manager's door demanding with even greater vigour proper accounting and its supposed stablemate more money. Inevitably, the Small Faces and Don Arden soon parted company completely.

In 1974, Arden told *Melody Maker*'s Rob Partridge that he had invested around £20,000 in the band. "After the Small Faces left me there were certain royalties owed to them," he claimed. "But they owed me management fees and equipment costs, so the two balanced out." This was not quite what accountants and courts decided. In October 1967, almost a year after they had separated from Arden, the Small Faces obtained judgement that Arden's company owed them royalties in excess of £4,000 (over £70,000 today). Obtaining that money was another matter. "We closed down his company, but couldn't afford to pay the lawyers to chase him," McLagan observes. "He was paying off in instalments," says Arden's son, who insists that while his family "always lived well," Don Arden was not rich. "He wasn't a multi-millionaire. That wasn't the business at the time. Nobody was." David Arden also insists that the Small Faces would have got the full sum eventually were it not for the man they had engaged to represent them. "[He] couldn't pay and he got a threatening phone call and that's the one thing that'd drive the old man mad ... Their lawyer was a guy called Victor Gersten. They went, 'Right, if you don't pay off this – it was like £2,300 in unpaid royalties – we'll put you in bankruptcy.' The one thing you couldn't do to my dad in those days was threaten him. He went, 'Fucking *put* me in bankruptcy.'" Arden says that his father's reaction was "the stupidest thing he could have ever done." Courtesy of Don Arden's bloody-mindedness, in February 1968 Contemporary Records went into liquidation. Many might not shed a tear for Arden but it also consequently meant that the Small Faces didn't receive the outstanding part of the debt until February 1977. "Of course, all the rights reverted to the administrator," reflects Arden. "I guess it must have been the Faces' lawyer." From Arden's point of view, it meant that the one Small Faces-related asset he had retained after losing publishing and booking rights in their transfer to other parties – the recordings he owned and leased out – were lost. "He stupidly cut off his nose to spite his face," says David. "In those days [his attitude was], 'There's another Small Faces 'round the corner, we'll find 'em' … At the time, he didn't realise how the music industry was going to go and how much he'd missed out on … He never thought there would be any life left in them. The album did about thirty thousand units, they hadn't broken in America, so there wasn't huge things to get excited about. He didn't feel that anything was going to be worth anything in five or ten years' time anyway."

Arden's obstinacy and irrationality also caused him to relinquish publishing rights on original Small Faces songs. "The old man had a huge row with Carlin Music, Freddy Bienstock, because they'd gone and done a deal behind the old man's back, or Stevie did. He lost his cool with Freddie."

Although clearly not blind to his father's faults, David is reluctant to accept the idea of grand larceny on his part. "Alright, let's say he nicked something," he reasons. "How much could he have nicked? … Their first album sold thirty thousand. The crappy royalty rates of the time and they were going out for two hundred pounds a night – you work it all out. They got the Beatles' chauffeur, they got a house in Pimlico with a maid. How much was nicked?"

Some, of course, would counter that petty larceny is still larceny, but David Arden does have a point of sorts. Compared to today, the music industry was much smaller and its revenue streams fewer. In the UK, radio broadcasts of records amounted to plays on the BBC, which had a monopoly of legal airtime. (Pirate stations may have been loved for their hipness but their solidarity with the emerging counterculture didn't extend to paying artists and songwriters.) That monopoly didn't end until 1973 with the arrival of local commercial radio. The money remitted to songwriters by the BBC via the Performing Rights Society (PRS) was – as might be expected of a monopoly – low. Moreover, the BBC had airplay restrictions imposed on it by the Musicians' Union ('needletime'), a measure designed to prevent professional musicians having their livelihood undermined by radio plays leading to reduced public interest in buying records or taking in live performance. *Saturday Club* – a huge programme at the time – was only allowed to play three releases per broadcast, while record programming on Sundays was restricted to *Two-Way Family Favourites*, with the rest of the day's broadcasting taken up with orchestras.

Not that, in one sense, the latter mattered much. By arrangement with the major record companies and the Musicians' Union, the BBC paid musicians performance royalties (i.e. remuneration for broadcasts of a song on which they performed, regardless of whether they were its composers). However, whereas today performance-royalty organisation Phonographic Performance Limited remits money to anyone who has registered themselves as contributing to a recording, the Sixties is a muddy period where in some cases these royalties were remitted to artists' management and in some cases to their record company, neither of whom necessarily passed it down the chain to artists. This was hardly compensated for by bands like the Small Faces being directly paid fees by the Beeb to perform on radio shows like *Saturday Club* and *Easy Beat* (with PRS going along with it if they were playing their own compositions).

Mechanical royalties – the royalty accruing to songwriters on every record sold – was usually handled by the Mechanical Copyright Protection Society, who then accounted to the music publisher. In that period, the 'mechanicals' amount, set by law, was 6¼ per cent of recommended retail price, as opposed to around eight per cent today. (That percentage was divided equally by the number of a disc's tracks, which was only two on a single but, less lucratively, much more on an LP.) Artist royalties – the money paid by record companies to musicians for sales of discs on which they played – were not set by statute but were a matter for negotiation between the artist's manager and the music label. They were notoriously low. The Beatles were initially signed by EMI on terms of a penny royalty per disc (at a time when there was 240 pence in the pound), which essentially meant they would have to sell nearly a million-and-a-quarter records simply to split a thousand pounds (equating to approximately £20k today) between the four of them. Pete Townshend says of the Who, "We were on a quarter of a percent (of which our managers took forty per cent, by the way). We were on nothing. I didn't make any money until after *Quadrophenia* [1973]." Other revenue streams had yet to be fully capitalised on (e.g., payments for music played in public spaces like hairdressers and supermarkets), were a much smaller market (for instance, use of music in visual media – 'sync licensing' – was of little relevance because soundtracking movies and TV with popular music was then almost unheard of), or had yet to be invented (such as streaming and sampling).

On top of those issues are ones unmentionable in any legal defence. Some of Arden's genuine expenses could never be put in his accounts: illegal activities like hyping records and bribing pirate radio stations are not tax-deductible. Then there are the type of things that become issues of dispute only when two previously friendly parties have fallen out. For instance, Arden, Sr. may not have intended to charge against record royalties for the band having "the run" of recording studios until such time as bad blood poured in upon their departure from his stable.

Even leaving all that aside, Arden says of his father, "I can tell you one thing: he never, ever that I knew of was [consciously] ripping off Small Faces, or indeed anybody else." He appends, though, "Accountancy, he never thought was important. 'What they worried about? 'ere – 'ere's some more money.' That's the way a lot of people were in those days. It wasn't until you got somebody like Allen Klein – an American accountant – who's started making it an industry. Up to then, people only got involved in entertainment because it was a bit of a laugh." But surely, a fast-and-loose attitude toward bookkeeping is a recipe for confusion and bitterness later on? "I wouldn't disagree with that at all."

Towards the end of 1966, Val Williams on behalf of Don Arden found herself making hand deliveries of several letters to various London addresses. Only gradually and with hindsight did she understand what this flurry of activity signified.

"I ended up getting this taxi with Ronnie and Kenney," she recalls. "The address was Regent Street and it was Harold Davison's office. There was a solicitor as well." Davison was a top pop booking agent. "I was taking these letters with contracts backwards and forwards to these places where they were negotiating the sale of the Small Faces." By the end of the year, even as 'My Mind's Eye' was still riding high in the charts, the Small Faces had left Arden and Contemporary behind. They had hired a lawyer and an accountant to tell Arden in person that they were departing his stable. Such well-connected and law-savvy people, of course, could not be intimidated in the way the likes of Robert Stigwood and Jimmy Page had been. "It was actually easier than we thought it would be and we were so glad to get away from him," says McLagan. In the first week of December, Marriott informed the music press of the split, enigmatically stating, "We've had a lot of trouble and one or two things have not been done quite how we would have liked." In that same week, the group declined to fulfil a commitment to appear on BBC-TV children's programme *Crackerjack*. The show's co-host Leslie Crowther gamely filled in by playing an instrumental version of 'My Mind's Eye' on piano.

The same month, the Small Faces vacated Westmoreland Terrace. That they were looking to move had been reported in September, the *NME* claiming that the fans who gathered outside and left so much devotional graffiti on nearby walls had been the subject of many police complaints by neighbours. "They just didn't get any peace whatsoever," their fan club explained. Of course, the reasons for a wish to disperse to their own London flats were intensified and complicated by the fact of them subsequently removing Arden – in whose name the one-year lease had been taken out – from their professional lives.

The rupture with Arden came as a shock to the fan-club administrators. Val Williams says, "Pauline at the time did not know anything about their arguments with Don. None of the office staff knew ... I don't ever remember any tensions or any arguments between the boys and Don at all. It's really weird. The first we knew was when [we were told], 'Right, that's it. The band have got new management.'" Made redundant by Arden, Williams was offered a job by Ron King as Galaxy Entertainments' junior secretary/receptionist in the agency's new offices in Denmark Street, also located in the West End. She accepted. "Ron was really lovely," she says, although does concede, "He was a villain."

The impression has subsequently been given that Don Arden was equanimous about the split, an impression conveyed not least by Arden himself in self-aggrandising media interviews. David Arden says, "No way. He always thought Stevie Marriott was the greatest ... Believe it or not, he was hurt ...

He was a tough guy, but he was also a very sensitive chap because he always thought he'd done his best."

The Small Faces had concerns other than whether Arden's feelings were hurt. "Really, we never got away from him," laments McLagan. He is referring to the fact that when Arden learned that the band had signed with Davison, he sent the agency a bill for £20k, a sum he claimed the band owed him. There was no incentive for Davison to challenge the invoice when he could just pass on the costs to the group. Accordingly, the band started out in debt to Davison and their new manager, Davison's associate Tito Burns. "So he didn't lose out," McLagan says. "He got paid. He did fine. And he was always getting royalties from our records, which we never were." That supposed £20k debt would be passed from manager to manager and would ultimately be picked up by the band themselves when the remnants of it bought themselves out of their final recording contract in order to start afresh.

Moreover, the Small Faces were not impressed with their new agents and managers. Although they secured them a prestigious spring 1967 support slot on a month-long Roy Orbison tour, it soon became apparent that booking gigs was the extent of their talents, not building on their recording success. "Harold Davison and Tito Burns pretty much shelved us," McLagan says. "They didn't do anything for us … Everything we asked for, they said, 'Well, that's going to be difficult because the state of the economy' or 'Your last record didn't do as well…' These excuses."

The band attempted to move on, but Kinks manager Robert Wace and Island Records supremo Chris Blackwell, after initial interest, both transpired not to have sufficient time to devote to them. McLagan always regretted not remaining with Arthur Howes, yet another agent whose retention of the Small Faces was announced in the music press (in this case in June 1968) only to be just as quickly declared to be at an end. McLagan adjudged Howes, one of the biggest promoters in the business, "a wonderful geezer." He explains, "Everything we asked for, he said, 'Yeah, we can do that.' 'We want to tour Europe.' 'Alright.' Everything was yes." Having said that, he recalls that the band moved away from Howes precisely because he seemed overly optimistic about what he could do for them.

When the Small Faces dispensed with Arden, they also lost a record company. They could conceivably have approached Decca directly to discuss a new contract, but it's also possible that they didn't want to, not just because of bad memories and unwanted associations but because there was a new label making a name for itself whose adventurous spirit was right up their street. Moreover, Immediate Records was helmed by Tony Calder and Andrew Loog Oldham, both men with whom their frontman was familiar.

Paul Banes started out in the Immediate label's accountancy department before moving into publicity. "They were already working together as PR," he explains of how Calder and Oldham came to conceive of Immediate. "They set up Immediate because they were working really closely together on the Beach Boys, Timi Yuro, Gene Pitney, you name it." The pair's vision for Immediate was never purely that of PR men, though: artistry was key. It was an attitude alien to the types who usually ran music labels at the time. The popular image of the latter was bald, besuited, bespectacled and long past any interest in popular music, if they'd ever had any at all. It's possibly an exaggeration, but probably not much of one.

Decca, EMI and Pye were the main components of the British record industry of the era, forming a trinity that was for musicians, especially younger ones, decidedly unholy. "The old farts were still running this industry," notes Malcolm Forrester, who became managing director of Immediate's publishing division, Immediate Music. "Edward Lewis and Joseph [Lockwood] and all those people got knighted, didn't they, for heaven's sake." "It could have been 1945 from the people that were working in there: old grey metal cupboards and radar on the roof," says Banes of Decca. "EMI in those days had somebody on the door with a uniform on who was a leftover from the war and the mentality in there was the mentality of people that were ten, fifteen years older than us: suit and ties and white jackets ... When I moved [to] Immediate, Tony I think was the oldest and he was 22." "They were taking on the established record companies of the time," says Keith Altham of Immediate. "It was the first independent record company of its kind, certainly to be run by people who were under the age of forty, maybe thirty. It was a revolutionary aspect of its time." "It was the Virgin of its day, Virgin when it first started," says Jones. "A free, independent label. If Immediate had stayed together and overcome their problems, it would have been as big as Virgin."

It's interesting that Don Arden – a friend of Oldham – had actually offered Immediate the Small Faces in the label's very early days. Oldham had turned him down, but he now rectified his mistake, signing the band to both the label and to a management contract. The latter was a significant fact: Oldham had proven his managerial nous by discovering the Rolling Stones and guiding them to stardom.

The good-looking Oldham was usually to be seen dressed in hipster styles and wraparound shades and often in a state of inebriation or intoxication or both. Both Altham and Jenny Rylance say he was "cooler" than the stars he managed. "He was one of those people who had a feel for what was going on and mirrored that with his selection with people on that label," says Altham. "He had some extraordinary talent. He had Rod Stewart at one time, he had P.P. Arnold, he had the Nice, Jeff Beck. Jimmy Page did a lot of work for Immediate. He had the pick of the crop. He was in tune with what they were doing. He had real flair. He listened to his artists." "Andrew was flamboyant, to say the least, and full of ideas," says Banes. "Andrew was a turning point in London for everything that was going on ... He was into the music." The label put its money where its artist-oriented mouth was, paying double the royalty rate of most record companies.

"Tony Calder was a bit of a drip to be honest," says Pete Townshend of Old-ham's partner. "He didn't really have Andrew Loog Oldham's flair." Jerry Shirley, an Immediate recording artist via his membership of the band Apostolic Intervention, says that Tony Calder was not as into-the-music as Oldham. "Not in the slightest." However, he adds, "Doesn't mean to say he didn't spot a hit." Banes says, "Tony was the businessman with ears and with experience."

"We made it up as we went along basically," says Banes of Immediate. "It was the place to be. Everybody was knocking on our door because [of] the vision of a generation the same age." The established music industry had a term for the Immediate staff. Banes: "They called us the Little Bastards. The record company formulas that they had at the time didn't correspond with what we were doing ... [Oldham] played on all of that." Behind the wild ideas and nose-thumbing irreverence, though, was a hard-nosed business approach. "I thought it was a seriously well-run office and Stan Blackman, who was our accountant, was seriously neat and tidy," says Forrester. "Tony Calder's first wife, Jenny, was absolutely brilliant at administration. My secretary Sam, she was sensational ... We were more serious and going-to-it than all your Pyes and Philips and all the other ones of the day ... All artist statements were sent out every six months on time, which is more than I can say for some of the other labels of the time ... I can tell you that every music publisher in town and every label in town had a drinks cupboard. We never had drinks cupboards. I would most probably be the only one that'd go to the pub. A little bit of smoking dope, but not even a lot of that. All I remember is everybody working. They'd be there, all of them – not so much Andrew but certainly Tony – sticking 45s in envelopes and doing mail-outs." "We would do a mail-out every month or every week, depending on what was going on," says Banes. "The fan club for the Small Faces, we did flyers for every record." It was left to Oldham to keep the decadence end up. "Andrew was, if you like, the artist," says Forrester. "He'd be in studios most nights or out ligging or something. He would come into the office about lunchtime, or as my old boss Freddie Bienstick used to say, 'At the crack of midday.'"

The first Immediate single – catalogue number IM-001 – was a licence of the McCoys' 'Hang on Sloopy', released in 1965 and a UK top five single. "Immediate went from [IM-00]1 to [IM-00]30 in a year with a whole bunch of different records, including people like John Mayall, Mort Shuman, Jimmy Page," says Banes. The turning point for the label came in Spring '66 with IM-035, Chris Farlowe's version of a Jagger/Richards song. "'Out of Time' was the first big, big record," he notes. "Every record after 'Out of Time' we put on the charts."

From what McLagan says, the Small Faces were impressed by Immediate and its ethos but not dazzled. "Mick was helpful when we were talking about going with Andrew Oldham," he says of the Stones' frontman. "He kind of clued us in to him but said, 'At least he's a good manager.'" McLagan adds, "I was suspicious of Andrew, but Steve was all gung-ho and Steve knew Andrew from years before, so we all just went along with it." He concedes, "It was definitely a step up from being with Arden." Banes offers of the new signings, "It was Tony going back to his roots almost. They fitted into the family."

The Small Faces signed with Immediate on February 10, 1967. "We were in a very funny position, where our management was also the record company", Marriott told Pidgeon of the all-encompassing deal. Although they weren't fully cognisant of it at the time, the band were plunged immediately into a veritable financial and contractual viper's pit. They were immediately in debt to their new label because the £25k Immediate paid to the Harold Davison agency in compensation for no longer being able to book them as a live act – note the increase of £5k from the compensation Davison paid Arden – was set down by Immediate as recoupable against gig fees.

A February '67 story in the *NME* stated that the Small Faces had signed to Immediate Productions and that their recordings would be leased to Decca. This was obviously an unsatisfactory situation for Immediate. Although they were successful as a production company and a song publishing company (no less an act than the Beach Boys were signed to their publishing arm), the crux of Immediate's business – or perhaps more accurately mission – was releasing records. It would have looked very odd if they were not issuing Small Faces product recorded under their aegis. Oldham got himself out of this situation in the obvious way. Paul Banes would give evidence for Oldham in the 1990s when his former employer tried to wrest back control of the Immediate catalogue from then-owners Sanctuary Records. "The lawyer said, 'Is it correct that you gave Don Arden 25 grand in a brown paper bag?'" recalls Banes. "If he did, it was out of his own pocket. We were all aware of the rumours, but nobody was going to walk around saying Andrew had given 25 grand to Don Arden, otherwise we'd have the tax man knocking on the door and everybody else. But it is very likely."

David Arden tells a completely different story. "I can't remember the whole top and bottom of the thing because I wasn't involved in the business on a daily basis, I was still at school" he warns. What he does recollect from what he has heard down the years, though, is that Immediate, Harold Davison and Freddy Bienstock/Carlin Music all "put into the situation to get it worked out," "it" being a sale of "agency, management and records." He also offers that any compensation paid to his father was almost an act of pity on the part of Oldham. "The old man loved Andrew," says Arden. "Don was one of Andrew's first clients." That fondness seems to have been reciprocated. "He said, 'Don, let me pay you. I'm not gonna let you lose out completely.'" Arden also insists, "There was no paper bags ... That is Tony Calder, God rest his soul, saying that. Codswallop ... The man who was Immediate's major business adviser was Allen Klein. There's no way he would have entertained brown paper bags. He was much too shrewd ... I know he got the cheque and I know exactly the bank he took it to deposit it: it was in the Strand and it was a bank called London & County." He adds, "I think it was ten grand." Whatever the amount, it has been said that the fee was recoupable against the Small Faces' record royalties.

There may be further twists to these labyrinthine intrigues. According to McLagan, the contracts his colleagues signed with Contemporary Records back in '65 weren't worth the paper on which they were printed. "They were all too young to sign," he says. "Parents never countersigned. So the contracts were bullshit." Although David Arden says he never saw the contracts, he says, "I never recall that ever being said and I find it hard to believe because, of course, the parents were being paid, so the parents would have presumably signed." Was his father savvy enough to arrange legally correct contracts? "Oh yes. As much as you could in those days." One has to come down on the side of David Arden on this score. McLagan himself admits he was hardly in the loop. "I joined the band later, so I never signed anything," he notes. Jimmy Winston – although mysteriously unaware that his three colleagues' parents were also receiving a Contemporary stipend – says, "All our parents signed. I do remember them taking contracts off to the parents." Then there's the fact that Jones says, "I'm sure those contracts were only limited to a short period of time. In those days, as a new band you were given three months and then you'd be nobody again." On top of Jones' acknowledgment here of the existence of formal contracts, his comments suggest – considering the length of time the band were with Arden – that the contracts would have been renewed at least once. Leaving aside all the fragmentary recollections and hearsay, though, is the compelling fact that the legal advisers engaged by the Small Faces to free them from Arden clearly didn't flag this up as an issue. Even in the naïve Sixties, it is inconceivable that any lawyer would have missed a flaw in Arden's paperwork – i.e., its illegitimacy – that would have enabled the Small Faces to walk away from him with no penalty whatsoever. It should be noted, furthermore, that it's said that the band's lawyer managed to nullify Frankie Langwith's civil case against them specifically by invoking the contractual point that Jones was underaged.

Meanwhile, Kenney Jones claims that in any case the band could have walked away from Arden with no penalty whatsoever through other means. The catch would have been Jones acquiescing to a suggestion that some of Arden's alleged methods be used on him. Although Jones is a preternaturally nice man, his upbringing in the East End meant he had relatives ready and willing to use extreme methods to exact justice on those who had done his family wrong. "[He] played the hard nut but I knew basically it was only a front, because my family are a lot harder," says the drummer of Arden. "[He was] lucky to be alive after what he did to us. I stopped my family going to finish him … My cousin Billy Boy Jiggins, he'd just got out of prison and he used to work for the Krays. He said, 'Kenney, I've just been talking to your dad. I hear your manager is ripping you off. I'll sort it out. I'll go and break his legs.' I said, 'No, no, I'll sort my own stuff out.' Because I didn't want to cause any trouble. With hindsight, I should have let him break his fucking legs."

Whatever the financial shenanigans and long-term ramifications thereof, there was one instant financial benefit to the Immediate deal, even if there is a sardonic element in McLagan's comment, "We went all the way up to fifty pound a week." The wage increase to half a ton (to use East End parlance) equates to a healthy £900 or so in today's money. Banes adds that this was not the extent of their Immediate-related income upon their signing terms: "They had a four-grand advance." The advance – which Calder put at £5,000 – was more money than the band had ever seen in one lump sum before. Calder – not necessarily the most reliable of narrators – said, "It was gone in a matter of days. Their drug consumption was unbelievable." The Small Faces Immediate record royalties were seven per cent on UK sales, six per cent for overseas. Banes adds, "They were probably getting a third of what Immediate were getting from distribution."

Separate to that was a publishing deal. Explains Banes, "When they bought the Small Faces into Immediate, we set up a publishing company called Avakak, which was Steve's name. Typical East End. Andrew and Tony co-owned the company with them." "Only Steve would come up with a company name like Avakak," notes Jones. It was a slightly wrong-headed pun. Aberbach was one of the biggest names in music publishing, familiar to pop consumers from its presence on countless record labels. Marriott would seem to have been under the impression that the word's final syllable was not pronounced like the classical composer but like the rear of the human torso. He decided to devise a name that supposedly echoed it but with a scatological twist. On a more serious note than cracks about having a cack, publishing was generally considered far more important and lucrative than royalties from physical record sales.

Jones says the company was set up on the advice of Oldham and Calder. He is glad that said advice was proffered. "I think we owned sixty per cent and Andrew Oldham owned forty per cent with Immediate," he says. In his autobiography *Let the Good Times Roll* (2018), he wrote, "The four of us were equal stakeholders, with Andrew and his partner Tony Calder also holding shares ... All those shares combined amounted to around 70 per cent of the company." The MD of Immediate Music demurs. "The Small Faces owned Avakak," Forrester says. "And it was administered – if that's the right terminology – by Immediate Music, which was 100% owned by Andrew and Tony. But I wouldn't know what that deal was. I'm running Immediate Music. We had quite a few deals where we administered other people's catalogues." Regarding Jones' conception of a 70–30 split between Avakak and Immediate Music, would it make sense that Immediate Publishing took from Avakak a 30% administrative fee? "It could have been, yeah." Andrew Oldham himself says regarding he and Calder owning part of Avakak, "I do not think so," adding, "What we did was co-publish in the UK with Avakak and publish to ourselves in the US."

Jones: "It was owned jointly and severally by the band, so everything that went through there was split by the band." McLagan confirms, "I owned a quarter of all those songs with Kenney and Stevie and Ronnie." Again, Forrester thinks the reality is slightly more complicated. In those days, publishing companies divided their profits fifty–fifty with their clients, so in fact each Small Face was guaranteed 25% of half of the revenue accruing from performances of songs. The other half of the revenue was passed on by the directors to the writers of the songs, which in this case of course was usually Marriott and Lane.

Although he was a colleague and close friend of Marriott, Jerry Shirley feels obliged to assert that such deals and figures undermine the claims of exploitation that have always run like a seam through Small Faces narratives. "Don't believe all this, 'We were always ripped off, always skint,'" he says. "Andrew spent a fortune on that band, and it was all out of his own money." It's certainly noteworthy that in April of that year, Marriott told a journalist that he was paying a rent of £40 a week on his Baker Street flat. The average Briton at the time had to find his rent out of a weekly wage of around £17.

Even the non-writers did well out of this publishing deal. Although Jones and McLagan (except on the infrequent occasions when they contributed to the composing) were only getting 25% of fifty per cent of publishing revenues, Forrester states that it was a very generous arrangement for non-writers. Jones also seems to agree. "It used to make me laugh," he says. "I used to get a cheque for, like, one and six [one-shilling-and-sixpence]. My standard royalty. Then about a month, six weeks, later I'd get a cheque for, like, three-and-a-half grand, my share of the company."

Whatever the nature of the Small Faces' finances, no one doubts that they were much, much happier at Immediate than they had been at Decca. The same could not be said for Pauline Corcoran, who made the move with them.

Arden had given the Small Faces' fan-club secretary the choice of staying within his professional orbit or continuing to work for his ex-charges. Although – unlike Williams – not a fan of the band, Corcoran had decided that her loyalties lay with them. "She enjoyed the job, she really loved it," reasons Williams. "She adored Steve as well." Although there wasn't a romance between Corcoran and Marriott, "She was his confidant. They were really close." The deepness of their friendship was demonstrated in the aftermath of a serious car accident in which Corcoran was involved while still working at the Carnaby Street office. "She was in a coma for a few days and she was drugged up on morphine," says Williams. "She was going out with Neil Jones from Amen Corner at the time. She said that when she woke up, the nurses said, 'Ooh, you're lucky – you had good-looking guys either side of your bed.' One was Steve and the other was Neil, and they were both holding her hand."

Whatever the shortcomings of the Arden era, they hadn't extended to dismissive treatment either of Small Faces' fans or those charged with cultivating them. "The new management did not like the fans coming up the office, so that had to stop," says Williams, who stayed in touch with her ex-colleague. "She was shoved in a little broom cupboard, a much smaller office than she'd been used to. Was not treated very well." Corcoran took a particular dislike to Tony Calder. "He didn't treat her very well and didn't like the fan club being there." Eventually, it proved too much for Corcoran. "I don't know how long she stayed at Immediate, but she did eventually end up working at home."

While the Small Faces may not have formally put pen to paper with Immediate until 10 February, that they had been very much in their orbit before that date is demonstrated by the fact, within weeks of signing, two singles written by Marriott/Lane, one of them produced by Marriott, had been issued on the label, '(Tell Me) Have You Ever Seen Me' by the Apostolic Intervention and 'My Way of Giving' by Chris Farlowe.

Marriott had recently participated in *Melody Maker*'s 'Blind Date', a feature involving a musician reviewing new releases without being told beforehand the identity of the artist. His comment on an Immediate Records act that he liked the way Oldham produced prompted a phone call from his old acquaintance and a meeting wherein Oldham told Marriott he was interested in working with him and an enquiry about songs he might have available.

Before Oldham re-christened them, Apostolic Intervention had been known as the Valkyrie. "I wanted to call 'em the Nice, but Andrew Oldham said, 'You can't use that name!'" Marriott recalled to Green. "Then later on he used it for Keith Emerson's band, who'd been backing P.P. Arnold. Andrew always steals with decorum..." Jerry Shirley was the Valkyrie's drummer. "We [were] a Small Faces copy band, pretty blatant about it," says Shirley. "We'd been to see them a number of times ... I was, if not their biggest fan, one of them." Naturally, the Valkyrie were thrilled when they were booked as support on a Small Faces gig. "We met again in a music shop on Shaftesbury Avenue," Shirley recalls of Marriott. "Our keyboard player, Dino Dines, flat-out said to him, 'Do you wanna make a single for us?' Steve was taken back by it and said, 'Yeah, alright,' gave us his number and said, 'Give us a call, stop round some time.'" When group members did indeed visit Marriott, they found that he hadn't changed his mind: "Steve was very friendly to young, unknown guys." With regard to '(Tell Me) Have You ever Seen Me', Shirley explains, "As we were doing it is when they were changing over to Immediate. I think one of the things Andrew did to appease them was listen to it and agreed to release it." Oldham denies that he was indulging Marriott and Lane's production ambitions in order to get the Small Faces' signatures on an Immediate recording contract. "They were great producers, and filled the void Mick and Keith left when they opted on not fulfilling my Holland, Holland and Dozier dreams," he says.

Not everyone was helping to facilitate the record, though. "When we came to do the sessions, Ronnie walked out," recalls Shirley. "He didn't think we were worthy. He was probably right. But Steve didn't care. We'd become his mates … Ronnie was more into cultivating a better class of people – famous friends. He was a good guy, though. The few times I met him, he was a nice man."

The lyric of '(Tell Me) Have You Ever Seen Me' is intriguingly oriented around reincarnation and/or pre-destiny and boasts interesting imagery like, "I see flowers breaking through the concrete." However, the fragmentary, sometimes unrhyming lines make it feel like the composers are groping for something to say. In any case, the song words are undermined by the tune. The writers got the idea for the melody after hearing a previous Small Faces recording played in reverse. It is as ungainly and stuttering as you'd expect a tune with such origins to sound, while its attempts to float into a surreal mood in the bridge are doomed to failure by the fact that it's always obliged to drop down to the clunky verses again. The guitar riff is lazily identical to one of its melody lines, which itself in its rhythmic, staccato quality sometimes resembles a football-terrace chant.

The record's B-side 'Madame Garcia' was another Marriott production. Some might assume it to be a Small Faces track as its occasional vocal yelps are clearly by Marriott, its organ work is highly McLaganesque and its structure very redolent of 'Grow Your Own' and 'Almost Grown'. Moreover, its publishing credit initially stated it to be a Marriott/Lane composition. Shirley, though, says, "Steve sang a bit on it and I think he played a little guitar too, but it was performed by the Apostolic Intervention and … written by my brother Angus and Dino Dines."

It's not really surprising that '(Tell Me) Have You ever Seen Me' failed to chart. Nor, Shirley says, was it too devastating for the credited artists. "We were all excited it was coming out, but we all knew that we were way down on the pecking order," he reflects. "There wasn't a lot of publicity on it and it only got a few plays on the airwaves. We did get gigs, though. It helped raise our profile a bit. But then soon after it had come out, and it was obvious it was a flop, the group's gigs started to thin out and before too long the group was broken up and I'd gotten another job with a band in Cambridge called the Wages of Sin."

Somewhat more was probably expected of 'My Way of Giving'. Farlowe's follow-up to his chart-topping 'Out of Time' was another Jagger/Richards song. However, 'Ride on Baby' was a slight creation by the Stones pair and climbed only as high as no.31. When one day Marriott and Lane played Farlowe's producer Mick Jagger 'My Way of Giving' the Stones man clearly felt he had a song to revive his charge's career.

'My Way of Giving' is far more of an adult love song than most pop creations of the day. It expresses the undying affection of the likes of 'Hey Girl' but in nuanced and poetic ways, the narrator vouchsafing doubts about romance even as he articulates a desperation for it. The first verse worries away at the issue for four tail-chasing lines, during which the multi-syllabic "nevertheless" is accommodated without awkwardness. There is also a yearning tenderness to the sentiments ("See confusion in my clouded eyes") of a type that would from here on be a motif in Small Faces songs, which in the Immediate era would veer far more toward big-heartedness than big-headedness, and to vulnerability rather than bluster. Musically, the song alternates stately verses with marching choruses and has a circular feeling without descending to a feeling of stasis.

Jerry Shirley happened to witness the Farlowe track's recording. "They needed a Harmony bass," he explains. "They couldn't find Ronnie's and they knew we had one, so we had to drive up to Olympic." What he found when he arrived at said recording studio was "a huge session." As well as the two composers and producer, he recalls the presence of Rolling Stones Keith Richards and Brian Jones, Oldham and "all these top session people." Not only were great artists and musicians present, but the man to whom Marriott and Lane were gifting a great song was one of the few in the country capable of standing toe-to-toe vocal-wise with the Small Faces frontman. Although the record's orchestration might be too ornate for some tastes, and Farlowe's singing overwrought, it's somewhat perplexing that the record did even worse than 'Ride on Baby', peaking in February at no.48.

Despite the disappointing chart performances, said discs provide an example of the artistic avenues Oldham and Calder were opening up to Marriott/Lane and their colleagues. As indicated by Oldham previously, Jagger and Richards had up to this point effectively been the house songwriter-producers of Immediate Records, but that year would see a rupture in their professional relationship with Oldham. Marriott and Lane, intentionally or not, were all set to replace them.

In February '67, Marriott became national news.

On the 24th of that month, the police stopped a cab carrying him and his current girlfriend Chrissie Shrimpton. That he made the front pages of the papers, though, may have been more to do with the fact that Shrimpton was the ex-girlfriend of Mick Jagger and sister of famous model Jean. This is something that can be gleaned from the headlines in question. "Chrissie: I Was Stripped in Drug Hunt" declared the *Daily Mirror*, while the *Daily Sketch* said, "Shrimp's Sister in Drug Probe." The hypodermic syringe and pills found on Shrimpton justified a raid on Marriott's Kensington flat. By what seems a small miracle, it turned up nothing illicit.

A couple of months later, Marriott fulminated of the incident to Chris Welch of *Melody Maker*, "They bust me just because I'm a name ... As far as I'm concerned there should be a distinction between hash and pot and hard drugs ... The only thing against hash and pot is that people can say they are a stepping stone to hard drugs, but that's only because the public are under the impression it's all the same thing. Why don't the newspapers wake up and give people the facts? ... If they invented whisky today, they would ban it. I know a lot of people who smoke, and they are all beautiful people. Old

Bill should leave it alone. What do they think they are going to do — stop it?" Many might agree with his analysis, but even those sympathetic to his cause may have blanched at the bare-faced cheek of a comment he gave to another media outlet: "I have never, never taken drugs in my life. My conscience is quite clear." There again, what had recently happened to his fellow pop artists makes his ultra-caution understandable.

It's difficult not to come to the conclusion that the reason the police mysteriously failed to find anything incriminating at the abode of such a prodigious drug consumer as Marriott is because of the raid that had occurred twelve days previously at Keith Richards' Redlands, Sussex home, the one that would infamously lead to he and fellow Rolling Stone Mick Jagger being jailed. It would soon become clear that there was a concerted London police campaign against pop-star drug use. It eventually took in not just Jagger and Richards but Brian Jones and the Beatles' John Lennon and George Harrison. Marriott would seem to have avoided becoming one of its casualties by realising which way the wind was blowing.

The Small Faces' next release was 'I Can't Make It' coupled with 'Just Passing', released in March 1967.

It featured the credit 'Produced by Steve Marriott and Plonk Lane for Immediate Productions'. The pair would be credited as the Small Faces' producers for the rest of the band's original lifespan. The publishing of both songs was listed as being by Immediate Music, while the record label stated the disc to be a Decca product. This confused situation was due to an outstanding claim by their previous recording home that the band still owed them material. According to Calder, Immediate Records considered this no loss: he told author Simon Spence that he and Oldham agreed with Arden's assessment of it as a "piece of shit."

Lyrically, 'I Can't Make It' is a descendant of 'All or Nothing', although this time the demand for unequivocal devotion contains a greater degree of humility. Musically, it's another expert meld of pop and soul, an uptempo affair with prominent drum flourishes and doo-doo-doo backing chants. Somehow, though, it's slightly sterile, reminiscent of the Beatles' similarly soul-oriented 'Got to Get You into My Life' in the way its surface gleam fails to disguise the fact that for all its tilts at passion it ultimately feels cold-blooded. It can at least be said to feature Marriott's slickest vocal to date, one which, incidentally, contains the first instance of his new signature, "Get yourself together."

'Just Passing' is a fleeting (1:15) acoustic ditty whose lyric about alienation might possess pathos were it not sung by a Lane stricken with a heavy cold and punctuated by the sound of him and Marriott cracking up. There again, possibly not, for its overall tone of melodrama has more than a touch of deliberate self-parody. Ultimately, it's simply an endearing wisp of a track. The track's composition is credited to Marriott, Lane and former housemate Mick O'Sullivan.

The record only made the lower reaches of the hit parade, peaking at no.26. Part of the reason for the relative failure was a ban by the BBC, who deemed the lyric "too suggestive." It was another illustration of the fact that Swinging England could be more myth than reality. Frank discussion of sexual intercourse was still taboo, especially pre-marital sexual intercourse, and especially in a medium with a young demographic like pop. Not only was the culture prudish, but at a time just before reliable contraceptive methods were available, keeping it a taboo subject was considered a way to help prevent what was then the sociological catastrophe of young, unmarried motherhood. Even so, it was an odd record for the corporation to take a stand on, being suggestive only if one was inclined to believe the title line was about the sexual act (in the actual lyric it's followed by the words "without you") and to furthermore believe that a line where the narrator implores the subject to open up her mind as well as her heart was one in which "mind" was a stand-in for "legs". "You've got to have a disgusting mind to think like that," Marriott griped to *Melody Maker*'s Chris Welch the following month. "'I Can't Make It', can mean anything." However, he then immediately gave ammunition to those who had detected in a previous single a why-won't-you-go-all-the-way? subtext: "If you want to be filthy, what about 'All or Nothing'?"

Marriott further lamented to Welch, "At that time we had no manager, and no one to hustle for us to get plugs. All the plugs were on [Radio] London and the BBC banned it, so not many knew it was out! It was chaos, chaos, chaos." On the same tack, Marriott would later tell Jim Green: "We were leaving Decca, so they just killed us on it." His bitterness was particularly deep because the track was one of the four Small Faces recordings that he told Green were designed from the get-go as singles.

It was a less than auspicious start to the new phase of the Small Faces' career, but at least it was a record that the band wanted released. The same could not be said of the next disc to bear their name. Don Arden naturally intended to exploit his ownership of unreleased recordings the Small Faces had made before they left his stable. He began with 'Patterns', released as a single on Decca in May 1967 c/w 'E Too D' from the first album. The Marriott/Lane written A-side is in 'My Mind's Eye''s vein of toytown psychedelia. It implicitly uses the motifs of the nascent flower-power movement – the invocation of bright and unusual designs that contrast with the utilitarian, grey shapes of everyday life – as a metaphor for a new type of consciousness. Instrumentation-wise, the track doesn't live up to such quasi-surrealism. Despite being draped in some dreamlike chanting, the music is perfunctory and basic, even if its opening, charging riff elicits some pleasure. As with 'My Mind's Eye', one suspects the strong influence of the spiritually minded Lane again, something underlined by his singing the lyric in tandem with Marriott. Any deep evaluation, though, is probably unfair and pointless as there is no way of telling how far along the group considered the recording to be. Leaving aside any aesthetic considerations, the band certainly weren't prepared to promote a record whose success would financially benefit a manager they had sloughed off in acrimonious circumstances. 'Patterns' is one of only two releases of the Small Faces' original lifetime – the other being 'I've Got Mine' – that did not chart.

Precisely one week later, the Small Faces finally properly inaugurated their Immediate recording career. In reality, it's probably far more appropriate that the first disc on which their billing shared a label with Immediate's distinctive jagged-lettered logo should be 'Here Come the Nice' for – in terms of spiritual approach and production technique – this track feels less like a recording than both a new dawn and statement of intent.

Marriott was known to publicly grumble that some people were openly sceptical about whether he and Lane genuinely produced their band's records. Such scepticism is understandable. Producing involves a certain amount of expertise and the Small Faces were very young (and looked younger) and – compared to many other British groups – somewhat inexperienced. Few other members of the pop elite were yet formally producing their releases, including the Beatles and (despite Jagger's production work for other artists) the Stones. However, Marriott and Lane's production creativity is not significantly disputed by those who worked with them.

"I think they were very interested in sonics," says Pete Townshend of the pair's ambitions. "Visiting them working at Olympic, they would appear to be very creative and always exchanging ideas." (Having said that, he appends a controversial qualifier: "Production is a non-existent role. It's been made up by engineers, I produced the entirety of *Quadrophenia*, which is probably the best-sounding Who album. It's really not hard.")

It should be said, though, that Marriott and Lane were assisted by what Banes terms "top-of-the-tree engineers." The principal one continued to be Glyn Johns, whose presence on the scene ensured in this respect a smooth transition from the Small Faces' Decca era. "Glyn was part and parcel of Immediate," explains Banes of the rollover from a period the band in all other respects might have wanted to dispense with. "He was working with Andrew all the time." Johns' pre-existing association with their new label, of course, was not the only reason the band were willing to have him at the console. "Glyn's a really good engineer, and he's really good at handling people," says George Chkiantz, a colleague. "He's great. I'm proud to have been trained by him." "Glyn is an original," says McLagan. "A lot of engineers stay in the control room and you'll play and they're trying to make a sound out of it. They don't hear what you're actually doing. Glyn would come in and put his head around the drums while Kenney's playing. Move his ears around and then he'd position mics so that he could hear [in the control booth] exactly what he'd just heard." "We were very fortunate to have known Glyn right from the start," says Jones. "What a great engineer he was. Way ahead of his time. Once you've got a great drum sound, it puts you into a different place."

Although Johns made many classic records, he was in some ways very un-rock 'n' roll. "He couldn't abide wasting time," recalls Townshend. "So if the band started to tell stories, or maybe rolled a joint, got the brandy bottle out, started to listen to other people's music, he would get restless." "I was his main assistant for a while," recalls Phill Brown. "He trained me, I suppose. He didn't mess about. He was anti-drugs. He was anti-wasting time. Even back then. I think he just got worse and worse as far as sharing his emotions and just getting pissed off easily. So he turned up there, he just wanted to make a record. He didn't want to be part of somebody's party ... But he was a worker. Glyn made some amazing records. He was probably the main guy in London really, because you had the Eddie Kramers and that, but his name came from Hendrix and a few other bits and pieces for Island whereas Glyn was right across the board. He was doing the Beatles, the Stones, the Move. Obviously, he was the flavour of the time, but he got good results. It's very hard for me to pick a duff album of his. And he came from that era of four-track/eight-track where you had to be a good engineer. It was about the sound in the room and the mics he used. It wasn't about the technology on the desk, because there was virtually no technology on the desk. Nowadays, it's more about the mix and sorting it out after you've recorded it. You had to get it right at source." Nor was Johns a square. In 1969 Neil Richmond worked as second engineer under Johns during what might be termed the Savile Row tranche of the Beatles' *Get Back*/*Let it Be* film/album sessions. In 2020, he recalled to *Uncut* magazine, "He arrived in his black E-Type Jaguar with a number plate: GJ1. He was one of the first cool freelance sound engineers. He had long hair. At EMI we weren't allowed to grow our hair long. We ... were working with Pink Floyd wearing jackets and ties!"

"He should have got co-producer's credit, actually," Lane later told Jonh Ingham of Johns' Small Faces work. "We should have realised that." Kenney Jones agrees that Johns' contributions were far too significant for the humble designation 'engineer'. Townshend notes, "He was their engineer before he realised that what he was doing was very, very close to production." The Who guitarist is surprised that Johns didn't insist on a co-production credit. "When we got to the *Who's Next* album [1971], he was very clear that he would only work with the Who if he co-produced." Johns himself exhibited no hard feelings. In 1982, he told Stuart Grundy and John Tobler for their BBC radio series *The Record Producers*, "The Small Faces were always looking for a new sound, or a new something – they were very energetic, and were always trying to get something new going, and were actually very fine producers of records. Ronnie Lane and Steve Marriott together were a force to be reckoned [with] ... I was involved in the production but they were just as much, if not more, than me."

At Immediate, Small Faces recording activity would be centred around Olympic Studios in Barnes, a semi-rustic area of south-west London. Phill Brown was at the time an Olympic recording assistant, aka tape operator, the bottom of a food chain that rose successively through recording engineer and producer. "It was very popular," he says of Olympic. "It was a new studio for a start. It was a non-union studio, so it was quite relaxed. It wasn't like working at Abbey Road or places that were very kind of corporate. It was very much a rock 'n' roll studio. It was basic. It was four-track when I started. It was eight-track when the Small Faces did *Ogdens'*. Homemade gear, but had a great-sounding live room. If you look at the clientele during that latter half of the Sixties, it was pretty much everybody at some point that worked there, including the Beatles, the Stones, the Steve Miller Band. Studio One was the main room. It held about 80 to 100 musicians." "Olympic Studios had a great echo room," reflects Jones. "It was dynamite sound if you put a little bit of delay on it or a bit of reverb. I very much used the ambient sounds, the room sounds. That's what makes the drumming really big. All we did was capture the actual sound of the drum kit rather than make the drum sound completely not like a drum."

Assisting Johns at sessions would be one of Olympic's resident tape ops, either Brown, Chkiantz, Keith Harwood or Andy Johns (brother of Glyn). Chkiantz, already a veteran of Rolling Stones and Jimi Hendrix Experience sessions, would assist on many Small Faces recording dates. "They suddenly sort of appeared with a bunch of tapes with a record half done," he recalls. Chkiantz found Marriott inspired and confident of his own talent. "He just [had] endless ideas." However, he had mixed feelings about both him and the group. He says of the Small Faces, "I liked them as a band" but also says, "I very much thought they were aping the Stones." Meanwhile, the very intensity of Marriott's creativity precluded much of a sense of fulfilment. "My memories mainly about the Faces were just the way Marriott pushed everything to beyond the reasonable limits. When we were trying to set up for the next session, he was still trying to put on some handclaps or do a mix. Trying to get him out of the studio was really difficult. I could really understand the impetus, but it was sad that you would go home from a Faces session, however good, sort of exhausted." Would Marriott not at least feel happy with his craft when playing back a finished master? "Only very briefly."

Chkiantz found Ronnie Lane "a much quieter person." He says, "He was a nice bloke. I chatted to him often. Bass players are in a funny position in a band. They're the worriers. I think he was downtrodden a bit by Steve. Steve was ebullient and pushy." Did he perceive Lane and Marriott as equally talented? "No. I have to be honest, I thought that most of it came from Steve." One person Chkiantz certainly doesn't think Marriott was able to tread on was Johns. "Glyn did not suffer from Steve pushing him too far, because when he'd done what he'd figured was enough, or he didn't think it was going to go any further, he just got up and left. People like me or Andy would wind up trying to dub on the extra handclaps or whatever."

Chkiantz doesn't recall spending much time talking with Jones or McLagan, but opines, "They were all nice guys." He noted that the Small Faces were unusually tight-knit. "As they came in the studio, they came in as a band. I got the impression that they spent time together." As with so many others around the Small Faces he had to, as it were, tell himself not to stare. "It was quite strange," he says of their symmetrically uniform height, or lack thereof. "That was an impression that kind of re-happened if you hadn't seen them for a while."

Asked whether Don Arden was still a source of grievance to the band, Chkiantz replies, "Yeah, absolutely. I think he'd held on to various tapes … Arden came up as a problem a lot."

'Here Come the Nice' is misspelt on many compilation tracklistings as 'Here Comes the Nice'. Music lovers have been less uncertain of its correct title than the fact that it's a fine and daring record. An anthemic melody is framed by acoustic guitar and soaring organ, and decorated with rousing call-and-response vocals. The lyric is delivered by a Marriott who alternates between delicate tones and a soul-man's bark. Similarly, the recording's aura of prettiness is peculiarly undermined by a climax which sees the instruments treated to make it sound like they've been dropped down a mineshaft, a cartoonish effect not too dissimilar to the elongated whistling and explosion noises traditionally soundtracking Wile E. Coyote's descent into a chasm after the Road Runner has tricked him yet again. The effect was achieved by the four band members simultaneously and heavily planting their backsides on the keys of an upright piano, the resultant discord then distorted further by tape manipulation.

The lyric ventures into even more audacious territory. The derivation of its phraseology is disputed. Tony Calder told Cliff Jones, "That came from a religious book Steve had found and the lyrics are about Jesus and speed!" Banes says it derived from a routine by cutting-edge comedian Lord Buckley called 'Here Comes Da Nazz' which the band heard on a record played to them by Oldham. Banes: "It became 'Here Comes the Nice'. Steve's vocabulary at the time was, 'Nice, man. Everything's nice, man.'" Shirley agrees: "The Nazz was a comedic record from a white guy that sounds black. There's a track on there called 'The Nazz', which is about Jesus. It's very funny."

As for the song's subject matter, according to McLagan when a Small Face shouted "Nice!" in public, it was a coded way of boasting about being stoned. Jones says, "Steve and Ronnie wrote it about the local pusher. He made you feel nice." Said pusher was none other than the man who had occupied the spare room of the band house in Pimlico. Shirley says, "The Nice was their nickname for the guy that used to get the speed for them: Mick the Nice. Mick O'Sullivan." In his autobiography, McLagan's viewpoint about O'Sullivan was fairly close to David Arden's designation of him as a "ponce": "He was permanently unemployed, and became little more than a ligger and a freeloader." Jones was a bit kinder in his own book, describing O'Sullivan as "a 'friend' of the band," and elaborating, "Every group has one, someone everyone knows, who helps out, hangs around, runs errands, is generally useful and makes things happen." Although Jones asserted that O'Sullivan played no instrument other than tuneless harmonica, he wound up getting two Small-Faces co-writing credits. His greatest contribution to the band, though, was providing the inspiration for one of their most iconic recordings.

The Small Faces had always been enthusiastic dope smokers, but they had now gravitated to methedrine, which they bracketed as "speed" along with another artificial-energy supplying stimulant, amphetamine sulphate. The song's sarcastic finale was meant to represent the famously dispiriting comedown from a speed high. Some might have a moral problem with them choosing to explore such territory when their audience was largely comprised of impressionable adolescents. That aside it was a real step forward, a move away from the received and stylised imagery in which they'd exclusively so far dealt. As Pete Silverton noted of 'Here Come the Nice' in a 1977 *Sounds* retrospective, "For the first time they'd tapped into their own cultural background rather than that of destitute blacks across the Atlantic."

It was on all levels a record whose release it's difficult to envisage Arden ever sanctioning. Essentially, Immediate were their enablers. Says Andrew Loog Oldham, "The deal with the Facettes, after their perceived torture with Don Arden, was to take them off the road, get them house, Glyn Johns, all the drugs they need, all the STD cleared up in Harley Street, and they would deliver us a breakthrough album with hits. They kept their word." "We came from making all these records that were highly commercial and our new-found relationship with Andrew Oldham gave us a new lease of life," says Jones. "When we were with Decca and Don Arden, we were touring so much that we hardly had any time in the studio. It was like, in and out. When we met Andrew, it was like, 'Take as much studio time as you like, do what you want' and we virtually lived in the studio. So for the first time in our lives we could experiment and really feel comfortable and explore what we really played like instead of doing all this chocolate-box stuff. Experiment with ballsier sounds."

Even ballsier words. The line "He's always there if I need some speed" is shockingly blunt for a Sixties pop single, even if the last word is disguised by dint of Marriott stretching it into a drum roll that serves to obscure its conclusion. Even so, it's quite obvious what he's saying because the word with which it rhymes is "need". That is, obvious to most listeners. Amazingly, considering the ban imposed on the innocuous 'I Can't Make It' and the later equally dubious censorship of 'Tin Soldier', there were no problems whatsoever with radio play of 'Here Come the Nice' nor any tabloid scandal surrounding it. For his part, Jones says, "It shows you how dumb the people were at the time. Half of them didn't listen to the lyrics. Unless you said blatantly 'Fuck off', they didn't get a clue." The mainstream broadcasters were not completely unworldly: eight months later, the Smoke had airplay trouble with their single 'My Friend Jack' because at least one BBC employee was hip enough to know that the line "My friend Jack eats sugar lumps" referred to the propensity of LSD lovers to dab 'acid' on cubes of sugar to aid ingestion. In a 1982 interview with Dave Thompson, Marriott suggested that their ingenue aura from the

asked us over for supper. Steve got Eddie, who was Andrew Oldham's driver, and Andrew's Roller, to take him over there. We had this very uncomfortable evening, with Rod wearing an old shirt that I'd bought him and playing sentimental songs on the record player."

'I Feel Much Better', 'Tin Soldier's' B-side, saw McLagan once again being allowed into the publishing parentheses with Marriott and Lane. Like 'I'm Only Dreaming', it's a singular but sometimes odd creation, with dubious properties like munchkin-like backing vocals and a pointless fade-out, fade-in (the latter another novelty of the era that soon became dated) sharing space with more pleasing and timeless aspects like mellifluous, hard-rock guitar and the brawniest rhythm section-work yet heard on Small Faces output (never has Lane's bass been so belligerent). Lane and Marriott, jointly handling vocals, trill surreal lines like "Times were so high they were low." The tableau is pleasantly lethargic, with the narrators exulting in writing rhymes, quaffing wine and taking their time.

The single was heralded by a January 1968 *NME* article with a headline reading "Small Faces Shatter Old Image". Although the feature may have involved a music journalist (Keith Altham) amenably assisting the group in image management, its message was also pretty much true. The difference between this record and 'Whatcha Gonna Do About It' was vast on every level. That debut had appeared just 2½ years previously. "It's amazing, innit?" says McLagan, although he does point out that lightning-speed development was then the norm in the pop universe. "Everybody – the Stones, the Beatles, all of us – everything was very fast." McLagan and Jones both say the group were not worried that they might lose their audience by releasing such image-shattering fare. "We were trying to make good music," McLagan shrugs. "The whole point of it was we would make the best records we could. We followed our hearts. We followed our ears. The Beatles and the Stones and the Beach Boys were all spending time in the studio. When we got to do that, it opens all the doors." Jones: "Never thought about it. All we wanted to do was lose our teenybopper image. Because we were great players. People like the Yardbirds and Zoot Money and all the bands that were around that were actually doing the blues and stuff like that, they knew we were great players, but we could never lose this image."

Of course, the fact that titans like the Beatles and the Stones had inspired enough loyalty to carry their audiences with them didn't mean that there wasn't a danger that other groups might move too fast for their own demographic. There is an implicit repudiation involved in recording something at a tangent to previous material. The spectre of what might be termed the Tremeloes Syndrome would soon be hanging over the music business: in 1970 the aforesaid British beat ensemble haemorrhaged a large section of their fanbase. Admittedly, this was perhaps less to do with the new direction of their music and more to do with the fact that they aggressively sold it by labelling the people who had bought their less complicated early records as "morons," but Marriott came pretty close to that kind of rhetoric himself when promoting 'Tin Soldier'. He told the *NME*'s Keith Altham, "We recorded rubbish like 'My Mind's Eye' because we knew it was commercial and it would sell. Now we can afford to do what we like." Certainly, upon its release on 2 December, 'Tin Soldier' did not enjoy the quicksilver chart progress of 'My Mind's Eye', even despite the fact that its first 50,000 copies came housed in a picture bag, then a rarity for singles in the UK.

Gered Mankowitz was the photographer responsible for the photo on the front of the sleeve, an artfully blurred colour band portrait. (The reverse featured a B&W stock picture of soldiers in a trench about to unleash a shell.) Mankowitz doesn't think he snapped the Don Arden Small Faces again after that early Jimmy Winston-era session, but being close to Andrew Oldham meant that from hereon he did much work for Immediate and hence multiple Small Faces sessions. He got to know their collective on-camera persona and found it different to the many other artists (including, most famously, the Rolling Stones and the Jimi Hendrix Experience) with whom he had worked. "I remember a lot of laughing, a lot of giggling," he says of Small Faces shoots. "I remember this thing of always performing for the camera, never just settling back and being moody musicians. That never seemed to be for them and if I tried to get them to do that, they'd dress up like spivs, they'd turn it into some sort of performance. There was a sort of spontaneity to them and to the way we did pictures whereas, with somebody like Hendrix, all you needed, all you wanted to do, was to put him in front of the camera and he did everything else. He just emoted and delivered. With the Small Faces, it always seemed as though that was hard so they had to perform and play around and I had to try and coordinate as much as I could ... There's some very funny pictures I did of them where they all just grabbed bits and pieces that were lying around the studio and become different characters. Steve had a flick knife and Mac has got what looks like some sort of club and Ronnie's holding a bottle and Kenney's holding a brick ... Ronnie's given himself a kiss curl. Mac's wearing what looks like a biker's hat and has pushed his hair back and he's doing his nails in a rather threatening manner ... Steve always wanted to make it into an event, dress up, use props. I think that came from Steve's actor thing ... Steve always performed. In fact, Steve's background as a young actor, in some ways, made him harder to photograph. Actors always struggle a little bit with their real personality. They always want to be something else. Always searching for a character to portray."

Mankowitz is doubtful that the picture that ended up on the sleeve of the 'Tin Soldier' single was intended specifically for that record. Despite it being "just another session," though, it involved some artiness unusual for pop imagery, although not unprecedented in Mankowitz's career so far. The month previous to the appearance of 'Tin Soldier' had seen the release of the Rolling Stones' *Between the Buttons* album. Its front cover featured a picture of the band on London's Primrose Hill that with its rather blurred, hazy ambience went against the grain of crisp and clear pop-LP sleeve photography. Of the 'Tin Soldier' shoot, the photographer says, "I'd used a version of my Vaseline filter that I sort of pioneered with *Between the Buttons*. That's a glass and black card, fixed in front of the lens, and then I smeared Vaseline on the glass. You could alter the distortion depending upon how you smeared the Vaseline, so I had several pieces of glass all with different shaped smears."

Mankowitz didn't choose the picture that was used. "Andrew was in control of all of that." Some might suggest that Oldham could have done with some guidance when it came to this particular decision. Despite that blurred effect on the *Between the Buttons* sleeve, and the fact that the billing was barely visible (at least on the UK version), one glance at it would have apprised anyone familiar with them that the artists were the Rolling Stones. The 'Tin Soldier' picture bag was the effect *in extremis*, so much so that, were the band's name not spelt out at the top of the design, it's doubtful that even fans would have been able to identify the group. "Andrew and Immediate were always trying to create some mystery," says Mankowitz. He says he personally had no problem with this. "We were trying to make a contribution to the image process and trying to make the image reflective somehow of the band at that moment or the music, but not necessarily conforming to a sort of accepted formula of how you present a band. I would have been thrilled about that."

The disc's slow sales start wasn't helped when the BBC insisted to DJs that the penultimate line of the record be cut because it seemed to suggest sex. (Marriott protested that he said he wanted to "sit" with the subject but that seems as unlikely as the BBC's accusation that he sang "sleep".) However, the single began to gain traction after some incendiary TV performances, not just on the BBC's tried-and-trusted *Top of the Pops* (happily, the ban that the programme had imposed on the group the previous year had been lifted, even though Johnnie Stewart was still *in situ*) but also ITV's recently inaugurated pop show *New Release* aka *Time for Blackburn*. "We needed to sell 'Tin Soldier' live – it's a very visual record," Marriott told Altham. "It's nice to be able to vent your feelings on something like 'Tin Soldier' – really let go. That *Top of the Pops* where we were all on stage together with Pat dancing behind us was the seller." There was also the boost of a promo film which offered the dynamic vista of a beautiful, bopping and strangely beatific Arnold and a guitar slinging, legs-splaying Marriott. It was the first colour Small Faces video, and the minority who had non-monochrome sets at the time could veritably wallow in the lavish sight of Arnold's bright pink mini-dress and Marriott's red crushed-velvet trousers and yellow ruffled shirt.

Even so, 'Tin Soldier' took two and a half months to edge into the top ten, and only managed a peak of no.9, a respectable position but not one quite befitting a titanic classic. It would have to wait many years for full validation, such as being selected in 2007 as his Castaway's Favourite by Paul Weller on *Desert Island Discs* and in 1997 being voted by the readers of *Mojo* magazine the tenth best single of all time (putting it ahead of anything by the Rolling Stones or the Who).

Rylance's memory of its chart ascent is intertwined with recollections of her own illness and Marriott's thoughtfulness. "I'd started to take the Pill, which didn't suit me at all," she explains. "I've got a very strange system and I got very ill. I was rushed to hospital. I was in the NHS, which was absolutely fine, nice lady opposite. Then Steve arrived with a flourish and wheeled me through to a private room in the hospital chair. 'Tin Soldier' was on *The Pops* when I was in hospital. When he was on *Top of the Pops*, he said, 'This is for you in your private room.'"

Just nudging into the domestic top ten with this masterpiece was one thing, but 'Tin Soldier' made a showing on the Billboard chart no higher than no.73.

That the USA remained one of the few markets the Small Faces were unable to crack was almost certainly because, even post-Arden and even after the success of 'Itchycoo Park', the country was never the subject of an attempt of any kind to break it. This secured them the unenviable achievement of being surely the only Sixties UK group of note to not manage to become part of the British Invasion that saw even lightweights like Herman's Hermits and the Dave Clark Five enchant American music fans.

"We didn't go there because Mac had a drug bust basically," says Jones. "In those days, it was very serious and you weren't allowed to go in at all." In November 1967, McLagan received a fine of £50 for possessing a controlled substance after being caught trying to fly out of Heathrow Airport with 85g of cannabis resin in his underpants. However, the keyboardist denies that this was the reason for the Small Faces only being successful in what the music industry terms the 'Rest of the World'. "That stopped us for about six months, that's all," he says. "It wasn't the reason we *never* went, because other artists managed to pay good lawyers and get through to the Americans and convince them that it would be silly to stop us going over there. Donovan told me one day, 'Well I've been busted – I go over there.' So I told Andrew and Tony, but nothing happened. We could have toured, and we should've." So what, in his view, was the real reason? "None of our managers wanted us to go over there because our managers also controlled our agency, our publishing, recording. You wouldn't allow such a scene today. You can't be an agent, a manager, a publisher, a record company all the same time. Arden held the reins, as did Andrew and Tony, so the last thing they wanted was for us to go to America because they could not be our agent and could not be our record company and could not be our publisher. They could only be our managers, so it had no interest [for] them."

Jones says, "I'm convinced if we went to America, we would have conquered America," adding, if not quite logically, "And we would have been maybe still together." McLagan was as frustrated as his colleague. "We thought, 'The Who are over there – we should be over there,'" he says. "[I'd] always wanted to get to America. I wanted to be where the music came from." He also shares Jones' belief that it could have ultimately been the group's salvation. "Things would have been different. If we'd had a bit of success in America, we'd have at least seen America and been seen and people would have started buying our records."

Banes shares the belief that the band's music would have been to American tastes. "Because they were unique," he says. "If the Small Faces had toured in 1967, that would have opened the way probably for them to have been at Woodstock." Yet Banes says that Immediate were "absolutely not" to blame for that vista never materialising, instead citing the fact mentioned previously that the band now rarely wanted to be in motion. "Having to take Steve and Ronnie to Bremen was an event," he says, naming the filming location of the West German TV show *Beat-Club*. "We signed with CBS, who opened the door to America – they broke 'Itchycoo Park' – but I don't think the band were too keen to go and tour America, and that's what they would have had to have done to break the album … I can't remember which one of them, but one of them didn't want to get anywhere near an aeroplane. Didn't like flying." In 1969, Marriott owned up to that phobia to Keith Altham in *Rave*. "Planes are about the only thing that really scare me today," he vouchsafed. "It's no use people saying that it's no more dangerous than a car or taxi. If you're driving one of those you have a chance – and you're driving … It just gives me the horrors. After a flight on a plane I'm shattered. Everywhere by boat for me." Yet his own wife points out that this is unlikely to be the explanation for the lack of an American venture. "They went to Australia, for God's sake," says Rylance. "He didn't like flying, but if the opportunity had arisen I'm quite sure they would have gone to America because that was the big prize."

For his part, although Marriott claimed he was responsible for the Small Faces not touring the States, he didn't offer his fear of flying as the reason. Instead, in 1971 he told Jon Tiven of *Phonograph Record*, "We never toured America because I had such paranoia about my guitar playing. I was the only guitarist, and to stick me up front didn't make it." "That's bollocks," McLagan says. "He may have said it, but it's bollocks. So many times Steve would play down his guitar playing. He was the best fucking guitar player the Small Faces ever had or wanted. He was brilliant." Possible supporting evidence for McLagan's feelings on the subject is the fact that, after he left the Small Faces, Marriott himself publicly disdained emphasis on technique, telling the *NME* in May 1969, "When people get really freaked out on technique and electronics they should go and listen to an early Muddy Waters album. That man plays the world's most useless guitar but with such feeling that it doesn't matter. Feel is what it is all about."

Meanwhile, Peter Frampton was astonished by an incident he recalled witnessing in 1968 when he was frontman of the Herd. He told *Uncut*'s David Cavanagh, "Ronnie Lane comes running in and says, [Hendrix manager] 'Chas Chandler wants us to open up for Jimi Hendrix on his headline tour in

America!' I said, 'Oh my God, that's fantastic!' Steve goes, 'Fuckin' no way. He should be opening for us. We ain't doing it' ... It was, like, a golden opportunity and he short-circuited it! Why?" Marriott's mother, Kay, thought she knew. She told Mark Paytress of *Mojo*, "He wouldn't go because he couldn't face failure. If they went there and weren't accepted, it would have been dreadful for him. He was a coward in that way, bless him." Rylance is "sure" that her husband was scared of failing in America. "Getting out of a small pond into that enormous one is very scary," she says. She states that for all the validation one might think would be obtained from record sales, or even screaming girls, Marriott did not have confidence in his own talents. "I think he overcompensated by shouting a lot." Bizarrely, McLagan seems not to have been told of the Hendrix overture, him complaining in his autobiography that the band never had an American tour offer "worth considering." Of the latter, he told Pidgeon that the band ultimately rejected "maybe three" US tour offers, because they weren't prepared to lower "our standards of comfort" by acquiescing to long bus tours.

Meanwhile, Andrew Loog Oldham claimed that the lack of US touring was down to their "imagined ill-treatment at the hands of Don Arden and Decca." He later wrote, "...the Small Faces felt they'd paid their dues under Don's strict work ethic and refused to tour America. I disagreed and our relationship suffered."

Whatever the reason, the Small Faces' failure to ever play the States effectively closed off to them the biggest music market in the world and created a situation that persists to this day whereby even the popular-music cognoscenti of that country are very sketchily informed about one of history's all-time great bands.

In January 1968, the very month that 'Itchycoo Park' was making its debut in the Billboard Top 40, the Small Faces could be found in Australasia, not only a longer aeroplane journey away than the States but a relative commercial backwater.

Banes, though, points out that the Big Show Tour of Australia and New Zealand, which began on 20 January, made some commercial sense. "We were selling bucketloads of records down there. Every record I think we put out in New Zealand went to number one." In Australia, 'Itchycoo Park' had made no.2 and 'Tin Solider' no.3. However, he found the band as reluctant as ever to travel. "To get them to go on tour in Australia was on the condition that Tony and Andrew went with them."

Also making the trip were the Who. "We had joint billing situation," says Jones of a band with whom the Small Faces were then commercial equals. "One night we'd top the bill, the next night they would. That was the only way round it." There was a public impression of rivalry between the two groups predicated on them having both until recently been mod bands and Marriott and Townshend having both deployed feedback as part of their stagecraft.

"The press would say we hated each other's guts," observes Jones. "That was totally wrong. We actually got along like a house on fire ... It was like one band except that they were from Shepherd's Bush and we were from the East End."

Rylance didn't join the Australasian jaunt. "I was at home looking after the animals," she says. She laughingly adds, "They called me the night after they got there saying, 'Don't worry about anything you read in the papers.' They got arrested when they got off the flight." This alarming turn of events indicates not so much that villainy was afoot but that a culture clash was erupting. In the Sixties, Australia was a very conservative country and highly suspicious of the new age represented by bands like the Small Faces and the Animals. The latter had the previous year had a terrible time Down Under, but they at least hadn't had a drug bust hanging over them to bolster the media's insinuations of degeneracy and justify their aggressive behaviour. "We did anticipate the trouble," says Pete Townshend. "We went knowing that it was going to be difficult. When we arrived after a 32-hour flight, we were immediately attacked by the press. 'Go home, you scruffy little Herberts. We don't want you here.' A lot of that was aimed at the Who to begin with because of our guitar smashing." However, as a convicted criminal McLagan was also a natural target. "We got off the plane after 36 hours in the air and TV cameras, said 'Welcome to Australia. You're a drug addict, aren't you?'" he recalls. "That was our welcome to Australia and we all said, 'Oh, fuck off.' Then everywhere we went, the press hounded us. It was fucking awful."

This time, the Small Faces couldn't even take solace in their music. Only recently one of the most exciting live acts around, they were now embarrassingly ring-rusty – something that playing on the same stage as the well-oiled Who rapidly brought home to them. Oldham says of the 'road' that the band had lately spurned with Immediate's permission, "When they got back on it, they were unreliable. Home and being supported was just too comfy." "We weren't the band we had been and the Who were straight off an American tour," reflects McLagan. "They hadn't stopped working. We were right out of the studio, pretty much. It wasn't us at our best. They *were* at their best and they were great ... Steve was really jealous." So much so that Marriott couldn't conceal his frustration. Ironically, it manifested itself in behaviour that itself came over as an imitation of Pete Townshend's stage trademark and therefore provided another indication of inferiority: "Steve started smashing his guitars." "Stevie was pretty wild," says Townshend. "Stevie was pretty out of control drinking a lot ... Stevie was copying Keith Moon at the time."

McLagan had his own musical frustrations, these ones relating to his desperate attempts to provide an approximation of the phasing in 'Itchycoo Park', a song the Small Faces had unusually deigned to include in their setlist. "I taped a jet flying over the hotel in Sydney, so every time we'd get to that bit, there was a microphone on top of the organ and this little cassette machine with a tape [marked] 'Jet'. I used to press 'play'. You know: a big click, a big clunk and this sound would come out: *shee-ee-ee*. Didn't sound anything like [it]. Fucking pathetic."

When they flew from Melbourne to catch a flight to Auckland, the band found that the contempt of the press was shared by flight crew. Ex-Manfred Mann frontman Paul Jones was also on the bill. Recalls Townshend, "Paul Jones – very, very well brought-up, very well-spoken fellow – got up and said to [an] air hostess, 'Um, madam, why is it that everybody on the plane has been served drinks but we have been excluded?' And she went red, burst into tears and ran and got the pilot who came out and said, 'Which one of you fuckers has been having a go at Dorothy? I'll fucking kill ya!' And Paul Jones said, 'Well, actually, it was me. I was just asking why we haven't been offered a beer or something.' He said, 'Right, that's it. We're fucking calling the police.' It was a cartoon." McLagan corrects Townshend's memory on one point: "There was no beer served on planes back then. The Australian band who were backing Paul Jones on the tour had a bottle of beer and they were passing it around and the stewardess saw it and said, 'Right.' She didn't like the look of us anyway."

Townshend: "We landed and the police were there." McLagan: "When we got to Sydney we were told to wait, and they sent police on the plane and basically arrested us. They took us to the first-class lounge where the waitress immediately came over and said, 'Would you like a drink?' We said, 'Yeah!' We got drunk. We were escorted to the plane to go to New Zealand, where eight policemen waited for us because the Australian police had warned them that we were a bunch of drunken bastards. All based on a bottle of beer we never were drinking from. They took us to the gig and followed us back to the hotel." "From then on, the headlines were all against us," says Townshend. "We found it really, really hard."

"Stevie threw a fucking TV set out the window in New Zealand and it landed on top of a police car that was stationed outside for our protection," says Townshend. "The press were just printing absolute lies about us, so it was very strange. I think at the end of the day, it was frustration. The fact that we were being treated so badly."

Prompted by press sensationalism, the inevitable happened and politicians engaged in posturing. The premier of New South Wales let it be known that he had instructed the police to keep an eye on performers and audiences at pop shows. Meanwhile, John Gorton, the Prime Minister of Australia no less, said of the Small Faces, "We never wanted you to come to Australia. You have behaved atrociously while you've been here, and we hope you never come back." With Marriott having engaged with Keith Moon in a hotel wrecking spree and Immediate anxious to avoid charges being pressed, it transpired that the Small Faces and/or their label ended up losing £10,000 on the tour.

Townshend recalls the Australasian public's response to be diametrically opposed to that of their authorities and functionaries: "The audiences loved us. The shows were great." Moreover, even the authorities were sometimes friendly. The fact that the day after the Auckland gig Marriott was due to turn 21 hadn't escaped the attention of some who might be expected to be oblivious. Townshend: "We get a knock on the door, and I'm terrified because they say, 'It's the police.' The door opens and there are two young policemen there with a crate of beer. And they said, 'Happy birthday, Stevie. We love you, even though those Aussie bastards don't' and went away."

That nice gesture alone, though, couldn't compensate for an overwhelmingly distressing experience. McLagan: "There's actually a book about it come out in Australia. It was all about nothing, but the Australian press really shit on us. It was 'orrible."

The long journey home involved an unexpected stopover wherein the Small Faces planted their feet on the American soil that would otherwise remain out of bounds to them during their original lifetime. "On the way back, we landed in Honolulu and then we had to go to San Francisco and then something went wrong with the plane," says Jones. "We circled for ages … We couldn't take off … because of bad weather … So they took us all to stay in a Holiday Inn outside the airport." There was a worry that McLagan could be arrested for being an illegal alien, but Jones notes, "We never went through passport control, nothing. I could have walked straight out into America then." Instead, Jones contented himself with turning on his colour TV set, not a fixture in the sort of hotels the band were used to staying in. Finding himself watching a news programme, the drummer was immediately greeted with a somewhat disconcerting sight from Vietnam. "That famous shot came straight on, the guy getting his brains blown out. That was my first impression of America."

The tin hat was put on a miserable experience when, on the band's return home, Marriott, Lane and McLagan realised they had picked up an Antipodean dose of the crabs. They inadvertently gave it to Jones – as abstentious with extra-relationship sex as he was with drugs – when he shared towels with them in the recording studio. "Well, I certainly didn't catch them," says Rylance. Nor did she at the time discern the fact that, however much he adored her, Marriott didn't exactly take the concept of fidelity seriously. "I didn't know about it at the time, but he definitely did have all sorts of relationships on the road."

"Ronnie Lane and I flew back from Australia together on our own," says Townshend. "We spent a day in Hawaii and then flew back to LA and then to New York, and then home that way. I remember on that trip back Ronnie and I talked a lot about forming a band together. Because we were both unhappy with being in these bands that had such sort of unmusical images. It wasn't about the music. It was about in the Who's case ideas and aggression and the Small Faces this light-hearted pop thing."

Although that mutual dream never came to pass, the confidence-sharing had the upshot of the two becoming firm friends. "The people that have been important to me over the years as close friends have been people that don't take any bollocks from me," says Townshend. "I always felt that we were equals ... My friendship with Ronnie was a joy to me, because he was always teasing me and wouldn't take any bullshit from me and kept me level ... We argued very rarely ... We would just go out and have dinner together or go to art galleries or go to events and stuff. We just spent time together. His girlfriend Susie was a good friend of my girlfriend at the time, Karen, who I eventually married. We were a couple of couples."

Safely back in blissfully sleepy England, the band knuckled down to the only thing that gave them unequivocal pleasure: writing and recording. The result would transpire to be an album that was their masterpiece.

March 1968 saw the release of the first American Small Faces album, *There Are but Four Small Faces*. With state-of-the-art hi-fi equipment being far more widespread in affluent America than the relatively poor UK, it was released in stereo only, although there was a promotional DJ version with a mono mix.

The pastoral colour cover photograph of the group was the 'grown-up' version of the small-boys shot used for the 'Itchycoo Park' advertisement (seen on the LP's back cover, still in monochrome). Also taken on Hampstead Heath, it features the band in psychedelic finery: Marriott wears a homburg while Jones is swathed in something approaching a kaftan. Marriott is holding the Itchycoo Park street sign.

The fact that the album title was situated in the uppermost area of the front cover was deliberate: American retail outlets were oriented around displays whereby people flicked through album sleeves in racks and would pull out something that attracted their interest. Similar attention to the specific requirements of the market attended the track selection. Unlike Britons, Americans were not apt to feel that they were being denied value for money if previously released singles were present on an LP. In fact, they were grateful to have the hits they already knew and liked. Accordingly, a sticker was slapped on some copies which pointed out that 'Itchycoo Park' was included.[3] Also included were 'Here Come the Nice' and 'Tin Soldier' and B-sides 'I'm Only Dreaming' and 'I Feel Much Better'. 'Talk to You', of course, fulfilled the function of being both a B-side and an album track. There were six other tracks from that eponymous Immediate album present among the dozen selections. 'Green Circles' was represented in a slower version that may have been a mastering error but which some people prefer for its dreamy ambience.

---

[3] The market consciousness even seems to extend to the fact that McLagan's 'Up the Wooden Hills to Bedfordshire' loses the last two words of its title. Presumably it was feared that Americans wouldn't understand the pun involved in the name of the English county and the place one lays one's head at night.

McLagan wasn't impressed by the hodgepodge release. While he accepts that "this was a way of introducing us to America," he laments that the band had no say in the tracklisting. "I remember seeing it and going, 'What the fuck is that?' That's the way things worked then." As well as the traducing of artistic vision involved in mixing and matching disparate recordings, another way things then worked was not-quite-authorised stereo mixes. As ever with recordings originally laid down in mono, the ones here dilute the music a little, occupying the status of perfunctory postscripts put together by studio staff once the group had personally and painstakingly supervised the mono mixes they considered definitive. Setting aside such considerations, there's little disputing that *There Are but Four Small Faces* is a fine collection of music and a good introduction to the band.

Unfortunately the introduction was not made to many people. Although Immediate took out a front-cover spot for it in *Billboard*, *There Are but Four Small Faces* peaked at #178 on that publication's album chart.

It wasn't only billing about which the Small Faces had rowed with the Hollies. The Mancunian quintet who had been chart regulars since 1963 with a brand of pop decorated with intricate if slightly sterile harmonies had once had a conversation with their London rivals that took an odd turn – and resulted in a timeless song.

"I was having an argument with one of the Hollies, and I was saying to him, 'You don't sing in your own natural voice,'" Marriott later told Derek Boltwood of *Record Mirror*. "And he was saying the same thing to me. The thing is … it's not the voice you use for talking … It seems to be a sort of tradition that pop singers should sound American." In recent years, Britain had clawed back some of the national pride that had been severely dented by economic woes and the precipitous decline of its empire via its storming of American shores with pop music. However, the British Invasion involved selling back to the States a form of music that was perceived as rightfully America's, right down to accents. The only British singers who rendered rock and pop in cockney or Geordie or Scouse or any other accent indigenous to their isles were doing so for comedic effect, for it was widely considered laughable that post-Elvis popular music could be delivered in anything but a generic American drawl. British working-class accents just didn't sound right.

Marriott determined after that conversation to change things. "I've been intending to make a record singing in a cockney accent for a long time," he told Boltwood. His chat with the music journalist occurred in 1968 when he was promoting 'Lazy Sunday', the record that fulfilled his ambition. By then, others had beaten him to the punch, the Kinks having been making a virtue of their Englishness since their early 1966 single 'Dedicated Follower of Fashion' and the Beatles having been using the likes of the long "a" in their output since the previous year ("And though the holes were rah-ther small…"). Even Herman's Hermits had crossed this Rubicon with the likes of 'Mrs. Brown,

You've Got a Lovely Daughter' and 'I'm Henery the Eighth, I Am', even if both contained a tinge of that old British self-mockery/self-loathing. (Having said that, on 'I Feel Much Better', Lane and Marriott had pronounced "pass" and "glass" with a long "a".) Moreover, McLagan remembered the cockney approach on 'Lazy Sunday' as partly occurring by accident. He told Ken Sharp in 1996, "He was singing it straight, and he went out for a pee or something and we were just messing about and sending it up, and just taking the piss out of it. And he came back in and said, 'Okay, let's go,' and it just kind of evolved like that."

However, while they may not have been first, the Small Faces may well have been the best, for 'Lazy Sunday' is a sublime recording. Pete Townshend describes it as a song "I was very, very inspired by." He says, "I still think it's a real masterpiece. It sort of seems silly talking about a pop song in those terms, but it felt really, really important to me. Not just because it talked about getting stoned, but because in a sense it was an expression of freedom and of individuality and of recklessness. Adventure."

The subject of the song had a basis in real life. Says Jones, "It was a real piss-take of some bad-vibe neighbour." McLagan: "It's a true story of Steve's home life at the time. That was happening. People banging on his walls." The neighbours were ones at the Marriotts' Chiswick abode. "He went to the bog," Lane told Pidgeon in *Classic Albums*. "And he sat there and wrote, 'Wouldn't it be nice to get on with me neighbours, but they make it very clear they've got no room for ravers.'" "He had a toilet in the attic," says Shirley of Marriott. "It was a three-storey townhouse, modern-built. Downstairs would be the kitchen, then there'd be a living room and then above that the bedroom and then another bedroom and then on top of that there was this khazi that had a skylight in it. That's what he meant when he said, 'Sit on the khazi while I suss out the moon' – he could see a full moon through the skylight."

Although the way his colleagues and friends tell it, Marriott was responding in his inimitable impish way to unspeakably un-cool mojo-messers, in reality it was the family unlucky enough to reside next door to Marriott that was the party with a legitimate grievance, as Marriott's partner now readily admits. "It was about our neighbours in Eyot Green, the poor old Hasselblads," says Jenny Rylance. "We used to say hello at first but we were the nightmare neighbours, basically." By now, the cohabiting couple's menagerie had been augmented by another dog, Lucy. "When he was taking me back to the East End to show me around, we went past this pet shop [and] we see this tiny Alsatian puppy, really scruffy and obviously dying in the window, blood on her," Rylance recalls. "We got her home and she had all sorts of lethal dog illnesses, so we had to keep all our dogs in and they had to shit on the balcony." Although they would clean it up every day, Rylance admits that the situation must have been "pretty grim" for the Hasselblads. "But I think the main thing was that Steve got these giant Wharfedale speakers from Olympic (they were doing a clear-out). The walls used to vibrate. I felt guilty about them in retrospect." Marriott had form on such behaviour. In April 1967, the music press reported that he was obliged to move from his Baker Street flat because the volume at which he played his 'sounds' even upset the fellow recording artist who was his neighbour there, Cilla Black. Moreover, according to Jones one response by Marriott to the Chiswick neighbours' complaints was an irresponsible and potentially dangerous act: he and Mick O'Sullivan spiked their water tank with LSD.

However, those not au fait with the real-life situation behind would have perceived 'Lazy Sunday' as a song that powerfully but comedically portrayed intolerant older folk trying to prevent with-it kids having fun. As such, the composition brilliantly tapped into the zeitgeist of the Sixties, an era in which the gap between the values and mindsets of the young and the old was never greater.

The initial atmosphere is music-hall, the mid-tempo proceedings started with jolly keyboards and syncopated percussion. Yet thanks to Marriott's strummed acoustic guitar work and McLagan's mellifluous organ the aura is transcendent rather than rinky-dink. Marriott then treats the world to a grown-up version of the Artful Dodger tones he once employed on the likes of 'Consider Yourself' as he regales us with his tale of neighbours who just don't understand ravers. London colloquialisms – "khazi," "gor blimey," "suss out" – litter the first two verses and chorus.

Sound effects like a flushing toilet and comedic quoting of the Rolling Stones' '(I Can't Get No) 'Satisfaction' and 'Colonel Bogey March' pepper the proceedings. (The latter inclusion was mildly daring considering it was by now far more famous for its amended version, 'Hitler Has Only Got One Ball'.) Phill Brown notes that this experimental approach applied to the whole of the LP of which 'Lazy Sunday' would be part. "On that album if some mad idea came up: 'Let's try it out.' It was very relaxed as a way to work ... It was the most fun, silly track on it if you like, but it was great fun to do, running cables down to the toilets and all these sound effects."

The song is also dotted with autobiographical detail that's not limited to Marriott–Hasselblad clashes. The reference to lumbago stemmed from the constant gripes of Marge, who was – according to who was recollecting – either one of the cleaners at the Westmoreland Terrace house or an old lady living next door to it, while the "Roo-tee-too-tee-too" refrain stemmed from the band's Australian trip and a vocal habit of Who roadie Bob Pridden that the Small Faces found amusing.

The raucous first act gives way to a second part which, ironically, evokes the serenity that Marriott routinely denied the people whom the song lambasts, the lyric invoking the quietude of the Sabbath in an age when the streets of Britain were deserted on Sundays because large shops weren't permitted to open. After a lull filled only with soothing organ, Marriott either feels it would be inappropriate to go back to his exaggerated Lahndhan tones or else loses his nerve and he reverts to pseudo-American for the final verse. Another lovely lull is filled with seagull calls and washing waves before one final chorus leads into a fade-out sweetly overlaid with birdsong and church bells.

"It was this fun aside," says Phill Brown of 'Lazy Sunday'. "In context of the whole album, it made sense. I didn't think it would get released as a single." Neither, supposedly, did the Small Faces. "That was a bit of fun we had in the studio," echoes Jones, adding, "We left a load of these songs. Someone played them to Andrew Oldham while we were on tour in Germany. We were over there for about a month and we pick up *Melody Maker* or something only to find that we've got a hit record. He put it out without telling us. We all went berserk. What it done was put us back to where we were in the first place. We were concerned that it would be back to the days of the Sha-La-La-La-Lee sort of band." "It was really annoying to have to go and promote it," McLagan says. "It was okay on an album. None of us wanted that out as a single."

"We found out about it in Italy," Marriott told Pidgeon. "I rang him up and went mad. I said, 'No, don't do that. It's supposed to be just a little one-off thing.'" Although Marriott's memory differs from Jones in terms of both the country in which the band were located and the drummer positing the release as a fait accompli, Rylance's recollection tallies when it comes to her partner's reaction. "He was furious, absolutely furious," she says. "It was a wound that didn't really heal. And for Ronnie as well. I assume for the other two. From Steve's point of view it had set them back. He didn't want to be perceived in that light anymore. They were growing up. They wanted to do proper music." "In countries where they've never heard of you and you get one record out … they thought that's what we did," Marriott lamented to Pidgeon.

Yet others paint a much more nuanced picture. "It might have been done against their best wishes, but not behind their back," Shirley insists. Banes says, "In those days, before we took a record anywhere, we did an acetate and we'd go and play the acetate to the programme directors. The chart for us was Alan Freeman on a Sunday afternoon." Alan 'Fluff' Freeman presented *Pick of the Pops* on Radio One, a show that broadcast the BBC's rundown of their aggregation of the era's competing charts as well as new releases. "Fluff was a friend of Immediate," says Banes. Of the show's producer, Denys Jones, Banes says, "He used to give advice to us. The version of 'Lazy Sunday' I played him first did not have 'Satisfaction', it didn't have the bells and it didn't have the people whistling and everything else on it. It was a naked record. I remember [he] said, 'It could do with something else' and Andrew added on top 'Satisfaction', the bells because it was Barnes Common, bits and pieces that suddenly made it come alive." But did the band know about these additions? "Oh yeah. At the end of the day in the studio it was Ronnie and Steve … And I think you'll find that the bits and pieces added on was perhaps Steve's idea." Did Immediate release the record without the Small Faces' say-so? "No," Banes insists. "That wasn't Andrew's mentality. He was always consulting Steve." Moreover, Marriott was not consistent in his protestations. Although when talking to Jim Green in 1981 he was still peddling the line, "We didn't want to release 'Lazy Sunday' as a single," one wonders how that can be reconciled with the comment he made in the very same feature, "There were only four singles that we knew would be when we cut them: 'All or Nothing', 'I Can't Make It', and later 'Tin Soldier' and 'Lazy Sunday'." Moreover, back in May '68, Marriott told Keith Altham, "None of us wanted to release this record at first ... It was really the enthusiasm of people like Andrew and Tony, Michael d'Abo and yourself which won us round ..."

Whatever the truth, 'Lazy Sunday' was released as a single on 5 April 1968. Although this time there was no picture bag, the record did have the benefit of the first proper Small Faces video as that term is now widely understood: i.e., a promotional film for a music release that involves the acting out of fictional scenes. The scenes in this one included Marriott being throttled by an irate housewife and Marriott – toilet roll in hand – going into an outdoor lavatory (the latter in actual fact the one in Jones' childhood home). One scene involving Marriott dancing was shot in Chiswick, with the supposedly troublesome neighbours' house visible in the background. "He put those very large speakers in the middle of the green outside," says Rylance. Provocation? "I don't think he ever meant to provoke them. But they must have been hugely relieved when we moved out." The colour film even had sections involving revolving, multiple band-member faces, something that must have rung a bell for those who saw Queen's celebrated 'Bohemian Rhapsody' video seven years later.

In terms of other promotion, with the *NME* front-page ad he took out on 27 April, Oldham was up to his usual inflammatory if lateral tricks. That this date is several weeks after the record's release is explained by the fact that the interim had seen the famous Grosvenor Square London riot in which a demonstration against the Vietnam war erupted into violence. The fact that the date of the riot – 17 March – was a Sunday clearly caused a lightbulb to flicker into life above Oldham's head, hence the picture of mounted police in a face-off with protesters beneath the name of the record and the band. (Clearly, Oldham realised that this time his concept was too allusive-cum-fatuous for the ad to be run without mentioning what the product was.)

While it seems indisputable that at least some of the Small Faces for at least a certain period of time didn't want 'Lazy Sunday' to be commercially released beyond the confines of an LP, Oldham's conviction that it was a stone-cold smash in the making was proven correct. McLagan thought it would "never sell a copy," but in climbing to no.2 it became the band's most successful single in their home country since 'All or Nothing'. (It was kept off the top spot by Louis Armstrong's 'What a Wonderful World'/'Cabaret'.) However, its success ultimately transcended its chart placing. It gradually ascended to a status in the band's legend that Marriott described as "our theme song." It and 'Itchycoo Park' are the two Small Faces tracks most likely to be heard today on gold/heritage radio stations.

Nothing soothes disaffection so much as success, at least with some people. In 1982, Marriott was still seething to Dave Thompson, "If we'd done the song straight, like it was written, it would never have been a hit. But because it was this funny, jokey novelty thing, we were stuck with it." Had he lived long enough, he might have reached the position of equanimity that later descended on Jones and McLagan on the subject. Jones: "It wasn't what we wanted to put out [but] I'm kind of pleased that they did." McLagan: "It was the right move, though, wasn't it? … Doesn't piss me off anymore."

Part of Marriott's issue with the success of 'Lazy Sunday' goes to a contradiction at the heart of his character. He yearned to be taken seriously, but he was a natural comedian, and persistently played up his all-about/Artful Dodger/wideboy image, exaggerating his accent to exude studied uncouthness. "Steve was vaudeville," says McLagan. "He had all that going on in him and that's a part of him. He was a serious blues player, but he was also a very funny bloke and a very amusing piss-taking bastard." To some extent, there was in Britain in 1968 a certain strain of insurrection involved in proudly, vocally asserting proletarian origins: working-class tones were heard much less frequently in the media than they are today, whether in newscasts, filmed drama or popular song. However, that act could so easily tip over into the schtick of what is now termed the professional cockney, which often goes hand-in-hand with a certain court-jester quality, which itself implies servility. It can also make someone look intellectually insubstantial. "Dusty Springfield was such a soulful singer but when she was interviewed, she'd do all these Goon impersonations and then wonder why people wouldn't take her seriously," McLagan pointedly reflects.

The B-side of 'Lazy Sunday' was a track called 'Rollin' Over'. Its enigmatic subtitle, 'Part II of Happiness Stan', was a clue to the fact that the Small Faces were preparing something rather special for their next long player. "We were the first band to do a concept album," says Kenney Jones.

The category of first narrative album in post-Elvis popular music is as crowded a field as "first rock 'n' roll record" or "best Prime Minister Britain never had." Leaving aside the caveat that the story contained on the Small Faces' May 1968 LP *Ogdens' Nut Gone Flake* is restricted to only half its contents, Jones is on firm ground when he points out of the Beatles' *Sgt. Pepper's Lonely Hearts Club Band* (1967), "Sgt Pepper's wasn't a concept album. Ours was actually telling the story and going into another dimension."

He would also be correct if he invoked the Pretty Things' *SF Sorrow* (December 1968) or the Who's *Tommy* (1969), which are both story suites but ones released subsequent to *Ogdens'*. Fewer are cognizant of the claims to the first concept album title of Ricky Nelson's *On the Flip Side* (1966) or Nirvana's *The Adventures of Simon Sociopath* (1967). Nevertheless, the fact that the Small Faces were heading into novel territory isn't even predicated on the fact that they probably weren't aware of the Nelson and Nirvana works, both still little-known to this day. Moreover, the Small Faces project possessed a sense of humour and a *joie de vivre* that would be absent from pretty much every other concept album ever recorded.

Except for one or possibly two tracks laid down at Trident in central London ('The Journey' and/or 'Rene'), the album was recorded at Olympic. McLagan later recalled that the process took them "the better part of a year." Marriott had a similar recollection, telling Green, "We recorded backing tracks over and over in different studios to see which was the best, and rewrote words ... The editing alone took three months." Jones insists that this wasn't a solid block of work, claiming that – aside from an extended run in February '68 – it was a matter of slotting in odd days not filled with live work and promotional activity, and that one straight "hit" would have seen the album completed in three weeks. Part of the discrepancy is probably due to the fact that Marriott and Lane, being the credited producers, would have spent far more time in the studio than the other band members. (Glyn Johns got a thank-you on the label for his work on "knobs.") However, Phill Brown – who says he was tape op from start to finish – also recalls a fairly short recording period. "It was done over a week or two, because they had the songs," he says. "You'd get at least two, if not three, tracks a day down. There was no messing around. Sounds were got up quick, technology was basic. So the basic tracks would have gone down pretty quick and then the overdubs. Stanley Unwin coming in, that was probably a three-hour session ... The mixing took a while with the phasing and stuff like that, and there was an orchestral session at some point, but I don't remember it being dragged out." As this was the first time Brown had worked with the group, and as he worked on no other Small Faces album and rarely worked afterwards with individual Small Faces members, he's unlikely to be confusing these sessions with others. Yet as the band members are unlikely to be mistaken, it seems that McLagan and Marriott are including in their description of making the album a preamble to which Brown was not party.

Asked if, when they were making it, they felt their new album was going to be something extra-special, McLagan says, "Oh shit, yeah. Absolutely. We knew we were at the top of our game." For this masterpiece-in-the-making, the band were able to avail themselves of cutting-edge technology of which Olympic had only very recently taken receipt. "*Ogdens'* was the first album that we did on the eight-track machine," says Brown. "Eight-track rather than four-track made everyone's lives a lot easier." The benefits are quite easy to outline. McLagan: "We'd been on four-track at IBC and Decca Studios, so you had the band on one track, lead vocals on another, backing vocals on another, and if there's any solo instruments then that'll be on the other track. Whereas with eight-track, every instrument's got its own track." Even eight-tracking recording would seem unspeakably primitive just a few years later, but not having to resort to 'bounce-downs' – the process by which space was made on a recording for more instruments by squashing the four tracks of the first tape generation onto two tracks on the next tape generation, leaving two tracks free for further overdubs – meant a merciful absence of sound-quality degradation.

High ambitions and expensive equipment in no way prohibited people enjoying themselves, however. "By the nature of the album, the whole vibe of it, it was fun to make," says Brown. "They always seemed to be out for a good time. That was part of their make-up …. They were a very funny bunch. These pint-sized little Herberts from London all smartly dressed, but they had this brilliant sense of humour. They [were] always just messing about. You'd be out there with Marriott perhaps doing a lead vocal and everyone else getting involved with the backing vocals and they would just fool around, just trying to make each other crack up and things like that. They seemed a really tight unit. They liked each other, they got on well, there didn't seem to be any kind of in-band politics." Of Marriott and Lane, Brown says, "They were the two that were playing the vaudeville, messing around singing old songs in between what they should be doing. There was a lot of that kind of malarkey."

A contributory factor in this fun vibe was, of course, intoxicants. Brown: "They'd come in and the roadies would have it or they'd have it. They'd skin up somewhere. It's easy enough to take a pill without people clocking it too much. I don't remember Glyn ever saying, 'Don't smoke in the control room,' but it's quite possible. They'd stay out on the stairwell or in the studio to smoke." For Brown, these indulgences never impeded industry. "You might have a giggling fit for ten minutes, but that's about the worst it got." He adds, "We worked pretty long hours on the *Ogdens'* album."

Andrew Oldham would occasionally show his face at the sessions. Just as Brown saw absolutely nothing about the relationship between the Small Faces members that portended trouble, nor did he notice anything awry with the bond between band and record-company owner. "There was a lot of banter with that lot [but] they didn't give any impression that they were pissed off with him. It wasn't all mates and hugs and stuff, but it all seemed fairly amicable."

Rock 'n' roll mateyness and irreverence was somewhat counterpointed by officiousness when the time came for a session to lay down the classical parts that decorate cuts like the album's title track, 'Happiness Stan' and 'The Hungry Intruder'. Noted Marriott, "We used to work them out on the mellotron, and then get a guy that used to work for Immediate to come round and transpose it to music. None of us could actually write music, but we knew what we wanted, so the guy would put it into sheet-music form. We'd tell him what we wanted, how many cellos, how many violas." With the parts written, four members of the London Philharmonic Orchestra were then drafted in. "At this orchestral session, it was pretty straight-ahead," says Brown. "Keith Grant originally set Olympic up as a non-union studio, to get around the ATTT, the Union for engineers, but when session musicians came in, you had to live by musicians' rules. You could do four songs or twenty minutes of music in a three-hour session. You weren't allowed to do more than that. It applied to all classical musicians. Musicians' Union had a hell of a clout. If you overdubbed, you had to pay the whole session fee again."

Jones' recollection is that the songs that would form side one of *Ogdens'* had been laid down before the trip to Australia and that the suite that would make up side two was the consequence of a subsequent band outing back in Blighty. Although this seems an implausibly tidy methodology, McLagan at least agrees that a large chunk of side two – specifically 'Happiness Stan', 'The Hungry Intruder,' 'The Journey' and 'HappyDaysToyTown' – resulted from that domestic trip.

Despite its flash and modernism, *Ogdens'* was the archetypal album resulting from "getting it together in the country," the late-Sixties rock-band fashion that saw the likes of the Band, Bob Dylan, Traffic and Led Zeppelin retreat to a rustic setting to find inspiration for their next long-playing outing. By now, Lane, McLagan and Marriott and their partners were living in Jerome Cottage, a large, two storied house in Marlow, Berkshire. (Jenny Rylance recalls that the Marriotts had spent a short time with the Lanes at their flat in Spear Mews, Earls Court after the Chiswick lease had, presumably much to the relief of the Hasselblads, run out.) As well as Rylance and Sue Hunt, also resident was Sandy Serjeant, a mixed-race dancer well-known from the TV pop show *Ready Steady Go!* with whom McLagan was romantically involved.

"Quite a nice period, actually," remembers Rylance. "It was about a year or so. I arrived down there ill from hospital and Sue was lovely, sort of looked after me." Although she hints at friction with one couple when she says, "Sandy thought I was lying in bed all day. I was, but I wasn't well at all," she also notes, "Ronnie and Sue and I and Steve always got on well." She recalls, "Mick Jagger visited a couple of times. He liked Steve. We had lots of friends. It was a nice house to have visiting. Big rooms." Another visitor was flautist Lyn Dobson, probably most famous as a member of a briefly expanded Manfred Mann. "The two elderly sisters who owned it, they lived in the bit next door," Rylance recalls of the house. "We never saw them, but one night we'd all taken acid and stayed up all night and Lyn was playing the flute in the garden and we got a note saying, 'Beautiful flute. Could you possibly [play] it during the day next time?'"

Just like at Pimlico, Kenney Jones declined to join the communal household. Rylance: "He lived with his mum and dad. They sort of kept his feet on the ground, which was probably the right thing to do." Can we infer from this that Jones was slightly detached from the three other Small Faces? "I'm not sure, really. He didn't do drugs, which was really important. It differentiated people at the time. Most people smoked dope that I knew, not just in the music business, but Kenney just didn't. That's quite a lot of strength of character. But they all got on with him. You couldn't not get on with Kenney. He's a lovely guy."

McLagan later wrote wistfully of countryside stretching in every direction and nobody around to bother them. Jerry Shirley feels this was the closest the group came to a genuine hippie lifestyle. "They were all married [sic], but they were living communally," he says, adding the amused caveat, "High-class communal."

Even despite this idyllic and cooperative setting, someone felt the group's craft and productivity would benefit from a works outing, in the specific form of a sailing trip. It's assumed that Oldham cooked up the plan, but he says, "Not even aware of it. If it happened, probably something Tony and Marriott dreamed up." Although the river cruise that formed part two of the *Ogdens'* writing process wasn't technically in the country, it saw the group and their partners visit some of the more scenic stops along the River Thames. "We took some motor boats out for a week," McLagan says. "Cruising boats … We sailed down the Thames with our girls and dogs and everything. It was a fantastic time." "We ended up somewhere in Henley," says Rylance. The Marriotts' canine crew had now been augmented by puppies. Rylance: "Lucy and Seamus mated – not my plan – and she had lots of puppies and we kept one of them that we called Achilles because [of] this mark on his heel when he was born." She adds, "Mac and Sandy had one of the puppies. It fell in the water at the lock and Steve rescued it."

Rylance has memories that tally with McLagan's recollection that material was written on the trip, not as per the impression of Jones once the group were back in the studio. "Steve and Ronnie spent a lot of the time on the boat or on the bank writing," she says. "That's where a lot of *Ogdens'* happened … Sue and I desperately trying to get some food organised for the dogs as well as us, and the two of them were just on the bank with their heads down with the notebooks and guitars." Marriott told the BBC, "We had all these nice tracks with no words, so we went out and just wrote the words."

McLagan has good reason to remember the process as he asserts that this was the moment when he was finally, consistently let in on the Marriott/Lane songwriting process. "Mac had a lot of anger," says Rylance. "He seemed to be resentful about Steve. I think it's probably to do with the fact of not being the frontman. That's the old syndrome, that other people get more attention. There was a bit of resentment there every now and then. Sandy and he would get a bit upset about things because more attention was being given to other people." "They couldn't avoid me," McLagan says. "I had the biggest one, so we'd congregate in my boat and we'd stop for a drink and a play … We'd pull over to the side of the river and work on songs … I was there as songs were being written. I was helping to write them … I got a lot of songwriting credit finally on that."

Although Jones had little input into composition, he feels he provided important inspiration. In 1972, he told Jonh Ingham of *Phonograph Record* that *Ogdens'* "was my idea originally." He expounded, "I told the rest of the group and we wrote the story in one day." Not necessarily contradicting that assertion is the account that one evening a ruminative but whimsical Lane was lying on a patch of grass looking up at the crescent moon in the sky and suddenly posed the question to himself of where the other half of the lunar sphere had gone. Lane explained, "There's this kid, who kind of falls in love with the moon, and all of a sudden he observes the moon being eaten away by time … When it's gone, he's all down; and then the thing is that all of a sudden – boosh! – it comes back again, like life itself. And I thought that was something to pick up on really, because you can often get really brought down by something, and you're just being stupidly impatient usually." Thus was born the story of Happiness Stan, who sets off on a quest to solve this mystery. (The protagonist's name was probably a reference to Lane's own beloved father.)

The premise was, of course, fatuous. Had a grown adult like Stan, even one inhabiting the sort of fairytale land in which the tale would be set, never wondered about the phenomenon of the half-moon before? "It's meant to be fatuous, isn't it?" says Pete Townshend. Possibly so, and in any case its silliness is also irrelevant. As with all picaresque tales revolving around a McGuffin, the conceit meant that the protagonist could be made to encounter all sorts of interesting characters and scenarios during the fulfilment of his contrived mission.

Jones thinks the Happiness Stan narrative didn't go far enough. "The two sides [of the record] should have told the story," he reflects. McLagan agrees: "The only thing would have improved it is to have [the] Happiness Stan story be on both sides, but that was not to be. We had thought we might be able to develop it, but the other thing is we had all these other [unrelated] songs, so it made sense just to put it on one side … We should have developed it and left all those other songs for another album. It had been about a year anyway, so…" Marriott, though, thought otherwise, feeling that the "cockney fairy story" as he termed it should only occupy one side "so we wouldn't bore people with a whole album."

Immediate by now seem to have decided that albums with no singles such as their first Small Faces LP was a foolish notion and that the hit-studded approach taken on the American *There Are but Four Small Faces* album was preferable. At Oldham's insistence, the LP included 'Lazy Sunday'. Jones complains that it is "totally out of character to the style of the album." Banes is unapologetic on behalf of Immediate. "Don't forget we weren't in FM radio in England," he reasons. "The pirates were not playing albums. The only person that was playing album tracks at the time was John Peel."

Although the placement of 'Lazy Sunday' on the LP (tacked onto the end of the first, non-concept side) might almost be assumed to be pointedly dismissive on the part of the band, in fact the original plan was for side one to feature seven cuts, with 'Lazy Sunday' followed by '(If You Think You're) Groovy'. The latter plan might well have been put into effect were it not for a technical issue. Just days before the album's release, Lane was explaining to the *NME*, "The difficulty here is that we need a variable speed machine to mix '(If You Think You're) Groovy' … But as we can't get into Olympic at present, which is the only place we can get one, we may not be able to make it." Almost bizarrely, Lane added, "The alternative is the Ronettes' old hit, 'Be My Baby' which we recorded for a giggle one day in the studio." The latter recording has never surfaced. Lane didn't mention a smouldering version of 'Every Little Bit Hurts' on which the lovelorn Brenda Holloway Motown single written by Ed Cobb is treated to a dark, slowed down arrangement that features Marriott on piano. This track was originally intended as the B-side to a projected 'Rollin' Over' single but didn't see the light of day until the 1990s. Although at 38½ minutes the album has the most generous running time of any Small Faces album yet, it could have accommodated at least one more track without sound quality suffering. However, if Jones thinks 'Lazy Sunday' uncharacteristic of the album, it is as nothing compared to the jarring note that would have been struck by the inclusion of any of those three aforementioned recordings, no matter how good at least one of them demonstrably is. *Ogdens' Nut Gone Flake* can be characterised as rock, psychedelia and pop, but the only overt element of R&B/soul is Marriott's perennially gritty vocals.

Either way, the six tracks on side one of the album are just as delightful as the half-dozen selections on the concept side. Proceedings begin with the title track. That the writing of 'Ogdens' Nut Gone Flake' is credited to Marriott/Lane/McLagan/Jones is on the surface unsurprising in that it cleaves to the tradition of an instrumental's publishing being divided equally among the recording's participants. However, it shortly becomes eyebrow-raising when the track reveals itself to be a new, vocal-less rendition of 'I've Got Mine', whose composition was originally attributed to the four people who were in the band at the time, i.e. Winston's credit has been replaced by one for McLagan.

Having said that, there are some who would not have noticed the provenance had it not been pointed out or admitted down the years. 'I've Got Mine' was a fine record, but rendered in monochrome. 'Ogdens' Nut Gone Flake' – like the whole of the album it kicks off – is multicoloured, rich, lustrous and dazzling. It's also often otherworldly, as demonstrated by the way the riff and rhythm familiar from 'I've Got Mine' are subjected to multiple examples of distortion (including phasing on Jones' frenetic drum work) and embellishment (including the transcendent strains of the London Philharmonic). The track also has a newly sinister ambience.

'Afterglow' begins with a sleepy, mock jazz-blues acoustic introduction before moving into rock stylings of somewhat more solemn timbre as Marriott expresses his gratitude for his partner's love with an almost frightening intensity. The listener's heart melts as he belts out lines like "Love has come to touch my soul with someone who really cares." There is a clearly post-coital sensuality to 'Afterglow' (or "While you're smoking the cigarette," as Jerry Shirley describes it). Did Rylance – its inspiration – not find this mortifying? "I had to switch off from that," she says. "It can be embarrassing if you allow it to be but the fact that it's such a compliment and with the best of intentions,

Figure 1: Don Arden was the manager who catapulted the Small Faces to stardom mere months after their formation. The band would have an up-and-down relationship with him, but Steve Marriott is seen here with him in happier times. (Courtesy of Simon Neal)

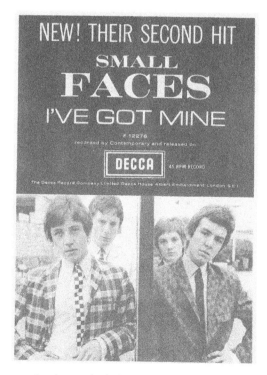

Figure 2: This music-press advertisement for the band's second single 'I've Got Mine' (1965) depicted the original Small Faces line-up that featured Jimmy Winston (second left). He was shortly to depart the band in acrimonious circumstances.

Figure 3: An advertisement for the eponymous debut Small Faces album which was conceptually apposite, depicting as it does the band's heads in miniature.

Figure 4: The cheerful cover of the Small Faces' first album (1966) fostered the butter-wouldn't-melt image that Don Arden moulded for them, for better or worse. Clockwise from top left: Ronnie Lane, Ian McLagan, Kenney Jones and Steve Marriott.

Figure 5: Pauline Corcoran was a teenager with a mature head on her shoulders who ran the band's busy fan club. (Courtesy of Simon Neal)

Figure 6: Although they were not romantically involved, Marriott was very close to Corcoran. (Courtesy of Simon Neal)

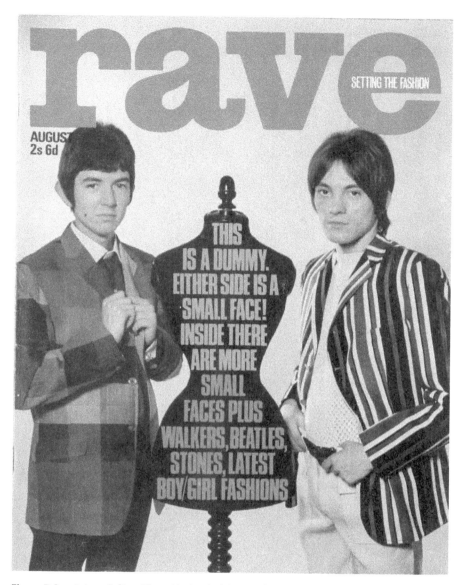

Figure 7: Ronnie Lane (left) and Steve Marriott (right) were a formidably innovative songwriting partnership but this cover of Sixties pop magazine *Rave* presents them merely as clothes horses. In time the band would come to weary of being, as Marriott put it, "a 10 by 8 glossy teen scream of the year."

Figure 8: In early 1966, Val Williams made a transition that millions of teenage girls fantasised about when she went from being a Small Faces fan to working with the band every day in Don Arden's offices. (Courtesy of Val Weedon)

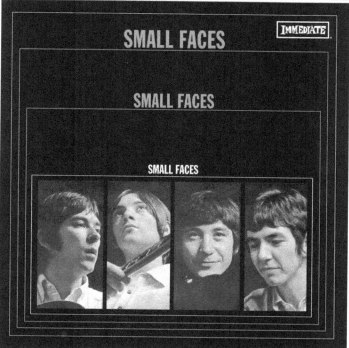

Figures 9 and 10: Released within weeks of each other in mid-1966, these two albums presented contrasting images of the Small Faces right down to their sleeves. The cover of Don Arden's hits-and-leftovers compilation *From the Beginning* featured an outtake from the jacket photograph session for their first album, whereas something classier was being aimed for on the front of the band's eponymous debut album for the Immediate label.

Figures 11 and 12: The publicity for the Small Faces' 'Itchycoo Park' single featured small boys standing in for the band due to their unavailability. A later picture taken in the same Hampstead Heath location by the same photographer, Gered Mankowitz, showed the real thing and was used on the American taster album *There are but Four Small Faces*.

Figure 13: The sleeve of the band's stunning 1967 single 'Tin Soldier'. Gered Mankowitz's Vaseline-smeared camera lens created a memorable if blurred image of the Small Faces that appeared on what was one of the UK's first single picture bags.

Figure 14: Andrew Loog Oldman exploited the furore surrounding an anti-Vietnam War demonstration in Grosvenor Square to provide some typically provocative publicity for Immediate Records, in this case the Small Faces' classic but decidedly unriotous 1968 single 'Lazy Sunday'. (Courtesy of *New Musical Express*)

Figures 15 and 16: The circular, ornate sleeve of the Small Faces' 1968 long-playing masterpiece *Ogdens' Nut Gone Flake* could be said to be revolutionary for the sake of it and was also impractical, but it was

undeniably beautiful.

Figure 17: Phill Brown, a young Olympic Studios tape operator who assisted engineer Glyn Johns in crafting the sonics of *Ogdens' Nut Gone Flake.* (Courtesy of Phill Brown)

Figures 18 and 19: These two 1969 compilations provided some consolation to Small Faces fans left bereft by the group's recent split. *In Memoriam* featured previously unreleased material but was blocked in the UK by the Small Faces, who objected to its morbid title. *The Autumn Stone* was a surprisingly rewarding and comprehensive mixture of new tracks and old favourites.

Figures 20, 21 and 22: Atlantic Records pulled out all the stops to promote the Small Faces' long-awaited reunion. However, the albums *Playmates* (1977) and *78 in the Shade* (1978) failed to live up to the band's legend.

Figure 23: The photograph on the cover of their 1977 reunion tour programme illustrated just how much the Small Faces had changed in their eight years away, right down to a totally unfamiliar member. L–R: Ian McLagan, Steve Marriott, Rick Wills and Kenney Jones.

Figure 24: The early-Eighties Marriott and Lane Majik Mijits project is for some fans a Small Faces-in-all-but-name proposition. Although completed and highly creditable, pursuit of a record company deal was abandoned due to Lane's deteriorating health. It would fail to see the light of day for two decades.

Figure 25: Such is their renown that even over half a century on from their original split the Small Faces are still cover material, as this 2011 issue of *Uncut* magazine demonstrates.

Figure 26: Sole surviving Small Face Kenney Jones keeps the flame alive with such projects as this 2021 live album. Its cover features the band's iconic logo, which he helped to devise back in the Sixties.

the embarrassment is a tiny, tiny part of it." Jones' performance on the track is like a muffled fusillade, but it no more spoils the vulnerable tone than Lane's propulsive bass or McLagan's soaring organ. A lull followed quickly by an urgent, double-time bridge, wherein Marriott likens love to a voice in his head, ratchets up the drama.

'Afterglow' segues – at a time when conjoined album tracks were rare – into 'Long Agos and Worlds Apart'. Aside from the title track, this Ian McLagan solo composition is the only non-Marriott/Lane song on side one. It finds the keyboardist immersed in just as much romantic bliss as Marriott had been in the preceding track, although this is not a blazing rocker but a lovely, gossamer ballad. Its woozy atmosphere is assisted by its every element being distorted or treated by studio trickery and by a lyric that plays with language and twists back on itself: one serpentine passage finds McLagan reflecting that if he could sit quite still and time could pass him by, he'd sit quite still and pass the time he had with his lover.

'Rene' concerns a woman who is the delight of dockers and a mother of children of every shape and colour. It's pure music hall, its beer-barrel rhythms, cockney vocal, singalong chorus and bawdy lyric ("You'll have a ball – she'll 'ave yours out!") conjuring up the often raucous entertainment provided to the British working classes before radio and television gave them a way to be diverted without leaving the house but which new diversion was necessarily much cleaner. Rather unfortunately, halfway through its four-minute playing time it becomes a jam involving Hammond organ, distorted electric guitar and mouth harp which is not only an abandonment of period authenticity but in truth largely dispensable.

"Renee Tungate her name was," Marriott claimed of the track's real-life antecedent. "Lived down Strone Road in Manor Park. And she did have a kid of every size and colour." Jones, though, says Marriott was telling porky pies. "It was about my aunt Rene, who was a bit of a flirt," he wrote. "I'd been telling the boys tales about her and about my boyhood explorations of the docks area, and Steve married the two into a song."

In the brawny, uptempo 'Song of a Baker', the band achieve the remarkable feat of turning a composition about the mundane subject of bread-making into possibly the album's most exciting cut. This is partly down to its thunderous base of crashing drums and reverberating piano. The excitement is also assisted by the way that Lane's lead vocal is buttressed on the more dramatic lines by a simpatico Marriott, and the fact that these passion surges are followed by pauses broken sublimely by, variously, a resounding piano chord and an infectious yell of "Yah!"

'Lazy Sunday' – contrary to Jones' misgivings – sits perfectly on *Ogdens'*, and its placement ensured that the first act/side of the original vinyl configuration drifted to a close on the lovely notes of church bells.

Instead of the album title, the label of side two of *Ogdens' Nut Gone Flake* bore the words "Happiness Stan". Even if *Ogdens'* was not the first narrative work in popular music, it remains probably the most coherent by virtue of the fact that it actually has a narrator. The band's first choice for this role was Spike Milligan, beloved to their generation for his pivotal role in madcap radio-comedy troupe the Goons. However, Milligan turned them down, possibly because of the fact that he was an inveterate rock hater. They went instead to Stanley Unwin, whose gobbledegook language 'Unwinese' had made him a fixture of radio and films and who had recently been prominent in the public consciousness via a television advertisement for Gale's Honey. Jimmy Winston notes, "The funny thing is, I introduced that to them. All the dockers and lightermen used to muck about with Stanley Unwin language: 'Deep joy and up chimney' and so on." "They'd always loved him," says Rylance. "All the band. They always loved that mad linguistic quirkiness of his. So that was great excitement. He came to talk about it. They talked about what they wanted to do and they were really ecstatic that he got it and what was needed." Phill Brown was not a little impressed to be working with Unwin. "He used to be on Hogmanay every New Year's Eve," he notes. "Working with him … was such a treat." Although a middle-aged balding man with glasses, Unwin entered fully into the far-out, youthful spirit. "Totally cool," says Brown. "He didn't seem fazed by it at all. He seemed to enjoy the whole experience."

Unwin didn't use a script. Brown: "They told him the story. 'We want to say something like…' Marriott went through the whole story of Stan with Unwin, who made notes, and then Stanley Unwin then just told the story in his language … There was a little vocal booth at Olympic and he just sat in there with a desk in his tweed jacket and it was recorded straight to a 15 IPS quarter-inch tape. Then that was spun in during the mixing … It was all pretty quick."

An indication of the unique way Unwin transposed and mangled words to form sentences that were simultaneously nonsensical and comprehensible is provided at the start of the suite where he greets the listener with, "Are you all sitty comfty-bold two-square on your botty? Then I'll begin…" To the Small Faces' delighted surprise his links also blended his usual schtick with the more contemporary argot used by the group members, exemplified by, "Oh blow your cool man … What is the thought of this half disappearing of the moony-most? … Absolutely smashed and flake-ed he was."

When at the start of the suite's opening track 'Happiness Stan' Marriott sings in a mannered voice and olde-worlde English to a background of elegant harpsichord, we immediately feel like we have been transported to the realms of a Disneyesque animated feature. We also feel we have been dropped into one of those generic mystical worlds populated by adults who are somehow childlike and where magic is an unremarkable facet of existence. However, the colourfulness and cuteness of a land where "the skies are silky-soft and full of coloured dreams" doesn't rule out a grit and a menace, not least when the titular Stan has his equanimity shaken by the moon being unexpectedly diminished in size, at which point the primary-coloured music takes on the hue of a sky just before a bad storm.

Stan sets off to find out why the missing lunar half is no longer "dangling in the heavenlybode", trailing in his wake the farewell message 'Rollin' Over'. Here the problems with the suite start, if one is inclined to let them. The track's hard-rock tones, earthly concerns and modern dialect ("Tell everybody there ain't nothin' gonna stop me!") hardly sit with the overarching antediluvian sexlessness and cuteness. However, the consistently high quality of the suite's music makes one disinclined to brood over such inconsistencies. More distracting on this specific track is the blatant plagiarism. Although the guitar work on 'Song of a Baker' owes a little to the Troggs' 'Wild Thing' it's not to the extent of it being distracting, but the riff of 'Rollin' Over' is clearly lifted from the Jimi Hendrix Experience's 'Foxy Lady' from the previous year.

Jones reveals that the track began in an ad hoc manner, starting with a visit by him to London emporium Drum City. "The guy said, 'Paiste have sent over this giant 26-inch cymbal.' I said, 'Oh, great'. I set it up, got quite excited. We were in Studio One at Olympic and we just did a jam. We were jamming any old thing that was the influence of the day and I suppose the influence of the day was a bit Jimi-Hendrixey. All I did was ride the cymbal heavy and played it on the edge. Glyn Johns just happened to turn the tape on and captured the moment." Surprisingly, George Chkiantz – who was tape op on overdub sessions for 'Foxy Lady' – doesn't see the Jimi Hendrix Experience connection ("I hadn't really thought of that"). He will also surprise some in not having a problem with the fact that in the track's final section horns jostle for attention with the guitar work to rather shrill effect. "It's just a fantastically rude brass. I admit it's overpowering but it's a brilliant sound."

Following those two Marriott/Lane compositions comes 'The Hungry Intruder' (officially Marriott/Lane/McLagan, but according to Marriott "Ronnie's little baby"), wherein Stan – having stopped for a bite to eat – finds a fly asking if he can share his packed lunch. Lengthy passages of swirling orchestration alternate with the vocals and dialogue to sweet effect.

Stan finds that virtue is rewarded when his generosity with his food yields him the information that the fly knows of someone who may have the solution to the mystery that perplexes him, even if he has no means to transport him to the person in question. Stan – having, naturally, "the possesey power of the magicold" – turns the little fly into a creature as big as all the flies in the world combined. Not only does the newly giant fly transport him, but he serenades him on the way with 'The Journey'. A dreamlike affair credited to all band members but sung by Lane, its philosophical ruminations begin with the observation, "If tomorrow was today, it would be yesterday." Despite the general weirdness, it features some almost funky bass, played by Marriott while Lane handles guitar. The second half of the song is essentially a jam which, though engaging enough, indicates – like the rather static back end of

'Rene' – that the Small Faces' once considerable prowess with instrumentals has somewhat deserted them.

The sage with whom the fly is acquainted turns out to be one Mad John. One can't help noticing the assonance with the handle of Ron King's employee, although this individual is cut from a more benign cloth than the psychopathic Tom. Cue a number that is musically gothic folk and lyrically of philosophical bent. Although credited to Marriott/Lane, it – surprisingly – is mainly Marriott's song. Even more surprising is his inspiration. A song revolving around a character who is considered loopy by a world that fears him but is in fact more enlightened than they are might have led some to assume that Marriott was taking his thematic cue from the Beatles' 'Fool on the Hill' from the previous year, but in fact the guitarist was provided his creative impetus by far loftier material. Marriott disclosed to Pidgeon, "That's reading books like *The Prophet* and all that, and getting something out of it, and realising there are these characters about that people were scared of through ignorance." Kahlil Gibran's *The Prophet* – a collection of prose poetry of a metaphysical and spiritual stripe – had been around since the 1920s but had recently been discovered by a new generation of truth-seekers, namely the type of people mocked in 'Itchycoo Park', with whom Marriott clearly had more in common than he usually let on or perhaps realised. Although Shirley acknowledges that Lane moved into spirituality sooner and deeper than Marriott, he says, "Don't forget, they were very close, so what one got into, the other one got into. It all started of course with the use of LSD … It was *Steve* that turned me on to *The Prophet* and Kahlil Gibran and all that stuff."

The song's brooding opening gives way in the bridge to a more playful – and cockney – ambience ("John 'ad it sussed!"). The track constitutes our first-ever sustained exposure to Marriott's acoustic guitar work and it is a revelation, starting from the opening ominous arpeggio and continuing with picking that is highly adroit throughout. It would have been nice to hear more of this, but the Unwinese re-emerges before the track has reached the two-minute mark and confines it to the background for the last minute-and-a-half. This raises another issue with the concept: after repeated listens, some will find Unwin's twitterings not so much enchanting as intrusive.

The song's denouement consists of the disclosure to Stan that part of the moon in fact becomes invisible on a regular basis before reemerging. Perhaps wisely – it being hardly a revelation to anyone else – it's dispensed with in a couple of lines of Unwinese, paving the way for another of the songs for which the whole storyline is an excuse. This one is 'HappyDaysToyTown' and involves Mad John letting Happiness Stan in on the secret to a good life to the backdrop of a celebratory party. The song is credited to Marriott/Lane/McLagan/Jones but, according to Marriott, is "Mac's song really." Lane sings the Mad John part while Marriott handles Stan duties.

These days, Toytown is better known as the name of a chain of shops, but to the Small Faces' generation was a decades-straddling fixture of BBC children's radio starring the characters Larry the Lamb and Dennis the Dachshund. The phrase "toytown" had entered the British lexicon as a pejorative to describe something that was inferior in a babyish way, and in fact the lyric of this number might be described as toytown philosophising, comparing as it does life to a bowl of All-Bran (probably an allusion to the Tin Pan Alley-era song ' Life Is Just a Bowl of Cherries') on the grounds that "You wake up every morning and it's there." Of course, others will say that the observation is jocular rather than faux, and McLagan in any case is co-opting the toytown phrase to invoke the uninhibited taking of joy from life that is characteristic of children. "I [used] it with my kids," Jones says of the crux of a song he loves. "'Happydaystoytown newspaper smiles' – that's brilliant. We thought of that in Stockholm in the back of a car, reading the papers. Lines like that [are] just stunning." It became another of the band's internal catchphrases. Noted Lane, "If you walked in and everyone was larking about, you'd say, 'Well, it looks a bit happy days toy town.'" Although the track has comedic and old-fashioned components – a beer barrel rhythm, jolly brass and shrill whistles – it's also grounded in the modern by raw electric rhythm guitar.

'HappyDaysToyTown' is another quintessential example of the life-affirming Small Faces spirit, this time with an additional anthemic quality. Its closing massed vocals and exhortation to laugh and sing reminds us of a thousand and one cartoons that end with a troupe of characters disappearing over the horizon while engaged in a singsong, one or more of them clicking their heels in the air as they go. Unwin's voiceover summation and farewell ("Oh, what a mind-blast … Stay cool, won't you?") captures the mellow, exuberant mood perfectly.

"We worked like mad on Ogdens' because it was a great project," says McLagan. With the LP's music assembled with such loving, painstaking care, it seems to have become unthinkable within the Small Faces camp that the product might be handed over to the record company to be put into another generic sleeve with an unimaginative title.

Faced with the happy but novel task of thinking up ideas for the way their product would be dressed, they were, according to Jones, struck by inspiration when, sitting around smoking joints, they noticed a tin of tobacco on a coffee table. In the Sixties, the majority of the adult UK population were almost certainly smokers (the Office of National Statistics didn't start collating figures on the issue until 1974, when they found that 45% of Britons smoked), and many of them still preferred 'roll-ups', cigarettes they assembled themselves with tobacco and rolling paper. McLagan recalled that it was Lane who suggested that they feature a tobacco-tin lid on their new album's cover. Ogden's was not as famous a tobacco brand as Golden Virginia or Old Holborn but the Liverpool firm was ingrained in British culture via a history dating back over a hundred years. When Oldham contacted Ogden's about the idea of using their name in the LP artwork, the firm were as enthusiastic as any company would be about the prospect of free publicity. Accordingly, they sent over scrapbooks of their historical packaging designs.

The story put about by the Small Faces camp is that Marriott, leafing through such a book, spotted a design for Nut Brown Tobacco and decided to adapt its name. It's possible that memories became clouded on this point. Ogden's manufactured brands like Juggler, Redbreast, St. Bruno and St. Julien, whereas it was Adkin who were known for their Nut Brown make. Whichever the manufacturer, Marriott was struck by a flash of inspiration on the level (whatever that level was) of his decision to call the band's publishing company Avakak. It being the case that the band preferred 'wacky baccy' to legal tobacco, he alighted on the pun "Nut Gone" – i.e., a brand of tobacco whose ingestion would cause one's head (nut) to be transported elsewhere. It was the apotheosis/nadir of the band's penchant for surreptitiously flaunting their drug use.

Product packaging of the Victorian era was often ornate and beautiful and the patina of antiquity such possessed by the 1960s only added to their allure. The Small Faces instructed Immediate staffer Mick Swan to develop an album-cover design in this mode. "He was a good lad," says Banes. "He did all our designs and whatever from the ideas that Andrew was passing onto him." Swan's design, like much Victorian product, was awash with bright colours, banner lettering, ornate fonts and exclamatory self-aggrandisement (the album's full title, in fact, could be said to be *Brightest Selection Ogdens' Special Nut Gone Celebrated Flake Tobacco*). Speckling the design were intriguing little illustrations: a military medal, a castle turret, and flowers. There were also coins, each of which bore the profile not of a regent but a Small Faces member, all of whom were given a pseudonym (Jones is "The Phantom Street Whistler", Marriott "George the Cleaner XVIII" [probably a reference to a photo of him with a mop found in the album's insert], McLagan "Maximiliam III" and the bassist "Leafy Lane," the latter apparently now the former 'Plonk''s in-house nickname following his introduction in this style at the beginning of 'All Our Yesterdays'). Cleaving to the tobacco-product concept is the statement that the record is 'Manufactured by the Small Faces'. The back cover carries a "1lb Box" declaration spotted by McLagan on another tin which, apart from being enlarged, was reproduced unaltered.

Ogdens' famously boasted the first circular album jacket. "See, it wasn't gonna be a round cover," McLagan said. "The idea was it was gonna be a tobacco tin ... It was a rectangular cover tin, you see. Most of them are." The sleeve's revolutionary shape had a genesis stemming from a conversation at the Trencherman hostelry on London's Fulham Road between Oldham and his close friend Sean Kenny. "He was the most famous set designer of his age and an extraordinarily creative character," says Mankowitz of Kenny. As well as designing the original stage set for the Lionel Bart musical *Oliver!*, Kenny had been responsible for Immediate's jagged-lettered logo. Mankowitz: "Sean Kenny and Andrew were having dinner and Andrew was telling him about the album and saying that he wanted to do something special for the sleeve. Sean Kenny came up with a basic design for a round cover that opened up to produce four circular panels and he scribbled it on a napkin. Andrew then took that and it became the sort of master concept for this cover." Oldham confirms this story, but one has to add the caveat that his memory may be playing tricks on him. He gave the following quote to Jon Tiven of *Sounds* in June 1974: "We started another label, Instant Records, a few months prior to our crash. It never really did anything; the best thing about it was the label that Sean Kenny drew. He drew it in a restaurant on a napkin and had it photocopied." There again, when asked about this now Oldham responds, "I do not recall him doing same for Instant."

However and by whoever it was thought up, a round record sleeve was unheard of, primarily for obvious practical reasons. Which, of course, was the kind of thing that was a red rag to Immediate. "It wasn't our [approach] to say it's impossible," says Banes. "It was, 'Let's get on with it.'" McLagan has postulated that Oldham (who, in fact, he was under the impression came up with the idea) would have been salivatingly aware of the extra press coverage the innovation would generate.

The left-hand side of the sleeve's first two-panel fold-out revealed a blown-up facsimile of the interior of a tobacco tin. It being the habit of smokers to tuck their 'skins' inside their tins, it was only natural that sitting on top of the ruffle border-protected tobacco was a packet of rolling papers. The brand on display, though, was not a familiar, commercially available name like Rizla or Swan but the non-existent 'Sus'. Any pothead would have immediately understood the reference: a joint constructed so that it could pass for a legal cigarette was 'unsuss'. This design involved photographic work for which Mankowitz was brought in. Meanwhile, on the fold-out's right-hand side was a colour illustration of remarkable beauty rendered by Pete Brown and Nick Tweddell, artist friends and former bandmates of McLagan. The busy design's abundance of butterflies, bees, pigeons, flora and concentric circles meant that some people didn't even register the prone figure partaking of a hookah in its centre.

Each of the four new panels that were revealed by opening out the sleeve again contained a monochrome Gered Mankowitz photograph of an individual Small Face. "*Ogdens'* was the biggest thing at Immediate at that time and everybody was incredibly excited about it," Mankowitz recalls. "I was down at Olympic with them when they were recording, so I felt quite involved. There was a feel that they were doing something special on lots of different levels. Andrew wanted to make the sleeve extra-special and I wanted to make the portraits extra-special. I came up with this idea of one of them in the foreground and the other three in the background in each portrait. And I wanted the portrait to try and reflect something about them, because it felt to me that the album was very much a personal journey."

The photo sessions (and by extension album sessions) stretched back to a point before the band's collective move to Marlow. Marriott's portrait was shot at his old Chiswick abode. In it, the behatted guitarist can be found gazing upwards at the lens. "It's a very grainy picture because I didn't have lights with me and I never used flash, so I just used available light," Mankowitz notes. "I think it was a pretty miserable day. Everybody was very stoned." Outtakes from the session reveal a mural of the Mighty Thor from Marvel comics drawn on Marriott's living-room wall, his speech balloon declaring, "Amazing gear!" (In humour typical of him, Marriott told a journalist that he was so "thor" he could "hardly thit down.") Lane's picture finds him cross-legged on the floor but gazing down at the camera, his expression almost superior. Mankowitz: "That's Ronnie in what he laughingly called the music room in his flat. You can see the egg boxes stuck to the ceiling." (There's perhaps a character detail to be read into this – Lane's deployment of this considerate sound-baffling measure is a stark contrast to Marriott's indifference to his own neighbours' peace being disturbed.) The at-home concept was abandoned for the McLagan and Jones portraits. "The flat that he lived in with Sandy was too small," says Mankowitz of McLagan. "Honestly, you couldn't take your jacket off without doing gymnastics. So we did a very crazy session in my studio for that." The crazy session involved McLagan's colleagues wielding props behind him – Lane a banjo, Marriott a mop – while McLagan's calm and apparently oblivious face fills the foreground. "Kenney wanted to be photographed originally with horses because he's horse-mad," says Mankowitz of the drummer. "So we went to Richmond Common to a stable there and we got four horses and photographed them. But in the end those weren't very successful. I think it was because they were too different from the others. So we ended up by doing some portraits at the office at Immediate of him in, I think, one of Andrew's chairs." Jones sports the type of floppy hat then in season.

All four pictures were treated after the fact. "I printed the pictures through a sheet of spun glass, which was a fibreglass filter that you put in front of lights to soften the light," Mankowitz says. The effect – which he terms "spiderey-web" and "vaguely sepia" – provides an olde-worlde atmosphere in keeping with the Victoriana of the front-cover design but incongruous for an artefact otherwise achingly modern.

"When you look at it fifty years down the line, it was absolutely brilliant," marvels Banes of *Ogdens'* design. "Things that we missed. The four little heads on the sleeve is one of them. Most people don't notice it. The way it opens up is just pure genius."

Some pre-CD vinyl re-releases of the album dispensed with the round sleeve, presumably to save on costs. Quite possibly all re-releases, though, have excluded the insert that originally came with the record which contained sleevenotes and additional photographs. For a brace of reasons, it was a quite daring affair. One of the pictures finds McLagan 'flicking the V's' at the camera. Performing the British equivalent of the American middle-finger was a then very undecorous pose for a pop star. McLagan later revealed that he was venting his frustration at his recent drugs bust. The inset also contained a parody of the Lord's Prayer reading:

Small Faces
Which were in the studios
Hallowed be thy name
Thy music come
Thy songs be sung
On this album as they came from your heads
We give you this day our daily bread
Give us thy album in a round cover as we give thee 37/9d[4]
Lead us into the record stores
And deliver us Ogdens' Nut Gone Flake
For nice is the music
The sleeve and the story
For ever and ever
Immediate

It's unlikely that retail outlets were as taken as Immediate with the notion that the revolutionary packaging enhanced the album's aura of specialness. The disc tended to roll out of the side of its jacket. Moreover, said jacket revealed itself to be fragile, the hinges on the fold-out panels quickly fraying. Banes says of UK retail outlets, "Because of the fact it was round, they could just pile it up," but adds, "In America they couldn't, because they had to put it in a rack." Bob Cato, art director and Vice-President of Creative Services at Immediate's American distributor CBS-Columbia Records, provided a solution. "He came up with the idea of having a plastic bag with a clip on it so they could then put it in the rack," Banes explains. That the plastic bag by its nature vaguely resembled a tobacco pouch was serendipity, but there were also drawbacks to this approach. McLagan notes, "In America, they got a lot returned, because the press stud would go against the record."

There were other transatlantic differences. The US edition of the sleeve was amended so that – unlike the UK edition – it bore a tracklisting, running around the circumference of the "1lb Box" design. This was to be expected of a market that then emphasised optimum sales over artistic whim and was probably something the Small Faces felt they could live with. However, the band weren't happy with the mastering of the American release, considering it too 'toppy'.

---

[4] Retail price of thirty-seven shillings and nine pence.

The UK edition of *Ogdens'* was released on 24 May 1968 in both stereo and mono. Of the stereo iteration, Brown says, "We put in quite a bit of time into the mixing because we were doing this live tape phasing during it being mixed to get the sound without having to record it on other tracks." However, he also says, "The stereo was almost a bit of a novelty at the time, so a lot less time was spent on putting the stereos together than doing the monos." Although monaural editions of music of the era are usually favoured by audiophiles as packing more punch, it has to be said that Marriott's vocals are less prominent in *Ogdens'* mono iteration.

Andrew Oldham had long specialised in provocative promotion. In 1964, the jacket of the second Rolling Stones album had to be revised because of sleevenotes in which he exhorted the public to knock a blind man on the head to obtain the wherewithal to buy the product. For *Ogdens'*, he authorised a music-press advert containing the parody of the Lord's Prayer from the album's insert. Today, the parody seems merely whimsical, even trite. However, while the UK of 1968 was already post-Christian, its populace had been raised in a society suffused with a primness and coyness that were the overhang of religious culture. Even to those people who didn't consider themselves believers, such irreverent usage of a hymn that was still recited by most children in school assemblies at some point during the week would have seemed on some vague level morally wrong. He of course was aware of the potential outrage the parody would provoke. Others were less gleeful about possible public complaints and outraged Fleet Street headlines than he: some music papers refused to run the ad. The Small Faces themselves came out with apologies and protestations as a minor scandal unfolded (Marriott: "We didn't know a thing about the ad until we saw it in the music papers"). However, there must also be a suspicion that they were of the opinion that all publicity is good publicity.

The *NME* would vote *Ogdens'* Album of the Year, an accolade in any circumstances, but especially so in an annum that saw the release of the Rolling Stones' *Beggars Banquet*, the Jimi Hendrix Experience's *Electric Ladyland*, the Beatles' eponymous 'white album', the Byrds' *The Notorious Byrd Brothers*, the Kinks' *The Village Green Preservation Society*, Van Morrison's *Astral Weeks* and the Band's *Music from Big Pink*. Over and above its success and excellence, a national pride could also be obtained from the way *Ogdens'* explored the Small Faces' own culture and musical traditions instead of exclusively proffering a facsimile of American strains.

The album attracted a degree of US interest, garnering a rave review by James Pomeroy in *Rolling Stone*. "It's wonderful, it's great, it's fabulous, and it's real!!!!!" he gushed. "It's full of fairy tales and groovy afternoons, of giant kissable flies and love, and mostly lots of happiness and joy. 'Brightest Selection' the front cover says and so it is, the brightest and craziest rock in too long of a time." He certainly hit the nail on the head when it came to the life-affirming essence of Small Faces music: "The music is happy and unabashedly so, the Small Faces don't have to make excuses or pretend to be cynical or even prophetic, happiness is enough for them ... 'Wish away your worries and problems,' they seem to say and in case you need help, they're ready and willing." However, the album remained only a cult proposition in the States. Commercially, it did better on the *Billboard* Top LPs chart than *There Are but Four Small Faces* but still peaked at a measly #159.

In the rest of the world, however, it was a very different story, nowhere more so than in the band's home country. The album spent six weeks at no.1 during its 19-week chart run. Banes encountered an all-or-nothing attitude from radio stations when he was plugging the record. "Either they played the whole lot or they didn't play it," he says. "But not playing it didn't change anything because we'd already started promoting that record and everybody [who] bought it went, 'What a great record.'" This excellent word-of-mouth is for him what led to it becoming Immediate's biggest-selling LP so far.

The album's success was assisted by a memorable television performance. Pop music was very sparsely represented on British TV at the time as a consequence of it being perceived by the older generation as adolescent-oriented ephemera whose rightful place was on the margins of airspace that was very limited (not only were there just three channels, but aside from school programming shows didn't start transmitting until the afternoon and came off the air before midnight). The BBC, however, were keen to demonstrate the validity of colour transmissions, which had begun in July the previous year on their secondary channel, BBC 2. The flash and youthfulness of popular music was the perfect way to do this, hence the show *Colour Me Pop*, a strand of their *Late Night Line-Up*. Rather than purveying the conventional magazine format of bite-sized contributions from multiple artists, it adopted what was a quite audacious policy of giving over entire half-hour shows to studio performances by one group or singer. The fact that they had just released a narrative suite made the Small Faces perfect candidates for this particular show. This wasn't the first time the band had been accorded this honour. The corporation's commercial rival network had given over to the Small Faces an entire special edition of its Granada regional franchise's *Scene at 6:30* in August '66. However, that programme had only been transmitted in Granada's north-west zone. Although the Small Faces' *Colour Me Pop* appearance went out at the relatively late time of 10:30 pm, the show's broadcast – on Friday 21 June 1968 – was national.

Despite the ostentatiously visible microphones and guitar leads – and although their movements were perfectly in synch with the sounds – the band's renditions were mimed ones. Technically, they were obliged to provide a new recording of their performance because trade-union rules designed to protect musicians' livelihoods prohibited miming to actual records. "We couldn't face it," Jones wrote in his book. Artists have often been understandably averse to lip-synching to quickly recorded approximations of works that had taken a long time to perfect. They had frequently got around the rules by simply handing over the original recording in the guise of a re-recording. Pop was now entering an era, however, wherein artists were not so much loath to re-record their product as virtually incapable. Although there might be some dispute about how long *Ogdens'* took to lay down, even Jones publicly said, "We recorded some of the tracks on *Ogdens'* perhaps ten times." The idea that a new, knocked-off recording could recapture the layered, polished, effects-drenched material on *Ogdens'* was ludicrous. Accordingly, the only elements on *Colour Me Pop* unfamiliar to anyone who didn't own the album were the mostly live vocal parts.

Whether despite or because of this, the Small Faces' performance is superb. A superimposed, shimmering fly silhouette during 'The Journey' is about the extent of the special effects, but none were needed in light of the band's mighty in-person presence. They are resplendent in the dandy fashions of the time, an amusing contrast to the sober suit sported by indulgent-parent presenter Mike Dean, whose squareness is compounded when he banally offers that *Ogdens'* is "one of the most idiosyncratic records on the market" and mixes up Toy Town with Enid Blyton's Toyland. The group give it their all as they proceed to prove that *Ogdens'* is a damn sight more noteworthy than Dean's oddly ambiguous encomium. Marriott – his shining, sculpted hair making him resemble a psychedelic Prince Valiant – dynamically spins and dips, strikingly employing his gimmick of holding his guitar vertically as he 'plays' guitar solos. It's notable how much the group are enjoying themselves, with much gesturing, verbal in-joking and laughing. One of their in-jokes is the cry of "Nice!" during 'HappyDaysToyTown'. A bethroned, crown-wearing, ermine-encased Unwin provides links for the *Happiness Stan* tracks (or as the closing credits would have it "Fairy Story told by Stanley Unwin"). He at least never makes the same sounds as on the record, it being impossible to replicate or mime to a narration for which improvisational isn't even the word. Side one of *Ogdens'* is represented by a performance of 'Song of a Baker' and the promo for 'Lazy Sunday'. The memorable show must have instantly converted many viewers unfamiliar with the Small Faces. The group even got paid more than was standard for it. Usually by this point they were receiving a collective BBC appearance fee of £100 (£1,300 in today's coinage), but *Colour Me Pop* yielded them £131 and five shillings.

On top of its high sales and critical acclaim, *Ogdens'* had a gratifying effect on fellow artists. Says Jones, "We influenced *Tommy*, without a doubt. Townshend even owns up. He says to this day, 'I didn't know what to write, so I'll write about this deaf, dumb and blind kid and there you go.' Out of simplicity comes a fucking masterpiece. Not only that, we were all hanging about together anyway. We were all telling each other what we were doing."

Townshend demurs on that point. "No, I was nearly finished with it," he says of his own rock opera. "I had a long, long, long collection of songs called 'Amazing Journey' before *Ogdens'* came out. I tended to work in my own studio at home for long periods before I even talked about [what] I had to the band. It needed to be finished, really, as demos before I presented it to the band. So I was well on the way." It should also be pointed out that he had already ventured into the territory of the rock opera in miniature form with Who album suites 'A Quick One, While He's Away' (1966) and 'Rael (1 and 2)' (1967). However, he doesn't deny that he was enthralled by *Ogdens'*, describing it as "a masterpiece." Back in 1969, Townshend raved, "*Ogdens' Nut Gone Flake* was a world-shaking record. When they first played it to me, the only material I had heard to which it could be compared were concept pieces like *Pet Sounds* or *Sgt Pepper's*. I was jealous of the Small Faces; they were becoming a real extraordinary sonic force to be reckoned with."

Asked if Marriott felt that he was now acquiring the same sort of esteem as the Beatles and the Stones, Rylance says, "I don't think he even really thought like that. It wasn't much about that sort of ego with Steve. He was happy it did well. They wanted to be a good band, they wanted to be producing good music. That's what it was about."

On the latter points, it can't be gainsaid that the group were achieving their objectives. More than that, though, in the second half of 1968, it seemed that the Small Faces were sitting on top of the world. They had critical acclaim and the respect of their peers. They had commercial success in the more respected LP format to add to their hit singles. They also had the potential for an enhanced standard of living. Jones told the *NME* that he had four cars. While that may have been partly down to his lucrative session work, Marriott, Lane and, to a lesser extent, McLagan would have been receiving or expecting to receive healthy PRS income. That there seemed little reason to believe that anything much could go wrong for the band is demonstrated by a quote Jones gave to the *NME* as *Ogdens'* was beginning its run at the top of the long-player chart: "Really this album is just the beginning of things. We're now free to do just what we want…"

5   Something I Want To Tell You

During the first half of 1968, fully three-quarters of the Small Faces got married.

On 4 January, McLagan wed Sandy Serjeant. Sue Hunt and Lane jumped the broomstick on 24 April. "Registry office," says Hunt. "Very informal. We kept it rather low-key." On 29 May, five days after the release of *Ogdens'*, Marriott tied the knot with Jenny Rylance, the two becoming husband and wife at Kensington Registry Office, south-west London. "It was very small, and very nice," Rylance says of the ceremony. "We didn't want a big deal at all, or I didn't. His mum and dad were there and my mum and dad came down from Manchester. Ossie had made me a dress with trousers to go with it. A few friends found out where it was, like Ossie. Gered Mankowitz was there."

No one who knew the story of Marriott and Rylance's courtship or the writing of 'Tin Soldier' – or even that Marriott dallied with groupies – would ever suggest that Marriott didn't truly love Rylance. However, it's a little eyebrow-raising that, once the ceremony was over, Marriott whisked Rylance off not on honeymoon but a few miles across town to Barnes. "We did a vocal overdub in studio two," recalls Olympic's Phill Brown.

Eyebrows meanwhile may have been raised in the pop fraternity at these weddings. At this point in history, the younger generation – especially the cooler end of it – while in no way disputing the power of love were beginning to question the validity of the institution of marriage. Rylance herself would have been perfectly happy to simply shack up. "He was the one who very much wanted to get married," she says. "I think possibly because Ronnie and Sue were married. It was his insecurity, I think." She reasons of her acquiescence, "By that time, I was committed to the relationship and we had a nice life together and we had our animals and we both had aspirations to get to the country. It just seemed the right thing to do."

Although the communal house in Marlow was vacated, two of the married couples would continue to live together. In the early Spring of 1968, Marriott and Lane bought Beehive Cottage, near the village of Moreton, Essex. "My lawyer told me to buy a house while I still had the bread," Marriott told Tony Norman three weeks after moving in. "Ronnie and I shared the cost of £15,000." Something about the nature of the relationship between Marriott and Lane is revealed by Jerry Shirley's recollection of the way the house was divided up between them: "They bought it together, so from Ronnie's point of view he probably saw it quite rightly as an equal share in the property. But Steve, being Steve, took the house with the bathroom and the toilet and la la la, and Ronnie, being Ronnie, took the loft above the garage that was turned into a house."

The pair were able to afford the house through an Avakak publishing advance. Immediate had taken up an option to extend the band's contract. (In a typical piece of wilful naiveté, Marriott later lamented, "They didn't tell us they had an option," as though he – or Victor Gersten – was unable to read a contract.) To placate the disgruntled pair – Gersten had suggested to Oldham and Calder that they were unhappy about revenue flow – Immediate stumped up a publishing advance in the form of a sum Jones recalls as £12,000 (over £200,000 today). Gersten has said it was lower, but still the princely-in-1968 amount of £10k, although he seemed to be under the impression that it went to Marriott alone. According to Jones, the Avakak advance caused the first major argument in the Small Faces' ranks. "Mac and I found out from Vic Gersten," says Jones. "He told us, 'You've got an advance here, but Steve and Ronnie have got [it] because they're writing the songs. Mac and I said, 'No, we're writing songs as well. That's supposed to be split four ways, because we're all shareholders in the company.' We were just pissed off about it, Mac and I."

Even so, the money was not quite enough to complete the purchase. "We had to borrow money to get the rest of the mortgage together," Rylance says. "Steve borrowed money from Arthur Howes. I do know that a while later Steve went to his office and paid him back in cash." Marriott himself put the figure stumped up by the Small Faces' booking agent as £1,200.

Beehive Cottage was a house as pretty (although nothing like as small) as its name suggests, white of wall and thatched of roof, standing in three acres, with the main building possessing three bedrooms and the outbuilding – formerly the stables – as big as an average house.

It was also very isolated and a world removed from the urban glitz associated with Marriott and Rylance, a couple comprised of a famous pop star and an eminent model. However, Rylance says that the metropolitan glamour image was never the reality even when the pair were domiciled in the capital, regardless of a fairly well-known photograph showing the pair entering the trendy King's Road shop the Chelsea Drugstore dressed in psychedelic finery. "We might occasionally go to a club like the Speakeasy, but we didn't go out that much," she notes. "We had our own life." In Chiswick, they would "play with the dogs, take them to the green," but things became even more scaled back at Beehive, with the trendy gear nowhere in sight as Marriott exulted in the sort of peace and quiet that he had denied Cilla Black, the Hasselblads and others. "We didn't really have neighbours. The only person I was in contact with was Mrs. Babbage, who was the next cottage down the lane, quite a way away. We just didn't see people, which suited me fine … I've always been like that. Make an effort to go out and that's your going-out defence face, so to speak."

Rylance says Marriott was perfectly happy in such isolation. "There'd be music every day, via his acoustic guitar. He was very, very focused when he was involved in a project. Not solely focused, but he was very committed to whatever he was working on at the time. He probably was a sort of workaholic. Music was the dominant force in his life."

Human nature being what it is, it wasn't complete isolation. "We had friends that would visit, and his family would visit. Occasionally we'd go to London for something." Rylance also says that sometimes she would visit the capital. She'd wait for the Small Faces to finish a recording session, then, "We'd take the long drive home back to Essex." Plus of course the Lanes were resident on the grounds. Workmates becoming housemates wasn't a problem according to Rylance, who says, "We couldn't have been closer."

Nor was idleness the order of the day even when Marriott wasn't working on music. "I was mainly in the country because we had lots of animals by then," Rylance says. "We kept getting strays. Being there all the time, we ended up with a sort of animal sanctuary, and at one point, before we could get them all neutered, with about 35 cats and kittens. We had to find homes for a lot of them. We had lots of ducks and geese as well. We had a kestrel with a broken wing and all that sort of thing, so he was always kept quite busy."

As to how the locals took to the glamorous pop star in their vicinity, Rylance says, "The local young guys, there was a sort of ambivalence there. I think they were quite interested and a bit resentful. [One of our] cats came back with lots of shotgun pellets. There was a resentment perhaps because we didn't mingle. If we'd have gone to the local pub that might have been better [but] I'm not a pub person. I think we were considered to be standoffish."

Marriott and Lane maintained a connection to the 'Smoke' by employing Liesel Schiffer, the domestic worker from Pimlico. "She got on the train," says Sue Hunt. "They loved her. I'm sure they paid her well."

Meanwhile, Jimmy Winston was getting on with his life. He had observed with amusement, though not surprise, the Small Faces' journey into a territory a long way from the blues. He says of *Ogdens'*, "I was never keen on that. In the times, a lot of drink, a lot of drugs about, and a lot of music was affected … I like the tracks one side, but the Stanley Unwin thing – although they love it and they live on it a bit – I don't know." Having said that, 'Real Crazy Apartment', the June 1967 single by his own outfit, Winston's Fumbs, released on RCA Victor, wouldn't have sounded too out of place on *Ogdens'*. "I like psychedelic rock," he says. The recording's frenetic surrealism had prosaic origins. "It was about a room I used to live in in the Ruskin. The stuff that went on in that room with my own band... We'd be there all night playing, writing, rehearsing, getting a bit merry. It was like, 'The books upon the shelf/ They give me wealth.' I've still got the volume of Shakespeare that I was looking at that night when that song came together."

'Real Crazy Apartment' b/w 'Snow White' (both sides Winston compositions) is now considered a highly collectible classic in the (admittedly limited) field of freakbeat-cum-psychedelia, but was no more successful than 'Sorry She's Mine'. Winston, though, had another talent on which to fall back. "I'd done three years at drama school and I wanted to go back and do some acting," he says. "I did quite a lot for Joan Littlewood at the Theatre Royal, Stratford. Did about six or eight shows there over a period of a few years. Then *Hair*." *Hair* was the US stage musical that encapsulated a late-Sixties *gestalt* involving, socially, cultural libertarianism and, fashion-wise, rising female hemlines and, as suggested by the title, descending male hair lengths. "I played General Custer," he says of the London production, although points out, "Everyone in *Hair* played half a dozen things and sung various songs." He was in the show for a year and clearly considers it the highlight of his professional life. "That was a phenomenon," he says proudly. He appeared on the 1968 London cast album co-singing 'Electric Blues'. He adds, "We got chosen – me and two other guys – to sing it at the London Palladium at a big charity gig in front of Princess Margaret."

Although the Ogdens' track 'Song of a Baker' saw powerful guitar work and backing vocals from Marriott, the latter's whole-hearted contributions served to disguise the fact that it was a solo Lane composition (Marriott later described it as "all Ronnie") and one that essayed territory – and a psychological journey – from which some claim Marriott felt rather excluded.

Hunt: "We had a lovely little house, Ibiza. We made very good friends when we would go there with this fellow who had another little house similar, not so very far away. This was all out in the countryside in those days. Would be very overpopulated now." In this exotic, tranquil setting, a neighbour named Chris Smith would bake bread in the traditional, local way. "He was an amazing baker and he was using the original oven that is in those houses from when they were built, and that's pretty old. The oven burned wood, heated up all the bricks inside. He was the baker. That was the inspiration." The exaltation of the simple, practical and humble to be found in the lyric of 'Song of a Baker' was something to which Lane connected his ever-growing spirituality. He explained to John Pidgeon, "If you're hungry, then you learn to become a baker ... I got the idea from a Sufi book, which was kind of a mystical book."

The brand of Sufism to which the Lanes were specifically attracted was that created and extolled by the Indian spiritual figure Meher Baba, then in the twilight of his life. Says Keith Altham of Lane, "I don't think he was an intellect, but I think his interest in spiritual things was quite genuine," As specifically regards Lane embracing the teachings of Meher Baba, Altham reflects, "I never thought that was a bad thing. I never met an unpleasant Baba person. They were never after your money."

Lane's interest had been piqued in Australia, partly as a consequence of him growing closer to Pete Townshend. The latter says he himself had been "following" Baba since the Monterey Pop festival the previous June, although adds, "I certainly wasn't trying to convert anybody around me to Meher Baba." Explains the Who guitarist of the Australian jaunt, "A girl appeared who spent some of the time with Steve Marriott. Then Steve dumped her and she came and hung out with Ronnie and me. I was wearing a Meher Baba button and she said, 'Fucking hell, Pete. Do you follow Meher Baba?' I said, 'Yeah, sort of. I'm new to the game.' And she said, 'You know there's a big centre in Brisbane? There's a lot of Meher Baba followers here and I follow him.' That sparked Ronnie's interest. So in the days that followed, he asked more and more about it and, when I got back to London, he started doing his own researches, met some of the older people that we both knew who had followed Meher Baba, some of whom were *very* old, had followed him from the Thirties. Both he and Susie started to follow."

Explains Hunt, "Traditional religion was so not us. In the Sixties, it was a complete renaissance. Everyone was searching and we were very interested in trying to understand about God and about how to do your life. So we were reading all these books, and then Pete Townshend started sending us in the mail little pamphlets and things about Meher Baba and meetings that were happening in his studio in Soho. I think he used it as a rehearsal space but he was lending it to this group of people who were following Meher Baba. It was a meeting that was happening weekly. In the end we said, 'Well, might as well go see what it's about.' So we did, and for both of us it hit home. We both wanted to explore it."

What was so fulfilling for the Lanes, though, was for Rylance something that her husband, and Lane's best friend, perceived as a threat. "Ronnie had this whole other life," Rylance says. "Ronnie was so committed to his spiritual quest, that's what drove the wedge. That's where the schism in their relationship began. Ronnie and Pete became great friends and Ronnie enjoyed that connection, and I think that's why Steve [felt] threatened. Ronnie was on this spiritual quest and that puts him in a slightly superior position when he says, 'Well, Steve doesn't get it.'" For Rylance, it was the resultant fissures in the pair's relationship that ultimately resulted in Marriott deciding to leave the Small Faces come the end of 1968. "Ah, that's bollocks," says Townshend. "It's bollocks. She's got to find some reason, hasn't she? I don't agree. The reason I don't agree is that I don't think Ronnie was as deeply committed to Meher Baba as I was, or as any other people in our group were. I think he never really made the immense commitment that he made to Meher Baba until in the middle of '69 he went with Mike McInnerney and his wife Katie to India and went to Meher Baba's tomb. When he came back, he was a changed man.

Before that, he was [merely] interested." It's notable, though, that when Kenney Jones is asked about whether Meher Baba created distance between Marriott and Lane he says, "Might have been a bit of jealousy, because the only reason Ronnie got into Meher Baba because he's got really friendly with Pete Townshend."

Townshend notes, "Meher Baba said, 'The use of hallucinogenics can open spiritual doors and lead to important pathways. A continued use will lead to mental illness.'" Asked if she and her husband started to lose interest in drugs as they gained interest in matters spiritual, Hunt says, "Oh yeah. Meher Baba didn't advocate taking drugs. In fact, he told people that it was no good." If indeed the days of Marriott and Lane publicly mischievously enunciating the codeword "Nice!" at each other were over, it would have severed another important bond between them.

If growing fissures within the band were one issue by which the Small Faces were confronted, another was the dilemma of how to follow up Ogdens' Nut Gone Flake. While the album was a triumph on many levels, it was a triumph that it was becoming apparent it might be impossible to capitalise on.

Keith Altham feels the stir the LP caused was "a superficial thing." He says, "The fact that they'd got something different – the round sleeve and Stanley Unwin doing the narration – made it an oddity rather than something of the future. It wasn't a step in the right direction so much as a step sideways." He might be in a minority on that, but there was something else that the band felt impeded the record being a stepping stone to something bigger. At the end of 1966, Marriott had blithely expounded to *Rave* journalist Dawn James, "There is a whole new outlook in sound now … You can use anything you want to get the right effect … It doesn't matter if groups don't use it on stage. The fans won't mind that sounds onstage are not exactly the same as studio sounds. It is old-fashioned to only record what you can reproduce with four crummy mikes in some badly built cinema. If you let this stop you, nothing new will happen." Within little more than a year, he might well have come to the conclusion that such an attitude was ill-informed bravado.

Human nature dictated that, while Marriott's comments might be accurate, the Small Faces wanted their masterpiece and latest product to be represented in their stage act as closely as was possible. The problem was in 1968 as closely as was possible was not very closely at all. That concert technology was very primitive had been demonstrated when McLagan had tried to approximate live the phasing on 'Itchycoo Park'. In addition to the issues involved in representing special effects, there was the fact that even miking up acoustic guitars was difficult, invariably resulting in teeth-grating feedback. Carting around a classical string section, meanwhile, was unwieldy and expensive. The alternative was to try to perform *Ogdens'* songs without the overdubs, strings or acoustic instruments, but that would be tantamount to a futile act.

As Marriott later noted of *Ogdens'*, "It was a terrible quandary to be in, because we couldn't really take it on the road."

Consequently, the band never performed the 'Happiness Stan' suite in concert. Whereas upon the release of *Tommy* the Who began giving over the bulk of their concerts to their rock opera, the Small Faces decided it would be too difficult to play at gigs anything off *Ogdens'* except for the rockers 'Rollin' Over' and 'Song of a Baker' (and the latter is a non-suite song). "That's one of the tragedies of the Small Faces," says Jones. Marriott agreed, terming it "our big mistake" as he told Pidgeon that the band had "let a lot of people down who wanted to hear *Ogdens'* on stage."

"It's very much like what the Who went through when we tried to perform *Quadrophenia* live," notes Pete Townshend. Before that 1973 concept work, the Who had had an advantage on this count in that, for all its conceptual grandiosity, *Tommy* is sonically a surprisingly skeletal album. "When we did *Tommy*, we went into a rehearsal room for three days and we played the whole thing from start to finish," Townshend says. "It played itself. With *Quadrophenia*, the recording studio process was so complex with synthesisers and brass parts and this, that and the other – sounds of the sea and all kinds of stuff going on – that when we came to rehearse it, we couldn't crack it. We couldn't bring it to life. So I really feel that it must have been really strange for them not to be able to play *Ogdens'* live. They had real trouble performing it and it worried them." He adds, "The other thing, of course, is that *Ogdens'* is only half an album, so it doesn't constitute a stage act, or even the major part of a stage act."

As well as feeling that the Happiness Stan suite could have been reproduced on stage, Jones also thinks that no less than *Tommy Ogdens'* lent itself to adaptation in other media. "If the Small Faces [had stayed] together, we would have definitely reworked *Ogdens'*," he says. "I'm convinced of it. As an album, as a film, as a project, as many different things. The Who are a classic example of what they do with their back catalogue."

The closest that the Small Faces came to bridging the gap between their gritty live work and their sumptuous studio recordings was their retention in spring 1968 of a six-piece brass section. Headed by the self-same Eddie Thornton who inspired 'Eddie's Dreaming', it featured trumpets, saxophone and trombones. Old hits like 'All or Nothing' and 'Tin Soldier' were embellished and – in Jones' eyes – refreshed by the horn charts. Jones said of playing with the brass, "I felt like I was in a band. I felt really professional." Unfortunately, this set-up wasn't sustainable. "By the time we'd pay the band we'd have nothing," Lane told Jonh Ingham. "You couldn't afford to do it."

There was also the issue of whether such ornamentation was wasted on their audiences. The Small Faces had lately been debating the idea of a live album. They recorded a November 1968 gig at Newcastle City Hall to see how the augmented line-up sounded. Marriott's memory was hazy on the issue when he spoke about it to Jim Green in 1981, but he thought that two sets might have been recorded, with and without the brass. Although the firm hand of Glyn Johns was on the recording-equipment tiller, the results were not very good simply because the gigs were, in Marriott's words, "real scream machines." The brass section, like the Small Faces themselves, are playing to people whose interest in their technique is negligible. There was clearly more than one reason it was impossible to represent the Small Faces' increasing sophistication in a live setting.

Being pop idols was now an aching, constant sore, a mockery of the band's very purpose. "We were desperately trying to lose this teenybop image," says Jones. Part of that teenybop image was their name, about which the group had now come full circle. While back in '65 they had decided – possibly in a spirit of contrariness – that they liked Annabelle's whimsical/mocking suggestion, as circumstances and fashions changed, 'Small Faces' was losing its shine again. "It's a bit of a naff name, innit?" Jones says. "At that time we were like, 'How we ever gonna lose this image with a name like the bloody Small Faces?'"

With a no.1 album and no.2 single in the Small Faces' very recent past and a public respect for their artistry that had never been higher, the pop world was naturally highly expectant about their next record. When it was released on 28 June 1968, however, it was to a chorus of derision.

One review of 'The Universal' said it sounded like a send-up of Don Partridge, a man who that year had parlayed his one-man-band television celebrity into a recording career with the top-five hits 'Rosie' and 'Blue Eyes' but who was also inherently a slightly comical figure. Penny Valentine of *Disc & Music Echo* opined of 'The Universal', "Complete lunacy ... the whole thing is chaos ... it sounds as though they've put it out to please themselves and without really considering what they're doing." This was tame stuff compared to another review which asked, "Have the Small Faces gone bonkers?" Chris Welch of *Melody Maker* simply declared it, "the worst record of their career" and "a catastrophic mistake."

At its heart, 'The Universal' is a number in the singer–songwriter genre, although that term was not yet in wide circulation. The words set to Marriott's acoustic strum are by turns melancholic, philosophical, romantic and ribald. The composition has a rueful, hungover tone. Marriott states he hasn't paid his rent yet ("Ain't feeling sorry but I haven't got the money anymore") and proffers a wastrel's viewpoint (he's decided his life will be devoted to play because working doesn't seem to be the perfect thing for him). Behind the rapscallion attitude, though, is something deeper. Says Jerry Shirley, "'The Universal' is all about you're living in the universal: you don't own it, you just rent it ... It's a light-hearted look at a deep subject."

The narrator (and for once we can definitively state that the narrator is the composer – Marriott even inserts his own Christian name into one of the lyric's reported bits of dialogue) disdains the namedroppers he meets and prefers to focus on the likes of birdsong and seashell roar. There's a couple of surreptitious drug references, with talk of a hippy-trippy type asking Marriott if he knows where to score. His worldview is also tender, him noting that he alternately foreswears and succumbs to romantic love, even if this worldview is shot through with a certain lewdness (his love is declared to be at the foot of his partner's hand). Marriott described the song to Jim Green as "one of the funniest things I've ever written … a very tongue-in-cheek, very English word-association thing." This amusing, interesting lyric, rendered the right way, might have consolidated their current success.

McLagan (who points out of the keyboards-less recording, "I'm not even on it"), says, "It's as much a novelty single as 'Lazy Sunday'." 'The Universal' indeed had a novelty-record vibe and the UK has always loved such releases. However, such recordings tend to be tidy and slick. 'The Universal' was anything but. Its basic track was not recorded in Olympic, Trident or any other professional studio but, Rylance points out, "in the garden at Jerome Cottage." Moreover, the recording equipment employed was primitive: you seem to be able to hear the clunk as the domestic tape recorder on which it's captured is placed on a surface. The acoustics are unmistakably open-air: a breeze can be heard blowing against the microphone. Then there is the fact of the Marriotts' dog Seamus barking prominently in the background. "It's a weird follow-up, which we recorded because we liked it and because it's different from anything else," Marriott said. "We wanted it to be the most terrible production. We wanted a really evil sound … It's supposed to be what I sound like when I wake up in the morning … It should have been called 'Hello the Universal' by the way, but it was released before we expected … That would have given the impression that we wanted, that the whole idea of the song was a kind of 'Good Morning' to life."

"It was completely different to what we normally were doing," reasons Jones. "It was like, 'Well, how can you use a track that you recorded on a little cassette player and put it out as a proper track?' We proved everyone wrong: yeah, 'course you can. That was the moment that we captured that we'd like to share with everybody else." Essentially, 'The Universal' simply sounds like a demo. The daring involved in this casual approach was the leitmotif of the age, of course, but on some level, such low fidelity and low production values may have communicated a certain contempt for the band's own product, or even for their audience.

Not that it wasn't completely bare and primitive. "I liked it before we put the [overdubs] on," says McLagan. "I liked the way it sounded just like that." "We brought it to Olympic Studios that evening and we all overdubbed it," says Jones. Clarinet, trombone, bass, picked electric guitar and oompah-oompah bass drum were the instruments overlaid. McLagan notes that these additions are incongruous compared to the record's fuzzy basic elements because they are "recorded so well and so loud." Their superimposition also sounds almost like an expression of lack of faith in the band's own iconoclastic decision to use the rough-hewn back-garden recording. The overdubs are also a little generic – particularly the clichéd guitar work – an orthodoxy that is something else that contradicts and undermines the studied scruffiness.

The record's flip, 'Donkey Rides, a Penny a Glass' (Marriott/Lane/McLagan), continued the longstanding Small Faces tradition of great B-sides and the newer Small Faces tradition of focusing on things distinctively British. Although it starts with distorted electric guitar and booming piano, the intro is not a precursor to contemporary rock – even though there's some modish shuffling backwards guitar in the middle – but an old-timey ambience. Lyrically, the song is a tribute to the simple pleasures of the seaside. "When we were all kids, we all shared the same holidays," says Jones. "The national holiday was to go down to Bognor Regis or Blackpool and you could ride a donkey for a penny." Marriott, mainly declaiming in British English although not his exaggerated gor-blimey voice, lists sun-dappled vacation pleasures ranging from idling away time in a caravan to scoffing the epicurean pinnacle of fishcakes, cabbage and mashed potatoes. Amongst the topics covered in a jolly bridge is the best method for dealing with nosebleeds. Despite the air of innocence (Marriott fondly recalls sharing the company of his lovely uncle Joe), the writers can't resist more ribaldry in the form of a silent dropout in place of "screw" – but then anybody who has ever seen a Donald McGill postcard knows that such sauciness is also part and parcel of the British seaside holiday.

The record was accompanied by a promo filmed by Alexis Kanner, also recorded in the garden at Jerome Cottage. Rylance is particularly pleased that it features much footage of Marriott frolicking with Lucy, Love and Seamus: "For me, it's a piece of live history and happy times." The promo depicts in a literal manner some of the elements of the lyric. Rylance: "They were going to get Emo, who was a friend of Dave Gilmour's, to do it to give him a bit of a break, but he wasn't up to it. So Annie Lambert, who was an actress, she was the sister of Kit Lambert and was a great friend of Sue's, was the hippy-trippy name-dropper knocking on the door."

Seamus barking in time to the music on the record may well have been accidental, but Jerry Shirley notes that he had other musical abilities: "Steve taught him to howl into a blues harmonica. They would sound like blues phrases. It was freaky. It was in tune as well sometimes. Amazing dog." The Marriotts' friend and near-neighbour Dave Gilmour roped in Seamus to howl on a track on Pink Floyd's 1971 album *Meddle* that was ultimately titled 'Seamus'. Seamus also had non-musical talents, as revealed to passers-by when Marriott and Rylance would walk him on the green near their previous Chiswick abode. "He was an amazing ball catcher," says Rylance. "Could leap miles in the air … People [in cars] used to slow down because it was so spectacular."

Although both Jones and McLagan liked 'The Universal', whether they were confident about its chart potential is another matter. Having said that, it's something they don't seem to have spent much time contemplating. "I don't know whether we thought it would be a hit or not," says McLagan. "It just seemed to be a good idea to throw it out. We were trying to be adventurous." Jones states, "I knew that it wouldn't be a big hit. It sounded a bit untidy and a bit messy." He adds, "But everyone missed the point. The point of it was, 'We'll just put this out for fun.' It's not as if it's commercial. It was just the humour of the band getting out there." Had 'The Universal' been reserved for a B-side or an album track, it would probably have been perceived as intriguing and charming. Unfortunately, it simply didn't fulfil the remit of manifesto that single A-sides are required to and therefore incurred the contempt or disappointment traditional for things perceived as misbegotten ventures. It climbed no higher than no.16, quite a comedown for a band whose last single was almost a chart-topper. If the lack of a picture sleeve might be assumed to suggest that Immediate weren't investing much in the record, it should also be noted that the fact that the label were prepared to put out such a patently uncommercial record and fund a promo for it could be posited as indicating long-term commitment to the band – and a resignation to short-term financial loss.

It being the case that 'The Universal' was pure Steve Marriott, it's understandable that he had keener commercial ambitions for the disc than his colleagues. To Dave Thompson, he simply said of the record's minimal success, "I did take it personally, because that song was the best I'd ever written, I thought." Jones considers the record to constitute a crossing of a Rubicon. Claiming that Marriott insisted on releasing it over the band's objections, he wrote, "He wanted to show that he could put out anything after *Odgens'* and it would be a hit, to prove a point … Either that or he had a death wish for the Small Faces … he knew it would crash, providing an excuse to split the band." "I don't know," says Rylance of that theory. "I'm sure he would have known it wouldn't have been a hit single like 'Lazy Sunday'. Just wanted to make a statement, I think." That it was lo-fi was "the whole point of it," she says. "He's saying, 'This is who I am right now.'" McLagan was thinking along broadly similar lines to Jones. "He told me in later years that the reason he left was he thought when 'The Universal' wasn't a hit that because that was all him he would just drag us down," he says. "I think that's bullshit. I think he was looking for something else to do at this point. He was already on his way out … He was off on his own, he wasn't thinking of the band anymore."

Lane told Pidgeon that 'The Universal' represented the disharmony within the Small Faces camp: "To me it's always been quite a sad little track, because it was the end. It was the last thing we did. And it was more or less recorded in that atmosphere. It was a total 'Fuck it!'" Rylance has similar feelings. "There wasn't anything else happening after *Ogdens'* so … they just decided, 'Let's put that out and see what happens,'" she says.

Jerry Shirley insists that Marriott's devastation over the single's failure was genuine and epoch-marking. "[It] really hit Steve hard, because he loved that song and up 'til then, everything he wrote was like the Midas touch – he just had to put pen to paper and it was a hit," he says. "It hurt him. He was shaken." However, Shirley says that Marriott's devastation was as much or more about artistic respect as commercial achievement. "It didn't matter to Steve [so much] that it wasn't a top ten, top five smash," he says. "What mattered to him [was] it was rubbished by the press [and] by his band members after they'd agreed to record it and release it." His words suggest that despite the kind things Jones and McLagan say about the record, the feelings they vouchsafed to Marriott at the time about it were somewhat harsher. Shirley: "This is the mistake that those guys made: they were dissing him and he's sitting there thinking, 'Well thanks a lot guys, if it weren't for me...' If they're disrespecting his songwriting but not coming up with anything themselves, if you were Steve, how would you feel?"

He suggests that if Marriott had any sense of self-worth as an artist, it was predicated on composition. "As cocky and as arrogant as he seemed to be, Steve was not a braggadocious guy," Shirley insists. "He didn't brag about his own achievements at all. He was very humble about his own abilities and, if you praised him, he would almost tell you off for doing it. You know in your passport it used to say 'occupation'? In Steve's passport, he always put one word: 'songwriter'." Rylance says that Marriott might not necessarily be euphoric if he had a number one but would be disproportionately deflated if something went wrong. "Lack of control, I think," she says. "He did have depressions."

Phill Brown, incidentally, provides some information about 'The Universal' that serves to back up the contention that the Small Faces were pressurised, at the very least, into releasing 'Lazy Sunday' as a single. In the early part of the twenty-first century he came into possession of a photograph of a BASF recording-studio tape box. Written on the ledger is some standard tape-box annotation: the Olympic studio used (one), engineering personnel (Brown and Glyn Johns), recording date (18 June 1968), client (Immediate), artist (Small Faces), and contents, complete with working titles and asides ("'Me You and Us Too', 'The Universal in the Garden (drop out near end of reel)' and 'Donkey Rides, a Penny a Glass' (B-side)'". All this, though, is accompanied by something decidedly non-standard. An NB at the bottom reads, "Don't let these masters go to Immediate. Must stay here unless otherwise told by the Small Faces." Brown: "It's my writing. I've obviously been asked to write it down on this label." This would suggest that the band were trying to ensure that their record company would have as little knowledge as possible about what they were recording. An inference that can be drawn there is that the band had found out to their cost that previous openness in this regard had led to a loss of control over their releases. Such skulduggery is sadly ironic in light of the fact that such considerations would soon cease to matter altogether.

Although they would stagger on for eight months further, the Small Faces had issued their swansong. 'The Universal' ultimately transpired to be the last officially sanctioned release of their original lifetime. It's astonishing to realise that this death knell sounded less than three months after the chart triumph of 'Lazy Sunday' and barely a month after the release of *Ogdens' Nut Gone Flake*.

The failure of 'The Universal' is by no means the only factor in the discord in the Small Faces' camp at this juncture. Another is the absence of money. Why it was lacking, though, is a matter of dispute.

"Steve and I frankly didn't talk about financial things very much," reflects Rylance. "I brought [to the relationship] what I had, which was from my brief modelling career and working at Quorum and selling a few antiques and stuff like that, but we struggled financially. We weren't on the breadline. There was enough to get the food in and buy dope. We'd get PRS. They seemed to come in quite often just before Christmas. That'd be quite a substantial amount and that would save us, but the fact that that was the case – that it was so important – you can tell that we just didn't have that much money." She adds of their circumstances, "As is often the case, that's when we were the happiest."

Sue Hunt has similar memories of being rich in life but not in purse. "We didn't have extra for the big fancy stuff maybe, but we still did okay," she says. "We had a nice lifestyle. It's difficult [to gauge] when you've got people around you who are just doing things for you all the time. I look back and we had a great life. No complaints. We could do whatever we wanted, more or less. We used to go to Ibiza. That could not have been cheap."

The non-songwriters in the band had a different perspective. Neither Jones nor McLagan had the cushion of a large publishing advance or regular injections of capital from PRS. As McLagan notes, "I was living in an eight guineas a week flat and finding it hard to find that money ... I had a house I was going to buy in Fifield. It was a double fronted Georgian house in two acres. £8,100. I couldn't get the eight hundred pound [deposit] off of Immediate as an advance off my royalties." He adds, "Andrew and Tony never paid us royalties. All we ever had was that fifty pound a week." Jones concurs on this. "It turned out that Andrew's liberating, 'Take as long as you want in the studio, lads,' should have been followed up with, 'because we aren't paying for it, you are,'" he wrote in his autobiography. "Immediate was ... giving with one hand and taking away with the other. We weren't aware of any of this." McLagan: "The fact that we were getting no money, that was kind of upsetting. We realised we were in a similar situation as we'd been with Arden and Decca, except our managers were our agents, were our record company, were our publicists, were everything: it was all Immediate. It was all Andrew and Tony and the team." "We put all our eggs in one basket, didn't we?" Marriott said to Pete Silverton. "We used to receive a sheet saying where all the money had gone to. That's all. It could have been done by any typist."

Immediate's management role at least came to an end, according to a 5 June 1968 story in *Record Retailer*. Under the heading, "Small Faces handling own management following closure of Immediate Artists," Marriott was quoted as saying that Immediate Artists wanted the band to sign with them again but, "We were saying, 'No, we want this much dough to re-sign,' and they, for some reason, decided not to pay us what they owed us, let alone what we were asking to re-sign."

While it's legitimate to object to such concentration of control and the multiple conflicts of interest it entails, the band's surprise that studio time would be recovered from their record royalties seems naïve even for an era when musicians were profoundly less business-savvy than now. Nor is the practice for most people unfair. As Shirley easily notes, "It's not refundable, but it's recoupable." However, Jones – vastly experienced in the way of recording contracts with not just the Small Faces but the multiple other bands with whom he subsequently enjoyed success – is still of the same opinion that he and his colleagues held in the 1960s. Asked if Immediate should have paid for the Small Faces' recording costs, he states, "Absolutely. Because basically, we have got a raw deal with the record company anyway. Of course they should have paid. They knew the only way they could get any records from us is to let us loose in the studio. So we went in the studio and recorded so many songs. The worst thing the Small Faces did was trust. We were all brought up to trust people. Not a pot to piss in, but the feeling of trust was spread in our families."

Yet tellingly, while the conflicts of interest that were commonplace in Sixties music contracts are today illegal, recoupable studio costs remain an industry standard. To be charitable, perhaps the band conflated such matters with more dubious activity by their label. For instance, according to McLagan when they had been about to undertake the trip to Australasia, Marriott and Lane (but not Jones and McLagan) were presented with insurance forms which made Calder and Oldham the sole beneficiaries in the event of their flight-related deaths. When McLagan pointed out that Marriott and Lane's families were not mentioned, the pair refused to sign.

"It creates a kind of a weird tension to have people telling you that you're rich when you're not," observes Pete Townshend. "Whatever the story is in the background, whether you've been ripped off or whether you've just got shitty deals. The way you're perceived and the way you want to behave … Keith Moon, I can't count the number of times he used to go into Jack Barclays and buy a Rolls Royce. He had no money." Yet Oldham adds another perspective. Although the Immediate co-head declined to cooperate with this book beyond some emailed answers to queries, he did offer this comment about McLagan's grievances in a different interview with this author: "What they sold and how much time they spent in the studio, the fact that they did one concert for sixty that everybody else was doing, and then you'd have an actual idea of what their income was. He has wonderful selective memory." He says of the Small Faces' grievances, "Artists believe what is convenient. It´s part of their make-up and their charm."

It should also be noted that when McLagan was busted in '67, his earnings were stated as being £200 per week (approaching £3,000 today). Jones has said that when he left the Small Faces, he had built up a nest egg of £800 – around £13k in today's money. Some of that pot will have been generated by his extracurricular session work and, as he was living at home with his parents, he may not have had the expense of rent. However, what seems to be the deciding factor in the health of his finances is the simple fact that, by all accounts, he was the sensible Small Face. When asked by Keith Altham in 1969 why the constituent parts of the now-defunct band weren't rich, Marriott trotted out his usual line of larceny ("We probably never saw a lot of the money we should have"), but also admitted, "We spent a lot. Never really knew the value of money – never really cared." The same year, McLagan told Chris Welch, "We messed ourselves up. We got into the habit of living well and didn't want to change. I lived in an eight guineas a week flat and we always used Daimler car hire. We lived like Bee Gees for years, but we didn't have the loot to back it up." (Note that in this anecdote, his eight guineas rent is presented not as a lowly figure he should rightly have had the means to readily pay but an extravagance.)

Then there is the issue of the relatively minimal amount of money sloshing around in the pop world *per se* at that point in history. Paul Banes puts the commercial success of *Ogdens' Nut Gone Flake* in context: "People forget that *Sgt. Pepper's* didn't sell millions, because people weren't buying albums to that extent. We were happy in America to go gold, and that was 500,000. The big, big records came a few years later when America started to buy albums by millions and millions instead of hundreds of thousands." An indication of why album sales in the UK were so low is the fact that often an LP cost up to a quarter of a working man's weekly wage (and even more of a working woman's). "An album sold at around £2," says Banes. "So *Ogdens'* grossed 200 grand for a hundred thousand copies sold. We did 90,000. Imagine the recordings costs offset against the band's royalty. Four per cent of £8,000 did not go far." It went less far when unusual costs are taken into consideration. Malcolm Forrester points out of *Ogdens'* round sleeve, "To have that printed up – that had some kind of guillotine made, whatever – that cost almost as much as it cost to make the bloody album." Even more unusual costs had to be put on balance sheets under alternative names. "Anything that came in was charged to them," Tony Calder told Simon Spence. "If they rang up and said, 'We want a block of hash that'll cost 300 quid,' you put it down for 'tip to driver'."

In the midst of all this disappointment, resentment, bewilderment and uncertainty, the Small Faces continued to record. They were working on their fourth album and even had a name for it, *1862*, a reference to the construction date engraved on a derelict church hall close to Beehive Cottage in which the band either practised or intended to rehearse or even record (accounts differ).

However, the *1862* sessions were desultory and seemingly half-hearted. In August '68, Marriott admitted to the *NME* that the group felt "a little gestation of the fourth album. "[But] there was no talking to Steve." The record instead disappeared into the realms of what-might-have-beens, or to use the more modern phrase, counterfactuals. One of the staples of music-industry what-ifs is hypothetical tracklistings. In the case of *1862*, there are such tracklistings, but one of them consists of something more than theory and wish-list. Toby Marriott, son of Steve, came into possession of what he termed a 'songbook' that his father had owned circa 1968. In 2008, he told blogger Mick Taylor that it contained ideas for the follow-up to *Ogdens' Nut Gone Flake*. Toby gave as the album's intended contents:

1. The Autumn Stone
2. Red Balloon
3. Collibosher
4. Buttermilk Boy
5. The Pig Trotters
6. Picaninny
7. Wide Eyed Girl on the Wall
8. Donkey Rides, a Penny a Glass
9. Blues Jam

Marriott's son conceded he was working from memory (the songbook had gone missing some years before) and it has to be said that some of the entries are questionable. 'Call It Something Nice' and 'Collibosher' are tracks now considered to be *Ogdens'* outtakes, while 'Piccaninny' goes back even further to late 1966. There again, perhaps Marriott considered them all to be worth excavating.

'Picaninny' is a rare Small Faces 12-bar blues, and even features some of the blues mouth harp Marriott was renowned for in the early days of his musical career but which was never a component of the Small Faces' sound. It suffers from the sameness of many blues recordings, although some fine piano work lifts it above the generic. 'Collibosher' is an affable mid-tempo affair pocked by blasts of brass and wistful interludes. It's the one vocal-less outtake that could conceivably have worked as an instrumental, albeit one not on the same level quality-wise as 'Grow Your Own', etc. 'Call It Something Nice' is the only one of this disputable trio with vocals. It features Lane and Marriott alternating vocals in a track whose lyric advises against perceiving the narrator as a saviour. Musically, it features a keening guitar intro and some more harp. Its major fault is that it feels less like a fully constructed song than a bridge.

Toby suggested that 'Blues Jam' might have been 'The War of the Worlds'. 'Buttermilk Boy' – a rocker about a country boy's desire to get romantic with a city lady – is another song that turned up on Humble Pie's first album, *As Safe as Yesterday Is*. Another surprise on the list is 'Donkey Rides, a Penny a Glass'. That is, it's surprising because 'The Universal', the song that it accompanied on single and which Marriott described as his best, does not appear. The absence of 'Wham Bam Thank You Mam' suggests that that number was still not on tape. Doubtlessly it would have been a contender for inclusion once it was. Other eventual contenders for the album could have been some of the songs that ended up on *First Step*, the 1970 debut album by the Faces, particularly Lane's folky, philosophical, fast-plucking 'Stone', which the composer had demoed in 1968.

Regardless of the putative fourth album, 'The Autumn Stone' b/w 'Wham Bam Thank You Mam' would have been a single in the realms inhabited by the Beatles' 'Hey Jude'/'Revolution' and the Kinks' 'Sunny Afternoon'/'I'm Not Like Everybody Else': stunning not just for sky-high quality but the breadth of ability displayed across two contrasting sides. Unfortunately, that also became a counterfactual. "Andrew didn't like 'The Autumn Stone' as a title or as a song," said Marriott. "They turned it down." Perhaps in one sense Oldham was right. The song's title is nowhere mentioned in its lyric. Additionally, the charms of 'The Autumn Stone' may have been slightly too gossamer for the environs of the singles market, where generally speaking some vigour – even with ballads – is considered needed to attract listener attention and create consumer momentum. 'Wham Bam Thank You Mam', meanwhile, would have been an inappropriate choice for the A-side for almost exactly the opposite reason: heavy metal and hard rock have not been complete strangers to the British hit parade down the years, but have also not exactly been considered friends there. Oldham's decision, though, may have been another nail in the coffin for the Small Faces. Even had the single been a flop on the level of 'The Universal', it would surely have been critically well-received. Such a noble-failure scenario might have been enough to quell the growing unrest in Marriott's soul.

Marriott wasn't quite right when he said that the tracks on the abortive 'Autumn Stone' single were the last Small Faces recordings. Perhaps what he meant was the last ones they gave a toss about. The final tracks laid down by one of the finest ensembles of all time were a job-of-work which involved backing the French equivalent of Cliff Richard.

Johnny Hallyday had been famous in France and pretty much nowhere else for a decade. On top of that, the fact that his career pre-dated the Beatles and their musical generation's reinvention of rock gave him a patina of squareness even in his own country. Hallyday, though, loved good rock music. He gave an early break to Jimi Hendrix when he invited him to tour France as a support act in 1966. His overture to the Small Faces to provide the backing on parts of his next album was made when the band had just completed a six-date UK tour in the company of the Who, the Crazy World of Arthur Brown, the Mindbenders and Joe Cocker. It came via Glyn Johns, who had lately been producing for Hallyday. A free trip to Paris involving what Jones recalled as "decent money" sounded to the band like a good idea. In those pre-internet days, there wasn't even the worry of stigma to inhibit the decision: if the news of their hired-hands activity should happen to filter through from foreign climes, it would have only marginally more gravity than rumour.

The resultant album, released in May 1969, was eponymous although is also sometimes known as *Riviere Ouvre Ton Lit* after its opening track. It's difficult to assess its quality simply because its lyrics are in French (and presumably a colloquial French that even foreigners versed in that language wouldn't much understand). The Small Faces appear on three of its tracks, on which the music certainly sounds powerful. Some of it also sounds familiar: 'Amen (Bang Bang)' is clearly Marriott/Lane's 'That Man' with a new, Gallic lyric. 'Réclamation (News Report)' and 'Regarde Pour Moi (What You Will)' would turn up in rewritten form on *As Safe as Yesterday Is*. Although none of the Small Faces' names appear in *Johnny Hallyday*'s credits as either performers or composers, it has been claimed that, courtesy of an honest publisher, the record generated the only Small Faces mechanical songwriting royalties Marriott or Lane ever saw in their lifetimes.

Anyone listening to the above-mentioned trio of tracks will notice mellifluous lead-guitar runs that are clearly beyond the capabilities of Marriott. That Glyn Johns was cognisant of Marriott's limitations on his instrument presumably accounts for the producer's decision to also invite Peter Frampton to the sessions (although Marriott was also quoted as saying, "I took Peter Frampton with me"). Frampton's band the Herd were releasing records written by Tin Pan Alley songsmith Alan Blaikley. He was also a pretty boy, recently voted by *Rave* magazine the 'Big Pop Face of '68'. Yet despite his lightweight aura, Frampton was a real musician's musician, a highly skilled lead player. So highly skilled, in fact, that the sessions seem to have confirmed a feeling on Marriott's part that he just had to be in a band with him. As he was already in a successful recording outfit, this hankering initially took the form of the notion that Frampton should join the Small Faces.

Marriott told Jon Tiven, "Then we would have had a fine lead player. I could have been the rhythm player that I wanted to be." It was a reoccurrence of Marriott's insecurity about his guitar abilities. McLagan says, "Steve was bitching about the fact that he wanted to sing or he wanted to play guitar, he didn't want to have to do both. But he was great at doing both. We were a great little four-piece band." Although Jerry Shirley says Marriott was a "fantastic player," he adds, "He was always insecure about his own guitar playing until late in life, when he really studied."

One can only wonder at the reaction to all this of Jimmy Winston, forced onto an instrument with which he was unfamiliar because of Marriott's insistence on being the group's guitarist, and ultimately forced out of the Small Faces partly because of his inadequacy on said instrument. However, there is the possibility that Marriott – who it can be assumed knew band psychology – was making the suggestion as a pretext. "It's like he protested too much," says McLagan. "Maybe he wanted to write with Pete, I don't know ... He wasn't silly: Pete was the Face of '68 and Steve was the Face of '66. A little bit of youth in the band wouldn't have been a bad thing." It should also be noted that Marriott said to Jim Green, "Peter Frampton was very upset with the state of affairs with the Herd; they'd killed themselves with bum records. He wanted to leave but didn't know how to, and could he join the Small Faces? I thought, 'Yeah, it'd be great.'" This suggestion that it was Frampton's idea doesn't tally with the account Frampton gave in his 2020 autobiography, although he did make clear that admiration was mutual. Stating that when he first saw Marriott with the Small Faces on *Ready Steady Go!* his immediate reaction was "I want to play guitar with him," Frampton revealed that his feelings about the Hallyday sessions were, "I recorded with the Small Faces and became part of the band for a week. And this is my dream come true." However, later on in the same text he seemed to have only vague intimations of the reasons for Marriott's exit from the Small Faces, saying, "I think Steve had wanted me to join the band, but they didn't want it, so he left – I guess after they had negated his idea, he wasn't enjoying it anymore."

Whether it was Frampton or Marriott who came up with the idea of Frampton joining their ranks, the other Small Faces were unanimously opposed. "No way," McLagan recalls their reaction. "Why fuck with something that's already perfect? As a band, we said no." In addition to that stance – which indeed might be posited as "There are but four Small Faces" – was a separate issue. "Pete's a lovely guy but he didn't have the fire like Marriott," McLagan asserts. "He wouldn't have been right for the band. It would have been such a softer sort of band." Although Jones says, "Personally I loved Peter Frampton's playing, I liked him as a lead guitarist, so it would have been okay by me," he also suggests that a fundamental problem would have inevitably arisen: "You've got two frontmen there," a situation he describes as a "recipe for disaster." Marriott saw it somewhat differently. He later explained to Green, "I asked the band and they didn't want him in. I think that's when I thought, 'Sod it! What am I doing? I've got to do something else myself.' Frampton's unhappiness made me feel I had to get out of the depressive rut I was getting into."

As far as Glyn Johns is concerned, the Small Faces broke up during the Hallyday sessions. He told Mojo's Wayne Pernu that at the Hallyday dates, "They had a huge argument, an enormous falling out. That was it." He could be right. On the last day of 1968, Marriott formally gave his notice to the Small Faces when the band played at London's Alexandra Palace on the night of their return from Paris.

The event was billed as a Giant New Year's Eve Gala Pop & Blues Party. Sharing the bill were Joe Cocker, John Mayall's Bluesbreakers, Amen Corner, the Bonzo Dog Doo-Dah Band, Free and an assortment of lesser-knowns. "The music was not going well in there," recalls Jenny Rylance of the 'Ally Pally' event. "The crowd was very noisy. Still some screaming, believe it or

had Shirley ready to abandon the project: "I assumed nothing was happening. But then all hell broke loose on New Year's Eve."

Rylance discussed Marriott's dramatic decision with him, but only briefly. "The most I felt I could say was – because if he felt it that profoundly – 'Are you sure?' I think by then he was already on the phone to Peter." Some people, like Jones, are a bit suspicious about how quickly Marriott was in touch with Frampton, and how swiftly he was absorbed into the ranks of the latter's musical project, a matter not of days but hours. "Maybe it was [in] his head, but he certainly hadn't said anything to me about it," Rylance says. "Peter and [girlfriend] Mary would come over and visit sometimes. But I honestly don't know. It does seem odd in retrospect, when you look at the timescale of what happened." Despite what occurred next, Rylance says that Marriott and Frampton were no Marriott/Lane in the friendship stakes. "They weren't as close. They got on well, but they were different sorts of people."

It was the Ally Pally gig that saw the final two pieces of the Humble Pie jigsaw slot into place. Spooky Tooth's Greg Ridley, who was recruited on bass, "just happened to be playing the gig," Shirley explains. "Steve knew him, loved his bass playing and said, ''ere, I've got this idea. I've left the band.' I don't know how he did all this, because you didn't have mobile phones back then, but he'd managed to call Peter and me, touched base with us, and he'd grabbed Greg at the back, because he said to me *and* Peter, 'I've got the perfect bass player.' All New Year's Eve." Some of Marriott's grand plans seem to have been marshalled from a public callbox. That evening Frampton was at Glyn Johns' home listening to the not-yet-released debut LP of Led Zeppelin, which Johns had engineered, when Marriott – somehow cognisant of his whereabouts – rang and said, "Hey, mate, I've just done me last gig with the Small Faces. Can I join your band? ... I just walked off the stage—that's it. And Greg Ridley's ready to leave Spooky Tooth...'" Says Shirley, "Steve was capable of thinking on his feet very quickly. No plans had been made. There was no prior knowledge about this. Greg knew nothing of it, Peter knew nothing of it and I knew nothing of it."

The sickest irony of the whole saga was yet to unfold. "A few days later I get a call from Ronnie Lane – awful feeling," Frampton told Max Bell in 2018. "Am I interested in joining the Small Faces because Steve's left! I said, 'You've left it a little bit late, Ronnie.' He wasn't too pleased when he found out why." Had the Small Faces initially accepted Marriott's proposal that Frampton join, of course, Marriott might never have left.

Before Marriott, Frampton, Ridley and Shirley could embark on their new musical venture, though, the Small Faces were compelled to execute a coda to their career. The two estranged factions of the soon-to-be-defunct band didn't even have the consolation of being able to not see each other because, notes McLagan, "We had obligations." He recalls these as including a tour of Germany and some British dates. In any event, honouring the existing contracts would be beneficial in one way, as the band members desperately needed money. McLagan, who by now had moved into his wife's mother's Kensal Green council house, says, "I took over as manager at that point." His assumption of management duties was down to more financial woes. "We had an accountant who ripped us off." When told by their accountant that for efficiency's sake the four should sign a stack of blank cheques, they had no reason to be suspicious up until the point where he shortly disappeared off the face of the earth. This added a tense layer of paranoia to the overarching glumness. There may be differing opinions about why the Small Faces were skint, but from their point of view the accountant was just another in a long line. "We had been ripped off by every fucker," says McLagan. "I wouldn't even give our road crew a float. I'd say, 'You wanna buy guitar strings, you pay for 'em. Hand me the receipt and I'll give you the cash.'" McLagan recalled that one morning at his address two "suits" tried to serve some papers on him. He assumed they were bailiffs working for Immediate because they had successfully served writs on the band at a gig in Scotland shortly before. (McLagan didn't explain what the writs were for.) Once he'd emptied a pot of urine on the visitors' heads, McLagan never saw them again.

The Small Faces were still big box-office even in their death throes. A January 1969 list of clients of the Commercial Entertainments agency in London reveals them to command among the highest prices on the roster, their £450 UK performance fee (approximately £7,500 in today's money) topping those of the likes of Joe Cocker, Jethro Tull and the Moody Blues. Only Fleetwood Mac could obtain more (£500). Note, though, that this isn't even half of the £1,000 a night McLagan (to repeat, then the manager) later claimed they regularly earned well before this point. Regardless of remuneration level, emotionally the tour was never going to match up even to something so recent as their enjoyable September '68 UK jaunt with Canned Heat and Tim Rose. "We were making decent money, but the fun had gone out if it," says McLagan. "We were just finishing up ... It was all over. It was horrible. When you're a pop star and haven't ever been on a bus in four years ..."

McLagan claimed that the last-ever Sixties Small Faces gig was in Devizes. It would indeed have been poignant-cum-pathetic if the career of a great and innovative band had stuttered to an end in a Wiltshire market town. However, that gig was in late February '69 and there was an equally incongruous and unglamourous sojourn to the Channel Islands that followed that. The 15 March 1969 edition of the *NME* reported, "The Small Faces bowed out of the pop scene on Saturday, March 8, as the last notes of 'Tin Soldier' faded away in the Springfield Theatre, Jersey." The paper reported that following their performance McLagan said, "This was definitely our final show." Although the keyboardist offered the conciliatory comment, "Really we're very glad this has happened, the group has done everything it can possibly do," his true feelings leaked through in another quote: "We're ... looking for a new singer–guitarist. But not as a replacement for Steve ... We will be a group now and not a backing group for a lead singer as we have been in the past!"

Ronnie Wood stated in his autobiography that he had thought Ogdens' an "amazing album" and that he and friend and colleague in the Jeff Beck Group Rod Stewart would listen to it all the time. The news of Marriott's departure from the band was therefore a "shock" that "made no sense" to him. Concluded Wood, "I can't imagine why he did that, except perhaps that's when he started to lose it." Quite remarkably for an outsider, he seems to have somewhat hit the nail on the head about what was going on in the Small Faces' camp. Many have tried to fathom how the Small Faces unravelled so quickly. In doing so, they seem to make the mistake of assuming that the motives of the member who caused their split were coherent.

Pete Townshend even seems to think drugs and/or depression were involved. Asked if he saw the Small Faces split coming, he says, "Fuck, no." However, he appends, "I got a sense that Steve was in trouble. I just felt that Steve was the one that needed some assistance, some guidance, and I get the feeling that maybe if I'd have been Steve's friend, and not Ronnie's friend, that I might have been able to see it coming and have been of some help." He mentions an occasion he thinks occurred in early 1968 when he visited Marriott's Essex abode. As he listened to records with him, he got the definite impression that "something major had happened." He explains, "He'd definitely lost his mojo. I remember coming away feeling really worried about Steve. My concern would have been that he'd been using heroin. He was nodding off. It felt to me like he was on the verge of it. And he was very, very, very depressed." He adds, "They went on to do quite a bit more work after that, so it may just have been a bad week."

Even if we dismiss Townshend's ponderings as a red herring, it doesn't mean that Marriott's true reasons were the product of a sound mind. "It's not really a very rational thing to do to walk off stage when you've just had a hit album," says Rylance. "I can't explain it myself." "It wasn't rational," Jones says of Marriott's desire to leave the group. He says that Marriott's issues were "a melee of things which built up into a boiling point." Although Jones acknowledges his colleague had issues such as dissatisfaction with Immediate, the difficulty of following up *Ogdens'* and a teenybopper image that the band felt powerless to slough off, he also says, "We were all concerned, but it obviously affected Steve far more." McLagan, asked if he can identify a reason for Marriott wanting to leave, says, "No, I honestly can't. It's his to know and ours to wonder." Marriott seemed to say as much himself to John Pidgeon. Just consider these extracts from a babbling rationale he gave him about his reaction to the failure of 'The Universal' and the part it played in his decision to quit: "I just went apart in my head. I just thought, 'I'm obviously going somewhere else, but I don't know what I want' ... I was a coward: I was very scared of what I was doing because I believed in it and yet there wasn't any trust in what I was doing, so I had to bale out ... I remember Mac saying, 'Do you have to leave? Do you have to do this?' and I said, 'Yeah, I have to leave,' and he asked why and ... I really couldn't explain why I had to leave. I just didn't believe in myself anymore. When you don't believe in yourself it's the worst thing that can happen, and I didn't, so I had to prove myself to myself."

Townshend thinks that one of the problems was that Marriott's personality hadn't been formed before he became famous. "He started very young," he observes. "He was a pre-teen performer. You see it these days with Britney Spears and Miley Cyrus and various other people that [have] been in showbiz since they were young. I think that was one of Steve's difficulties. I don't think he had his own world. I'd benefitted really greatly from the people around me in art college. It did help me at the time when the Who were struggling to find its *Tommy*, if you like, that I had this circle around me of smart, intellectual, cool people. It did feel to me like when I went first to meet the band, they were all living together like boy scouts. I think they only had each other. This may be why Ronnie Lane latched onto me. I suppose what I'm saying is that Stevie had great ambitions, and I'm not quite sure how focused they were or who supported him in it."

Marriott was not just young – he had only just turned 22 – but inordinately mercurial, impulsive and insecure, not the recipe for reasoned thought processes and decision-making, notwithstanding the fact that he was intelligent enough to be a bookworm. "Sitting down and talking through the tensions and working them out – that wasn't Steve's style," Shirley says. "He just, as was typical of Steve, threw a wobbler that night and no one talked him out of it. And there was no talking him out of it … At that particular time in his life, he didn't back down."

On top of that is the capacity of any human being for self-deception about their own motivations. McLagan gives a hint of his belief in Marriott's aptitude for the latter when he notes of his ex-colleague, "He had it all sewn up when I saw him again. He said he didn't want to drag us down and all that, but I don't think that's the truth. It's what he found convenient to say. It's like him saying, 'My guitar playing wasn't good enough.'"

Speaking to Keith Altham in *Rave* a couple of months after the final split, Marriott came out with an interestingly ambiguous comment: "I'm not a super-musician or anything like that, but I know I can do some better things with our new group. I do a little bit of everything – singing, composing, entertaining and playing. That enables me to get together a final product sometime, which with the help of better musicians I can improve upon." This instantly raised the question in some people's minds: did he mean better musicians than him or better than the Small Faces? It's presumably this quote to which Kenney Jones was referring when he later said, "I'll always remember reading, on the front page of the papers, 'Steve Marriott quits the Small Faces to play with better musicians,' which still annoys me to this day because we were great musicians." Asked if Marriott respected the other Small Faces' musical abilities, Rylance unhesitatingly says, "Yes, he did. Absolutely." Moreover, putting down his ex-colleagues on that score would be absurd – there were few better musicians around than Jones and McLagan, and as a matter of fact

Marriott was the least technically accomplished on his instrument in the band. It may all have been a misunderstanding caused by Marriott's clumsy phrasing or Altham's inexact reportage or both: no other comments from Marriott that could be viewed as putdowns of his Small Faces colleagues' musical abilities have come to light.

In any case, however he meant it, this was not the standard reason Marriott gave for leaving. If indeed there could be said to be a standard reason: his explanations down the years were several and varied.

In that same Altham interview, the main misgiving Marriott expressed about being a Small Face was the way it turned him from a musician into a "ten by eight glossy teen scream of the year." He is backed up a little by Altham, who has noted how refreshing Marriott found it in September '68 to tour Scotland with Alexis Korner and for the first time in several years play to an audience who were there simply to listen. Rylance accompanied Marriott on the trip. "They were like our auntie and uncle really," she says of the man she calls "'lexis" and his wife Roberta. Korner was not just an uncle figure, but the type of artist whose audience contained zero screaming girls. "That really appealed to him," says Rylance, who states that Marriott was past the point of finding the knowledge that he inspired ecstasy to be flattering. "You realise that it's not even personal. They'd probably scream at anybody that had a hit record at the time. And you want to be focusing on the music."

Marriott also complained to Altham of the obligation to perform past hits, some of which he would have preferred to forget. "We weren't playing for ourselves anymore," he said. He stated something broadly similar to Jon Tiven two years later, claiming that the Small Faces had been stagnating: "The music, the feel, the whole thing was that of a band that had been together too long. We'd been on magazine covers too long." To Dave Thompson in 1982, he complained of "crashing about on stage and putting up with the screaming, and it was horrible. Andrew was losing interest in Immediate, so he didn't give us any pointers; all we had was this awful formula." He told Jim Green in '81, "I thought, 'Well, if there's a time to leave, it must be now, 'cos it's on a high' — rather than waiting for a low and splitting up because we hated one another ... Whatever you read in print, it was in fact a case of, 'Marriott was scared.'" Yet Marriott even gave Green a different reason in the same interview: "I couldn't see how we could follow *Ogdens'*. It was a worldwide hit that wasn't really a true picture of us live." Marriott claimed that the split was good for *Ogdens'* legacy. "It made perfect sense to knock it on the head after that. I think it was the best thing that could've happened. It left a nice taste in the mouth, because that album was the last legitimate album that we made ... And I'm sure we wouldn't be sitting here talking about it, like we are now, if we'd gone on to try and better it." To be fair, Jones also expresses the last thought, saying, "It was like, 'How do you top this?'"

After the split, McLagan was also prepared to admit that their image problems may have been insurmountable. "We fought to get a mod image ... and it worked," he said. "But eventually it worked back on us when we were trying to be ourselves." Much later, McLagan told this author, "I think we had run our course … We were glad to see him go at that point. It's like in a marriage. If your wife says, 'I don't love you anymore,' you don't want to be with them."

"I think it was an incremental disillusionment," says Rylance of Marriott. "He was not happy for quite a long time. Nor was Ronnie. It wasn't an overnight thing. [He] didn't like who he was in that context and didn't want to be the frontman. And he and Ronnie were not getting on in the end." The latter is certainly something on which she and Lane's wife agree.

Some arguments between Marriott and Lane were rooted in the strapped finances of the Small Faces. Rylance: "That obviously didn't help. That would be a major pressure. He and Ronnie bickered about who wrote what at that point and who was getting more, probably because we were broke." "That was an element," says Hunt. "It was painful because they didn't agree anymore." "The main thing was the music," Rylance says of Marriott. "He wanted to be in a band that played the sort of music he wanted to play … But also, there was something possibly quite self-destructive about Steve."

For Shirley, the multitudinous reasons/issues/problems that Marriott gave for wanting to leave are not contradictory but simply part of a continuum. "They'd all happened to him in quick succession and they devasted him," he says. He also emphasises a couple of issues that don't usually get focused on. One is that Marriott's bandmates were increasingly unimpressed with his attitude. "He had a bad habit of screaming at the band on stage," he notes. "I used to watch it as a fan and think, 'That's not good.'" Shirley opines, "At that time, he was capable of being as close to impossible as anyone I've ever seen in this business. 'Overwhelming' was the word that was often used. They were all exhausted from it. They'd had to put up with hissy-fits and his freaking-out." He notes that there was another side to this coin. "Steve was noticing that when you fly off the handle at your bandmates like that time and time again, if they can't flat-out come back at you for fear of you pissing off, they start to grumble behind your back. It's human nature … There was a lot of Chinese whispers going on. They would be making fun of Steve behind his back. He wasn't stupid. He got frustrated by some of that." Another issue is one to which Shirley has alluded previously in this text: that Jones, Lane and McLagan were increasingly unimpressed with Marriott's musical ideas. Marriott, he says, was "wanting to go in a certain direction that they were putting a damper on." He elaborates, "They'd run out of ideas that they collectively agreed upon … He wanted to get tougher … 'Wham Bam Thank You Mam' was something that Steve was very proud of, but it was described by one of them as being a bit heavy or something … They had lost their overall direction … They were at each other's throat. They didn't want to do what he wanted to do, and that was always trouble in Steve-world."

"Steve always had a tremendous ego and it was inevitable that if he couldn't get his own way, then he'd walk out," says Keith Altham. "He certainly had an eye on the American market and he didn't think the Small Faces were going to crack it. I think that once *Ogdens'* didn't make it in the States, that was their last throw of the dice." Altham's insight into Marriott's mentality at the time derives partly from his subsequent experiences acting as PR agent for Humble Pie. He seems to feel that Marriott did indeed hanker for a higher class of muso. Of 'Wham Bam Thank You Mam', he says, "There was a kind of anger associated with doing stuff like that with him. It was a kind of desperation, almost. I think he wanted to extend the musical capabilities of the band with some superior musicians, as he felt, and he felt that the Small Faces had come to the end of their run. He felt that they weren't musicians of the nature that would enable them to progress in the direction to which rock music was heading in America. That's a market that he saw as being the most lucrative and the most in tune with his own ideas. He also wanted to extend himself as a musician and he didn't feel extended within the Small Faces ... Bands were trying to do things that were more progressively challenging, and he saw that as the way to go and he thought the Small Faces were too poppy ... There was always a certain musical respect [from the public] for the Small Faces, but it was a much more pop-music direction. Steve was growing out of it faster perhaps than the others were and I think he wanted to hit that market while it was still available to them and the only way he could see of doing that was to form a group of like-minded people or people that he felt he could control."

Shirley does state, "Steve did call the shot right. At that moment, they had blown their lot. They had done this remarkable three-and-a-half, four-year stint that culminated with that wonderful record. They'd run out of ideas." Even so, he says, "I'm astonished that they broke up so quickly, and that I was right there when it happened." Although he benefitted from the split, he insists, "The last thing in the world I personally wanted to see happen was the Small Faces to break up. It was such a weird position to be put into, especially at my age. I was fucking sixteen. Watching Steve and Ronnie's remarkable relationship collapse right in front of me and these are heroes of mine ... It was just very, very strange and brilliant all at the same time."

In the end, one should never forget how young Marriott was, and not just in the chronological sense but in the sense of lack of breadth of life experience in his cossetted profession. In 1977 he told Pete Silverton, "I had to leave before my nut went. I dunno. It was just growing up, I suppose."

Although she remained professionally loyal to the Small Faces to the end, their split may well have come as a relief to Pauline Corcoran.

"She said that while they were at Immediate, the fanbase dropped quite dramatically," says Val Williams. "Because they weren't touring so much, and then they changed their musical direction ... It switched from the screaming girls ... There might have [been] a lot more people liked that type of music, but they don't necessarily want to join a fan club." Williams could be said to be a microcosm of the band's fanbase. "I'd lost interest when they did the

Ogdens' thing," she admits. Although she says, "Now, as an adult, I've found a new appreciation for that sort of music," she says the reaction of her younger self was that "it was a bit too hippified, it was a bit out-there." Says Pete Townshend, "The thing about the Small Faces [was] that all four of them conformed to the mod look of the day and therefore maybe it explains why they were a bit short-lived. The Small Faces were so identified with the mod movement that as the movement started to fade, it caused tremendous difficulties." Whatever the reason, the under-employed Corcoran found her job disappearing from under her.

There was another problem. It's unclear whether or not Immediate ever picked up the tab for the Small Faces fan club, but it is indubitably true that when Corcoran started working from home the band formally became her employers. The group's pockets, though, were not deep. "She told me sometimes they would pay and sometimes they wouldn't," says Williams. "She said to Steve, 'I can't continue to do this. I've got to earn a living.' Her mum was nagging her by this time. She was living with her mum and two brothers. I think her mum wanted her to go out and get a proper job again. Steve understood, but obviously they weren't getting that much money. They paid her when they could."

The news of the Small Faces' rupture revealed Arden's human side once more. Says Williams, "He phoned Pauline up and said, 'You're going to be without a job. Would you like to run the fan club for Amen Corner?' So that's what she did."

She also married their drummer. She and Dave Neal – who would also drum for Suzi Quatro – had two children, although later separated. She lost touch with both Williams and the members of the Small Faces, although years later the two women reconnected with each other and Kenney Jones and Ian McLagan. Corcoran went on to work in hospitality before retiring. She passed away in 2016 following a short illness. Williams – these days Val Weedon - got married in 1969 and had two children. She returned to college and graduated in 1987, going on to do a Periodical Journalism course and ultimately becoming a freelance journalist in 1990. A noisy neighbour motivated her to start the Right to Peace and Quiet campaign, whose patron was Spike Milligan. Five years of media interviews and lobbying of politicians for improvements to the law culminated in 1997 in her being awarded the MBE.

With possibly their biggest cash cow now history, Immediate Records set about figuring out how to wring some last drops of profit out of the Small Faces.

Their first expedient was a double A-sided single released on 7 March 1969, the very day before the band's final gig. The songs involved were 'Afterglow' and 'Wham Bam Thank You Mam'. It was obvious that the first track being listed as 'Afterglow of Your Love' was deliberate, and embarrassingly clear that the second track being billed as 'Wham Bam Thank You Man' was accidental. It wasn't just the title of the *Ogdens'* cut that had been changed. The mock jazz–blues acoustic intro had been excised. This was arguably an improvement, as the track now started with an explosive swirl of instrumentation. Although it had lost some matter at the top, the track had gained some material at the back end, it now boasting a blazing fade-out that had originally been clipped on *Ogdens'* to enable the segue into 'Long Agos and Worlds Apart'. The recording may also have been sped up a fraction. The fact that the single was mono added another element of unfamiliarity for some. Whatever the philistine motives and methodology, one can't help but feel that this is a more powerful iteration of the song than the standard one. It also to some extent *became* the standard one, as the single version began turning up on Small Faces greatest-hits packages.

An exploitative, fag-end release though it may have been there was no getting around the fact that the pairing of the songs made for a cracking record. However, it was just as unauthorised as 'Patterns' had been and the disintegrating Small Faces were even less interested in promoting it than they had been that Decca 45. Even so, a combination of artistic excellence and public sorrow over the loss of the band caused it to make the UK top 40, it climbing to no.36.

In November 1969, the exploitative final single was followed by an exploitative posthumous album. Oldham may not have liked 'The Autumn Stone' for the title of a single but he now decided to use it for an LP. *The Autumn Stone* was a double album which featured three live tracks from the Newcastle City Hall recordings ('Rollin' Over', 'If I Were A Carpenter' and 'Every Little Bit Hurts'), previously unreleased studio material ('The Autumn Stone', 'Collibosher', 'Red Balloon', 'Call It Something Nice' and 'Wide Eyed Girl On The Wall'), every authorised Decca and Immediate single A-side except 'I've Got Mine', both sides of the 'Afterglow of Your Love'/'Wham Bam Thank You Mam' single (the latter track now spelt right), and one B-side ('Just Passing'). If the sequencing had a logic, it wasn't apparent. The collection was housed in a sleeve whose cover design was simply Mankowitz's four cracked-lens photos from inside *Ogdens'* slapped into a leaf pattern presumably meant to allude to the title season. The back cover featured an outtake from the same photographer's blurred-picture photo session that had resulted in the 'Tin Soldier' picture bag.

It was a bizarre piece of product on several levels. The live tracks were mastered at the wrong speed, leading many purchasers to jump up to try to see what was slowing down their turntable. The inclusion of 'Just Passing' was seemingly random. Why this fleeting cut in preference to any other B-side, or indeed to the A-side of the 'I've Got Mine' single? Although the public wouldn't have known this at the time, the selection of the unreleased studio material was lazy. Why the exclusion of an exquisite finished master like 'Don't Burst My Bubble' instead of meaningless backing tracks? The set was also parsimonious: at 66 minutes in length, it could have easily accommodated another fifteen minutes' worth of material (up to around five songs). In mitigation, though, the album was sold for the price of a single LP.

The band were even less interested in promoting this album than its precursor single, particularly – it must be assumed – Marriott, whose new band had already released its first album. *The Autumn Stone* failed to chart.

Despite its ragbag and shoddy nature, though, the album is surprisingly well thought-of. As with its precursor single, there is no denying that it's a thoroughly pleasant listen. Who could resist an almost complete collection of the 45s of one of the greatest hit merchants of the decade, even if they were both arbitrarily shuffled and mixed in with unreleased material? Moreover, although the unreleased material was of varying quality, it was clear that some of it was up to the high standards of the Small Faces' best work. Additionally, the album was, up to a point, comprehensive. Courtesy of Immediate taking the trouble to licence material, it was the first Small Faces compilation to feature selections from both the Decca and Immediate years, and for many decades would remain one of the few examples of such. Simon Frith described the album as "very enjoyable indeed" in his review in the prestigious *Rolling Stone*. The LP was only available in the US on import, but that was beside the point as he was clearly using the article to provide Americans an introduction to the Small Faces. Another UK journalist writing another primer to the band for Americans – Pete Silverton in *Trouser Press* in 1977 – described *The Autumn Stone* as "almost certainly the best Small Faces album."

Although the rounding up of all those A-sides was useful for those not in possession of some or all of the original singles, there were some British Small Faces fans who did own the entirety of the previously released stuff. If those people were averse to paying twice for these tracks in order to avail themselves of new material, they could opt, if they could find it, for a Continental release called *In Memoriam*. This May 1969 album was blocked in the UK by the band, partly because they objected to a title that suggested they were all deceased. Its second side featured the five previously unavailable studio tracks and its first side the three live cuts, plus the bonus of live versions of 'All or Nothing' and 'Tin Soldier'.[6] The cover design also evinced more thought than the UK counterpart, including a mystical-looking wino on the front rumoured to be a heavily made-up Oldham.

Whatever their qualities, The Autumn Stone and In Memoriam were never going to constitute consolation to Small Faces fans for the notion that they

---

[6]   The screams of Small Faces concertgoers were hived off to a separate first-side track titled 'Small Faces Live', a trick Oldham had pioneered with a Rolling Stones in-concert EP. In that instance, the track had been credited to 'Nanker, Phelge', the attribution for collective Stones compositions. In this case, the recipient of the publishing royalties was 'Jimmy Avakak'.

could have lasted several more years and released much more great music. They might even have endured for several decades à la peers like the Rolling Stones, the Who, the Kinks and the Hollies.

It all makes even less sense for those apprised of rock-group lore. Pete Townshend might have been jealous of the Small Faces' *esprit de corps*, but it was the rancorous ranks of the Who that persevered where the generally harmonious camp of the Small Faces did not. Moreover, it's not widely appreciated that since the late Seventies at the very least the Rolling Stones' camp has not been a happy one and their continued existence is down to Jagger and Richards gritting their teeth to endure each other's company long enough to make new studio albums and undergo tours, with them maintaining a careful distance when not required to be in each other's vicinity. "I do have a certain amount of envy for the Who and the Stones just because they carried on," says McLagan, who toured with the Stones. "We could have done some great things. We did do some good stuff, but it might have developed, and it might have been really, really great. Look at the Grateful Dead, for example. I'm not a fan, but whatever arguments they might have had they just sort of went, 'Well okay' and carried on. A band is like the universe: constantly exploding. Too much time spent together. You can't help but want to do something that nobody else wants to, so you have to go off, either make a solo album or you leave the group. I like the idea of a band like the Stones who just get on with it." Jones, who also acquired a close knowledge of the dynamics and compromises of a long-lasting band, in his case by becoming a member of the Who, says, "That low ebb, if we could've gotten over it like many bands that stay together like the Who and the Stones and the Hollies and various other bands... They're all still together and I'm really jealous, I'm really envious that we didn't do it and I'm very angry that we didn't do it because we had so much more to offer ... They had more of a positive, powerful management. They all stuck together and overcome their problems. We were a little younger and a little bit more impatient and a little more frustrated."

Jones and McLagan also concur that touring the States might have made the crucial difference. "Everyone kept hearing about everybody else like the Who, who cracked America, and great stories, and there we were with the teenybopper image not achieving anything," says Jones. McLagan: "We'd been doing England and Germany constantly for four years or so, so it would have been a breath of fresh air – a kick up the bum – to go to America and seen some other bands and play against some other bands."

For Jones, the knife was twisted in the wound when he heard the first offerings from Marriott's new musical venture. He acidly notes, "Humble Pie, when they started, I kept thinking, 'Well fuck me, *we* can play like that.'"

6 Wham Bam Thank You Mam

"Ronnie and Mac were so bitter about it," says Jenny Rylance of Marriott's ex-colleagues about the break-up of the Small Faces. "They couldn't even approach each other. I think he spoke to Kenney sometimes. But Kenney was angry as well."

Several years – and a substantial amount of post-Small Faces career success – later, Lane was able to tell Pidgeon, "In retrospect you can look back and say we all knew it was going to happen. No one would look anyone in the eye by that stage, and in actual fact when Steve turned round and quit, apart from the first initial second of total horror, there was a rush of relief afterwards that someone had killed it at last." However, he would seem to have been telescoping events. His initial horror lasted somewhat more than a second and for him the Small Faces split was considerably more traumatic than it was for McLagan and Jones.

Like the latter pair, Lane had lost the band he loved and potentially his livelihood, but on top of that he lost a dear friend. "When he went off to joining Humble Pie, I was staggered," Lane said to the *NME* in 1970. "I felt a huge personal loss because we had been very close … Just after Steve left, I was in a right state." "They were very close and then they fell out horribly, and it was brutal to watch it," recalls Shirley. Intertwined with this is the fact that Lane lost his home and the investment he had ploughed into it.

When Lane and Marriott had been colleagues and friends, residing in a house together had seemed the most natural thing in the world. In the rancorous circumstances of the Small Faces' split, however, continuing to share living space would be somewhat awkward to say the least. After a period that Marriott estimated to be around three months, Lane moved out of Beehive Cottage, no doubt thinking he could put a deposit on another property when the money he had invested in the house was reimbursed. He thought wrong. "When they split up, Steve didn't want to pay Ronnie back any money," says Shirley. "Sadly, it's what really screwed their friendship up. Steve told him,

'Well, seeing as how I wrote most of the hits, I don't really think I owe you anything.' Which is pretty cold … Steve sent him a PRS statement, which tells you which songs were hits and which ones weren't because of how many times they're played on the air. He got a red pen and put it through the songs that were making all the money: 'I wrote this, I wrote this, I wrote this – therefore I don't owe you anything.'" Did Lane not threaten legal action to claim back his investment? "Hippies didn't sue each other." Rylance adds a comment that reveals what may be a point-of-law reason for Lane's inaction over and above countercultural values: "It was on our property. It was in Steve's name." Lane instead opted to air his frustrations with what Shirley terms a "beautiful letter." "He said, 'Dear Steve, waffly whiffle wiffly barse, diddley doo bibbley fucking bollocks fuck bollocks waffley boo, fiddly barr fitchley, boddley fiddly fuck fuck fuck bollock, up your arse, spots on yer bum …' Just waffle, pages of it, and then signed it off by saying, 'Forget it. That's what you're best at. Ronnie.'"

Divorces are complicated and nuanced. An illustration of this is the fact that, despite all the bitterness and recrimination surrounding Marriott's decision to leave, Ian McLagan actively considered working with Marriott and Frampton in their new band. "Pete and I became firm pals and he asked me to go down and join Humble Pie," says McLagan. The Pie were currently rehearsing near Beehive Cottage (not incidentally in the 1862 building, which Jerry Shirley thinks the Small Faces never used either). "I went down there and played with them for a day, but I didn't really enjoy it," says McLagan. He said his lack of enjoyment was partly down to not being impressed by the Pie's musical chemistry. It also seems reasonable to assume that beneath that lay a complex mixture of emotions including festering resentment about Marriott's departure and a conviction that joining him in his new venture would constitute a betrayal of Jones and Lane. His statement above is ambiguous about whether it was his decision to not accept the implied invitation to join the band, but he told John Pidgeon, "I said yes. And Greg Ridley said no." Shirley's recollection is that it was Marriott's idea that McLagan be invited down to play, although adds, "Peter would have been into it, because Peter and Mac got along well." Shirley notes, "We were polite to him, he was polite to us, and then he left and that was the last of it. It was never going to happen because something went on between him and Greg years before that would have prevented it from happening, some personal thing with a girlfriend." McLagan told Andy Neill that Ridley "didn't take to" him because Ridley had "gone out with Sandy years before."

Despite not getting the gig, McLagan found Marriott executing what he interpreted as another attempt at peace-making. McLagan had recently written a song called 'Growing Closer', which Frampton had been helping him demo. To his complete surprise and pleasure, it featured on the UK version of the Pie's debut LP *As Safe as Yesterday Is*. McLagan adds, "Not that I ever got a penny out of it, because I didn't get publishing for some reason."

Someone else who was invited to rehearse with the nascent Pie was Brian Jones, only recently sacked by the Rolling Stones. "He knew Steve," says Shirley. "They got on well. He also knew Peter and Greg. It came out of a phone call that Brian made to Steve asking how things were going and Steve suggesting he came down for a jam the following week. We were all excited about the idea but a little apprehensive too, as Brian's reputation in recent times wasn't the best. However, this was a Rolling Stone we were talking about, so everybody thought it was worth a try." The prospect of the multi-instrumentalist Jones being a fixture of a band that also featured Marriott is enough to make the mouth of any music-lover water. Sadly, Jones never made it down. Shirley: "We heard, a day or two later, possibly the very next day, the tragic news that Brian had gone for a swim and died." Although the entire band was unanimous that Jones should become a permanent member if it worked out, Shirley adds, "Speaking personally, had he lived, I don't think it would have worked because we had such a strong feeling between the four of us."

Asked if it was a frightening period for the Small Faces after Marriott left them, McLagan says, "Oh yeah. We didn't know what we were going to do." Jones, Lane and McLagan found themselves clinging to each other almost in desperation, although only after a hiatus. "When the Small Faces split up, we split up completely," recalls Jones. "We all went our separate ways. As far as we were concerned, we were finished. We were looking for gigs for ourselves somewhere, whatever." But then: "Ronnie Lane, Ian and I got together after a bit and said, 'Well we've got nothing else to do, let's have a little jam, a little play' ... To be honest, we were lost." "We decided that, if we could, we'd stay together because we liked each other," says McLagan. "We liked the way we played." Despite their desperation, the trio retained the fortitude of character to turn down an offer to be Donovan's backing band.

In contrast, Marriott's fortunes almost seemed assured. As soon as he became part of the Humble Pie set-up, the band were a de facto 'supergroup', a neologism recently coined to describe musical ensembles comprised of people whose principal members had already achieved fame in other bands. Perhaps inevitably, Marriott reacted against the grandiose term by choosing for the ensemble the name 'Humble Pie'. It was related to his wish to no longer be a main focus. "And he really didn't," says Jenny Rylance. "He found it too onerous to be this other person. He had to be tough and brittle and manly." However, Keith Altham doesn't buy it. "He let Peter believe that," he says. "I think it suited his purpose in terms of the fact that he had to ring up and ask Peter if he could join the band. He didn't want Peter alienated by the fact that this monster had come in and was going to take over his stage and his direction and everything else. So that was the role he played for a while. Softly softly, catchee monkey ... Steve took over, inevitably, by force of personality."

Supergroup they might have been, but Humble Pie were another Marriott band whose average age was extraordinarily young. Marriott was 22, Frampton nineteen and Shirley seventeen. Greg Ridley was the grizzled veteran of the bunch at 27. However, Marriott was moving between major life stages when most people are just embarking on their first one, and that's not even to mention his unusually eventful childhood.

It's interesting that whatever his previous and indeed subsequent misgivings about Immediate, Marriott via the Pie was prepared to sign a new contract with the label. Paul Banes observes, "We piled a lot of money into the Small Faces and we piled a lot of money into Steve so that he could do what he wanted to do with Humble Pie." The Pie emphatically did not let the grass grow under their feet. Within five months of the Small Faces' formal split, Humble Pie had released their debut album. Within another three months, they had issued their second album, *Town and Country*. In between, they released the standalone single, 'Natural Born Bugie' (on which, significantly, Frampton, Ridley and Marriott alternated vocals). Shirley reveals that it was planned at one point that 'Wham Bam Thank You Mam' would be resurrected to be included in this busy release schedule. "I remember him playing it to me and saying, 'This is our next single.'"

Even then, Marriott was frustrated at what he considered the slow release pace. "We did *As Safe as Yesterday Is* and *Town and Country* before the first was released," Marriott later complained to Green. "Delays, delays — I don't know why." This impatience would seem to be explained by Marriott's genuine and preternatural enthusiasm for the Pie. "I've never been so excited about anything as I am about this group," he told *Melody Maker* in April '69. Shirley, though, thinks the rapid turnover was a mistake. "I always felt that what we should have done was taken the material from both those albums and looked very closely at what was the best and made one album out of them," he says. "Possibly re-record some of it."

Humble Pie found a market, but slowly. Although the chugging 'Natural Born Bugie' was somewhat derivative of Chuck Berry, it was also catchy. It climbed to no.4. in the UK chart in September 1969. It was the band's first and last hit single, but it's probable that Marriott was viewing the Pie as an albums-oriented act. Yet the first LP only made no.32 in the UK and the second failed to chart. *As Safe as Yesterday Is* failed to chart at all Stateside, while *Town and Country* initially failed to obtain an American release.

An interesting post-script to the debate about heavy metal in this text is that *As Safe as Yesterday Is* became quite possibly the first recording to be labelled as such when Mike Saunders said in the 12 November 1970 issue of *Rolling Stone* that it marked Pie out as "a noisy, unmelodic, heavy metal-leaden shit-rock band with the loud and noisy parts beyond doubt."

Much bigger success for the Pie was just around the corner. For many Small Faces fans, though, whatever appeal the group did have was mystifying. Those first two albums seemed to labour heavily but achieve little. The tunes seemed rather vague and shapeless. Moreover, it turned out that Marriott's gritty voice sounded less impressive when not juxtaposed with the Small Faces' contrasting bright pop melodies. On top of that, lyrics like that of 'Buttermilk Boy' showed an unattractive earthiness that the Small Faces had not dealt in. Maybe Marriott's writing would have gone that way in any case – exulting in a new freedom to be sexually frank would be a keynote of the Seventies, and the Small Faces had more reason than most to embrace it after having endured that butter-wouldn't-melt image for so long – but somehow one can't imagine Small Faces songs featuring lines in which a man is urged to lose his country ways to ensure that the object of his affections "lets her knickers down," the sauciness of 'Rene' notwithstanding.

Marriott inadvertently confessed the limitations of Humble Pie when he told Jim Green, "The first Small Faces albums consisted of our going in and doing our stage act, but in the Pie we started going in and creating the stage act — getting the songs down that we wanted in the set, instead of coming out scared: 'Oh shit, how we gonna play that motherfucker?'" It was effectively an admission that the band would never try to record anything particularly adventurous.

While Marriott was engaged in a whirlwind of activity, Jones, Lane and Mc-Lagan were trying to get their bearings. They listlessly but gratefully took up an offer by Ian 'Stu' Stewart, roadie for the Rolling Stones, of the use of the Stones' neglected rehearsal space in Southwark, south-east London. The use was gratis on the understanding that it would be paid for when, and if, they secured a recording contract. There, the trio began a rehearsal process so loose and aimless that, as well as including guitarist Leigh Stephens, it also involved another drummer, Micky Waller, which must have seemed odd and disconcerting to Jones. There was one thing the trio were sure about, though. "We didn't really want a singer," says McLagan. "That was the whole plan."

In the end, it wasn't Stephens who got the axeman vacancy but Ronnie Wood, a sharp-cheeked, dark-eyed man known to all and sundry as 'Woody'. Although currently bassist with the Jeff Beck Group, his preference was for guitar, on which he had a unique crow's-caw sound. McLagan: "We met Woody through Steve, funny enough, at the 'Lazy Sunday' house ... We thought, 'Well this'll be great because Ronnie Wood can sing a little bit, Ronnie Lane can sing and Ian McLagan could sing a little bit.'" However, McLagan also admits that this line of thinking was a bundle of self-deception and wishful thinking. Jones puts it more bluntly: "Ronnie Lane had a great voice [but], after Steve Marriott, I didn't think it was strong enough."

This juncture of the story contains another indication of just how nuanced was the Small Faces' divorce, at least if Jerry Shirley's theory is to be believed. "It was Steve that suggested Ronnie Wood in the first place as his replacement, and he wasn't stupid: he knew that if Ronnie came along, chances were Rod'd come with him," he says. Rod Stewart was currently the lead singer of the Jeff Beck Group but like Wood had issues with what he felt to be the titular guitarist's dictatorial methods. He was also Wood's best mate and as such would sometimes accompany Wood to Bermondsey. Shirley notes of Marriott, "He's left, he's trying to figure out [how] he can help them get themselves back together. He could be a bastard sometimes, but he wasn't the devil incarnate." "I'm not surprised if that's the case," says Rylance of Shirley's suggestion of Marriott's machinations. "He was fundamentally wanting to be a good person." Some credence to Shirley's theory is provided by comments Wood made to Andy Childs of *ZigZag* in September 1974 which suggest that Marriott and Wood were in each other's orbits at this juncture. Wood had been fired (it turned out temporarily) from the Jeff Beck Group at around the same time as the news emerged of the Small Faces' split. "I went to see Ronnie Lane because I thought there's only one other band I would join and that would be the Faces, 'cos Rod and me really dug the Small Faces," said Woody. "I went to see Steve too because I really got on well with Steve and I nearly formed a band with him. But I thought no, Steve's ... going to be alright, but the other three maybe won't. They might split up and I thought that would be a shame. So as they were still together we had some workouts."

For Shirley, this benign Machiavellianism makes the Small Faces' bitterness toward Marriott unreasonable. "They were a young bunch of brothers that had had this fantastic success and out of nowhere he drops them in the shit and I don't blame them one bit for being pissed off," he says. "I do, though, think that once they had steadied their ship and Ronnie's come in and then Rod had come in, they carried on with the bitterness towards Steve way, way longer than was right."

Not that Stewart joining the band that sought to rise from the ashes of the Small Faces was an instantaneous thing. "Rod used to sit on the amps waiting for us to finish and then we'd have a break and go up the pub and have a laugh and we'd come back and play some more and we'd go up the pub again afterwards," recalls Jones. It was obvious, though, that Stewart wasn't hanging around just for the convivial company or the piss-up: he was waiting for a question to be popped. "I kept thinking, 'This is nuts,'" Jones says of a situation of mutual coyness that lasted several weeks. "We had to get real instead of just jamming and going up the pub. He's one of the greatest singers around. So when we went up the pub one time, I said to Rod, 'Do you fancy joining the band?' He said, 'Oh, do you think the others would be alright with that?' I said, 'Yeah, no problem.' And then I got a shock."

In the mid-Sixties Stewart's natty suits and closely-sculpted hair had earned him the sobriquet 'Rod the Mod'. However, the Small Faces were somewhat less interested in the matter of him having once inhabited the same youth cult as they than the fact that the gravel-throated Stewart happened to occupy the same exalted blue-eyed bluesman bracket as Eric Burdon, Chris Farlowe, Stevie Winwood and – yes – Steve Marriott. Nor was Stewart just a great singer. He was a charismatic and unselfconscious frontman, able to command a stage or a TV screen. Yet the fact that they had had their fingers burnt by Marriott prevented the group from seeing what was staring them in their small faces: that they were hugely fortunate to have the option of securing the services of one of the few singers in the country who was Marriott's equal. Jones: "Ronnie and Mac just felt that they didn't really want to compromise things and have another Steve Marriott in the band who would just walk out." Eventually, though, Lane and McLagan had to capitulate to reason. McLagan recalls, "I thought, 'Oh well, fuck it. We need this. We need a front man.'" "They replaced one massive ego with another massive ego," notes Altham of the Marriott–Stewart changeover. "I thought that was extraordinary, really."

Songwriter Ian Samwell may or may not have been the party that first brought the Small Faces to the attention of Don Arden, but it seems indisputable that it was he who aroused the interest of Warner Bros. in the remnants of that band when Immediate indicated they had no interest in issuing any product with which they might come up. Martin Wyatt of Warners has confirmed that Samwell – who was just about to take up a job with the label as a talent scout – sang their praises. Rod Stewart told *Disc & Music Echo* in 1971, "Warner Records didn't want to sign us up – it was only Ian Samwell saying, 'This band's going to be big one day' that did it." Although the Faces were also technically a supergroup, it was a decidedly ersatz one, made up of Small Faces leftovers and blokes estranged from Jeff Beck. Stewart has admitted that an according sense of inferiority afflicted the band in its early days: they were convinced that few members of the public wanted to know about such a sub-par ensemble. Dismal attendances at their early UK gigs seemed to bear out their feelings.

Nonetheless, the band's new manager, Billy Gaff, secured them a quite lucrative advance against royalties. "We got thirty grand, which is a lot of money those days," says Jones, who claims it was he who suggested that Gaff ask for such a large sum. However, the band immediately lost a big chunk of that package. McLagan: "When we got out of Immediate, we had to pay twenty thousand pounds to pay off our contract, which was the same contract as the Arden thing."

Euphoria in the camp was further dampened when they were informed that they were to remain chained to a handle they now had greater cause to resent than they ever had previously. "Ian Ralfini, who was the boss of Warner Brothers, said … 'We want you to be called the Small Faces because that's a well-known name,'" recalls Jones. ""It never crossed any of our minds to call it Small Faces, never in a million years. We said, 'No, we're a completely new band. We want to call ourselves something else' … He said, 'Well, you can't have the money, then.'" The band were not in much of a bargaining position. McLagan: "We had no money to pay off Immediate until we signed with Warners." Desperation for the finance necessary to start a new life made the group cave in, although they did wring a concession. Explains Jones, "We said, 'Okay, the first album we'll let go out as 'Small Faces', thereafter we'll call it the 'Faces'." The diminutive prefix appeared on the cover of their first US album, but not the British iteration – somewhat ironic and illogical considering that the Small Faces had never had any significant success in America. Leaving aside issues regarding preconceptions and brand names, the (eventually) shortened name made more sense considering the normal heights of Stewart and Wood. For those cognisant of the abbreviated way to which the Small Faces had colloquially been referred (admittedly, almost no Americans), it was all not just ironic but immaterial. As with the Small Faces, incidentally, there was never a definite article to the name on record sleeves.

Once Stewart and Wood had disentangled themselves from the Jeff Beck Group, the Faces set to work recording. With what would come to seem perfect symbolism, the band members played on Rod Stewart's first album before the Faces set about assembling their debut LP. The recording careers of the Faces and the solo Stewart were very intertwined even though Stewart had his own loose solo-album band. As well as consistently using Faces personnel in various configurations on his albums, Stewart would use the Faces to collectively mime to his solo singles on TV shows regardless of which of them had played on them. During the Faces' lifetime, Stewart would never play concerts under his own name but only as part of the Faces. However, behind the all-for-one bonhomie, there was no disguising the fact that Stewart cared more about his solo work than he did the Faces' records. This was manifested most obviously in his dispensation of songs. Not only was Stewart as good a singer and as charismatic a stage performer as Marriott, he had in common with the ex-Small Faces guitarist a penchant for writing tender and life-affirming compositions, even if he was never as prolific as Marriott. The Faces didn't often feel the benefit, though: his best songs (often written in collaboration with Wood) ended up on his own albums. "He never admitted it at the time, but it's a hard thing to admit," says McLagan. However, nobody was in any doubt that it was true. "I felt that all the Faces were left with was a bunch of riffs that we had to string into songs," says Jones. "We made some good songs, don't get me wrong, but really there was more to choose from in Rod's repertoire."

Perhaps it's the fact that Jones and McLagan had no idea of his writing powers when they hooked up with Stewart that leads them to evince tolerance on this score. "Look, if I was in a band and I also had a solo deal, obviously I'd save the best stuff for me," says McLagan. "I understand it." "Rod was [always] under pressure to deliver an album and a good one," reasons Jones. The Faces also had the consolation of the fact that Lane and McLagan both wrote.

Despite the crossover of personnel, Stewart's own work sounded very different to Faces product. His solo albums always possessed a distinct folkie and Celtic tinge, courtesy of the frequent use of acoustic guitars and fiddles. As for the Faces, they sounded nothing like anybody expected them to. Their long-playing entrée, *First Step* (March 1970) was mystifyingly hesitant and confused. The focus and tightness of the band that three of the members had recently been part of was nowhere to be seen. To an extent, this problem would never be rectified. It partly came down to work ethic, or lack thereof. Whereas the Small Faces, given the chance, lived in the studio, the Faces couldn't wait to get out of it in order to go down the pub. Consequently, although Faces records improved, the band's sound would always be slightly sloppy and scraggly, a far cry from the vital and sheened Small Faces hallmarks. "It's funny, looking back because it's the same guys really," concedes McLagan. "Woody and Steve played very similar too." He proffers one explanation in saying, "When we formed the Faces, we kind of were eager to not be a pop band anymore. You grow up a little bit. Also, it's hard to write pop songs as you get older. It's really a young person's medium." There would also seem to be a certain element of deliberately distancing themselves from the old sound, which to an extent went hand in hand with an image they had never much cared for. "Small Faces were forever trying to run away from our teenybopper image and that sort of thing and the Itchycoo Parks," says Jones. "Even though they're great tracks, they didn't represent the band. When we got together with Rod and Woody, we had a chance to break free. The same with Marriot when he had a chance to break free with Humble Pie."

The Faces steadily increased their concert attendances by gigging prolifically. Unlike with the Small Faces, their audiences were attentive. The teenagers who had hitherto drowned out concerts had matured into young adults who were prepared to listen. The in-concert prowess of the Faces quite remarkably, and quite quickly, became on a par with that of the Rolling Stones and the Who. "They were a good live band – a good, *fun* live band," says Altham. "They created a good atmosphere on stage." Stewart draped himself in tartan, kicked soccer balls into the crowd and made a trademark of dramatically twirling his lightweight aluminium microphone stand. Collectively, the Faces brought to any venue they played an amiable ambience that was intertwined with their unashamed – even ostentatious – imbibing of alcohol. Within two years of their formation, they were selling out the 20,000-capacity Madison Square Garden. The fact that they were on a plateau far above the one the Small Faces had occupied made some within their ranks form the opinion that the Small Faces had been merely a rehearsal for the Faces. By 1973, Lane was talking of the Small Faces' catalogue like it was juvenilia. "I walked into a store in 'Frisco and they had the lot – embarrassing," he sneered to the *NME*.

The Faces' camp was famously characterised by an *esprit de corps*, but – contrary to what American journalists imagined – it wasn't unique. Had they known more about the Small Faces, they would have understood that a group who genuinely loved each other's company was something the Faces had in common with the Small Faces. Moreover, that camaraderie didn't go as deep as had the precursor band's. It's noticeable how the tone changes in Kenney Jones' autobiography when the narrative moves from the Small Faces to the Faces, with anecdotes of tenderness within the Small Faces' ranks giving way to tales of the quite malicious pranks played on each other by the Faces. It's also worth noting that one respected music journalist claimed that beneath the Faces' onstage bonhomie was an attitude toward their audiences of thinly veiled contempt. Certainly, they thought nothing of taking to the stage an hour or more later than billed.

Stewart's very good second album, *Gasoline Alley*, appeared in June 1970. It contained a track wherein it could be said the Small Faces met the Faces: his rendition of 'My Way of Giving' happens to feature the playing of Jones, Lane and McLagan. Jones' blazing performance trumps his playing on the Small Faces' version. The Faces' own second LP, *Long Player*, appeared the following February and was a clear improvement on *First Step*. Although uneven, it boasted several gems, including the lovable scamp of a song 'Had Me A Real Good Time' and 'Richmond', the latter an example of the sort of effortlessly poignant acoustic numbers with which Ronnie Lane would habitually grace Faces albums. *A Nod's as Good as a Wink... To A Blind Horse*, which followed in November the same year, is the closest the Faces came to a long-playing classic. It's no coincidence that the album marked the first time that the Faces did not produce themselves, them having previously baulked at the cost or because Glyn Johns had turned them down (accounts vary). "Once we got Glyn in, which was Ronnie Lane's idea, things turned around for the Faces," says McLagan. Through Johns' efforts, they now sounded as sleek and streamlined as was possible for such a proudly raggedy-arsed aggregation. The album alternated powerful rock ('Too Bad') with endearing downbeat whimsy ('Debris'). The album's 'Stay With Me' was a *tour de force*, a strutting, frayed-riffed anthem which suggested a band ready to take on the Stones on their own turf, even down to its misogynistic nastiness. It was the Faces' first hit, making no.6 in the UK and reaching the US top 20.

What bliss it was to be alive for a Rod fan that year: Stewart's 1971 solo album was *Every Picture Tells a Story*. It remains one of the greatest albums ever released. Among its highlights is an achingly beautiful version of 'Reason to Believe', written by old favourite of the Small Faces Tim Hardin. The album and its single 'Maggie May' – a co-write by Stewart and one of his regular songwriting partners, Martin Quittenton – topped the UK and US charts simultaneously, making Stewart the first artist in history to achieve this quadruple-whammy. It was quite a way for the been-around-the-block Stewart to finally become a star at the grand old age of 26. "On a plane once he was looking through his fan mail," recalls McLagan. "I took the piss out of him. We'd sort of got over the novelty of having fan mail and it was like a fresh thing for him and he was excited."

Marriott told John Pidgeon of his decision to leave the Small Faces, "I don't think it was a mistake, because everybody benefitted from it in the end." That this wasn't bluster is backed up by Keith Altham. Asked if Steve Marriott ever expressed to him any regret about leaving the Small Faces, the journalist turned Humble Pie PR man unhesitatingly says, "None at all. I think he was absolutely delighted with what he'd got with Humble Pie."

Paul Banes thinks the band constituted the perfect marriage of the professional yearnings of Marriott and Frampton, both of whom felt they had been hampered by their previous outfits. He says, "When they went out as Humble Pie, Steve was playing Dr John, which was a million miles away from *Ogdens'*. Where Peter wanted to go with the Herd was a bit like where Steve wanted to go with the Small Faces and the two sort of matched up." For Banes, Marriott was returning to the blues roots he'd seen back at the Ilford Pally. "Having seen Steve playing 'Hoochie Coochie Man' and everything else, we knew where his music came from." This hardcore element to the Pie's sound was underlined by Marriott's frequent demonstration of the mouth-harp skills that most Small Faces fans were completely unaware he possessed.

It was only once he was in the environs of this new ensemble that Marriott finally consented to take his music to the United States. "I didn't see much fear of flying creep into it when he was with Humble Pie," notes Altham. Rylance: "He knew it had to be done. He wouldn't have not gone somewhere because of the fear of flying." However, getting on planes came with a price. "He got out of it," says Rylance. "He never used to drink much, but he was a drinker in the end. He had to have something."

Banes' memories of the 1969 inaugural American Humble Pie tour verge on the ecstatic. "Steve insisted that I go on the road with them," he recalls. "They were a support act ... I took them from New York all around America on a shoestring. I tell you, when they got on stage in the Fillmore in New York opening for Santana, who'd just come off the back of Woodstock, the people went bananas because they'd been waiting to see Steve Marriott since 'Itchycoo Park'. When he went out on stage [with] an acoustic guitar and sang 'Hallelujah I Love Her So' and a country song, they loved it. They were on, I think, eight dollars a day. We weren't getting paid a lot of money, but we were supporting the biggest acts you could play with at the time. We kicked off with Mountain. From there, Santana. From Santana, Chicago and Chicago, Neil Diamond, who'd just come off a number-one record. The Kinks. The Moody Blues. We landed up in San Francisco for the last major dates, with the Grateful Dead and the Rolling Stones playing down the road in Altamont. They tore the place apart." Banes adds, "There were not a lot of original songs on that first tour but they were dammed good ... That tour opened the door for the live album that broke them. They were huge in America. They did the spadework."

Rylance recollects of the Pie's US tour the following year, "He called me up saying, 'I can't stand it – there's girls sleeping in the corridor. Please will you come over?' because he was sweet like that." However, Rylance acquiescing to his wishes brought about a difficulty. When Rod Stewart had joined Marriott's old band, it had been yet another overlap in the life of the two men that involved Rylance. However, that was not particularly an issue for Marriott, (especially if, as Shirley claims, Marriott had engineered the whole thing). However, when Rylance travelled across the Atlantic, it was to find that songs were being played on the airwaves from Rod Stewart's current album *Gasoline Alley*. "That was difficult," she reflects. "I was told that 'Lady Day' was about me and that's the song that happened to come on the radio. So there was [a] terrible silent atmosphere." It wasn't this, though, that subsequently led to Rylance accompanying Marriott on the numerous US Pie tours only "occasionally" and "not for the whole thing." She explains, "I hated being on the road. And some of the other wives in the band didn't like me for that because if I'd gone they could have gone, but I didn't like being an appendage, sat around in hotel rooms."

"Some of the music they recorded was great, but it was the stage performances that people remember," says Rylance of the Pie. Marriott's mesmeric live presence made logical/inevitable the in-concert album to which Banes refers. *Performance: Rockin' the Fillmore* was a double set released in November 1971, the band's fifth album overall. That two of its inclusions – versions of 'Rollin' Stone' and 'I Walk on Gilded Splinters' – each last an entire vinyl side gives an indication of how quintessentially first-half-of-the-Seventies a band Humble Pie were. Meanwhile, the dominance on the record of Marriott demonstrates how his initial, and apparently sincere, wish to take a back seat to Frampton had dissipated, admittedly largely at the behest of the Pie's new manager Dee Anthony, who felt that Frampton's more fey persona and approach was not likely to fill arenas. Rylance: "When he first joined Dee Anthony, he said, 'I don't want to be the frontman, I want to be part of the band' and Dee Anthony was saying in the end, 'You're the one. You've got to get out there and give blood. That's what this band's about.'" Excited by enthused American audiences, Marriott was by now ready to step up to this responsibility. "When my confidence came back, it came back with an almighty bang," he told Pidgeon. Rylance: "So it ended up it was always his personality and how people perceived him was defeating the objective that he wanted, because he had to become that person again." Of that "tough and brittle and manly" persona, she says, "It sort of took him over. He had to give blood every night on stage, which is why he started doing more and more coke."

Anthony was cut from the same sort of cloth that Don Arden's critics claim he was – only on a far larger, darker scale. Keith Altham says of Anthony, "I was introduced to him quite early on and I said to Steve afterwards, 'You do realise he's probably Mafia, don't you?' He said, 'Yeah, well, better on my side than against me.'" Echoing David Arden's claim about Marriott, Altham adds, "He was one of those guys that liked strong figures around him, whether or not they were borderline criminals." He also says, "You had to be a strong character to take care of Steve Marriott anyway, otherwise he would take *you* over." "He certainly had some connections to the Italian lot in New York," says Rylance of Anthony. "*The Godfather* had just come out. They were all incredibly impressed by that … They were very impressed by Dee when they met him because he was a big, strutting guy … It's like the manager became the father figure."

Although he appears on it, Frampton had left Humble Pie by the time *Performance* was released. He had been a valuable contributor as both songwriter and guitar foil, him and Marriot engaging in impressive lead interplay. However, his increasingly subservient status is illustrated by the fact that the band's eponymous third album (1970) had been the last where he and Marriott were working on equal terms. By the time of the following year's *Rock On*, Marriott's heavier songs were being given, Frampton thought, preferential treatment: Frampton's poppy 'Shine On' was mysteriously overlooked for single release while the hard-riffing 'Stone Cold Fever' was showcased in concert. "He was no longer prepared to share the limelight with anybody," Frampton later said. The disaster that Jones claims would have occurred if Frampton had joined the Small Faces had come to pass in Humble Pie: all had been harmony with Marriott and Frampton before it became obvious that two frontmen meant two competing musical visions.

One of the Faces' shows in 1972 was at the Great Western Festival in Bardney, Lincolnshire in May. Also on the bill were the post-Frampton Humble Pie. By this point, the two former constituent factions of the Small Faces had both done spectacularly well for themselves. That very month, Humble Pie scored their highest US album-chart placing when *Smokin'* made no.6 on *Billboard*. *Lost and Found* – a two-fer consisting of *As Safe as Yesterday Is* and *Town and Country* – appeared in the US top 40 that year too. Come the following year, Humble Pie set an attendance record: the 117,000 souls they drew to a Milwaukee fairground was the highest number of paying punters for a single concert yet recorded. Meanwhile, on the Faces' 1972 'Rock'n'Roll Circus' American tour, the band were averaging $75,000 per show (approaching half a million dollars in today's money). Life now looked rosy indeed for Marriott, Lane, McLagan and Jones alike.

There was trouble in paradise, though. First was the dissolution of the Lanes' marriage. "We were all in this Baba group," recalls Hunt. It was a scene centred around Richmond, a leafy district just outside London where Townshend had a house and Lane owned a cottage on the grounds of Ronnie Wood's house the Wick. (The latter was an arrangement strangely similar to the one that had existed with Marriott and Lane at Beehive Cottage.) "It was just a lovely period where we would be in and out of each other's houses along the river," reflects Hunt. Also part of this circle were Mike and Kate McInnerney, with whom she says the Lanes were "really close friends." Mike McInnerney was an artist probably most famous for the Who's *Tommy* album cover. One momentous day, however, Lane abruptly transferred his affections from his wife to Kate. This came as something of a shock to Sue ("Everything was fine"). "He fucking just upped and left," says Townshend. "Katie had been living like a hippie, making nettle stew and listening to Van Morrison while Mike McInnerney did the cover for *Tommy* in the corner. Suddenly she was wearing jewels and high heeled shoes and expensive Coco Chanel outfits. It was just very strange. Katie and Ronnie were completely changed." One could suggest that what Lane had done becomes even more dubious when considering Kenney Jones' claim that he knew better than most the agony of abandonment: in 1966 the bassist tried to kill himself in the Pimlico Small Faces house after being dumped by a girlfriend.

The outsider might aver that Lane's actions constituted him comprehensively failing to live up to his spiritual ideals, but Townshend demurs. "I don't [think] there's a contradiction," he says. "It's not up to me or you or anybody else to make a judgement about whether or not Ronnie Lane was some kind of fucking hypocrite because he followed Meher Baba and then went off with his best friend's wife. That's for Ronnie to sort out with his maker. I don't think Ronnie ever proselytised about Meher Baba, so I don't think we have to forgive him for anything. The Jewish way of looking at this makes some sense to me, which is that we're constantly in conflict as human beings in that we're looking on the one side for some kind of sense of complete being and on the other side we're looking for pleasure and safety. So we're constantly torn. Why people turn to psychiatry, to drugs, to outrageous behaviour, to overspending, to all kinds of things, is not because of anything that's exclusive to one type of business or one type of religious or spiritual following. It's universal to all of us. We just happen to know the stories in detail of people who become famous."

Perhaps surprisingly, Hunt also declines to see hypocrisy in Lane. Although she describes Lane leaving her as "completely and utterly a life changer," she also says, "Things aren't that black-and-white." She offers a "karmic" rationale for her non-judgmental stance. "We come in with impressions from past lives and sometimes there are connections between people and things that have to be resolved between those people. When someone does something to someone else that is apparently bad, it might be something that is balancing out some other event that happened in past lives between those two people." Townshend: "Meher Baba's view of that would be that the karma that Ronnie and Katie were living out could well have been settling karmic debts that had been created by Sue and Mike McInnerney against them in their previous life. One just doesn't know." Hunt: "Yes, it was reprehensible. Yes, I was devastated. But it's just part of life experience. Something that I had to go through, he had to go through, she had to go through. Reasons and motivations, accountability – all that is not up to me. It's up to the divine and the balance of people evolving."

In the midst of what might be termed his cruelty, Lane also managed to be caring. "I was a little beside myself and sometimes I asked him if he'd meet with me and he did," Hunt says. "He was kind. He was trying to move on and do his new life. He took care of me. He bought me a flat on the Wandsworth Bridge Road and he bought me a car. That helped me go on with my life."

If Hunt and Mike McInnerney's treatment is the most tragic element of this particular saga, coming not far behind it is the fact that it is all ultimately a story of futility. While Lane and Kate McInnerney had several happy years together, their relationship didn't survive the decade.

There were some fine moments on Ooh La La, the Faces' 1973 album and the first not to feature covers, whether they be on the rock-oriented first side ('Borstal Boys', 'Cindy Incidentally', the latter a UK no.2) or the rustic second side (Lane's 'Glad and Sorry' – replete with exquisitely rippling McLagan piano – and the beautiful, melancholy title track). The album was also infused perhaps more than any other Faces album with that quintessential Faces bonhomie. Nonetheless, it felt insubstantial, and not just because of the paltry thirty minutes playing time. The Faces were becoming a bit predictable: the over-familiar boogie patterns, Wood's fat, slurred electric guitar and McLagan's mechanical tendency to come in on the third or fourth bar were now less trademark, more cliché. In *Melody Maker* shortly after the album's release, Stewart did his bit for promotion by declaring it a "stinking, rotten album."

In May 1973, Lane and Stewart had a fistfight backstage at a Rhode Island gig. Just over a week later, Lane announced he was leaving the group. Hunt avers that Lane was never as happy in the Faces as he had been in the Small Faces. "Ronnie was always discontented," she says. "He wasn't ever settled down. It wasn't the same as working with Steve. He and Rod got on fine – very talented guy, beautiful voice and they did some wonderful things together – but Ronnie was always looking to go on his own path to do his kind of music. Which he did."

"He had a chip on his shoulder about Rod's grandiosity," is Townshend's explanation for Lane's departure. "What then happened – so it's kind of evidence, isn't it? – Rod moved to California and started to play in Las Vegas once a week. It's a very different world from the one that he started at, which was being in a small R&B band playing the Scene Club with Long John Baldry. He was a really authentic blues man, and also a mod face. He became like the guy who teeny girls had posters of on their walls. He was a heartthrob."

Lane's initial apprehension about recruiting a lead singer who might turn out to be a diva had, from his point of view, been justified. McLagan was increasingly feeling the same way. Asked if, when Stewart was acting up, he experienced Marriott-related déjà vu, the keyboardist says, "Yeah. 'ere we go again." He points out that there was an additional element with Stewart: "He was having the big success."

Townshend also says, "It must have been difficult for them both to get used to the fact that Ronnie's role was he was the bass player in the band. He had a bit of talent as a songwriter." "Ronnie Lane had to leave because all the songs he was writing, he could never do them live because we had a singer," confirms McLagan. "It was rotten for Ronnie." In another scenario that recalled the Small Faces, Lane fulfilled the remaining Faces live commitments before making his final exit (in this case in early June). He was soon releasing often lovely records of his own with his band Slim Chance (which name had been a contender for that of the Faces in the beginning).

Tetsu Yamauchi, formerly of Free, came in on bass, but there was no replacing the group spirit that gradually seeped from the Faces over the next couple of years. Lane had asked McLagan to bail with him, but McLagan declined. The keyboardist soon had cause to regret his decision: "When Ronnie left, the Faces were just then basically Rod's touring band because he wouldn't record," he laments. "He had a solo career and didn't give a fuck for the Faces." The band would never manage to scrape together another studio album.

They still managed to put out some fine singles. The first came at the end of 1973 in the shape of the uptempo low-life tableau 'Pool Hall Richard', which made the UK top ten. In 1974, despite their internal fissures, the paucity of their product and a declining stage ability that motivated critic Charles Shaar Murray to label them "a painful travesty of their former selves," the Faces worked extensively and lucratively. Moreover, in November came a superb single, 'You Can Make Me Dance Sing or Anything' (whose composition was credited to all five current Faces). For the first time ever, the Faces' sound was widescreen and polished, high production values that only enhanced an already lively and tender piece of soul–pop. The record (a UK no.12) indicated that this new incarnation of the Faces most definitely had a future, yet it would prove to be the final Faces release.

The Faces had for a long time all lived close together but April 1975 saw Stewart become a tax exile in the US and a man who could only be reached by his colleagues via telephone calls that – courtesy of the primitive communications technology of the time – took an hour to set up. At the same time, he jettisoned his usual solo-album collaborators, both musicians and songwriters. Ronnie Wood, though, was not exactly inconsolable. While Stewart was preparing what would become the LP *Atlantic Crossing*, Wood went on tour with the Rolling Stones. The acrimonious departure of Mick Taylor from that group in late 1974 had left a hole that had still not been plugged. Publicly, Wood was absolutely insistent that his presence on the American Stones trek in June through August was just a matter of someone helping out his mates until such time as they acquired a proper replacement, but the tour would be extended (cutting into Faces rehearsal time for their own tour) and Wood would also agree to another Stones jaunt after his next Faces commitments were met. He was one of several outside guitarists who played on Stones sessions in the first few months of '75 and would eventually appear on two tracks on the resultant 1976 album *Black and Blue*.

On 19 December 1975, Rod Stewart announced his departure from the Faces. His press officer Tony Toon stated, "Rod feels he can no longer work in a situation where the group's lead guitarist Ron Wood seems to be permanently 'on loan' to the Rolling Stones." Following Stewart's announcement, his abandoned Faces colleagues decided to carry on regardless and make a record without him. Wood told Barbara Charone in *Sounds*, "I'm looking forward to it just as much 'cause it's more of a challenge now. Now we know he's not gonna be there instead of hoping he's gonna show up." However, when McLagan attended a meeting with Mo Ostin, then the head of Warner Bros., it was to be told that the record company wasn't prepared to finance this putative LP because it was just about to be announced in the press that Wood had joined the Stones. "Mo Ostin knew before I did," McLagan reflects. Sure enough, Wood duly publicly confirmed he was now Mick Taylor's permanent replacement. Without Wood, the Faces now consisted of an occasional co-songwriter and a non-writing rhythm section. This stub was clearly unviable. The Faces were finished once and for all.

Jones blames the split on a combination of Wood's obvious desire to be in what might be termed the genuine article (i.e., the band whose template – five-man group playing scruffy, riffy rock 'n' roll fronted by a singer of huge charisma – the Faces had aped) and "Rod moving over to America and that transatlantic gap."

Stewart's decision to leave undoubtedly released Wood from the horns of a dilemma – he has been a Rolling Stone ever since. His absorption into their ranks was somewhat more successful than his joining the Small Faces. Whereas his becoming part of the latter band helped turn a brilliant pop–soul–psychedelic group into a ramshackle boogie outfit, he reinvigorated the Rolling Stones, at least initially: *Some Girls* (1978) was their best album in years. A real twist to the tale came years later when he found out he could have joined the Stones the last time a similar vacancy had existed. Back in 1969, Ian Stewart rang the Bermondsey rehearsal space he was permitting the ex-Small Faces and friends to use in order to sound out Wood about replacing Brian Jones in the Stones. Ronnie Lane took the call and craftily rebuffed the offer without Wood's knowledge.

Another twist to the saga is the bit-part played in it by Steve Marriott. The Stones role that Wood obtained was originally Marriott's for the asking. "He was the first one up for the job," says McLagan. "Keith's [Richards] number-one suggestion. The reason he didn't get it was he had a better voice than Mick." At his audition, Marriott is said to have disregarded Richards' advice to not upstage Jagger and to restrict his contributions to guitar. "Last thing Mick needed was someone singing that good, because Steve was not good at being in the background," observes McLagan. Those inclined to doubt this story as the sort of apocrypha with which rock 'n' roll is littered are directed to the fact that after this juncture McLagan got to know Keith Richards well through both touring and recording with the Stones. Moreover, essentially the same story has been told by Marriott's second wife, Pam, and by Wood himself. Manon Piercey, onetime beau of Marriott and subsequently second wife of Joe Brown, says she heard it directly from Wood. A footnote to the footnote is provided by the fact that, according to Marriott, this wasn't the first time Jagger had vetoed him joining the Stones: Marriott claimed publicly that he was considered by Richards as a replacement for the disintegrating Brian Jones back in the late Sixties. Meanwhile, musician and Marriott friend Joe Brown opines that whoever thought of Marriott becoming a Stone "must have been bloody mad." He notes, "Jagger couldn't hold a candle to him when it comes to singing."

Humble Pie recruited Clem Clempson in Frampton's place and built on their existing success.

Rock On had been the first Pie album released on A&M following the bankruptcy of Immediate. "Immediate went under when I decided I had better stop supporting it with what was left of my Stones income," says Oldham. "It wasn't because we weren't having success," says Banes of the company's dissolution. He blames it on an American distribution deal agreed in 1967. "We had a terrible collision between Andrew and Tony. With 'Itchycoo Park', everybody was running after us and Tony signed the proposal with United Artists in America at the same time that Andrew, out in Monterey for the festival, did a verbal agreement with Clive Davis to sign with CBS. We ran into a mega lawsuit and to settle the lawsuit, we signed with CBS and we gave a guaranteed debenture to United Artists for a huge amount of money, which sank Immediate at the end of the day." He also blames the distributor the label had for every territory outside the US: "We were left to die by EMI," he says of Immediate's collapse. "All they needed to do was give Andrew fifty grand and they would have a record company that would still be flourishing. Somebody said to me they didn't want that to happen because they were in the process of forming Harvest Records. They would have seen Immediate as a conflict."

Banes also claims that Oldham – when he became aware that Immediate was finished – provided a life raft for Marriott and his band. "Andrew turned round to Humble Pie and said, 'We got a problem. I'm gonna recommended you for a deal with A&M.'" This may sound like a loyalist's tall tale, but Marriott essentially confirmed this story to Jim Green, whom he told, "Andrew gave us the nod on Immediate. He said, 'You've gotta leave now 'cause we're going under,' and suggested ways of getting a record deal, which was really nice 'cause I'd had no idea. We could have … wound up as assets to the liquidator." More than that, as Shirley observes, "When we went to A&M, we got paid a huge advance."

Immediate Publishing lasted a little bit longer than Immediate Records. "Carried on for most probably eighteen months after that," says Forrester. "My secretary and myself, we moved to Andrew's house." However, that situation proved unsustainable when the loss of Immediate Records revenue was compounded by Immediate Publishing having to relinquish the Beach Boys' Sea of Tunes catalogue once their contract with them had come to an end. "There was certainly not enough revenue to employ people once you take away two massive income streams," Forrester notes. The debenture that for Banes and Forrester doomed Immediate now benefitted even further United

Artists. Forrester recalls, "Andrew and Tony put the Immediate Music catalogue up as security against monies owed to UA. When [Immediate] Records folded, UA enforced the handing over of all of [Immediate] Music's works to UA London." "United Artists got a publishing company for nothing that is now turning over a million," says Banes. Forrester recalls a nice gesture by Don Arden in this period. "When Immediate Music folded … he phoned me to see how I was. Nobody else phoned me … I liked him a lot. Thought he was a great character."

Smokin' might have pandered to the unsubtle tastes of the hard-rock arena crowd, but *Eat It* (1973) evinced more ambition, even if Marriott's 'cocaine ears' ensured it went out with a bad mix. A double album, it boasted a rock side, a covers side, an acoustic side and a live side. The soul and R&B flavour that had always been part of the Pie's sound was now accentuated by the presence of black female vocal trio the Blackberries. It was the band's last top twenty – or, come to that, top fifty – US album.

By now, Marriott's personal life was unravelling, and cocaine was the culprit. "Coke definitely does something to people's heads," says Rylance. She was no innocent about drugs. "I knew about acid a bit. I knew about smoking dope. We used to have masses of it at the cottage. We used to keep some of it down a rabbit hole. They busted Greg [Ridley] in Epping, who called us up and said, 'They might be on their way to you.' Fortunately, the dogs could appear to be uncontrollable and when somebody strange was at the gate they would go berserk. So these two guys arrived at the gate saying, 'Mrs Marriott, can we come in?' I'm saying, 'No, I'm afraid I can't control the dogs.' They looked very fierce and two of them were Alsatian and half-Alsatian, so they weren't risking it." For all Rylance's anti-establishment, drug-savvy hipness, though, Marriott's latest drug of choice was foreign territory to her.

"That wasn't part of our life," she says of cocaine. "He was different when he came home. At the time people didn't think coke was that harmful but, of course, we know now. And the coke was getting worse and worse, because the more insecure and unhappy, the more coke he'd be doing." It all had a profound effect. "I fell out of love with him," she says. "There was a point when he was going away for another tour and instead of feeling bereft I felt relief because he was just a bit of a nightmare.

"It was made much worse by his reaction when he thought I was seeing this guy … I didn't have an affair with the guy but someone who was keen on me, a photographer, brought a bit of sanity into my life. Steve was beside himself with fury and jealousy, even though he'd had so many things over time. I was followed, the guy was followed, threats and everything … That's the thing that finished it for me. If he could resolve it in a better way … But neither of us were able to do that. Those weren't the days when you had those proper discussions about things." Rylance found Marriott's mother unamenable to discussion too. "I tried to talk to her when things were going wrong, and she didn't want to know. I thought she could have helped a bit."

Of the ultimate split with Marriott, she says, "It was gradual because I started to see old friends. I'd go up to London just for the day – had to get back to the animals – and I saw there was another life out there. It was very painful for him, but I had to get out. I left finally at the very end of 1974."

Rylance stayed in touch with Dee Anthony, to whose English wife Val she was close. Frampton had continued to be managed by Anthony. She recalls, "Peter Frampton was doing a tour here and it was a big deal. Dee sent his huge hired Rolls round and took me to the concert with him and said he was going to make Peter bigger than David Cassidy." Anthony did far more than that. *Frampton Comes Alive!* (1976) became the biggest-selling album in history up to that point. Some people remain suspicious of the fact that a double in-concert set by an only moderately well-known musician should rack up this achievement and rumours continue to abound of Anthony using his Mafia connections to bring it about. Whatever the truth of that, Frampton handled his success far better than did Marriott. "They're obviously very, very different people with different backgrounds different genes, different upbringing," reasons Rylance. "He was able to take a step back whereas Steve didn't. He didn't have much of a grounding in his upbringing."

"I continued to hear from Steve for a while," says Rylance. "That last tour [by] Humble Pie, Dee was calling me up saying, 'You've gotta come, because he won't go on the road without you.' I knew that I couldn't possibly go, so I encouraged this other girl who used to come and visit at the cottage to go, and she happened to be slightly going out with this person called James, who she brought round to see me. That's how I met James, who I was with for about eighteen years. But Steve continued to call. When I was with James, he called usually at two or three in the morning. James would answer the call and he'd say, 'Can I talk to my old lady?' It was awful. James couldn't understand why I wouldn't go back and see Steve, but I knew I probably wouldn't be able to leave."

Marriott's father later reported that he had visited Beehive Cottage to find Marriott screaming across the surrounding fields, "I want my wife back!" Of Pam Land, the woman who became Marriott's second wife in 1977, Rylance says, "He called me up the day before he was due to marry Pam, saying, 'Hi darling. I just wanted you to know I've got to marry Pam tomorrow because her visa's going to run out, but if there's any chance of us getting together, it won't happen.'" The last time Rylance and Marriott spoke was just after she'd come back from hospital after giving birth to her and James' son. "The phone rang and it was Steve saying, 'Hi, darling. I just want you to know I've bought this cottage in Idaho' – or somewhere, I can't remember where it was – 'and it looks just like Beehive. I'd really like you to see it one day.' I said, 'Steve, I've just come back from hospital with a baby.' He said, 'Oh. Well that's it then, isn't it?' and just put the phone down. It was very sad. I felt so much guilt about it because it was a situation where somebody thinks that you're the key to their happiness and well-being and you really have to in the end take responsibility for your own happiness."

Marriott's music seemed to sag along with his spirit. *Thunderbox* (1974) was an unimpressive covers-heavy set. So too was the following year's *Street Rats*, but that was the least of the problems with an album allegedly bastardised and bowdlerised at the behest of A&M by, of all people, Andrew Loog Oldham. One or more tracks on it are alleged to have been co-opted without Marriott's permission from an unreleased solo album he recorded at Beehive in 1974 with Clem Clempson, Greg Ridley, Jerry Shirley and keyboardist Tim Hinkley. Gered Mankowitz was asked to take some photos at the latter's sessions. It was the first time he'd seen Marriott since a shoot for *As Safe as Yesterday Is*. "He seemed frail and he seemed to be a bit lost," Mankowitz recalls. "Pretty stoned, pretty drunk ... The place was in a pretty filthy state." Nonetheless, he says, "It was a good session. I got some great portraits of them all and we had a great day." Unfortunately, the pictures weren't used in the way intended. "A&M rejected the album and I think that was very humiliating for Steve," says Mankowitz. The full recordings would not see the light of day until 1996 when they were issued as *Scrubbers*, whereupon they were hailed as what would have been a refreshing departure from Marriott's Humble Pie formula.

Marriott effectively admitted he knew of this ossified Pie routine at the time. In 1977, he observed of Humble Pie to Chas de Whalley of *Sounds*, "We were one of the first rock 'n' roll bands to be doing that heavy good-timing stuff back in 1969–70. But it got very stale, didn't it?" However, before he could formally bring down the curtain on the decayed proposition that the group now consisted of, it – a familiar motif – had to go through with preexisting touring commitments. Worse was to come, though, than grimly fulfilling the obligations of an enterprise in which some or all participants no longer believed anymore in the company of people one no longer wanted to be around. By now, punk was on the horizon and a terrible fate awaited Marriott's Seventies work. Post-punk, Humble Pie became one of those bands whose appeal suddenly became inexplicable, even to those who had once proudly bought their wares. Their catalogue's sudden presence in remainder racks and the group's abrupt status of dinosaurs has worked to almost completely eclipse the fact of how big they were, while the mesmerising but intangible Marriott stage presence that was the reason for so much of their appeal now resides only in the memories of those who witnessed it in the flesh.

"Our paths crossed a couple of times in America," says Kenney Jones of the Faces and Humble Pie. Although Humble Pie had initially seemed the more successful band, the two groups ended up being perceived as level-pegging, and possibly with the Faces being on a higher plane. "All of us conquered America, but independently," notes Jones. For him, this situation was "ironic," "weird" and "not right" – he wishes the successes had not been "independent" of each other but had come for them collectively within the Small Faces. He was also never too impressed by the self-conscious virtuosity of Humble Pie and Marriott's increasingly mannered and bombastic vocal style. McLagan was another of Marriott's ex-colleagues not enamoured with the Pie. "All he did was replace Kenney and Ronnie and played keyboards himself," he says. "He talked about wanting to go heavy, and Humble Pie were heavy, but they weren't very good in my opinion. Nowhere near as good as the Small Faces." Echoing a Little Richard song title, McLagan observes, "I don't know what he wanted, but he got what he wanted and he lost what he had."

The Faces and Humble Pie did have one thing in common: their songs were all too often bereft of the zip, flash and discipline of those of the Small Faces. Basically, on record they were both a bit boring. The Pie, though, were ultimately more boring than the Faces. However inconsistent the Faces were, a good half of each of their albums was good-to-very good. There are few songs in Humble Pie's canon that fit that description, and that canon is larger than those of both the Small Faces and the Faces. Moreover, Marriott's voice deteriorated alarmingly across the course of the Pie's career, changing from soulful to merely hoarse, almost certainly another consequence of heavy co-caine usage.

In his autobiography, Glyn Johns, who produced their early albums, summed up Humble Pie's deficiencies by saying, "This band was loud, extremely energetic, using variations on the same riff, with very few good songs … they lacked the substance that I had hoped for, particularly knowing what Steve was capable of as a songwriter." How ironic in light of Jones' comment, "It was Glyn Johns' suggestion that Peter Frampton and Steve get together. We found that out afterwards." McLagan felt Marriott missed Lane's songwriting help, however occasional, partial or sometimes nebulous. "Ronnie Lane was like the glue that kept Steve anchored," he told Ken Sharp. "When he wasn't writing with Steve, Steve's stuff wasn't half as interesting."

There are a couple of other unfortunate ironies surrounding Humble Pie. One is Marriott's rap in *Performance: Rockin' the Fillmore* wherein he states that his woman wanted a ring on her finger. "Meant a lot to her, didn't mean a [expletive bleeped] to me," he says to testosterone-fuelled audience cheers. Although Shirley says the anecdote doesn't refer to Jenny ("That's about the tart in Manchester that gave him so much grief"), it's still a dismaying contrast to that touchingly romantic story about 'Tin Soldier' impressing Jenny Rylance so much that, to his joy, she agreed to marry him. It also demonstrates the very different demographics of the two bands: Marriott would never have felt obliged to pander to a Small Faces audience with such macho posturing.

The other irony is 'Wham Bam Thank You Mam'. Listening to that superb Small Faces track, one is struck by the fact that Humble Pie never recorded anything either as heavy or as good. It is the starkest proof possible that everything Marriott needed to fulfil his musical visions had always been available to him within the Small Faces.

7 It's Too Late

During the 1970s, Jimmy Winston continued to successfully ply his trade as thespian, graduating from the stage to television where he appeared in episodes of *Doctor Who*, *UFO* and *Hazell*.

It was appropriate that his turn in the latter cockney private-eye series saw him combining his two main talents – he played a musician – as he had always maintained a foot in the music industry. "In between a year or two of acting, I'd do a record," he says. One of the records he made was 'Princes Ball' released in 1975 on Decca under the name Jestaband. Another was 'Sun in the Morning', a 1976 release on NEMS, which was not only a label at that very moment having success with Small Faces re-releases but was it so happens run by the son of Don Arden's former employee and possible discoverer of the Small Faces Pat Meehan. Winston seems to have been broadly oblivious of these coincidences, but his life would shortly bisect his Small Faces past in a much more direct way.

Despite a start in the motor-vehicle profession that one might term rather painful – i.e., his gainsaid transportation arrangement with the Small Faces –Frankie Langwith had continued to be involved in the business. In the mid-Seventies, he was running an Essex garage selling connoisseur automobiles. By coincidence, Steve Marriott's Beehive Cottage was located not far away. "The band had made some money out of Humble Pie at this point and [were] all buying nice cars," says Winston. "Stevie ended up going down and buying a couple." The path was set for a reunion between Winston and Marriott.

"He got in touch with me and I went out to see him," says Winston. "We went out quite a bit and we were having a bit of fun and talking about things." His mild surprise at being contacted by Marriott was as nothing compared to how he felt about the change in Marriott's appearance and personality. "He was more cocksure," Winston recalls. "He was more aggressive. He was never an easy guy to get on with, but [now] he didn't give a fuck. You could catch moments when he was a bit more thoughtful and you could discuss something quite sensitive and it was a bit easier. He had those moments and then he'd get off his head and the rough-and-ready would come out." Winston's surprise was to a large part based around what might be termed the 'common' character Marriott had adopted almost full-time. "It's funny, because when I first met him, he was really quite well-spoken, like he had just come from a kids' drama school. But at the end of his life, he became quite gross. Very East End, "allo, son' and all that. He changed his nature … As he put weight on, he became like that kind of person." That weight problem got more pronounced, to such an extent that "he got quite a big, plump guy."

Someone else who got a flavour of the studiedly objectionable character Marriott seems to have devolved into was his first child. Lesley, daughter of the young fan Sally Foulger, never met her father. Lesley revealed, "Steve apparently … once rang Sally to get her to bring me round so he could see me. However, it was about 1 a.m., so Sally decided to stay at home." Although the adult Lesley subsequently went to see Marriott in concert several times, she never worked up the courage to approach him, possibly because an overture by her boyfriend in a bar when she was present in one particular small venue led to Marriott responding, "What do you want me to do – mind me fucking language?"

Asked about his 'professional cockney' persona, Marriott's friend Joe Brown – well-known for his cheeky-chappie-from-the-capital image – provides a rationale which seems suffused with self-doubt but perhaps unwittingly gives an insight into why Marriott went that way. "Well, that's the deal innit, mate?" he says. "I mean, I don't know. I've been at it so long I'm not sure who I am. I've performed all over England for sixty odd years. I'm a Londoner. You're trying to get yourself over from the stage and so you develop your own voice." Pete Townshend offers: "I suppose there's another possible thesis, which was that when he was playing that character in the Dickens thing as a little boy, that became a formative character for him and he went back to it again and again and again. When you're vulnerable, perhaps sometimes what happens is that you do resort to old tricks."

Despite his misgivings about Marriott's new persona, Winston couldn't help but envy his current circumstances. "He had a lovely set-up," he reflects. "The sort of thing that musicians long for. A nice proper thatched roof cottage and a little cottage in the garden with a studio in it." Said garden cottage was in fact the former abode of Ronnie and Sue Lane. When the couple moved out, Marriott converted the building so that he didn't need to rack up costs at the likes of Olympic in order to work on his musical ideas.

Winston also found that there were gratifying elements about the new Marriott. One was a greater sense of self-criticism about their past tussles. "It's the only time he ever said, 'Look, I know I've been a prat.' Bit more realistic … We put all our wrongs to rights and we were okay." However, the conversation didn't ever turn to how Winston came to leave the band. "That was then." The two gravitated to the activity that tends to occur when more than one musician is in a room: collaboration. "We wrote, come up with ideas and discussed things."

Winston realised that despite Marriott's lovely set-up there were dark financial clouds on his horizon, as demonstrated one day when Pam went to answer the door. "She was a bit of a hippie flower child," says Winston. "All soft and relaxed. She's called out, 'Stee-vie. It's the tax man here saying you owe "X" amount of money.' He was a bit inebriated, Stevie. He said, 'Oh, tell 'em to fack off!' and she shut the door. I think that was the beginning of a problem … Unfortunately, in America, he'd been cheated and robbed."

At the close of the Humble Pie story, Marriott was possibly no richer than he'd been at the conclusion of the Small Faces' career. Clem Clempson later said of the band's final days, "We came home to England and found ourselves skint … From being one of the biggest-grossing acts in America, overnight we had nothing."

Laurie O'Leary succeeded Dee Anthony as Marriott's manager at this time. "I did it on a handshake," he says. "His affairs was really in a terrible way … I went to Beehive Cottage and he didn't have any electricity … He was, as he would say, hungry and looking. He was with Pam. She was pregnant. It was sad really."

Once again, Marriott was blaming his lack of remuneration on the larceny of third parties, but this time there does seem to be more truth than usual to his claims. Jim Leverton would later collaborate with Marriott in the Majik Mijits project. One song that emanated from it was 'How Does it Feel', whose subject was Dee Anthony. "There's a line in there, 'I heard that you spent Peter's ninety per cent,'" Leverton says. "In other words, a massive-selling record that Peter Frampton only got ten per cent [of] and Dee Anthony got ninety." Rylance notes, "You would think he would have learned from Don Arden, but to go from Don Arden on to Dee Anthony and end up having Dee's lawyer and accountant – not having your own – just seems extraordinary to me." "[He was] ripped off by Dee Anthony," agrees O'Leary. "He and all of the band. They all said that he bought them houses with their money and he owned all the titles." Leverton: "The band had three or four beach houses in Nassau that [were] bought by Humble Pie and when the band disintegrated the Italian people copped all the assets. In the small print all the beach-front houses belonged to Dee Anthony and not Humble Pie." According to Pam, when Marriott tried to lay claim to his monies Anthony arranged a meeting at which was present notorious mobster John Gotti, a man later reputed to have – amongst other things – got revenge on a man who accidentally killed his son in a road accident by ensuring he was cut in half with a chainsaw while still alive. After said meeting, Marriott discontinued his claim.

Yet while there is a consensus that Marriott's allegations about Anthony are not complete baloney, the line in 'How Does it Feel' that reads "You took all my money, you took every bit" wouldn't quite seem to capture the full nuance of the saga of Marriott coming away penniless from Humble Pie. Asked whether Marriott was left broke because of Dee Anthony, Leverton says, "Well, and his own indulgence. He did spend a lot of money on himself." When in August 1975, Marriott told the *NME*, "I'm as skint as skint is," he also noted, "I blew all my money on a studio" (clearly a reference to the converted outbuilding at Beehive) and "I bought me parents a house." Asked whether, regardless of his IRS issues, Marriott burnt through a lot of income himself, Winston says, "Oh God, he did. Like you've gotta believe it. On all sorts of things which we won't go into." Moreover, A&M's Larry Yaskiel has recalled a point as early as 1970 when he was unable to reach Marriott on the phone and discovered that it had been cut off for non-payment. This was at a juncture when Marriott had not only just received a $100,000 advance from his label but also had Small Faces publishing royalties coming in. Dee Anthony had yet to enter Marriott's life.

It should further be pointed out that some might suggest that Marriott ripped *them* off. Jerry Shirley asserts that one of the reasons Marriott claimed he was defrauded was to cover up his own profligacy and dishonesty, and that he had personal experience of this. He has recalled being astounded when told by band accountant Bert Padell that the Beehive studio had cost $100,000 to build. Shirley wrote, "He used the studio as a red herring to draw us away from the real issue of his overspending ... He insisted that that money being spent on the studio was a fraction of what we were told it was and this was a sign of our money being systematically ripped off." While Marriott's claim may be plausible if one believes tales of conflicts of interest surrounding accountancy in the Pie stable, Shirley also notes, "The group's money financed the studio, but no sooner had it been built then all of a sudden it became Steve's studio."

Yet despite all his financial woes, self-inflicted or otherwise, Marriott was never someone who would lunge for a payday. "I got a call from Andrew Lloyd Webber," says O'Leary. "Would Steve like to do Che Guevara in this new musical? ... The initial thing was to do the album ... I talked to Steve about it. I said, 'Come on, we'll go and see them. He's a nice enough chap and Tim Rice is alright.' Classic Steve – he picked a shirt out of a bag and it was silk. He said, 'What do you think?' I said, 'Well, it looks alright but isn't it meant to be ironed?' He said, 'Nah, fuck me, that's how it is now.' I'm sure he brought the fashion in [for] crushed silk, because I'd never seen it before. He put it on and we went up to see Andrew Lloyd Webber. They made the biggest balls-up ever by playing the whole score of *Evita* to us, and at eleven o'clock in the morning saying, 'Would you like a drink?' thinking coffee or tea or water or something, and Steve said, I'll have a large VSOP, Remy if you've got it.' They came out with a bottle. They went through the whole procedure. They were loving it. You could see it was their baby. Instead of playing the two songs that they wanted Steve to sing, they went through the whole thing, which ballsed it up. Steve was quite pissed. We got in the car. Driving along, after about twenty minutes, he said, 'Fuck that, mate. That's not for me, is it?' They said Che Guevara in *Evita* was a disinfectant salesman. He said, 'Fucking disinfectant!' Steve missed a golden opportunity, but then Steve's Steve. He said, 'I couldn't do that if it gets on the stage, fucking seven nights a week.' He was honest."

What saved Marriott's financial bacon was the reunion of the Small Faces that resulted from the roughly simultaneous implosions of the Faces and Humble Pie. "It was basically an excuse to pay off Steve's debts," McLagan later claimed of Marriott's participation in said reunion. One could understand a feeling of schadenfreude on the part of Marriott's ex-Small Faces colleagues at his desperate state of affairs and consequent willingness to work with them again. It was certainly a marked contrast to the way that Marriott's departure from the Small Faces back in '69 left the rest of the group lost and frightened.

It would be oversimplifying matters to posit the band coalescing in the wake of the end of their respective post-Small Faces (Act I) projects as a seamless transition. If the second act of the Small Faces' life might be compared to a car, it took a few turns of the ignition before its engine started – and, even when it did, the vehicle was shortly missing a wheel.

The seed for the reunion was planted at that London meeting with Mo Ostin at which Warner Bros. dropped the bombshell that Ronnie Wood had followed Stewart out of the Faces exit door. "We had some time booked in Brittany," says McLagan: "We'd booked our studio there because it was somewhere different. We had our crew, we had everything organised. He said, 'You know, I'm not keen on you doing this. Why don't you and Ronnie and Kenney get back together with Steve? I'd put that record out.'" The response to Ostin's suggestion was a flat rejection. McLagan: "I said, 'I don't want to work with Steve again – we did that. And Ronnie [Lane] doesn't want to work with any of us.'"

However, the impetus for a Small Faces reunion was in the ether courtesy of a confluence of events that suggest a certain predestination, something that puts one in mind of the "something a little bit magical" about the Small Faces' story that Marriott was not alone in their ranks in believing in. Jones had told *Disc* in June 1974, "Ronnie Lane and I were talking about the old band recently and thought we'd like to do a reunion gig. Then we talked to Steve and Mac and they agreed. I don't know when we will get the time, that is the only problem." Cosmic forces seemed to be at work to provide an incentive to create that time. Not only did the Faces and Humble Pie disintegrate over the following eighteen months, but in December 1975, 'Itchycoo Park' began climbing the UK chart. (Since the last time the record had been on the hit parade, there was now one official, universally recognised singles chart in the country and 'hit parade' had become an antediluvian term.) Although the re-released 'Itchycoo Park' (its B-side now not 'I'm Only Dreaming' but 'My Way of Giving') boasted the distinctive white label and jagged-lettered logo of Immediate, it also bore, albeit smaller, the logo of NEMS Records. A company that had started issuing records after the death of Brian Epstein – of course, the most famous person ever associated with North East Music Stores – its latest owner Patrick Meehan, Jr. had bought the Immediate catalogue and was keen to exploit it. In an even more incestuous twist, he recruited Tony Calder to help him do this.

It's presumably this turn of events that led Jones and McLagan to travel up to the Fishpool, a sixty-acre farm owned by Lane on the Welsh border. That the visiting pair were hopeful for the prospects of a full reunion may have not least been due to the fact – as McLagan remembered it – that the trip was made at Lane's suggestion. When they got there, however, they found Lane resistant to the suggestion of a revived Small Faces. McLagan told Wayne Pernu, "Kenney'd already spoken to Steve about getting back together, but Ronnie didn't want to. So then Ronnie talked to me and Kenney and wanted us to get back together with him and call it Ronnie Lane's Slim Chance. Like we'd be his band. So we left very disillusioned." However, there were momentous changes afoot that would help shift Lane's perspective.

7 January 1976 saw the Small Faces congregate in the same room together for the first time since the 1969 parting of the ways. The venue was Jones' Kingston home, where they met to discuss Small Faces possibilities, both mere ideas and concrete proposals. "Tony Calder offered us something like a thousand pound each if we would get together and make a video of 'Itchycoo Park' and 'Lazy Sunday'," recalls McLagan. Although they agreed to the promo shoot, they declined the suggestion of David Enthoven of EG Management to cut some new material to offer Calder as bonus tracks for a Small Faces compilation.

Although Britain still had the same number of television channels that it had had in 1967 – three – TV ownership was now nigh-universal and society was consequently much more visually oriented. Meanwhile, *Top of the Pops* was far more important than it had been then. As the only regular music show on British TV, it was the meeting place for all pop lovers, regularly watched by a third of the country's population. An appearance on it was virtually guaranteed to send a record higher up the chart. Hence the suggestion of a promotional film to give the 'Itchycoo Park' re-release a boost. As the other one of their most famous recordings, 'Lazy Sunday', was also a potential re-release, NEMS decided to include it in the scheme.

Both promos were very similar, clearly shot in the same session. In an enclosed, darkened space, the Small Faces ham it up to back tracks. They certainly look different to the last time they did promotion for said records, their psychedelic finery having given way to un-ironed, casual attire and their mugs no longer quite so angular and fresh. In the case of 'Itchycoo Park', these informal Seventies visuals bore absolutely no relation to the far-out Summer of Love soundtrack. In fact, *Top of the Pops*' resident dance troupe Pan's People did somewhat better when they mimed to the record on an edition of the show. Leaving aside their habitual literalness (they were seen to place steepled hands against tilted cheeks to the part of the lyric that talked of resting eyes), the visual accompaniment that they provided a playback – pixie outfits against a vista of a rainbow and a giant toadstool – was much more apposite, even if idiotic. Still, it was the exposure that television provided that increased sales, not necessarily the quality of the visuals, and the public responded positively.

'Itchycoo Park' peaked at no.9 on 17 January 1976. 'Lazy Sunday', didn't do quite so well, but its apex of 39 on 3 April the same year was still impressive in a day and age where the superlative 'heritage artist' was yet to supplant the pejorative 'has-been' in the culture.

Marriott was closer to that latter concept these days than his three ex-colleagues. While the Faces had racked up three top-ten UK chart singles and a No.12, this was the first time in this decade that Marriott had occupied what was no longer called the hit parade.

In terms of remuneration, though, the Small Faces must have felt like they were not in the 1970s – where artists were increasingly powerful and well-rewarded – but back in the exploitative Sixties. "The motherfucker never paid us," seethes McLagan of Calder. "Did the video, the records got in the charts again, never got paid again. All the same bloke."

Back in 1967, 'Itchycoo Park' had shared the top ten with the likes of the Move ('Flowers in the Rain'), Traffic ('Hole in my Shoe') and two other – though non-piss-taking – Summer-of-Love anthems ('Let's Go To San Francisco' by the Flowerpot Men and Scott McKenzie's 'San Francisco [Be Sure to Wear Some Flowers in Your Hair]'). Its re-release saw it nestling cheek-by-jowl with a new generation of pop stars, including ABBA ('Mamma Mia'), 10cc ('Art for Art's Sake') and Demis Roussos ('Happy to Be on an Island in the Sun'). In the top spot was Queen, approaching the end of their marathon nine-week run in pole position with 'Bohemian Rhapsody'. Could the Small Faces still be relevant and viable in such an altered landscape?

Some people clearly thought so. O'Leary was shortly approached by David Enthoven with another proposition. EG Management – which had guided King Crimson and Roxy Music to stardom – also happened to be the company currently overseeing the affairs of Ronnie Lane's Slim Chance. "They said, 'Do you think Steve would go and do a couple of numbers with Ronnie?'" O'Leary recalls. "I said, 'What's in your mind?' They said, 'Well, we can probably get the Small Faces back.'" That it was Lane's camp now making a more-or-less formal long-term reunion overture was clearly a turnabout. The concert in question took place in Colchester at Essex University on 24 January. O'Leary: "Ronnie did his set completely and I've got to stand there with Steve. He's going, 'The bastard ain't gonna let me get up.' There was still that kind of hostility. Right at the end, Steve was called up on stage." Marriott rendered 'All or Nothing' and then stayed on for 'Whatcha Gonna Do About It' and two covers. "Rough as it was, it was still good, and everybody loved it," says O'Leary. "That was the nucleus of it."

By the following week, *Melody Maker* – in an edition published when 'Itchycoo Park' was around its chart peak – was reporting that "The Small Faces' reunion is on." However, from what it said, it was set to be a limited affair: "The Small Faces … will play at least two gigs this summer, probably at football stadia … The Small Faces will not record any new material but following the summer gigs the four members will pursue their individual directions." A spokesman was quoted as saying, "They're doing it for fun, basically."

McLagan explains that goodwill had been engendered by the promo shoot, but only up to a point. "We had such a good time that day," he recalls. "We said, 'Let's get together. Let's do one gig. We'll film it, record it. So we won't have to be together as a band or anything. Let's not dwell on the past. Let's have as nice time as we're having today.' It seemed like a perfect idea. It would be cashing in but, also, we'd be having fun." Marriott's recollection was that things snowballed from there in that a concert or concerts would be too limited. "We thought – what we gonna play?" he said. "I don't wanna play all the old shit. There were some good numbers there, but you can't have an hour-and-a-half of them."

Meanwhile, Marriott had an outstanding obligation to deliver a solo album to A&M. The label very much called the shots on *Marriott* (1976), a sessioner-dominated affair. The record is admired in some quarters for its slickness but was dismissed by others – including Marriott – as antiseptic. The latter tendency seems to have held sway when it came to public reception. "The album came out and it nosedived," says O'Leary.

Meanwhile, new Small Faces activity was nudging ever closer to a full-scale reunion because of Lane's cash-strapped situation. While Lane was the only one of the four with an active ensemble, he was in deep financial trouble. For a while, he'd been a rich man, with money rolling in not just from Faces work but from the Lane Mobile Studio. An Airstream Trailer converted at a cost of approximately £60k to accommodate a Helios mixing console, Studer and Revox tape machines, and Tannoy monitoring, it vied with the Rolling Stones Mobile for being the portable recording studio of choice for Seventies rockers. Led Zeppelin, Bad Company, Eric Clapton and the Who numbered among the clients to whom his investment was lucratively hired out. Lane had also had a solid post-Faces solo recording career. *Anymore for Anymore* (1974), *Ronnie Lane's Slim Chance* (1975) and *One for the Road* (1976) were all sweet, rootsy and acclaimed. Even the album *Mahoney's Last Stand* (a 1972 collaboration with Ronnie Wood belatedly released in 1976 that was the soundtrack to a film co-written and co-directed by the same Alexis Kanner who directed the Small Faces' 'Universal' promo) had an inordinate number of fans.

Things started to go wrong when in Summer 1974 he set up an ambitious live concept called the Passing Show, in which music mixed with circus-like entertainment criss-crossed his home country. "He was always obsessed by it," says Townshend. This obsession would appear to go as far back as – and possibly precede – 1968, when the Rolling Stones mounted their similarly themed *Rock and Roll Circus*, albeit in stationary form for television broadcast. "Mick Jagger nicked it," avers Townshend, who played at the latter event with the Who. The concept seemed to be a musical extension of a rustic lifestyle Lane embraced wholeheartedly. Once the most flamboyant of pop stars (Calder said, "He'd go into shoe shops, find something he liked, then order the whole stock, all 180 pairs, to be delivered to his house"), he adopted the appearance in the mid-Seventies of a neckerchiefed, Wellington-booted squire. As well as buying the Fishpool, he attended agriculture school alongside teen-aged farmers' sons.

A circus-like revue that spurned the star-billing and cossetted trappings of celebrity for ad-hoc performances under a big tent on muddy greens may have sounded very romantic and spontaneous in theory but the Passing Show ended up a logistical nightmare of limited public appeal that drained Lane's finances. "When Ronnie walked away from the Faces, he became a casualty," says Townshend. "Because from that day onwards, he was completely and utterly, totally broke. He never had any fucking money ever again. He was living close to the knuckle." As such, Lane's situation was one where the right circumstances could tempt him to do something to which he might otherwise be hostile. Those circumstances arose when Joe Brown offered the Small Faces a deal similar to the one Ian Stewart had extended to the band after Marriott walked out in '69.

Joe Brown was a celebrity from the first wave of British rock 'n' roll. The famously spikey-haired blonde guitarist had had a succession of hit singles (including three top tens) before moving into family-entertainer mould. Part of the reason for his friendship with Marriott can be discerned in the name given by producer Jack Good to Brown's backing band: the Bruvvers. "He said to me that I'd had an influence on him," says Brown of Marriott. "I think that's why we met up in the first place. Because there wasn't many bloody cockney singers around anyway … He was a good friend. He had a bit of a troubled life I thought, but when he was straight, he was great."

Another thing the two men had in common was home-studio facilities. Brown considered the set-up at Beehive a little primitive compared to what he had, however. "It was quite a lot smaller," Brown says. "It was more of a groove room. I don't know whether he actually made any records there at all. I think he did a lot of his own stuff there, wrote a lot of songs and stuff, but when it comes to a studio layout with your drums and all the mics and a Neve desk and all the whole bit, I don't think he had all that." It being the case that the Grange – the studio located at Brown's Chigwell house – had all the things he lists, it was capable of turning out state-of-the-art finished masters. Moreover, Brown's friendship with Marriott meant that he was prepared to give a reformed Small Faces use of it on a conditional-fee basis: he would be paid in the event of them landing a record deal. As such, it was the ideal venue for them to begin laying down tracks. With nothing to lose and a lot to gain Ronnie Lane consented to turn up there in the early summer of 1976.

Things started reasonably well, but Lane's mood deteriorated and darkened remarkably quickly. Part of this seems to have been down to Marriott's behaviour, which Jones described as "overly confident and arrogant." This would probably have been annoying in the best of circumstances, but these weren't the best of circumstances. "Ronnie got the needle because Steve was writing with me," says McLagan. Shortly after the promo shoot, McLagan had accepted an invitation by Marriott to visit Beehive. There, Marriott and McLagan engaged in something they never had in the Small Faces: direct and exclusive collaboration. "We wrote four or five songs one night," McLagan recalls. "I'd written with Ronnie but never with Steve." These demos of Marriott and McLagan's joint compositions were made in the home studio that had once been Lane's home. Although Lane may not have known this, it must be assumed that another part of his increasing belligerence was festering anger at the way his investment in Beehive Cottage had effectively been stolen from him, something of which he must have been painfully reminded when the Small Faces did a few days' rehearsal there after the Essex University gig. Another element of his dark mood must have been the dawning realisation that he was afflicted with a terrible and incurable disease, the same one that had rendered his mother so frail. "Years later, he told me that he thought that the MS was starting around then," says McLagan. "He didn't know at that time, but after that the symptoms became more obvious."

The band had worked through the night of 16 June – assisted in the cases of McLagan and Marriott by cocaine – and the next day retired to the local pub for lunch. There, Lane got drunk. (This was a quicker process for men of the Small Faces' stature. As Lane's oft-time drinking buddy Townshend points out, "He, being much smaller, tended to get drunk quicker than me.") He then started making noises about returning to Wales. The dark mood seemed to pass but resumed back in the studio. "Ronnie blew a gasket," recalls McLagan. "He said, 'Well fuck the lot of you.' While we were doing backing vocals on a track, he [said], 'Fuck this.' I said, 'What!'" Lane threw down his headphones and made to depart. "We chased him up the alley," McLagan recalls.

Recountings of what then transpired tend to be clouded by mealy-mouthed obfuscation. In his autobiography, McLagan seemed to skip a section of the story, vaguely saying, "It was horrible and it should never have happened…" In his own book, Jones was also imprecise as he said of Marriott and Lane, "The two of them clashed. Verbally and physically." McLagan's account makes it sound like an argument, Jones' like a fight. Speaking to Chas de Whalley in 1977, Marriott was more upfront about the fact that what occurred was basically an assault: "There was an insult given out and I still take it as one today. At which point I whacked him, and Ronnie said goodbye." Perhaps some kind of kudos was due Marriott for his honesty, but hardly for his rather self-pitying addendum: "It'll obviously turn round to be all my fault." The insult in question has been said to be that Marriott hadn't written a decent song since the Small Faces split, a contention which some of the band's fans might consider uncomfortably close to the truth. Quite possibly in his heart of hearts Marriott did as well, hence his extreme reaction. Incredibly, this doesn't seem to be the extent of the abuse and humiliation to which Lane was subjected that day. McLagan told Rod Stewart biographers Tim Ewbank and Stafford Hildred, "He had a couple of brandies and got very nasty, very bitter and very angry to the point where I physically kicked him up the arse and out of the studio, and told him to fuck off and not come back."

Lane's roadie and aide Russ Schlagbaum wrote in his diary that Lane had phoned him and said, "Russell, come get me out of here, fucking Marriott is insane." The deal from which Lane had walked (or perhaps run) was not negligible. EG had taken on the role of the reformed Small Faces' management at the insistence of Lane. (O'Leary was happy to continue as Marriott's manager but just as happy not to have anything to do professionally with the Small Faces.) Mark Fenwick, Enthoven's partner in EG, had been negotiating a five-album deal worth $1m, of which the Small Faces would receive 25 per cent. When the Small Faces reunion transpired to be a 24-hour one, EG also bailed.

In fairness to Jones, McLagan and Marriott, they did have some cause to be disgruntled with Lane over the events that led up to Lane's departure, however ugly and inexcusable the circumstances of the latter may have been. As McLagan told Silverton, "We'd ditched our projects, but he wanted to keep on Slim Chance. We agreed to go with his management company. We'd bend with the wind."

What with the time and emotional energy they'd by now invested in the idea of a reunion, it's perhaps understandable that the remaining three should elect to continue with the project. "I heard that Steve had given Ronnie Lane a backhander or something," says O'Leary. "I'd go to the studio and suddenly, 'Where's Ronnie?' 'Oh, he's left. Never mind, I've got someone else – Rick Wills.' I said, 'He's the tallest Small Face I've ever seen, mate.'"

Rick Wills had been recruited by Marriott literally overnight. He was a more than competent bassist, having already played on Peter Frampton albums and toured with Roxy Music. He would later find fame with Foreigner. "Rick was a lovely bloke," recalls McLagan. "We got on with him straight away and we continued cutting the album. We had a lot of fun." That Wills was of normal height was hardly a fatal flaw. However, the fact that he was a good musician didn't mean he could fill the hole left by Lane. "Rick Wills was virtually a session man," notes O'Leary, presumably a reference to the fact that the newcomer was not a habitual composer. Lane had brought a singular stripe of philosophical and wistful songwriting to both the Small Faces and the Faces. Within the sometimes real, sometimes notional Marriott/Lane songwriting partnership, he had acted variously as collaborator, foil, rival, sounding board and impetus to creativity. Not only could Wills not fulfil any of those functions, but there was no one else who could pick up the baton. As McLagan says of Marriott, "He was writing with me, but he wasn't writing anything classic. I was trying, but I couldn't be his Ronnie Lane." The Small Faces were about to run into the same issue that the Faces had when Lane left them back in '73: although the member they had lost was not the most important in terms of input – whether it be definable songwriting contributions or indefinable spiritual ones – he was essentially irreplaceable.

On top of that were issues of legitimacy. Jones' opinions of band reformations is that, "There's no point unless you're the originals." Today, when a band can boast just one member of its classic line-up – even just the drummer – and still make a living thanks to the power of the brand name, it would not be particularly controversial for a group to be missing a key member. In the mid-Seventies – an era still in the right-on shadow of the Sixties – such ventures were often dismissed as fraudulent or desperate. Still, it wasn't as if the band members had anything else to do.

The album's production would be credited to "Kemastri" (i.e., Kenney/Mac/Steve/Rick), with the exception of the sole cover version, the old Valentinos' song 'Lookin' for a Love', written by J. W. Alexander and Zelda Samuels. For this cut the band decamped to Roundhouse Studios in London and engaged the services of Shel Talmy, who was credited as the track's co-producer. Talmy – legendary producer of the Kinks, the Who, the Creation and others – actually recorded around half a dozen tracks before walking out in frustration at Marriott being incapable through drug use.

The album was completed by September, but it would be quite a while before the band were able to even notify the world of its existence, let alone release it. Just before Christmas '76, Jones was involved in a bad car crash which derailed the project by two months. Marriott later said that the band had been "as skint as arseholes all that time," adding, "And we couldn't even tell anybody we wuz skint cos we couldn't say we were together, you know. It's been difficult." Mel Bush, manager of David Essex, was brought in to shop around the album and an accompanying tour. The logical first stop was Jerry Moss at Humble Pie's label, A&M. However, according to the *NME*'s Steve Clarke, Moss said he would only be interested if a big-name producer like Bob Ezrin was brought in. The band then successfully turned to Ahmet Ertegun of Atlantic Records, who facilitated a deal with Atlantic subsidiary Warner Bros. "The deal with Warners was $300,000 an album," says O'Leary. This was a large amount of money even by today's standards. However, the euphoria was short-lived. Marriott hadn't told the others that he already had obligations elsewhere. Consequently, £250,000 of that windfall had to be sacrificed to untie his contractual bonds. "They [gave] Dee Anthony and [A&M records'] Jerry Moss quite a bit of money for Steve to come out of his recording contract with them," says O'Leary. The Atlantic advance was also to be staggered, with tranches released only on submission of each album. Coupled with Marriott's superhuman profligacy, it all meant that, as the Small Faces were preparing to reintroduce themselves to the world, Marriott could be found dismantling Beehive's state-of-the-art studio and selling off its component parts at rock bottom prices, as well as some of his guitars. This may also have been partly to do with the aim (at the time unfulfilled) of leaving Britain, him having married the American-born Pam in March '77.

Fortunately for the reunion, the public's interest in the band was kept alive in '76 by the release of a quite splendid Small Faces compilation. *The Singles Album* – subtitled *All the Decca 'A' + 'B' Sides* – was an entry in the much-admired Rock Roots series devised by Decca employee Alan Fitter. It was an early example of an archivist approach to popular music which is now common but was then rare. Explains Fitter of the line, "Decca had so much superb material in the vaults that wasn't being released – Genesis, Them, the Zombies, etc." He doesn't believe the go-ahead to release the Small Faces album came as a consequence of the recent reissue hits. As for units shifted of *The Singles Album*, he says, "The sales were pretty good for most of the series. I think they exceeded expectations."

The release also exceeded the expectations of the time in terms of thought and care. Although *The Singles Album* was restricted to the Small Faces' pre-Immediate days, in every other way it was impressively comprehensive. In an age of shoddy best-ofs designed only to make money, it was astonishing to find a compilation that didn't restrict itself to A-sides and which furthermore spurned watery simulated-stereo mixes for the power and authenticity of original monoaural iterations. As such, the LP was a delight for old fans who had gaps in their collection, aficionados who didn't have gaps but simply liked the convenience of the songs all being on one disc, and newcomers who had recently been alerted to the band's virtues by the radio. The band's profile was sustained the following year via NEMS releasing the Immediate-era compilation *Small Faces' Greatest Hits* and a reissue of *Ogdens' Nut Gone Flake.*

In April 1977, the band finally began granting interviews to announce their reformation and to promote a forthcoming British tour. A feature in *Sounds* that month found Marriott revealing to Chas de Whalley the insecure character he increasingly kept hidden behind a wall of buffoonery. "I'm really nervous about this one," he said. "It's like you made a model aeroplane and you don't know whether it's gonna fly … In rehearsals it works. It's what I've always wanted to do. But I get these terrible nightmares that everything blows up when we do a gig … Until you get in front of a crowd, you don't know." He boasted of having written a new song called 'Has-Beens in Harmony' which he adjudged "smashing," yet its very title sounds like a double bluff. (The track was never released.) At the same time, he seemed genuinely euphoric to be a Small Face again. "As far as we're concerned, this is it. It's got to go on for the next five, ten years. It's great to hear a guitar and a Wurlitzer together again … With this band it's … like grinning at one another all the time … The attitude right now is like … almost too happy." He was even able to take some satisfaction from his straitened circumstances. "I don't want to be a superstar again … As long as I've got enough cash to keep my family, what more do I need? I don't want what Rod Stewart wants. No way. There might have been a time when I did. But I was younger then and I learned … When you get that heavy star trip laid on you, you start believing it."

Presumably through the Mel Bush connection the Small Faces secured a prestigious guest slot on the BBC television show of current pop idol David Essex (who, incidentally, had secured the role in *Evita* of Che Guevara that Marriott had spurned), on which they performed 'Whatcha Gonna Do About It'. Essex would be one of the attendees at their live shows, as would Elton John and Michael Jackson.

However, when the tour opened in Sheffield, it has to be said it was in decidedly shaky fashion. The band had serious technical difficulties, with McLagan's keys out of tune and Marriott at one point dropping his guitar. Their version of Chuck Berry's 'Don't You Lie to Me' seemed apropos of no Small Faces musical tradition. (McLagan later spoke of them having recorded a studio version of the song in this period, but it was never released.) Marriott and the restless crowd engaged in banter that only just stopped short of nastiness.

The gigs did improve, partly because his bandmates read Marriott the riot act about taking to the stage drunk. The last night of the tour at London's Rainbow Theatre was well received, with the band and guest P.P. Arnold clearly having fun. However, a motif in reviews was that the new songs with which the band interleaved the old hits were not overly impressive. This misgiving could be dismissed as simply the inevitable consequence of the later songs not having had the same chance to embed themselves in the public's affections – until, that is, the new album made its appearance.

Said album was titled *Playmates* and released in August 1977, more than a year after the band had started recording it. It came housed in a sleeve with a distinctive antediluvian-looking illustration by Dan Fern featuring doe-eyed, doll-like children. The image was slightly bizarre but might for long-time fans vaguely invoke the spirit of 'HappyDaysToyTown'. The band's logo for the record was designed by Barney Bubbles, the graphic artist of the moment, mainly through his work for Stiff Records. Bubbles was an old friend of McLagan's from art school. Perhaps ominously, he declined to take credit for the logo because these days the Small Faces weren't cool. This wasn't because of anything specific they'd done – it was something that could be said of any artist of the Small Faces' generation at that moment in time.

The musical landscape had changed yet further since the re-released 'Itchycoo Park' had charted. While Sixties veterans might be able to understand ABBA, Queen and even Demis Roussos, they were less equipped to deal with punk rock. The Small Faces may have taken the piss out of the Beautiful People in 'Itchycoo Park', but the attitude toward same by the Sex Pistols – standard-bearers of punk – was somewhat more malicious, exemplified by their slogan "Never trust a hippie," an inversion of the hippie mantra, "Never trust anyone over the age of thirty." An indication that punk's agenda couldn't be further removed from the vulnerable love songs that had made the Small Faces so endearing was the fact that the Pistols were apt to play a live cover of 'Whatcha Gonna Do About It' in which lead singer Johnny Rotten changed the first line to "I want you to know that I *hate* you, baby." "These kids take what we were doing but they go a bit too far," Marriott observed of punk to de Whalley. "They take all the fun out of it." He was, inescapably, sounding exactly like the kind of old fart punks despised.

Yet there's no getting around the fact that the reason punks had a 'year-zero' attitude to popular music was precisely because of a decline in the craft of the Sixties generation that the contents of *Playmates* perfectly epitomised. The heart veritably sinks at the opening bars of first track 'High and Happy', written by Marriott. With its choppy guitar riff, female backing singers, pedestrian horn charts and hoarse Marriott vocals, it both sounds nothing like the Small Faces ever had. More importantly, aesthetically it's utterly ordinary. (Some might also have an issue with its exaltation of refuge from life's problems via drugs use and the effect this proselytising might have.)

A trio of songs demonstrate Marriott's increasing predilection for country music. The Marriott-written 'Saylarvee' features barrelhouse piano from its composer and a nimble electric guitar break from Saul Sheckner. The other examples are Marriott/McLagan collaborations, 'This Song's Just for You' and 'Smilin' in Tune'. All three are perfectly competent (if hardly glittering) examples of the genre but must have been bewildering to old Small Faces fans. Moreover, 'Smilin' in Tune' is clearly supposed to serve as the anthem for the Small Faces reunion: not only does its title echo Marriott's happy-vibes sentiments about the reunion as articulated in his comments to de Whalley, but it pointedly constitutes the closing cut and name-checks in its lyric 'Itchycoo Park'. This slice of country pie only serves to draw attention, though, to the fact that the distinctly British nature of much of the original band's music is nowhere to be found.

Another thing that gives the album an unmistakable mid-Seventies aura of decline and decadence is a clutch of the type of somnambulant ballads that proliferated in the era and had helped drain rock of the rebel image that had previously been thought an integral part of it. Marriott and McLagan are responsible for one of them, 'Never Too Late'. Another brace – 'Tonight' and 'Drive-In Romance' – are provided by the pair of McLagan and journalist/author John Pidgeon (who wrote the 1976 book *Rod Stewart and the Changing Faces*). McLagan plays acoustic guitar on 'Tonight', which surprisingly was later the recipient of a cover version by no less a figure than Ringo Starr, who included it on his 1978 effort *Bad Boy*.

The uptempo 'Lookin' for a Love' has a sprightliness that marks it out from the surrounding material, but that's the only way it shines, and in any case Talmy's production is no less muddy than the Kemastri mixes. 'Playmates' (Marriott) is a soulful seduction song that doesn't really go anywhere.

'Find It' (Marriott/Lane/McLagan/Jones) closed the first vinyl side. As can be seen from the publishing credit, it's the sole clue herein to what might have been if Lane had stayed the course. With the distaff soul singing plastered over it, though, it doesn't feel that different from the rest of the material. It's also a groove rather than a song. Blues harp from Marriott takes it into the fade without the feeling of anything having been achieved despite it going on for six minutes.

The only other track the band laid down with Lane's involvement was 'Lonely No More'. Although in its melodiousness and slickness it would not have sounded out of place on a *Rumours*-period Fleetwood Mac album, it's also very Small Faces in its vulnerability and thankfulness for love. It had genuine potential to be a hit single, something which could have profoundly affected the fortunes of the reunion. It's bizarre but symptomatic that it wasn't included on the album.

It has long been a dichotomy that the decline of pop musicians' craft runs parallel to their improvement in technique. It's one proven on this album. However, the universal fact that popular-music recording artists do their best work in their twenties is compounded by some specific individual declines. It isn't only Marriott's voice that has deteriorated since the last time the Small Faces released a record. Jones' drumming changed considerably during the lifetime of the Faces. Although he still sometimes shone – his performance on '(I Know) I'm Losing You', which features on Rod Stewart's *Every Picture Tells a Story* album, is easily equal to that on 'Tin Soldier' – it steadily became less urgent and less interesting, and this is noticeable here.

The fact that this is no longer the Small Faces the listeners had known is constantly underlined by elements unfamiliar from Small Faces fare, whether it be collective female backing vocals, blasts of mouth harp or strains of mandolin (the latter contributed by Joe Brown, who also provides some acoustic guitar). Meanwhile, although horns – supplied on this record by Mel Collins – weren't a complete stranger to previous Small Faces fare, never have they sounded so uninteresting and rote as they do here.

Of course, to some extent change, experimentation and bucking expectations were what the Sixties incarnation of the Small Faces were all about. The group, though, had run into a resurrection conundrum that would become familiar over the coming years as defunct groups increasingly reassembled: getting the band back together inevitably leads to fans expecting them to sound a certain way, but that expectation is illogical and impossible. The Small Faces that the world had known – in reality, in concept, in spirit, in circumstance, in sound – were gone forever. However dominant Marriott had historically been within the Small Faces, Ronnie Lane was always more than one quarter of the band. On top of his missing songwriting skills was loss of chemistry. Alchemy within bands is indefinable, immeasurable and impossible to mathematically, consciously construct. It exists nonetheless, something proven by how slick and skilful the Small Faces had been literally within weeks of their formation. On top of all that, however, is the fact that even if all the constituent parts of the Small Faces had reassembled, it would not have magically enabled the band to pick up the thread from 1969. Eight years on, they were different people with different motivations, tastes and techniques – as demonstrated by McLagan's previous comment in this text that, after the Small Faces' original split, he, Jones and Lane were no longer interested in the "young person's medium" of pop songs. Much the same problem had afflicted both the Byrds' reunion album of 1973 and *Before We Were So Rudely Interrupted*, the reunion album by the Animals released at exactly the same time as the Small Faces' effort. Where Small Faces fans were disappointed by the absence of the bright, impish, melodic, Hammond-dominated Small Faces sound of yore, 'Byrdmaniax' were upset at the lack of jangling twelve-string Rickenbackers and ethereal harmonies and Animals devotees were perplexed by the non-appearance of percolating, commercial R&B driven along by Vox Continental organ.

The you-can't-go-back lesson was underscored by the group photo on *Playmates*' inner sleeve: Rick Wills' unfamiliar face seemed almost an effrontery, Marriott's walrus moustache was just as disorienting, and Jones' swept-back barnet was the almost absurdly over-stylised product of an era that was definitely not the 1960s. Only McLagan looked impressive: his handsome and sharp-cheeked appearance a bit of a turnaround from the days when the keyboardist's jug ears and depressed tooth made him stick out uncomfortably in Small Faces pictures.

The album was by default doubly deficient through its timing: in the wake of the studiedly British and frenetic punk scene, non-urgent tempos, country digressions and Americana (e.g., references to things like drive-ins), only seemed to prove that the Small Faces were out of touch. The band might have dodged this perception had the record been released within a normal timeframe after its completion, but getting in under the wire before the punk revolution was not to be. (By a yet further curious coincidence, the Animals LP had also been held up for a considerable period by contractual obligations on the part of their lead singer of which the rest of the group hadn't been informed.)

The *Playmates* album was accompanied by a single, 'Lookin' for a Love' backed with another McLagan–Pidgeon co-write, the noirish, horn punctuated 'Kayoed (By Luv)'. The 45 came in a picture sleeve, something now common even in the British market. However, this one unimaginatively featured the same band picture as seen on the inner sleeve of the parent album. Like *Playmates*, the single failed to chart.

Reviews of the album were poor. *Sounds* adjudged it "limp, flabby and muted." Across the Atlantic, *Creem* said, "Those pintsized ravers and giddy hucksters are now, on this set, a bunch of plodders, playing by rote." Small Faces members were just as unforgiving about what they'd conjured up. "I don't think it was a very good record," McLagan admits. Jones said in 1994,

"When we jammed in private it was just like the old days, but the album was piss poor."

The mediocre sales were in spite of heavy promotion. Not only was the album the recipient of full-page UK music-press advertisements, but the group played several festival shows in Germany and in the same month embarked on another, longer UK tour. They were by now a five-piece, with Jimmy McCulloch having been poached from Wings to provide lead guitar. (His mellifluous work can be heard on 'Kayoed [By Luv]'.) For McLagan, the new addition was like the attempt to recruit Frampton to the Small Faces all over again, predicated on Marriott's insecurity about his own guitar ability and a desire to infuse some youth into the set-up. "A big mistake," he said. "McCulloch [was] a great guitarist and all that but a pain in the neck as a bloke and we didn't need him." McLagan was probably destined never to be happy about McCulloch's presence. In 1974, the guitarist had tried to pull Kim, McLagan's new partner and soon-to-be wife, right in front of his face.

Live, McLagan was dismayed that Marriott tended now not to soulfulness but to vocal gymnastics, the type of singing that would much later become familiar from TV talent shows, a showboating style designed not to communicate emotion but demonstrate technique. Additionally, despite the high number of new songs in the repertoire, the keyboardist was dismayed by the *de rigueur* oldies. "We had to do 'Itchycoo Park' and all that," he laments. "I fucking hated it. It was going backwards. So much of the show was history." Jones was also not having a good time, mainly because of Marriott. "When Steve was nice, he was lovely to be around, but when he was in one of those moods and 'orrible, you didn't want to be near him," he says. He adds, "He was not the pretty boy that he was. He'd let himself go because of whatever drugs he was taking and bits and pieces." Marriott's receding hairline and overweight state might not have been so noticeable had it not been for his apparent determination to bring attention to his physical decline by lack of pride in his appearance. O'Leary recalls one particular gig: "Kenney Jones said, 'Can't you get him to put something nice on?' I said, 'You tell him.' He went out in a pair of wellingtons, dungarees and a red shirt."

Then there was the 'gobbing'. Despite his reservations about punk, Marriott for some reason proceeded to adopt one of its hallmarks. McLagan says his abiding memory of the Small Faces reunion is, "Steve spitting at the audience. Every night." It left the keyboardist bewildered. "Somebody should have said, 'But Steve, it's the audience spits on the band.' Just stupid. Imagine being in the audience and having someone spit on you … I think he was getting in first. I don't really know. It was the strangest thing." "Steve was in a different place," says Jones. "His head was up his arse. It wasn't a professional attitude."

The depressing circumstances were made worse by the poor state of Marriott's health. Whether it was because of drug use or Marriott's highly-strung personality or both, after a gig at the Edinburgh Playhouse McLagan found himself in the alarming position of having to give Marriott the kiss of life when the singer suddenly stopped breathing as they were enjoying a nightcap in Marriott's hotel room. He subsequently found out that Marriott had experienced several such episodes previously. He was then just 30.

Despite its poor reception and lack of chart action, Playmates apparently sold in sufficient quantities to make it worth Atlantic's while to give the reunited Small Faces the go-ahead for a second album.

The album was recorded at Beehive with the assistance of Island Records' mobile recording unit, 'Kemastri' once again acting as pseudonymous collective producer. It's unclear, though, how much of the album was the result of new sessions, with some tracks dating from the original Joe Brown studio work and some from the Talmy recordings. By the end of the process, Mc-Culloch – a tempestuous character destined to die in 1979 of heart failure at the age of 26 – seems to have made himself *persona non grata*. Although he appeared in a promotional film for the album's single, his name is buried in the "our thanks" section of the LP's back-cover credits. The band, *sans* Mc-Culloch, get their faces on the front cover this time, but only in a small monochrome picture on the wall of a living room – the room rendered as a comic book panel-like illustration – in which a record is playing on a turntable. The same photo appears on the back cover in colour, but not much bigger. If this bespeaks a nervousness, it's unwarranted. Although the hair is generally of an unseemly length for the post-punk era, Marriott for one looks younger than on the last outing, having shaved off his moustache. Not that any of this mattered much: the band had effectively split up by the time of the set's August 1978 release.

The uptempo opener 'Over Too Soon' (Marriott/McLagan) is a pleasant but slightly boring love song. Its mediocrity is dismayingly underlined by the fact that it's a sort of inferior 'Lonely No More', which once again is mystifyingly absent. 'Too Many Crossroads' (Marriott/McLagan) is a slow-cooking bad-luck anthem. It comes to a close without having inspired any emotion on the part of the listener. 'Let Me Down Gently', a McLagan–Pidgeon collaboration, is a Cajun-inflected mass singalong but still average.

Wills gets his own compositional track with 'Thinkin' About Love', although Marriott handles vocal duties rather than the bassist/'false face'. It's perky and likeable and no worse than anything else on offer. Marriott's mildly pop-oriented pledge of devotion 'Stand by Me (Stand by You)', which closed the first vinyl side, is probably the LP's highlight in the sense that it's the one song present that listeners find themselves humming afterwards.

'Brown Man Do' is Marriott's tribute to the perseverance of people of colour in the face of hardship. While mildly moving, it's a little shocking that the swathes of organ from McLagan – such a welcome presence on so many previous Small Faces recordings – are actually rather tedious. Also shocking is the fact that the McLagan vocal on 'Real Sour' – a dissection of a dying relationship written by him and John Pidgeon – is a bit of a relief after Marriott's gone-to-pot hoarseness and self-parodic overwroughtness.

'Soldier' is a composition by Joe Brown. "It's just a song that occurred to me about people sending their bleeding kids off to war and not wanting to go there with them," says Brown. Peculiarly, this grand statement is given not a dramatic setting but – a female chorale aside – a down-home treatment, a conceptual deficiency for which Marriott's histrionics don't compensate. That the muscular 'You Ain't Seen Nothing Yet' carries the publishing credit Marriott/McLagan/Wills/Jones simply leads to the cheapskate reaction that it's befuddling that it took four people to write such a nondescript song.

With the closing 'Filthy Rich' (Marriott) we finally have, after two albums, a reminder of a major element of the old Small Faces sound, in this case cockney and music hall tones. Unfortunately its humour – a hankering to create an artificial woman with "Mitzi Gaynor's arse and Jayne Mansfield's posthumous tits" – is merely crass where 'Rene' was pleasantly ribald. This is something of a shame, for otherwise the tune possesses some vitality, Marriott for once finds a range where he doesn't sound like he's straining and the track marks the first time on the LP that the soundscape doesn't seem suffocatingly crowded.

78 in the Shade is no particular disgrace and is often well-crafted, but there is nothing exceptional about any of it. It's all overlaid with that patina of soporific dullness that seemed to afflict the output of all thirty-something musicians in the second half of the Seventies. McLagan says of the album that it's "even worse" than *Playmates*. For his part, Marriott opined, "*78 in the Shade* was a bit heavier [than *Playmates*]. Like Humble Pie. I think it would've gotten heavier and heavier had it gone further on."

Perhaps mercifully for the memory of the Small Faces, "it" didn't go "further on." The taster single was 'Stand by Me (Stand by You)'. It was backed with 'Hungry and Looking', a not-bad group-composed instrumental named for what O'Leary remembers as Marriott's on-his-uppers catchphrase. It features some greasy mouth harp, a competent sax solo and some slick McCulloch guitar runs. The disc got nowhere, and not necessarily because Marriott ostentatiously, and somewhat predictably considering his recent behaviour, picked his nose in the promo. Second single 'Filthy Rich' b/w 'Over Too Soon' dribbled out in June '78 to similar public apathy. The dismissive title given the parent album (by McLagan) was lived down to by its chart non-performance upon its September 1978 release. It's to be doubted, though, whether the Small Faces reunion would have continued (or more accurately been revived) even had it been a hit.

Jones told McLagan that Marriott's behaviour had led to a situation where he was cringing every time he stepped out on stage with the singer. "He agreed," Jones recalled. "We fulfilled our contractual obligations, then we were done." "I stopped taking Steve's calls," McLagan says. "I just got bored listening to him on the phone. I wasn't interested." Marriott seemed to have been cheerfully oblivious of his bandmates' disgust with him. "The reunion wasn't financially viable," he claimed. "Too many of us had too many tax and other financial pressures to do what we'd've had to do — take it street level and play all the clubs and support gigs."

"Small Faces Part Two was never going to happen," says O'Leary. "They were in it for the money ... If Ronnie and Steve had been doing the thing, whether they would have got on or not, certainly there would have been a better content. It would have been a more saleable venture. It didn't work. The punters at the end of the day are not stupid." Neither Jones nor McLagan, though, are prepared to even allow that better results might have been obtained by Lane being involved in the reunion. "I think it was doomed," says McLagan. "I wasn't that keen on it in the first place ... It was a hopeless idea really because it was all about money." While Jones laments, "It really wasn't the same without Ronnie Lane," he also says, "You can't turn the clock back and expect it to be the same."

It wasn't even as if the band ended up with any of the money that everyone concedes was the motivation behind the reunion. Jones has recalled that at the end of the project, each member was theoretically owed £15,000 (around £85k today). Marriott's share was eaten up by his existing contractual problems, while Jones and McLagan had to pick up the tab for the two albums' production costs ("We did get paid eventually," says Joe Brown of the studio time he'd donated). This left them each with "pennies." Only Wills was remunerated fully.

"I wish we'd never done that," summarises Jones of the reunion. "One thing I regret in life is the reformation of the Small Faces. I really didn't like it at all and I should have walked out when Ronnie Lane walked out. I like to wipe that part out of my life."

8　Own Up Time

The now two-times splintered Small Faces proceeded to seek work where they could find it.

Ian McLagan became a session musician and sideman, his talents and reputation ensuring gigs – in concert and in the studio – with both peers (the Rolling Stones, Carly Simon) and musicians who had grown up listening to his bands' music (e.g. the Rich Kids, formed by ex-Sex Pistol Glen Matlock). As well as this, he secured a solo deal and by 1981 was on his second album.

Marriott resumed his career with the chaotic approach that had always characterised it, lurching from penury to fortune and back again. "Steve was always able to get some money from somewhere," notes O'Leary. A case in point is the fact that by the end of the decade he was being paid to participate in a project that at the height of punk nobody would have imagined ever being possible: a reunion of Humble Pie. The reunion was essentially the deployment of a brand name: only Marriott and Shirley had appeared on previous Pie fare. However, it resulted in two albums. When *On to Victory* (1980) was released it created another ostensibly unimaginable vista: it appeared on Don Arden's label Jet. David Arden – who was, he says, "more or less" his father's "right-hand man" by then – explains that the hook-up came at the recommendation of CBS Records president Walter Yetnikoff, who told the Pie's management "That's the best little record company going. If you want Humble Pie to happen with this new album, take 'em there." Was there a big reunion between his father and Marriott? "No, there wasn't. He was off doing his thing." He also says, "I saw Stevie on a few occasions. I can't say we were great mates, but he was the chirpy little chappie. Most of the time." How well did *On to Victory* do? "It wasn't great at all actually, but we had very little promotion from them. We didn't make money on it, that's for sure." However, that was not the reason Humble Pie only recorded one album for Jet. "Polydor offered them a deal that took in a lot more territories. We only had the UK, Ireland, Germany and a couple of other small European territories."

The second album, *Go for the Throat* (1981), featured a new version of 'Tin Soldier'. While the very notion was questionable to say the least – why try to match perfection? – it bizarrely saw the song become a semi-hit in the States, climbing to #58 on *Billboard*, fifteen places higher than the peerless original had managed.

As a non-composing drummer, Kenney Jones might have seemed the ex-Small Face least liable to do well, but he proceeded to become the most comfortably-off of all of them. The stroke of luck that led to this, however, was one tinged with trauma and tragedy, for it involved the shocking death of an old friend. In September 1978, Jones attended the premiere of biopic *The Buddy Holly Story*. "They had the reception before the film," he recalls. "We all met in Peppermint Park off Leicester Square and had drinks." Who drummer Keith Moon was one of the guests. Moon's work had been unimpressive on *Who Are You*, the Who album released three weeks previously, but the drummer was making an attempt to deal with the excesses that had led to the diminution of his vast talent. Jones: "I was talking to Mooney. He said, 'I've been straight. I've not had a drink for a long time and I've been taking these pills that if you do have a drink they make you violently ill, so there's no way in a million years I'm gonna go near it.' He was in great shape. Then we all walked *en masse* round to Leicester Square into the Odeon cinema and watched the film. I remember saying goodbye at one o'clock in the morning. I went home, went to bed, woke up the next morning, put the TV on and the news came on and they announced that Keith Moon had been found dead of a drug overdose. I thought, 'What the fuck's he up to now? Another prank. He can't be dead – I just was with him.'" The report, though, was true. Possibly accidentally, Moon had taken a fatally high dose of the very drug prescribed to cure his alcoholism. "I found that one very difficult to take at the time," reflects Jones. "A massive shock."

The story shortly took another unexpected turn when Jones was contacted by the Who's manager. "I got the call about three months later from Bill Curbishley saying the band have had a meeting and they want you to join the band, they won't consider anyone else. I said, 'I'm sorry Bill, that's very kind, thanks for the offer, but I can't.'" On the night of the premiere, Jones had arrived back from the US where he'd gone in pursuit of a plan to form what he terms as "the Eagles done English." The project was to be put together by him and Glyn Johns in partnership with Atlantic Records. Jones explained this to Curbishley. "He was quite taken aback that I said no. He said, 'Well, Pete's coming into the office about six o'clock this evening, why don't you pop in?'" Jones took up the offer to reconnect with Townshend. "Curbishley and myself and Pete just sat around talking for about an hour-and-a-half just having a laugh about the good old days. Then Pete said, 'You've gotta join us – you're part of the mod band, you're one of us.' They worked on me a little bit. I said, 'Let me go and talk to the band.' They all were great, said, 'You got to do it.'"

Although Jones joining the Who might seem a fanboy's logical fantasy – the Who were a mod band, the Small Faces were a mod band, ergo he was a natural choice – Townshend confirms that there were more rational reasons for it. "I'd done a lot of recording with Kenney," he says in reference to demos he'd long recruited him to play on. "I didn't work with many other drummers. I'd done a bit of work with Charlie Watts, but apart from that… I'd always admired Kenney's workman-like approach to rhythm and song construction and keeping it simple. There's something that's very difficult to carry with a drummer. Keith Moon was a decorative drummer, but he also had immensely sharp concentration so it balanced it out. He would always be listening. But a lot of drummers white out. They start to play a rhythm, they get an adrenaline rush, and they kind of leave the building, but they're still unfortunately playing the drums. Kenney was a really down, solid, grounded drummer, and he managed to stay awake and aware and in the room. Whatever he was playing therefore, whatever kind of phase he was going through as a drummer, I just loved it."

After confirming to the Who that he would be taking up their offer, Jones threw a celebratory party at London's Stringfellows nightclub. He was surprised to find Marriott and Lane turn up together and that they seemed to be getting along well. Jones: "Steve said, 'Lend us a few bob, Ken.' Obviously now I was doing better than them."

Jones' tenure in the Who spanned two studio albums and three years of live work. It was not in any way an unequivocally happy period, continuing as it did the decline in the quality of Who product and featuring clashes with Roger Daltrey, who didn't feel Jones' drumming style was appropriate for the group and made no bones about saying so. For his part, Townshend says, "Although Roger says that he didn't really enjoy the Who period with Kenney, I fucking loved it. It was a great sadness to me when it all fell apart."

Not even Daltrey could deny that in one sense at least it was highly fortunate for the Who that they hooked up with Jones. The group were at that time negotiating a recording contract with Warner Bros. Curbishley told Jones that he was intending to ask for a five-million dollar advance. Jones – who'd recently read about substantially higher deals granted to David Bowie and Paul Simon – told him he should go for fifteen. Curbishley didn't obtain quite that amount, but the twelve million he secured – two million of which was non-recoupable – was far bigger than he would have gotten had he not had that conversation with the drummer. It was an action replay of Jones' advice to Billy Gaff a decade earlier about the Faces, albeit adjusted for inflation and the massive increases in remuneration made possible by the exponential expansion of the music industry. With his share, Jones was set up for life.

Ronnie Lane, meanwhile, had been steadily moving in the opposite direction. "I got a phone call from Ronnie saying, 'I'm completely and totally broke, will you produce a solo album for me?'" recalls Pete Townshend. "I said, 'No, I can't do that, it's too much of a call. But I'll do an album with you if we can persuade Glyn Johns to produce.' So I called Glyn – all within an hour – and he said, 'Yes, I'd love to do it.' And we went and we did *Rough Mix* together." *Rough Mix* was an intermittently excellent collaboration between Lane and Townshend released in 1977. Presumably, some of the album's Lane contributions would have graced *Playmates* had he continued with the Small Faces reunion. "It did okay, but it wasn't a huge hit," says Townshend. By the time of its release, however, Lane had problems on his mind other than chart stats and record royalties.

He had lately found himself more and more afflicted by the type of mysterious and debilitating physical problems that had manifested themselves during his short-lived tenure with the re-formed Small Faces. "His legs would give way, his speech was slurred," says McLagan. "He didn't know what was going on." Townshend says that it was during the sessions for *Rough Mix* that Lane received the formal diagnosis that he had inherited multiple sclerosis from his mother. This was real life-changing stuff. The degenerative condition would shortly take away his ability both to walk unaided and to play bass. "I never heard him complain," says Keith Altham, who remained close to him. "He was that kind of character. Had a lot of courage. Kept a brave face on everything." Good cheer though couldn't make his condition go away. Although Lane subsequently released the 1979 solo album *See Me*, on which Eric Clapton guested, it was to be the final release of his lifetime.

In 1982, Kurt Loder of *Rolling Stone* wrote, "Lane puts part of the blame for his condition on drugs and alcohol and the rock 'n' roll lifestyle he knew with the Faces," quoting Lane as saying, "I did a lot of really unreasonable things in those days. I'm ashamed of myself for the way I've gone on, very ashamed." It's not clear from that statement whether Lane is specifically referring to the way he treated Sue Hunt. Asked if Lane was the kind of person who would assume he was being punished by a higher authority for the way that he'd lived his life, Townshend says, "I don't know. I suppose it's possible." In any case, Townshend points out that this instant-coffee version of karma wasn't in Meher Baba's teachings. "Meher Baba did not talk about punishment or heaven and hell," he says. "Karma can only be made sense of if you accept that there's a programme of endless reincarnation in which we live again and again and again, trying to work through karma that we inherit from our last life."

Laurie O'Leary accompanied Marriott on a visit to see Lane. He was shocked by what he saw. "Ronnie looked pretty bad, pretty pathetic, poor sod. His looks had gone. At this point, he was able to walk with a stick, but he was very weak." Some reports say that when Marriott first saw Lane in a wheelchair, he burst into tears.

A gig by Marriott's latest band Blind Drunk at the Bridge House in London's Canning Town in September '81 featured a guest appearance by Zoot Money on which Lane contributed backing vocals. The show and Marriott's own shock at the condition of his erstwhile best friend sparked an idea in his mind. "The emotion got in, the sympathy," says O'Leary. "He put aside all of

which featured the playing of both Marriott and Lane – Leverton says, "The version on the Majik Mijits record was done from scratch." The smooth-rolling music on this track is complemented by the sentiment of awe in the face of love that had always characterised most of Marriott's best songs: the heart melts when he notes, "Got a woman, got a kid, Lord got a whole lot more."

Marriott's marital bliss also informs 'Toe Rag', a paean – if rather a bantering one – to Marriott and Pam's young son Toby. "A lot of fun doing that track," notes Leverton. The cockney vocal and acoustic guitar-led music was recorded in a crowded students' bar with a piece of cardboard serving as a baffle board. The same happiness seems to inform the lovely ballad 'Be the One', although Leverton describes it as "a guitar idea that Steve had and I came up with some lyrics that fitted it."

Leverton, in fact, recalls Marriott's domestic happiness with new wife Pam at this juncture eclipsing any lingering grievances he had about Dee Anthony. "Very optimistic character. Just get up and start again." However, he adds, "But he had to have his say about it." Said say took the form of 'How Does it Feel', whose narrator declares that he hopes the unnamed addressee burns in hell and asks him how he can sleep with the lies that he tells. It's a powerful and moving invective and a sprightly piece of music. Of the growling-riffed Marriott–Leverton co-write 'You Spent It', the bassist says, "That's basically about ex-wives that spent all the money and then cheated on you at the same time … He had this guitar riff and some angry words and I helped him with the lyrics."

In January 1976 Lane told Chris Welch in *Melody Maker*, "When we started the Faces it was just for a loon. And then they had to turn it into something else. All the rock bands turned into the very thing they were supposed to be kicking against. It all became an industry, and that's what really nauses me." Throughout 1976, such sentiments would take firmer hold amongst musicians a generation younger than Lane, resulting in the phenomenon known as punk rock. Although Lane's sentiments can retrospectively be read as a hankering for a new wave, that the form it took displeased him is something explored in 'If the Cap Fits (Chicken)'. Leverton says, "Mick came up with some of the music for it. It's directed at punks. The words go, 'Don't you call me old man, punk/You're yellow to your liver/You stink of smack and rock 'n' roll.'" Of Lane's opinion of the musical movement that had designated musicians of his and Marriott's generation has-beens and sell-outs Leverton says, "There was a lot of pretenders, a lot of people not really that talented getting away with it and calling everyone else old farts."

With its snarling guitar riff Lane's hard-hitting 'Last Tango in NATO' ironically sounds a little like Humble Pie, although Lane's declaration of disgust about the posturing of the Cold War's two nuclear superpowers was the type of political commentary that the apolitical, hedonistic Marriott would never have essayed.

In 'Birthday Girl', Marriott's pays humorous tribute to a relative. "That's about Steve Marriott's auntie in Georgia," says Leverton. "He went to visit her and by coincidence it was her birthday and she was in this cabin in the woods all on her own on her birthday with her hair all done and her dress on and everything and there was nobody there just to wish her happy birthday, so he wrote her a song."

Lane contributes a trio of songs about his own relatives. 'Bomber's Moon' humorously describes his singularly crowded nuptials. "He went to America on his honeymoon and his wife invited her mother and her brother and her sister and her father along," explains Leverton. "Ronnie picked the bill up for all these people." The folksy 'Ruby Jack' could be said to be a companion piece to 'Toe Rag'. Leverton: "That's about Ronnie's son Reuben, just wishing him all the best in his life. [He was] about four or five when that was written." With the jolly 'Son of Stanley Lane', Leverton says, "He makes reference to blue plaques, but he wasn't self-centered enough to say, 'Ronnie Lane lived here.' It's like, 'Once lived here the son of Stanley Lane,' who was his father. I think it's got a little bit of fatality about it in as much as, 'When I'm dead and gone they'll put a blue plaque to say that, yes, he was a man to be reckoned with.'"

On 'That's the Way It Goes', Marriott and Lane alternate cockney lead vocals over a barrelhouse piano. "I said, 'Steve, there's a hit there you know,'" recalls O'Leary. "I really thought we'd get our money back by putting [it] out. Thinking of Small Faces and 'Itchycoo Park' and 'Lazy Sunday' and the old East End and all that. But Steve dismissed that."

Regardless of whether 'That's the Way it Goes' had hit-single potential, the Majik Mijits now had a cache of high-quality songs with which to try to secure a record deal. With Lane's wife Boo – the project's administrator – keeping hold of the masters, Marriott ran off some cassette copies with which to drum up record-company interest. The plan was to target Stateside labels. "I couldn't make out why they would want to do this in the States, but maybe they had a hook into a record company," says O'Leary. "They were both quite well-known in the business." Moreover, O'Leary had his own reasons for encouraging the Atlantic crossing. He says Marriott was under "intense pressure" in the UK. Said pressure related to the fact that he hadn't paid the income tax he should have in his native land, which may be down to corrupt management or Marriott's own negligence or – as was so often the case in Marriott's financial affairs – a combination of the two. O'Leary: "I had to say to him, 'Steve I can't really stand up being your advisor and manager because even your accountants are now putting me in the frame as the man who knows all about your business. You're best off going to the States and sort yourself out.'" Thus did Marriott combine his quest for a Majik Mijits deal with a fleeing of his country's shores, something of course facilitated by Pam's American nationality. O'Leary: "He sold Beehive and then bought a place up in Wood Green, and then sold up Wood Green and went to the States." "I went with him," says Leverton. "We wrote a few tunes in New York. He used to ring Ronnie every single day, let him know what's happening. It was still an ongoing thing then. That would have been October of '81."

The Majik Mijits aroused some interest in the industry, and moreover from significant figures. "Arista were quite interested and possibly the Rolling Stones' label were interested," recalls Leverton. Arista's founder and president Clive Davis may have inadvertently had a hand in the demise of Immediate Records, but he was both a legend in the business and fondly regarded. Formerly president of Columbia Records for six years, Davis set up Arista in 1975. He had already signed to the label Barry Manilow, Patti Smith, Lou Reed, Heart, the Kinks, the Bay City Rollers, Eric Carmen, Donovan, the Grateful Dead, Graham Parker and Al Stewart. "Clive Davis was a big noise," Leverton notes. It goes without saying that the same description could be applied to the Rolling Stones, even though Rolling Stones Records – a vanity label distributed by third parties – hadn't done much since its 1970 founding. Apart from Stones product (group and solo releases), it had only released fare by ex-Bob Marley cohort Peter Tosh and the now-forgotten band Kracker. However, any release attached to the label featuring the band's famous lapping tongue logo – and furthermore one that had the distribution muscle of Atlantic (US) and EMI (UK) – had more than a fair chance of success.

No sooner had this record-company interest been obtained, however, than Marriott had gone off the Majik Mijits project. After his own return home, Leverton didn't hear anything from Marriott for a while. "You start getting on [with] other things," he reflects. "Then I had a call from Steve that as far as he was concerned, he wasn't going to take it any further because it could be damaging to Ronnie. That would be the winter of '81." "He could see it wasn't going to happen purely because Ronnie was worse than he ever thought he was," says O'Leary. Leverton's understanding is that Rolling Stones Records had expressed concern about Lane's ability to promote Majik Mijits product. Whether the Stones' concern precipitated or followed Marriott's loss of interest in the project, the latter was now convinced that Lane's health issues made it unviable. Accordingly, when Clive Davis consented to a meeting with him he found that he was more enthusiastic than Marriott. Leverton says, "I believe he was quite impressed, but Steve declined. There'd be gigs, there'd be TVs, radios and things like that. The usual stuff that you have to do. He didn't feel that Ronnie was up to it and he didn't want to be responsible for dragging him through [it]." He adds, "Ronnie had a different view."

"They followed him over there," says O'Leary of the Lanes. "When Boo came back with Ronnie, they were very anti-Steve. Obviously, they'd had an altercation." The couple's main grievance centred around a sum of money that had recently been passed from Keith Richards to Marriott. O'Leary, who refers to the Stones guitarist by the s-less version of his surname that he used in the Sixties, says, "Steve borrowed some money off Keith Richard. They came back with a story that he'd got a quarter of a million dollars and just left them with no money and nowhere to go." Pam Marriott remembered the sum in question to be the somewhat lower (and more plausible) figure of $5,000. O'Leary: "They were very unhappy and tried to create a problem between Steve and I ... They said 'Oh, Steve's this and he's even pissed off with you and he reckons you should have given him some money' and all this ... It didn't work, because Steve never did me any harm."

"He thought the money that he'd borrowed from Keith was Majik Mijits money," says Leverton of Lane. "There was a bit of a misunderstanding over all of that and some pretty hostile telephone calls between the two of them. I think Steve was quite hurt by it ... I know it was a personal loan because they were quite close friends, Marriott and Keith. It [was] a personal loan to move his family to Georgia. I think the words were, 'Here's some money, get yourself out of New York, down to Georgia, get yourself a band and go out on the road' ... Sometimes you have to save yourself before you can save other people." It does seem unlikely that, after all he'd done for Lane, Marriott would have then ripped him off. Having said that, while there doesn't seem to be evidence that Marriott defrauded Lane when it came to the Majik Mijits, considering what he had done to him with regards Beehive Cottage it's easy to understand why Lane became convinced that he'd been cheated.

"Steve formed a band to go out and get some money," says O'Leary. "He said to me, 'I've got a baby to keep and a wife to keep', but he also had a habit I suppose. They started gigging out there. I think he felt he'd done sufficient for Ronnie ... Steve would turn quickly." Leverton says that his phone call announcing the end of the Mijits mission found Marriott neither devastated nor resigned. "He wasn't that sort of bloke. If you've reached the end of something, you've reached the end of it and you just move on. He was just very quick at picking up and starting again. He was very matter-of-fact: like – what's next?" O'Leary was less sanguine. "No way did I feel happy about losing seven grand," he says. However, he adds, "At the same time, I always had the feeling, 'Well, there're about four tracks on there that I know are worthy of the money and eventually, if we do a catalogue thing, yes, something will happen.'"

Meanwhile, Lane had his deteriorating physical condition to address. He tried various cures of the alternative variety, including decompression chambers and snake venom. When Altham and Ian Stewart were in New York on Stones work, they heard word that Lane was in a rattlesnake-venom clinic in Fort Lauderdale and travelled down to see him. Altham: "We knocked on Ronnie's motel room door. He wasn't going to let us in at first because we were pretending to be the vice squad. The door opened: 'You bastards.' We said, 'How's the treatment?' He said, 'Well, it doesn't seem to be having a lot of effect, but there's a very good side effect. As soon as a mosquito bites me, it dies instantly.' Took him out on a porter's trolley, because he couldn't walk. He loved it. We took him around to his favourite bars."

Altham and Stewart decided to see what they could do for their old friend. "Stu and I were at a party," explains Altham. "I think it was Jeff Beck's fortieth.

Ronnie was there as well, not in earshot. We were saying, 'He's broke.' We knew he hadn't got any money and he had this terrible diagnosis. We said, 'We ought to try and put a concert or something together and get him some money.' Jeff overheard us and said, 'I'll do it.' We said, 'Great. Who else can we get?' With that, Clapton, who was also in the party, came over and said he would do it and before we knew it we'd got a whole bunch of people. Hammersmith Odeon was our initial idea and just give the proceeds to Ronnie to help him with his medical expenses and general life. While we were doing that, it just kind of grew. I think they got in touch with [promoter] Harvey Goldsmith. He said, 'We ought to do something bigger.' Before we knew it, we were talking about a concert at the Royal Albert Hall and then one in Madison Square Gardens and one in Los Angeles. Ronnie got to hear about it inevitably and we had to confess to him what we were doing. He said, 'No, don't do it for me, do it for the MS charity. That's where the money should go.' Typical Ronnie." Thus was born the 1983 star-studded concert titled The Ronnie Lane Appeal for Action into Research for Multiple Sclerosis (ARMS). At the concerts Lane would usually appear on stage at some point.

Sadly, the good intentions were ultimately stymied. "I knew as soon as it started to get overinflated it was going to go wrong somehow, because the bigger these things are the more they tend to get out of control," Altham says. "I flew out to New York to see the Madison Square Gardens gig. I was wandering around backstage and all these superstars were there. Charlie Watts came up to me and said, 'Wot you doin' 'ere?' I said, 'Well, I've come over to support the concert.' He said, "oo paid for your ticket?' I said, 'I did.' He said, 'Well you must be the first bugger that's actually paid for their own ticket because everybody else seems to be on expenses.' He wasn't too happy about it – and with good reason, because expenses by their very nature in these situations become elastic and people were making money out of it. Money started going adrift and astray and I think at the end of the day a lot of the money that had been made for the ARMS charity found its way into individuals' pockets."

It would have been logical for Marriott to be a star turn at one or more of the ARMS concerts, but no invitation was extended to him. "He was hurt by that and it showed the animosity," says O'Leary. He and Lane were never reconciled. The schism was symbolically demonstrated by the width of the Atlantic Ocean continuing to lie between them even though they each changed location. O'Leary: "Ronnie went to live in the States and he got married out there. Steve came back."

In the late Nineties, tapes of the Majik Mijits sessions found their way into the hands of Kenney Jones who – flush with his earnings from his lucrative if difficult period with the Who – had by now established himself as the custodian of the Small Faces' legacy and affairs. "I rang him," says O'Leary. "I got wind of it that he had the masters and I said, 'Ken, they don't belong to you, they were nicked' … [He said] he would have a vested interest in adding to the masters with Mac because then they could put it out as the Small Faces."

Although such an artificially constructed Small Faces album might have disgusted the same purists who had misgivings about the project's lack of genuine Marriott/Lane co-writes, many other Small Faces diehards would have been intrigued, even delighted, at the idea. O'Leary, though, wasn't prepared to enable such Fantasy-League vistas: "I said, 'No, it's cheating, I wouldn't allow it' ... I mean, what could they add? The Majik Mijits were the Majik Mijits." Leverton says Boo and/or Jones' notion was "a hare-brained idea" and "scandalous." Even McLagan says, "It was a rotten idea. If they'd wanted that, they would have asked us." Jones, in any case, denies everything. "For a start I hated the name Magic Mijits," he says. "I fucking couldn't stand it and still can't stand it, so I would have no part of it." He states it to be part of a strand of Marriott humour to which he was averse. "'Packet of Three' and all that. Spitting, gobbing, and all that. That's what I didn't like about Steve."

In the end, the "catalogue thing" for which O'Leary had always held out a vague hope did materialise. Nearly two decades after the Mijits recordings, he was approached by reissue/heritage label New Millennium Communications, who had possibly been apprised of the recordings by the bootlegs of it that were floating around. "I've got part of the money back," says O'Leary. "I did a deal for five grand." Although he had still lost out, he was able to be philosophical about it on the grounds that a project he believed in had finally obtained a release and it was now a tribute to his "extremely good" friend Marriott.

With both Lane and Marriott by now dead, Leverton was commissioned to ensure that the recordings were released in a state as close to how they were intended to sound as was possible. "There were solos that hadn't been played," says Leverton. "I remember at the time both Steve and Ronnie saying, 'We should get a good saxophone player to fly over the top of it all.' It's terrible when you're second-guessing people, but I got Frank Mead, who's a tenor sax/alto sax player. He came in and did a fantastic job." Once a fine-tuning had effected such changes as bringing up the handclaps on 'Lonely No More' and pushing down the organ in which the rough mix of the whole album had been somewhat drenched, the recordings were almost ready for the market. "There was a worry about it being too short," Leverton says. A suggestion was made to include a Lane composition called 'Beguine'. Leverton: "A nice track, but Ronnie didn't have all the words finished. He'd sing a few words and he'd hum a bit. We felt it wouldn't be doing him any justice to stick out a half-written song." Instead, Leverton elected to end the set with a fragment of 'All or Nothing' as performed by Marriott and Lane at the Bridge House gig that kicked off the entire reunion. "It played at a really slow pace, so to have featured the whole track would have been laborious for the listener," Leverton says. "It's a bit of sentimentality on my part, because it is Steve and Ronnie. It's the only number one that the Small Faces ever had. Ronnie is on there singing backing vocals. [It's] just a little postscript. I find it a bit spooky."

The twelve tracks preceding it on the released CD studiously alternated Marriott and Lane songs. The sequencing was, again, designed to be authentic. "When we were bringing cassettes out of the studio to play to people like Clive Davis, that's the way that it ran," says Leverton. "I always thought the title should have been *Six of One, Half a Dozen of the Other.*"

With neither principal around anymore to promote it, *The Legendary Majik Mijits* – released in the summer of 2000 – was never destined to make a big splash. Moreover, it might also be said that the years it had spent in the vaults gave the album a mystique to which it was impossible to live up. The album suffered to some extent from the same problems that afflicted *Playmates* and *78 in the Shade*: it was the product of Sixties artists who were nowadays able to proffer professionalism rather more than they were vitality. However, the songs were uniformly better than those on the two Small Faces reunion LPs. Lane was both taking up some songwriting slack and complementing Marriott's contrasting approach. The smoothly galloping 'Lonely No More' (used to open proceedings) is pretty damn close to being a classic. The sweet ode 'Be the One' and the coruscating 'Last Tango in NATO' also touch greatness. While there's nothing else present quite as good, neither is there anything awful on what is a thoroughly enjoyable collection. It can also hold its own with products by Marriott and Lane's peers. It's interesting to note that at the time of the recording (as opposed to release), the Rolling Stones issued *Tattoo You* and the Who *Face Dances. The Legendary Majik Mijits* is as good as either of those, something that we can take as some form of evidence that Marriott and Lane – had their partnership not been ruptured back in the Sixties – could have kept artistic and commercial pace with their contemporaries.

The Majik Mijits project is at the very least as genuine a Small Faces reunion as the iteration of the band featuring Rick Wills. If it must serve as a group epitaph, it's a pleasingly decent one.

9 Afterglow

"He became a cult figure playing gigs through the Eighties," says Laurie O'Leary of Steve Marriott.

The phraseology puts one in mind of the manager of movie-spoof band Spinal Tap explaining away his charges' declining ticket sales with the words, "Their appeal is becoming more selective." In the 1980s, the man whose group had set an audience attendance record as recently as 1973 began scraping a living by playing in pubs and bars. The names he chose for his bands added an infantilism to the aura of sadness: Blind Drunk, Packet of Three, the DTs. There was an exception to this exultation in adolescent hedonism, but it carried its own pathos, as O'Leary explains: "When he came back in eighty-something, I said, 'Steve, you know the official receivers are after you?' Went to see his band, which at the time was Packet of Three, and they changed the name onstage. He said, 'Er, we are the Official Receivers.' I thought, 'Oh fu-u-uck.' He was really rubbing their nose in it." Furthermore, the man who implied he'd been able to name his price when Humble Pie signed to A&M was now and permanently would be without a meaningful record contract. From 1982 up to his death in 1991, Marriott's only album releases were live records released on obscure labels like Zeus, Mau Mau and Bellaphon.

Marriott's life was further blighted by his excesses. O'Leary's comment "He was into cocaine quite a lot" is something of an understatement. Marriott's drug use habitually wiped out the money that O'Leary was occasionally able to rustle up for him from promoters or publishers. "He did forty thousand pound in 2½ months," O'Leary recalls. "He moved out of his house up into [a] hotel. It was pathetic to think he'd done forty grand in 2½ months." An anecdote about Marriott from Jerry Shirley – who with Jim Leverton made up the rest of Packet of Three – gives a flavour of Marriott's reduced circumstances. "He had a moment of inspiration one night where he offered a job as a rhythm-guitar player in the band to Mick Green from the Pirates," says Shirley. "Jim Leverton and I had a cow, because we couldn't afford a fourth member. We could just about make it as a three-piece." Shirley's addendum demonstrates how infuriatingly self-absorbed Marriott could be: "Steve says, 'Well, can you call him and tell him he can't join?' I thought, 'Oh, thanks a lot, Steve.'"

Joe Brown and his wife Vicki were godparents to Toby Marriott. "When he was around, he was a good father," says Joe. "But he worked a lot. Very difficult to be a decent father when you're away all the bloody time." Nor was Marriott an attentive partner. He never seemed to have trouble acquiring women, but did seem to have difficulty keeping them. He split with Pam in the early Eighties, following which the closest he seems to have come to happiness is in the mid-Eighties when he hooked up with his childhood sweetheart Manon Piercey. Brown – who later married Piercey – says, "I heard not just from Manon but from other people like Jimmy Leverton and Davy Hynes that Steve was a totally different guy when he was with Manon. He was a really nice, home-loving guy. He used to do all the cooking and he was great. But when he was out on the road, I suppose it all got a bit different." When his relationship with Piercey faltered, Marriott's next long-term union, which lasted until his death, was a purportedly abusive and troubled one with the fourteen-years-younger Toni Poulton.

The story of Marriott's sad final years, though, is more nuanced than it might appear. Marriott's hedonism, for instance, did have its limits. O'Leary recalls, "I saw him refuse something. I asked him what it was. He said, 'Smack – don't get into that.'" He was even able to forego his worst vice. "When I got back together with him in Packet of Three, I'd noticed a wonderful change in him," says Shirley. "Simply put, he'd stopped putting things up his nose."

Moreover, it was far from the case that the big paydays were necessarily all in the past. If Marriott endured penury, it was often through choice. Invited in the early Eighties to audition to replace the departed Paul Rodgers in Bad Company, Marriott turned up inebriated and distracted and essentially acting in a similarly infuriating way to that of drummer Simon Kirke's deceased ex-Free guitarist colleague Paul Kossoff. His failure to get that gig might be something that could be put in the category of involuntary were it not for known incidents of self-sabotage. Joe Brown remembers a "very strange" incident from 1986. "He came over to see me," he says. "He brought Manon with him. He was supposed to go and meet these record people and he just didn't bother going. They'd come all the way over from Germany. He was one of those guys: easy come, easy go. I think that's how he run his life: all or nothing. That's the kind of character he was. He sailed through life. He wasn't bothered about anything."

Not that Marriott spurned all gigs: at the turn of the Nineties, his voice could be heard in a brace of TV advertisements. The Inland Revenue wouldn't have necessarily known about them: he insisted on cash payments.

By that juncture, it was adjudged by the type of people who invested in such things that a professional Frampton–Marriott reunion was a viable proposition. At first, Marriott seemed enthusiastic about the overture, so much so that he abandoned his activities with his current band, which included Jim Leverton. "He went to California early in '91 to do some stuff with Peter Frampton," Leverton recalls. "We were all pissed off because we were working hard with Steve and he just dropped it." However, the ever-mercurial/irrational Marriott ultimately chose not to forsake his current hand-to-mouth existence for theoretical ease and comfort. Says Leverton, "The story I heard was that it was going pretty good and then contracts were laid out on the table and the words 'Humble Pie' appeared and he said, 'Nah. I'm not signing anything along those lines. If we're going to do something, it has to be now and not trading on what went before.' And of course business people don't see it that way. It's a brand name, like Heinz Baked Beans."

Keith Altham saw a Marriott gig in Epsom in 1991. "He was still a good performer," he says. "It was a good band." Marriott went back to Altham's house afterwards for a few beers where Altham observed that "he'd put on a bit of weight," but it was Marriott himself who drew attention to another change. "He saw that I'd lost most of my hair and said, 'When did you lose yours, then?' I thought, 'What does he mean?'" Altham took a closer look at Marriott's scalp. "He looked like he'd got a full head of hair, sticking up in a spike. I realised it was a hair weave." Did Marriott seem upset that he had to resort to such a cover-up? "No, not in the slightest." Nor did Marriott seem distressed by his reduced circumstances. "He was a survivor, and he loved being on stage and performing. At least people were listening to him. He was frontman, and he got pretty much his own way with whatever they wanted to perform. He seemed very content." Joe Brown observes, "He was always happy. Always." "There is some truth in that," says Shirley. "There was times where he was more at peace with himself in Packet of Three."

Although Ian McLagan continued to record and perform under his own name whenever the opportunity arose, he mostly subsisted on his sideman activity. His CV was ultimately highly impressive. Among the luminaries with whom he worked in the studio or onstage after the Small Faces reunion were Billy Bragg, Jackson Browne, Joe Cocker, Bob Dylan, Melissa Etheridge, Buddy Guy, John Hiatt, Bonnie Raitt, Bruce Springsteen and the Stray Cats. Despite the star-studded résumé, though, he didn't end up wealthy. McLagan told this author that he had been tempted to buy Bill Wyman's 2002 book *Rolling with The Stones* but that its price tag (£30 in the UK) was beyond his means. The reason for his relative poverty was his own drug problems, in his case revolving around crack. It accounted for the better part of the $100k advance he obtained for his 1979 solo album *Troublemaker*. Nonetheless, he was generally speaking a happy man, having found long-term domestic bliss with Kim Moon, the ex-wife of Keith Moon. "Richard Barnes, who was my best friend from art college, was seeing Kim when Moon was behaving badly towards her," says Townshend. "I pleaded with Barney to end the relationship with Kim because I was afraid Keith would commit suicide if he lost Kim. He was apparently absolutely, deeply besotted with her. Barney did step back just for a couple of days in deference to me and she went straight to Mac. It lasted and it was very, very solid."

Kenney Jones had a difficult start to the Eighties. Townshend, increasingly afflicted by hearing problems caused by the Who's huge stage volume, thought that the band only had a future as a studio outfit and that they should cease live performance. His colleagues disagreed. Daltrey, meanwhile, continued to state, and with ever increasing force, that Jones was not working out as Moon's replacement. The upshot was dissolution, preceded by one last big payday in the shape of a 1982 farewell tour. Once that was over, Jones found he no longer had the option of returning to the sessions that had previously provided him a lucrative side-line. Courtesy of drum machines, he says, drummers had all of a sudden become "a thing of the past and slightly redundant."

However, whereas Lane, McLagan and Marriott blew the Seventies fortunes they all made, Jones – as ever – was the prudent exception. The only man to have come out of the Small Faces with significant savings predictably not only held onto the bonanza that came via his Who membership but expanded it. "The last time I saw Kenney, he was playing polo and Prince Charles was on his team," says Joe Brown. Jones set up his own polo club in 1994 after having been smitten by the sport in the mid-Seventies. The wheel of fortune even eventually turned for him musically. Come the millennium, he was racking up chart placings as part of supergroup the Jones Gang.

There is but one Small Face. Although of a younger average age than most Sixties bands, the Small Faces have a shockingly high attrition rate: discounting Seventies stand-in Rick Wills, Kenney Jones is now the only surviving member of any line-up of the group.

Marriott was the first to go. His heart problems meant that he was almost certainly not long for this world. However, when his premature death did come, it was in an unexpected and horrific way. On 20 April 1991, he was burnt alive in a fire at his cottage in Arkesden, Essex. It is theorised that, in an inebriated state, he had fallen asleep with a lit cigarette and had woken up to find the house ablaze but was helpless to save himself. He was just 44. "A lot of people have written about Steve being obnoxious, nasty," says O'Leary. "Under the [influence] of booze and whatever, I suppose, yeah. I never experienced that Steve. He was always great with me ... My wife knew a lot of people in the music business that I've handled. She burst into tears. When he died, she just couldn't believe it. She said, 'He was a real person.'" "It's just so sad that we lost this fucking immense talent, this incredible shining light of a ball of energy," says Townshend. "And to some extent, is it possible that without Stevie, we wouldn't have had Ronnie Lane? His relationship in the beginning with Steve was very, very, very close, and it must have helped build something in both directions for them."

There were some crumbs of comfort for Marriott fans. His death could just about be posited as having some poetry: just like the tin soldier of his greatest song, he had expired in flames. Meanwhile, despite lately being a man whose star was felt by many to have waned – which number seemed to include him: he exhibited signs of jealousy over the fame and success of both old rivals (Rod Stewart) and old friends (Kenney Jones) – his death was deemed important enough to make the headlines. The front page story of the massive-circulation UK tabloid *News of the World* declared "Ciggie Blaze Kills Rock Legend".

When told about the tragedy, Lane is said to have observed, "I wish I was with him." Although friends testify to Lane retaining his humour and stoicism as his life steadily got worse, glimmers of despair such as that occasionally came to the surface. In 1990, Lane told the *NME*'s Martin Aston, "I soldier on, though for what reason, I don't know." Neither decompression chambers nor snake venom nor removal of his mercury fillings nor elimination diets nor any of the other increasingly desperate cures for MS that he tried prevented his incremental physical deterioration. Jones was heard to publicly lament that every time he saw him another piece of Lane's body wasn't working. Symptoms of his decline humiliatingly included lack of sphincter control. Perhaps it was a blessing that on 4 June 1997, aged 51, Lane succumbed to a virus that, without the MS, would not normally be lethal. His place of death was Colorado, which had been his home since 1994 after a period domiciled in Austin, an artistic and bohemian enclave in the otherwise conservative state of Texas.

Austin was also the domicile for the last part of his life of Ian McLagan, who lived considerably longer than Lane but still didn't quite make it to his seventies, passing away aged 69 on 3 December 2014 after suffering a stroke. He had been talking of a Small Faces reunion to mark the band's fiftieth anniversary in 2015. Following some recent heart problems, though, he had issued do-not-resuscitate instructions.

He had been preceded to the afterlife by his beloved Kim, who was killed in a car crash in 2006. "It was a fucking tragedy what happened to Kim," says Townshend. "Unbelievable." Kim's death seemed to bring a belated mellowness to McLagan. Although generally a friendly and decent man, he was by common consensus also the most bitter and hot-headed among the ex-Small Faces. By August 2014, he was telling this author that his days of brooding over the injustices he felt had been done to the Small Faces were over. "I've spent too many years hating people and being angry," he said. "It's a long time ago. The money's gone." He still retained a residue of fury, though, on behalf of his fallen comrades. "The worst part about it is that Steve and Ronnie never got a penny for all their hard work, all their songs, all the recordings," he lamented. "Not one penny. The widows get some money now, but they got nothing. That's not right, but no one can sort that out."

This is not for the want of trying, at least on the part of Kenney Jones. As the baby of the band and a 'mere' drummer, Jones seemed the least likely person to set out on the trail of missing Small Faces monies, but it is he who has had the wherewithal – in terms of both finance and time – to nose around and cause trouble. It was a mission he began in the 1970s. The good money he was making in the Faces meant that he hadn't felt much motivation to investigate why Small Faces-related revenue streams had stopped flowing, but a chance conversation apprised him of the need to be seen to be doing something. "If you don't do anything about it, it's called sleeping on your rights," he explains. There was little progress, though, for several years. "All these paper trails are quite complex," he points out. However, he remained determined. "I kept a reasonable track of the paper trail so I can prove anything that goes on and I can definitely prove fraud in certain issues … They didn't bank on me being successful in my own right. I've got my own money I can throw at it and, as far as I'm concerned, I can match theirs. Any big company – EMI, anybody." "We had help and we pay for that: every time we get a cheque, that person gets a cheque too," said McLagan. "But the point is Kenney's diligence and tenacity. He hasn't stopped. He's still in there fighting for the Small Faces and he's really done wonders." Altham isn't surprised that Jones has taken on this custodian role. "Kenney was always the toughie," he says. "People underestimated Kenney's resilience. Also, he had a bit more of a business head than the others. Kenney was a terrier. Once he got his teeth into something, he made sure he'd see it through."

Jones' achievements in this area are all the more remarkable for his intemperate nature. In his autobiography, he admitted, "Being an only child I was used to getting my way." This is made evident in several places in said book, not least in his recounting of a meeting in the early Nineties that his accountant managed to set up for him with Terry Shand, owner of Castle Communications. Castle were the current owners of the Small Faces' Immediate catalogue, having bought it off NEMS. Jones admits he was stand-offish at the meeting and that, when all parties went out to lunch, actually had to be restrained as he began jabbing his finger at Shand about the "pittance" Castle had been paying the Small Faces and their heirs. Luckily for him, Shand seems to have been an obliging soul, something perhaps related to the fact that he was at that point planning to sell his business. Shand offered a lump sum of £250,000, a 15 per cent royalty and an obligation on the part of Castle to get the surviving Small Faces members' approval for any future releases. Although a massive improvement on the current terms, Jones saw this as simply a starting point, convinced that the threat of an audit would see the quarter-million lump sum doubled. However, when his father shortly thereafter died, Jones was too traumatised to continue negotiations and acquiesced to McLagan's request to settle for what had already been offered. Castle's properties have subsequently been sold on three times and now reside with Universal Music, with whom the Small Faces representatives have a good relationship. "Eventually I'll own it, because I'll just buy it at some point," says Jones of the Immediate Small Faces catalogue. "I'll share it with everybody else that's legally entitled to it. It's not the possession I'm after. I just want to protect it."

As regards the other Small Faces record company, in 2002 McLagan said of Decca, "We finally signed a contract with them last year. They never paid us anything until '91. It's Don Arden *and* Decca's fault. They never apologised. That upset me as much as not getting paid. The least they could have done was say something like, 'Well, we apologise for the years that our predecessors never paid you, but here's a cheque.'"

Separate and in addition to mechanical royalties are publishing and performance revenues. Jones says of Avakak, "It's incredibly valuable to us collectively and to the two estates of Ronnie and Steve." He deduced "highly suspect" activity in this area, although doesn't seem to have suspicions about Tony Calder and Andrew Oldham, whom he says gave up their shares when Immediate folded. Jones has asserted that it was after that bankruptcy that money stopped coming in from Avakak. "United Artists were looking after the publishing and we had a 50–50 with them," says Jones. "When Immediate went bust, I was now in the Faces and I still used to get my cheques for Small Faces royalties, publishing, for the first six months, a year, then suddenly it stopped. I thought, 'What's going on here?'" This got worse in the late Seventies. "We found out United Artists sold our company, Avakak and their entire catalogue, to EMI. When you do that, and you're directors of a company, the ombudsman or the receiver – whoever's doing the deal with the lawyers – should have actually said, 'Do you want yours?' They never told us about it. So that's where a fraud is being committed. They just swept it under the carpet, thinking, 'Okay, the band's split up, no one will ever know.' If we'd caused a legal problem, it would have stopped the sale going through." The scale of the stakes involved are suggested by Malcolm Forrester's comment, "The actual liquidation was a big event, there was hundreds of people there."

McLagan said in 2003, "We just found out recently according to EMI, who now supposedly own the rights, that Steve signed a contract giving them his share, which is very unlikely when you think about it. Why would anyone sign it away?" Jones: "They couldn't have done it [without] us signing too." A legal action was instigated to demonstrate that the shares should sit with the band alone. However, Jones was rather vague in his book about the upshot ("At the time, however, it wasn't possible to make our case and we had to park the claim"). "I'm still fighting it now," says Jones. "They [owe] us an absolute fortune of publishing." What was once EMI's problem is now Sony's, the latter media giant having become the latest baton-bearer in the publishing ownership relay. Jones: "They've bought the problem, so I'm going to them. I know I can prove fraud. The best thing to do is do a deal. A settlement. Life's too short. But not short enough to fucking give up on it."

When it comes to record royalties, some contend that the free rein that the Immediate label gave their artists in the studio has backfired on them: their onetime artists bear a grievance about the lack of remuneration caused by their own high studio costs. Moreover, Andrew Loog Oldham asserts that no record royalties were forthcoming to the band because of the means by which those records made the hit parade. "Immediate bought every record into the charts," he says. "That's the reality. Because of our buying records into the charts, we had a break-even figure of a hundred thousand. A silver disc was quarter of a million and you were inside the top three. Mickie Most says in my first book, 'A hit doesn't earn you any more than three thousand pounds' (in that time)." "It's possible," concedes McLagan. "I'm accepting the fact that that must have happened. But my heart doesn't grieve over that – he's in the record business. He could have paid us some royalties."

Banes acknowledges that Immediate had to hype records into the charts ("We had the list of the record stores from EMI that were the chart shops and we'd go and buy the records. We spent money when we needed to") but denies that this prohibited a profit ("We weren't spending that much. It wasn't a thing we were doing all the time, but it was done, because everybody else was doing it"). Instead, he lays the blame solely on the Small Faces' insistence on being holed up in the studio.

It should also be pointed out that the villainy of the people with a hold over purse-strings was not always unequivocal. In Decca's case, it may even be non-existent. As the Small Faces were signed not to them but to Contemporary Records, the label's only legal obligation would have been to provide royalties to Arden's company. That Arden's alleged failure to pass on his charges' cut of said royalties was hardly the fault of Decca is something implicitly admitted in the fact that the band did not include Decca in the suit they brought against their ex-manager in 1967 over unpaid royalties.

Don Arden appeared to eventually come to the realisation that it was possible to become wealthy without denying his clients their rightful share. In the Seventies, he guided Electric Light Orchestra to superstardom. There seem to be no major misgivings on the part of ELO members about his handling of their finances. "ELO I think got the best out of Don Arden," acknowledges Jones.

In 2000, McLagan told *The Independent*, "Don Arden is a confused old man now, a sad case. He's had the cheek to want to negotiate with us about back royalties. I will not meet the man." The contrition this comment suggests on the part of Arden about whatever misbehaviour he *was* responsible for seems borne out by Jones' recollections. In the early Nineties, Chris France – who was assisting Jones in "investigating the back catalogue and publishing and God knows what" – made contact with Arden and set up a luncheon between him and Jones. The drummer was shocked to find out that Arden lived in the village of Lye, between Rygate and Dorking, which he himself had only recently moved from. "He lived at the end of the road, less than a mile away and he'd lived there for three years whilst I was living there," Jones recalls. "When we went to lunch, I said, 'Why didn't you contact me if you knew I lived up the road?' He said, 'I thought you were gonna kill me.' He was very helpful, trying to help in any way." Arden may have been humanised by his own recent travails: "His wife was upstairs really sick, obviously dying, so he was running upstairs and looking after her."

With regards the suggestion that his father began to feel contrition about his treatment of the Small Faces, David Arden says, "Contrition for what? Look at the big picture of things. What did he do? Contrition for what? Seriously."

Andrew Loog Oldham desired to make amends for the Small Faces not being paid, although this didn't amount to admitting to any wrongdoing. In 2002, he launched a High Court action to claim ownership of the rights to the Immediate catalogue. McLagan for one was not impressed. "He promised us he'd pay us this time when he releases all our stuff again," he scoffed. "I thought that was quite funny because he never paid us before. Why would we trust him this time? And anyway, he doesn't have the rights. He signed them away, and the people he signed them away to have been paying us regularly." "What was being disputed was Andrew's ownership of the masters because of the fact he financed them," says Paul Banes, who gave evidence for Oldham "When Immediate went to the wall, it was bought. The override that Andrew had on all these records, he should have been paid irrespective of whether the company had gone down or not." "They laughed him out of the High Court," said McLagan. "He's now on the run. They froze £400,000 of his money." Banes offers, "He found out 24 hours before that his lawyer had represented Sanctuary, so he couldn't represent Andrew." Banes says other things about the fairness of the hearing that are not included here for legal reasons.

As to why he waited so long to lay claim to the catalogue, Oldham said, "The fact is that sometime between 1967–1969 I went 'out to lunch' and did not return until the summer of 1995. During that time many aberrations manifested themselves." Either way, McLagan notes, "It took him another nine [sic] years to be not out to lunch, then he sued Sanctuary."

Despite the pleasure he seemed to take in Oldham's misfortune, McLagan ultimately had an emotional reunion with him. In 2002, he was reflecting on his last meeting with Oldham at a Los Angeles Rolling Stones gig in 1985. "I was walking back from the stage to go and get a beer and I heard this voice from the shadows behind me: 'Hey, Mac.' I said, 'Andrew Oldham, you thieving bastard, how the devil are you?' 'I'm fine!' Keith [Richards] still loves him. Keith won't have a word said against him. Mick [Jagger] has different feelings, I think." In 2014, McLagan was remembering an Oldham encounter with a different timbre "two or three years" before. "He would come to Austin to do panels [at] South by Southwest. One year Andrew Oldham took the stage at this panel. The first thing he said was, 'I'd like to apologise to Ian McLagan for things I said in my book.' I had his email address from a mutual friend and

I emailed him and I said, 'Andrew, next time you're in Austin, let's bury the hatchet, and this time not in your head.' He responded immediately saying, 'I'd like that.' The next year he came up while I was signing some books and I said to the lady I was signing [for], 'Scuse me for a minute.' I went up and we hugged and kissed. I said, 'It's great to see you, let's have dinner.'"

Today, Oldham says, "Immediate was formed for all the wrong reasons and produced some very bright music. The Small Faces were children. I had been spoilt by the Stones. I am not interested in proving anything." Others are happy to try to do the proving for him. There is a large school of thought that, while the Small Faces may well have been ripped off by Immediate, Tony Calder rather than Oldham was the villain of the piece. P.P. Arnold has said, "Tony Calder was a big-time crook, a gangster, really." Jerry Shirley opines, "I am defending Andrew, but Tony Calder – I don't know. If anybody was messing with money it would be far more likely to be Calder." Kenney Jones concurs, although admits he can't cite anything more specific than not liking the cut of Calder's jib. "Don't agree with that," says Forrester, stating he found both Calder and Oldham to be honourable men. He adds, "What happened after the liquidation is any man's guess."

"Andrew would be more likely to be guilty of risk-taking that was perhaps out of control," opines Keith Altham. "He had the creative flair and creative ability. He didn't keep sufficient control over some of his partners or employees." However, this is not a preamble to a denunciation of Calder. Although he says of the latter, "I'm sure he wasn't guiltless" and that "he could be easily persuaded that cutting corners was the way to go," he also claims, "He wasn't quite the crook that he was [made] out to be." As support for this, Altham says, "I had dealings with Tony Calder over the years where he left me in the lurch financially on fees and things, but he had a strange kind of loyalty in that when he next got involved with something that was making money, he'd pay you back." If Calder was corrupt, he took that secret to the grave with him. He died of pneumonia in 2018 aged 74. He and Oldham had remained friendly. Don Arden passed away in 2007 aged 81, the causes being Alzheimer's and pneumonia. His daughter Sharon had also become a music-business manager, but no suspicion of malpractice seems to hang over her stewardship of the affairs of the likes of Lita Ford, Gary Moore, Motörhead, post-Mercury Queen, the Smashing Pumpkins and, of course, her husband Ozzy Osbourne.

Jimmy Winston, meanwhile, managed to get his own rightful share of Small Faces monies independent of Jones. "In the very early days, when Ian McLagan joined and I went off and did my own things, I got no royalties from Contemporary or Don Arden for a long period," he says. "That was a bit annoying, but I just [thought] 'Oh, fuck it' … It wasn't 'til later that I thought, 'Hang on a minute.' In about 1976, Universal Music/Decca got the copyright back from all the other little things that Don had probably done with them. Don had bits of companies all over the place … I've got publishing with about two or three different publishers where bits and pieces of it ended up … Universal/Decca … had a long case going and they got it all back, the majority of it … I had to take them to task and got a big back payment and thereafter royalties. I wasn't going to bother about it, then this journalist came to talk to me one day. He said, 'Do you know they're re-releasing this, doing this, doing that?' He had all the information which I hadn't bothered to follow. He said, 'You should chase this up.' So I got in touch with Decca, went up to see the legal people and had a long period of taking it all to task … You could deal with Decca. They were too big to be too sneaky."

Winston says that at the beginning of 1998, "I had to go up and sign fresh, and we got a much better deal … I had to go through all the songs that I was on." Some compromise was involved. "I get a relative percentage to what I was on, as opposed to all of them. To get the deal in the end I had to do it the best I could. It's like 'You Need Loving' – that's not credited to me, but I was definitely a part of it originally." For the same reasons of practicality, he didn't pursue the fact that the title track of *Ogdens' Nut Gone Flake* bears McLagan's name as a co-composer instead of his. Very gratifyingly, the new settlement did not start at the point when it was signed. "There was a backlog which they'd managed to win as well. It was good, because it was like being paid for something you did years ago but you never got paid for then. It was the best couple of months' work I ever did. It also justifies what you do, because we did sit and suffer together and write and do stuff and there was good times."

It should be noted that, although Kenney Jones is a public supporter of the Conservative Party, he is no clichéd capitalist. Financial self-interest seems to have always been a secondary motive in his determination to lay claim to ownership of the Small Faces catalogue. When this author discussed with him in 2006 his failure to register for royalties for his playing on Rod Stewart's version of '(I Know) I'm Losing You' and mentioned that the money would have consequently been put into a central pot, he replied, "Well as long as it goes to someone needy."

One mission he has is to give greater prominence to the band's masterpiece, specifically by his quest to make an animated motion picture of the 'Happiness Stan' story. "It's a full-length feature animation film," he says. "A $50m epic. It leans more towards *Fantasia* than anything." Another indication that Jones has high ambitions for the project is the fact that he approached the most successful filmmaker of all time to make it. He would almost appear to have gone into his meeting with Steven Spielberg with the assumption that Spielberg would be more impressed by him than the other way around. "I was banking on the fact that he would be a fan of *Ogdens'* – most people are," he says. "He'd never heard of the Small Faces or *Ogdens'*. He said, 'I wasn't into music at all – I was a kid making my own experimental films.'" Shocking as the director's ignorance of the Small Faces' existence may have been, his reaction at least wasn't a flat-out 'no'. "Basically, they had no problem making it into a full-length animation film but because I'd taken the bare bones of it – I said, 'In this bit we need a new song', 'In this bit we need a new character' – he said, 'Go away and do all that and bring it back to us, then we can work on it.' And 'What was the message?' I didn't really have a message, but I've got a message now and it's powerful … When you write the lyrics out, the story is actually incredibly thin, so you've got to think more commercially. There's only Happiness Stan in it and Mad John and the fly. There's other people got to be in there, so I've invented a whole journey of different characters … So it's almost 'Influenced by *Ogdens*'." Jones says a new element of the storyline is, "The moon influences your personality. The tides rise and fall. The moon can influence a lot of things." However, he insists, "We're not tampering with the original. We're not going to go too far away from *Ogdens*'."

What with all his other ventures, Jones has only been able to work on the putative film on a piecemeal basis. Moreover, the project has encountered multiple hiccups. "I sat down with a friend of mine and scripted some of it. I said, 'Whatever you do, don't do anything without me there', and he did. He went off completely in a different direction, so that was it. Stopped that one." With regards to the issue of a professional scriptwriter, Jones has sometimes been petrified by indecision. "I could spend hundreds of thousands on writers and still not like it and then the problem is, if anyone else writes anything, we use anything similar to what they've done, then you've got a legal problem." This itself has a domino effect on production: "We can't really write the new songs until that storyline is done."

Jones estimates that the project needs "four or five new songs" to augment the six on the second side of *Ogdens*' plus an unheard, lyric-less Small Faces outtake that he has snaffled for the film. "I've got Pete Townshend," he says. "Every time I see him, he says, 'What's happening with *Ogdens*'?' because he's going to write a couple of songs on it … Townshend sees it completely and he's just champing at the bit to write the songs, but he can't write the songs until the story's finished … The seven tracks will be rearranged and God knows what and the other five songs will complete the story." Visuals-wise, Jones says, "I've got Uli Meyer, the world's top animator in my book. He did *Space Jam* and *Aladdin* and all that lot. He loves it. I've got Una Woodruff, who's the illustrator. Her artwork is just second to none. She's England's top wildlife artist. She's an old hippie like the rest of us. She's very *Ogdens*'." As for the voice artists, Jones says, "Phil Collins is going to do lead voiceover on it because he's a bit cockney. He'd play Happiness Stan."

Unfortunately, the project has dragged on over such a protracted period that other items on Jones' wish-list are no longer possible. At a time before George Harrison's passing, he said, "'The Journey' is very Beatley. It would be nice if I got Ringo and Paul and George to come into the studio and do that track." Stanley Unwin died in 2002. Jones' next-best choice for narration was Robin Williams, not least because he was a big fan of Unwin. The comedian's suicide in 2014 put an end to those plans. A death two years later stymied another casting ambition. "I want him to sing the voice of the Fly," said Jones of David Bowie. "He'd be stunning." Meanwhile, McLagan's demise has ruled him out of contributing to the music, an idea the keyboardist was keen on.

There has been an upside to the extended gestation, however. The animation technology that has developed during it has made it probable that, if it does happen, the movie will be commensurately better than first envisaged. "I've said that I don't want to use computer animation, but now I seriously have to look at it because it's come on so much more," notes Jones. "You've got two-dimensional now and three-dimensional coming in and it really is great. Now they've got facial expressions and muscle movement." Jones, in any case, is unapologetic about the time it has taken. "You've got Steve Marriott and Ronnie Lane and their memory to contend with. It's very important for me to get that right: somebody that sees *Ogdens'* the way I do and the way it's meant to be."

One can only look forward with keen anticipation to Happiness Stan's quest for the missing half of the moon sharing the multiplexes with the latest Pixar and Disney extravaganzas and bringing the Small Faces' music to an unsuspecting new demographic. ("Mommy – what does 'John 'ad it sussed' mean?")

"The Small Faces is an institution," says Jones. "It's got so many fans. I can't believe how many bands we influenced. I find out something new every day."

Although it's no great surprise that such a great band as the Small Faces have a legacy, what is arresting is how early it started. Its newsletters listed some remarkable, not to mention unlikely-seeming, names as honorary members of the Small Faces fan club, among them Sonny & Cher, the Walker Brothers and the Hollies. Val Williams confirms this was all genuine. She states of Pauline Corcoran, "If she saw anybody that really liked the band, she would add them to the list. Sonny & Cher were at *Ready Steady Go!* and met them and heard their music and really liked it. Pauline met them. She asked them if they'd like to be honorary members." Corcoran would seem to have missed a trick, however, by not approaching the Byrds. In 1966, said American ensemble namechecked the Small Faces in their phantasmagorical single 'Eight Miles High', cooing in their ethereal three-part harmonies, "In places, Small Faces abound." McLagan met the Byrds' David Crosby several times down the years and in one of their encounters Crosby confirmed to him that the line did indeed refer to the keyboardist's former ensemble, whom the Byrds "loved" when they first heard them on their '65 British tour.

Many long-term Small Faces fans were startled by the opening track of *Led Zeppelin II* (1969). 'Whole Lotta Love' seemed to be nothing more than a cover version of 'You Need Loving', albeit with a galvanising new guitar riff. Their amazement was shared by Marriott. "I couldn't believe it. I was astounded, quite astounded," he said. "The phrasing was exact ... He took that [vocal] note for note, word for word." "It's virtually identical," says Jones. "They openly say that. Robert Plant would come to our gigs all the time." Marriott told Tiven, "When we were in France, we played a gig with the Yardbirds, when Jimmy Page and Jeff Beck were with the group. After we did 'You Need Loving', Jimmy came back to me and asked what it was."

The Zeppelin track's composition was credited to all four of that band's members. Of course, the Small Faces couldn't complain too much about the plagiarism, it being the case that they openly admitted that the Marriott/Lane writing attribution of 'You Need Loving' is hardly justifiable. McLagan reveals, "When my book came out, I told the story and Willie Dixon's daughter Shirley – or their lawyers – got on to Decca and asked them to stop and desist until they'd paid them the money. And Decca got in touch with me: 'What's this all about?' I said, 'Yeah that's right.' I mean, Steve and Ronnie are dead anyway. I said, 'Yeah, fuck it, they nicked it. It's Willie Dixon's. You should pay Willie Dixon's daughter, for Christ's sake.'" The relevant lawsuit may have pre-dated McLagan's *All the Rage*, but Zeppelin had to cede monies to Willie Dixon's estate. "Great, innit?" said McLagan. "Fair's fair."

On David Bowie's 1972 breakthrough LP *The Rise and Fall of Ziggy Stardust and the Spiders from Mars*, the track 'Suffragette City' featured the line, "Wham, bam, thank you ma'am!" Of course, the Small Faces no more coined this phrase – meaning the practice of brief sexual congress with no thought of emotional attachment – any more than they were the first to deploy "all or nothing" to signify absolutism. However, it's perfectly feasible that Bowie was paying tribute to one of his favourite recording acts in much the same way he nodded in song to the Pretty Things and other heroes. "When we first started ... David Jones, as he was called then, was a folk singer," recalls Jones. "We used to drink in a little coffee shop in Denmark Street called the Giaconda ... We used to take him along to the gigs with us and he was like a fifth member of the Small Faces." Bowie played onstage with the Small Faces several times and Kenney Jones is convinced he would have been invited to join the band were it not for the fact that he was primarily a vocalist rather than an instrumentalist.

Vocal duo and ex-Turtles Flo & Eddie recorded 'Afterglow' on their eponymous 1973 album, while Australian singer–songwriter Daryl Braithwaite released his take on the same song as a single in 1977 and secured a top-40 chart placing with it in his home country. Despite their ostentatious disdain for old-guard musicians, many Seventies punks loved the Small Faces. The fact that the Sex Pistols traduced 'Whatcha Gonna Do About It' hid a soft spot on their part for these old farts: Pistols bassist and chief melody writer Glen Matlock has admitted of their 1977 single 'Pretty Vacant' that "the chord sequence for the chorus ... came straight from the Small Faces' 'Wham Bam Thank You Mam'..."

Watching the 1981 BBC comedy sci-fi television series *The Hitchhiker's Guide to the Galaxy*, Jenny Rylance found herself put in mind by its title theme of the orchestral opening of the title track of *Ogdens' Nut Gone Flake*.

She says, "I thought 'God, are they using...?' It sounds exactly like..." If her suspicion is correct, it means that the Eagles were inspired by the Small Faces: the music behind the programme's titles was 'Journey of the Sorcerer', an instrumental from the American country-rockers' 1975 album *One of These Nights*.

Nineteen seventy-nine saw the UK mod revival. While the whole movement might have been nebulous (a patchwork, never quite logical or consistent avowal of adherence to Sixties mods' musical and fashion interests) and contradictory (nostalgia for the values of 'modernism'), it nonetheless existed. This mini Parka-clad army naturally gravitated to a band with a long association with mod. Osmosis saw this new interest in the Small Faces' back catalogue spread beyond its borders to others of that generation: it wasn't unusual to see the era's skinheads buying Small Faces compilations. At this particular juncture in history, they could avail themselves of *Small Faces Big Hits*, an excellent 1980 Virgin Records release that was the first mainstream compilation since *The Autumn Stone* to represent both the Decca and Immediate years, with much of it in glorious mono.

As new generations of musicians rose to prominence, musical homages to the Small Faces proliferated. The first major one – indeed series of them – came from the Jam. The Jam's 1982 song 'The Gift' blatantly lifts a part from 'Don't Burst My Bubble', recently released for the first time after languishing in the vaults since its recording. The opening guitar line from their 1982 single 'The Bitterest Pill (I Ever Had to Swallow)' is a lift from 'Tin Soldier'. The Jam's live version of 'Get Yourself Together' appeared on an EP given away with initial copies of their 1983 compilation *Snap!* 'Wild Wood', a song released early in the solo career of the Jam's ex-frontman and main songwriter Paul Weller, feels suspiciously (if vaguely) like his take on 'The Autumn Stone'.

The homages didn't stop with the music. Weller commissioned a Jam band logo whose jagged lettering was deliberately in the style of the old Immediate Records logo. In the Jam's latter days Weller took advantage of the fact that he actually looked a little like Marriott, teasing his barnet into an approximation of the off-centre parting, ears-uncovered early Small Faces hairstyle. Via his publishing house Riot Stories, Weller was responsible for the first-ever Small Faces biography, if a slim one, in the shape of Terry Rawlings' magazine-format *All Our Yesterdays* (1982).

"They were the most complete band," Weller told John Hellier of Small Faces fanzine *The Darlings of Wapping Wharf Launderette*. "They had a great look but that alone is no good if you can't play ... The music, well that was just fantastic." As mentioned, in 2007 Weller chose 'Tin Soldier' as his favourite piece of music when he appeared on radio programme *Desert Island Discs*. Although Weller wouldn't like it, there is even a Steve Marriott comparison to be drawn from the fact that in 1983 he split up the Jam at the peak of their success in order to pursue other musical directions. The Style Council were to the Jam what Humble Pie were to the Small Faces: a group that never matched the standards of the band that was sacrificed to make way for it.

Weller was sometimes more of a fan of Small Faces music than were the Small Faces members themselves, as demonstrated by an amusing conversation he once had with McLagan. "Paul Weller said to me one day, 'My favourite Small Faces song is "Get Yourself Together",'" McLagan recalls. "I said, 'Really – how's it go?' He said, 'What the fuck are you talking about?' I said, 'Paul, surely you write a song and you record 'em and you play it once or twice in the studio and never play it again? Thirty years later, why would you remember it?'"

In the late Seventies, American heavy metal band Quiet Riot covered 'Tin Soldier' on their first album and 'Afterglow' on their second. When for a brief period in the mid-Eighties Quiet Riot became one of the biggest bands in the world, the Small Faces' name was being bandied about in print again. Kevin DuBrow – the band's singer and lyricist – publicly expressed his love of Marriott to anyone who would listen. In January 1984, he told Mat Snow of the *NME*, "Steve Marriott's my favourite singer. He's my idol! ... I know every song he ever did with the Small Faces and Pie – every single, every obscure fuckin' B-side, live tapes off the BBC Radio which people sent me ..." Marriott had recently opened the show for Quiet Riot at El Paso Coliseum in Texas and sat in with them when they performed 'C'mon Everybody' during their second encore. "This year we sold a lotta records, went number one in the States, but the greatest thing was Steve Marriott jamming with my group," DuBrow exclaimed. "Without a doubt!"

Some Small Faces fans (although possibly not Humble Pie devotees) would have cringed at the fact of Marriott being championed by the unsubtle likes of Quiet Riot. They would have been less leery of the tributes paid by post-modern pop band Blur, who came to prominence in the Cool Britannia wave of the 1990s. For a while, Blur were incapable of releasing an album that didn't engender reviews that namechecked the Small Faces, principally because of the group's simultaneous love of sweet tunes and crunching instrumentation but also because of the intermittently 'mockney' singing style of vocalist Damon Albarn. The fact that Blur released a song called 'The Universal' was also grist to that particular mill. Blur's contemporaries Oasis were also Small Faces fans, although this was evident more in public pronouncements and members' participation in tribute events than any directly identifiable element in the gleeful bouillabaisse of retro influences their music constituted. Something similar could be said about Ocean Colour Scene, albeit with the additional complication of their love of the Sixties being partly filtered through the prism of the Jam's take on the decade's music. "Noel Gallagher told me that they put a live album or single out," says McLagan of Oasis' chief songwriter. "He said, 'The audience sound wasn't so good, so we stole the audience track from the live "Tin Soldier".'"

Quiet Riot covered 'Itchycoo Park' in 1993. Two years later, the song was the subject of an even more unlikely interpretation, this one by the British dance-music outfit M People. This version, which combined pulsating artificial percussion with a female choir, made no.11 in the UK chart.

Buzzcocks, Gene, 60 ft Dolls, Dodgy, Ocean Colour Scene, Primal Scream, Ride and Paul Weller, amongst other Small Faces lovers, appeared on *Long Agos and Worlds Apart*, a 1996 album of Small Faces covers designed to raise money to help pay Ronnie Lane's medical bills. That same year, the Small Faces were given an Ivor Novello award for Outstanding Contribution to Music. Jones and McLagan attended, while Lane's brother Stan and Ronnie Wood collected the awards for their fallen comrades. In 2002, the Small Faces and the Faces were jointly inducted into the Rock 'n' Roll Hall of Fame. This prize had a suggestion of tokenism in the fact of the Small Faces being hitched to their successor band, who meant far more in the US where the awards are based. Nonetheless, both awards constituted deserved recognition and will have ignited interest among these who hadn't previously heard of the Small Faces. So too the blue plaque installed on Beehive Cottage in 2017 ("Steve Marriott 1947–1991. Singer, songwriter and vocalist with The Small Faces and Humble Pie: The Rock and Roll Hall of Fame Inductee lived in this house 1968–1977"), even if it was a BBC Essex award rather than the 'official' English Heritage grade granted to Jimi Hendrix's ex-abode. It's, so far, the closest thing to the fulfilment of Ronnie Lane's jocular statement in the Majik Mijits track 'Son of Stanley Lane' that one of these days his fame will be commemorated with a blue plaque outside his basement.

In 2012, the Small Faces became the latest subjects of the recent phenomenon of the jukebox musical in the shape of *All or Nothing*. Author Carol Harrison was an ex-mod and a childhood acquaintance of Marriott. Harrison interviewed members of Marriott's family and friends of the band in her research. The show – which was subtitled *The Mod Musical* – went on several UK tours and had a short run in the West End. It was then recalibrated as an 'experience', which stripped out the drama and had the cast perform the songs from the musical, plus other numbers by Sixties acts.

Acting as voice coach on the project was Marriott's daughter Mollie, soon to be a recording artist herself. As Joe Brown married her mother Manon Piercey, this makes her Brown's stepdaughter. "Mollie has got a great voice," Brown notes. "She's caught something off of him."

Small Faces fans – famous or otherwise – have been able to purchase their heroes' wares quite readily in recent years.

The Seventies were rather a wasteland for Small Faces product. While the first Immediate album was the only one of their LPs not in print, the band's excellence was clouded by the fact of the racks being awash with confusing and sub-standard compilations boasting what purported to be rarities. "Tracks that are 'unfinished' or 'alternate versions'," notes McLagan with disdain. "Which there weren't really any of. I mean, there's only one 'Tin Soldier'. If you hear 'Tin Soldier' without Steve singing on it or without the guitar, that's Andrew Oldham's fuck-up. There's one stereo and one mono. Same take. But apart from stereo and mono, there are other tracks that are just jams. I don't want them out. People can get that on bootlegs. When people hear about the Small Faces and they go and listen to all this *crap*, it's just so annoying. Andrew Oldham and Ken Mewis – the guy who worked in the office – they went into a studio and re-mixed everything we did on Immediate. Every single thing. Sometimes they took vocals out or took a keyboard out or took drums out, took the bass out. Just to make other tracks. Gave them different titles and then got twice the advance from CBS or Columbia. I know for a fact. Ken Mewis admitted it to me. You see 'em in truck stops in America. Every now and again a cassette or CD [will say] 'Rod Stewart and the Small Faces'. There was no such band called Rod Stewart and the Small Faces. It'll be maybe a couple of cuts of Rod – because he was on Immediate – and the rest of 'em are 'Tin Soldier', 'Donkey Rides, a Penny a Glass', but with different titles, and it's just a remix of the same tracks. It's bloody annoying."

Things began to improve a little in the early Eighties as the archive industry – which can be defined as reissue programmes helmed by people motivated as much by music as money – properly kicked into gear. Courtesy of Charly Records the first Immediate Small Faces album finally became available again, albeit in its horribly diluted stereo iteration. By the early Noughties, the situation had improved so much – assisted by the advent of CDs and their vastly greater playing times compared to vinyl – that Castle Communications were proffering a two-disc version of the same album which featured both mono and stereo versions as well as contemporaneous singles and B-sides, as well as miscellaneous (genuine) alternative versions and mixes. Said format – essentially a snapshot of an artist at a particular point in their history rather than a straight reproduction of an album's original contents – became standard for reissues, acquiring the generic term 'Deluxe Edition'. There have been deluxe editions of the Small Faces' first Decca album, *From the Beginning* and their two Immediate albums, all of which come with informative liner notes that – in some cases for the first time – give precise details about recording dates and personnel.

In 2000, *The BBC Sessions* provided the first unheard Small Faces material in decades, albeit most of it taking the form of live-in-the-studio radio performances. A version of Rufus Thomas' 'Jump Back' and studio renditions of 'If I Were a Carpenter' and 'Every Little Bit Hurts' complemented versions of more familiar Small Faces material.

Charly's box set *The Immediate Years* (1995) sought to round up everything Immediate-related that had been commercially released. It was admirably comprehensive but at the same time a mopping up exercise that by definition drew no distinction between the worthy and the worthless, imperishable masters sharing space with the phony alternatives McLagan spoke of.

It's not to be confused with *Here Come the Nice*, the 2014 Sanctuary box set comprising four full-length CDs, plus some additional novelty discs, which also concentrated on the Immediate years. It featured every A- and B-side released anywhere in the world on Immediate Records (including mono versions of songs only familiar to most through stereo album iterations) plus unreleased material that included outtakes, breakdowns, alternate versions and studio chatter. It was bundled with a certificate signed by Jones and McLagan, a 72-page hardback book, a lyric booklet and Small Faces miscellanea like press-kit facsimiles, posters and prints. Some aspects of the package were dubious. The alternative versions might be less fraudulent than the ones McLagan complains of but are hardly a great listening experience. Moreover, the set was limited to 3,000 copies, retailed at $150 and was only available in the United States. Nonetheless, at the very least such prestige treatment was pleasing for any Small Faces aficionado in the way that it implicitly recognised the band's import. A similar comprehensiveness as regards the Arden era attached to the 2015 set *The Decca Years*.

More suitable for those broadly unfamiliar with the Small Faces and who just wanted to dip a toe in the water was the 2003 double-CD set *Ultimate Collection*. Not only did it straddle the Decca and Immediate years but, because of those extended CD lengths, was able to go considerably further than *Small Faces Big Hits*, which had only featured A-sides, and even than the double-LP *Autumn Stone* release. "There's been compilations before," McLagan said. "It's the first one that's been done with our co-operation and involvement. Previously, it's just been put together and whipped out and that's the end of it. We only know about it until we read about it or see it in the record store in Australia. This one, we've been consulted right from the beginning and I've actually made a couple of changes here and there and corrected the liner notes where there were slight inaccuracies or spelling mistakes. It's nice to feel involved in our own product." By now, of course, technology had to some extent bypassed the record companies and the Small Faces' disagreements with them: people were well able to both compile their own professional-sounding best-ofs and to disseminate them worldwide in seconds. However, spanning over two hours of music with its fifty tracks, *Ultimate Collection* was both a great listen and incredible value for money. So much so that it became the first Small Faces product to reach the top 30 of the UK albums chart since *Ogdens'* 35 years before.

Gratifying though the recognition of their familiar material is, more exciting are bona fide, never-before-heard Small Faces recordings. In 2021, Jones oversaw the release of *Live 1966* on his newly formed Nice label. A January 1966 performance before an attentive audience at the Twenty Club in Mouscron, Belgium, it is not only a rare snapshot of the group captured onstage without the impediment of a wall of screams but, for Jones, a valuable testament to the real essence of the band. "We did things like 'Ooh Poo Pah Doo'. That's the kind of thing we loved playing before, then all of a sudden we got a hit record and had to drop all the songs we loved to play." He promises more in the way of both reissues and previously unreleased recordings. "There's a few more little aces up our sleeve. I'm just slowly finding them all."

The Ruskin Arms, where the Small Faces first came together, is now gone, having closed its doors for the final time in 2008. "The room I used to live in has become an Indian restaurant on the side of the pub," Jimmy Winston says. "I took my son and we went in and had a curry."

In the 1980s, Winston began moving away from acting and music-making. However, he managed to maintain a place in the music industry in an unexpected way. "Back in the Sixties, it was a dream that someone would ever put you in a studio and you could record," he reflects. He was after a fashion able to turn this dream into a day-to-day reality. "The late Seventies was when home studio recording started to appear," he says. "I had the very first four-track recorder that came over from TEAC. Then the eight-track. Started a little recording studio at home. By 1980, I was getting stuff for other people and I just evolved into a business called Sound Business Audio Systems selling recording equipment and did that solidly for about thirty years. That was a great time to actually make money from working hard. It kept me in touch with music and recording. I always had nice equipment to record on and I was also able to run a business and get life together properly. I did well." Considering the financial travails that famously afflicted at one point or another all the other ex-Small Faces except Jones, there must have actually been times when he was more solvent than they? "Oh, much more solvent."

Speaking in 2019, Winston added, "And, dare I say – and I say this with full respect – I'm glad to be here alive. Three of them are not. It's the saddest thing in the world for that band what's occurred." He was not only talking about premature deaths. "I would have hated to linger on in a band that earnt nothing, ended up in debt and was always falling out … I feel sorry for the band because they got stuffed more than me. They stayed for all that extra time, they had success and got nothing out of it, really."

Winston became an in-demand presence at the various conventions now held in tribute to the band. "It always amazes me how long all this goes on," he marvelled. "It's good for the Small Faces. The last convention I went to was at the 100 Club with the Small Fakers. They are earning far more money than we ever did as a band and they're our tribute band. They earn really good money because people do want to hear the songs. I just got up and did 'Whatcha Gonna Do About It' with them and I played an acoustic song. The audience were my sort of age, the majority." Yet: "I remember one convention. I turned up there and there was actually scooters outside – Lambrettas and things like that – so there was young and old."

Winston – who in later life went by 'Jim' – said he was "much, much happier," than he would have been if he'd remained in the band. "Small Faces was one little moment. I'd have given all that up to be in *Hair* for a year." However, he was anxious to point out that his relationship with the group couldn't be defined by the way it ended. "You got to remember, up until this point, we'd been having a great time. We actually became a success. You can't only look at a marriage break-up. We had a lot of fun. We never stopped laughing." Winston passed away aged 77 on 26 September 2020 following a battle with lung cancer.

To posit the Small Faces' story as one with a happy ending would mean ignoring inconvenient facts. Marriott's decline into a parody of his Artful Dodger stage role and his financial irresponsibility and health issues; the health issues pertaining to Lane, which were far worse and, unlike Marriott's, in no way self-inflicted; the financial problems both men experienced toward the end of their lives which – even though the story is more nuanced than either of them ever let on – were partly to do with them, as well as Jones and McLagan, not getting their rightful share of the monies due to them.

Yet when this author spoke to McLagan in 2014 – 3½ weeks before his unexpected death – he refused to view the story as a tragedy. "The Small Faces story's all about the music," he insisted. "The finances, that's another thing." Jones agrees: "I think people remember us for what we achieved and what we were and all the great songs that we made."

That music is something of which Jones and his colleagues were proud. "It's pop, it's rock, it's soulful, it's mod," McLagan summarised it. "It's different. It was music of the times really – but it seems to last." "It's kind of weird because I've become a fan of the band," says Jones. "I can stand back and look at it." At over a half-century's remove the drummer can finally see beyond the mistakes and what he felt to be the frequent gaps between ambition and achievement. "At the time I kept thinking, 'What do people see in us?' Now I know. I think the band was way ahead of its time in so many different ways … What amazed me standing back from it is the arrangements and the creativity."

The band's last surviving member summarises, "I view the Small Faces catalogue as important as the Beatles'. It is a statement – and I'll stand by it."

Acknowledgements

The author would like to extend his thanks to the people listed below for granting interviews. Some interviews were conducted specifically for this book. Others were for various magazine features on the Small Faces, although much of the latter material is itself seeing print for the first time here.

Keith Altham
David Arden
Paul Banes
Phill Brown
Joe Brown
George Chkiantz
Jenny Dearden (née Marriott, née Rylance)
Alan Fitter
Malcolm Forrester
Kenney Jones
Ron King
Jim Leverton
Kenny Lynch
Gered Mankowitz
Ian McLagan
Laurie O'Leary
Jerry Shirley
Susanna Tacker (née Lane, née Hunt)
Pete Townshend
Val Weedon (née Williams)
Jimmy Winston

The following people declined to be interview for the book but graciously responded to emailed queries:

Glyn Johns
Andrew Loog Oldham

Additional assistance was kindly provided by Larry Crane and John Bacciga-luppi of Tape Op Magazine and Simon Neal.

Selected Bibliography

Books

(Editions stated are ones author personally referred to.)

Arden, Don; Wall, Mick. *Mr Big. Ozzy, Sharon and My Life as the Godfather of Rock*. London, England: Robson Books, 2004.

Badman, Keith; Rawlings,Terry. *Quite Naturally: The Small Faces*. London, England: Complete Music Publications, 1997.

Frampton, Peter; Light, Alan. *Do You Feel Like I Do?: A Memoir*. New York City, USA: Hachette Books, 2020.

Grundy, Stuart; Tobler, John. *The Record Producers*. London, England: BBC Books, 1982.

Hellier, John; Hewitt, Paolo. *Steve Marriott: All Too Beautiful*. London, England: Helter Skelter Publishing, 2004.

Hewitt, Paolo. *The Young Mods' Forgotten Story*. London, England: Acid Jazz, 1995.

Jones, Kenney. *Let The Good Times Roll: The Autobiography*. London, England: Blink Publishing, 2018.

McLagan, Ian. *All the Rage*. London, England: Pan Books, 2000.

Neill, Andy. *Had Me a Real Good Time: Faces, Before, During and After* (Updated Edition). London, England: Omnibus Press, 2016.

Pidgeon, John. *Rod Stewart and the Changing Faces* (Electronic Edition). London, England: Backpages Ltd, 2011.

Schmitt, Roland; Twelker, Uli. *The Small Faces & Other Stories* (Second Edition). London, England: Sanctuary Publishing, 2002.

Shirley, Jerry. *Best Seat in the House: Drumming in the '70s with Marriott, Frampton and Humble Pie*. Michigan, USA: Rebeats Publications, 2011.

Spence, Simon. *All Or Nothing: The Authorised Story of Steve Marriott*. London, England: Omnibus Press, 2021.

Stafford, Caroline; Stafford, David. *Anymore for Anymore: The Ronnie Lane Story*. London, England: Omnibus Press, 2023.

Websites

https://www.americanradiohistory.com
https://www.billboard.com
https://www.discogs.com
http://www.everyhit.com
https://www.officialcharts.com
https://www.rocksbackpages.com
https://en.wikipedia.org

Index

Taylor, Mick (Rolling Stones guitarist), 205, 206
'Tell Me', 7, 14
'(Tell Me) Have You Ever Seen Me', 85, 86, 96, 98
Thank Your Lucky Stars, 10, 34, 35
'That Man', 96, 175
That's All, 99
'That's the Way It Goes', 237, 238, 240
Theatre Workshop, the, 13
Their Satanic Majesties Request, 111
Them, 224
There Are but Four Small Faces, 128, 129, 139, 151
'Things Are Going to Get Better', 99
'Thinkin' About Love', 230
'This Song's Just for You', 226
Thomas, Rufus, 263
Thompson, Dave, 94, 102, 134, 164, 183
Thompson, Denis, 13, 23
Thornton, Eddie 'Tan Tan', 100
'Thumbelina', 116
Thunderbox, 210
Tibetan Book of the Dead, The, 68
Tim Hardin (album), 169
Tim Hardin II, 169, 170
'Time Has Come, The', 110
'Time Is on My Side', 50
'Tin Soldier', 1, 57, 94, 110, 111, 112, 113, 116, 117, 118, 120, 121, 122, 128, 133, 154, 160, 180, 187, 188, 211, 227, 234, 260, 261, 263
Tiven, Jon, 61, 123, 147, 175, 183, 259
'Tobacco Road', 20
Tobler, John, 91
'Toe Rag', 239, 240
Tommy, 1, 134, 152, 160, 182, 202
'Tomorrow Never Knows', 68
'Tonight', 226
'Too Bad', 199
'Too Many Crossroads', 230
Toon, Tony, 205
Top of the Pops television programme, 28, 29, 65, 66, 95, 121, 122, 217
Tosh, Peter, 241

Town and Country, 193, 202
Townshend, Pete, 2, 9, 10, 11, 17, 18, 27, 42, 48, 76, 80, 90, 91, 108, 124, 125, 126, 127, 128, 130, 139, 152, 153, 158, 159, 160, 167, 181, 182, 189, 202, 203, 204, 213, 219, 220, 221, 234, 235, 236, 248, 249, 250, 257, 267
Traffic, 111, 218
Tremeloes, the, 119
Troggs, the, 7, 143
Troublemaker, 248
Trouser Press magazine, 6, 50, 64, 188
Turtles, the, 259
Tweddell, Nick, 147
Twice as Much, 99
Two-Way Family Favourites, 75

UFO, 212
'Ugly Duckling, The', 116
Ultimate Collection, 264
Uncut magazine, 91, 123
'Understanding', 64
'Universal, The', 161, 162, 163, 164, 165, 166, 169, 173, 174, 181, 219
Universal Music, 251, 255
Unwin, Stanley, 135, 142, 144, 145, 152, 156, 159, 257
'Up the Wooden Hills to Bedfordshire', 98, 100, 128

Valentine, Penny, 161
Valentinos, the, 223
Vendome, Michel, 49
Village Green Preservation Society, The, 150
Vincent, Gene, 19, 74
Volt Records, 52

Wace, Robert, 78
Walker Brothers, the, 258
Waller, Micky, 194
'War of the Worlds', 169
Waters, Muddy, 6, 39, 61, 123
Watts, Charlie, 235, 243
'We Love You', 108